MAKING ANGELS IN MARBLE

David Walsh

Making Angels in Marble

*The Conservatives, the Early Industrial Working Class
and Attempts at Political Incorporation*

BREVIARY STUFF PUBLICATIONS
2012

A BREVIARY STUFF PAPERBACK ORIGINAL

Published by Breviary Stuff Publications,
BCM Breviary Stuff, London WC1N 3XX
www.breviarystuff.org.uk

A CIP record for this book is available from
The British Library

ISBN: 978-0-9570005-0-6

Contents

Tables

Preface

This piece of work began life as a doctoral thesis in the late 1980s. Its objects were two-fold. At the outset I was interested in the reasons why the apparent political solidarity of the working class of the industrial north-west, (a region at the forefront of the transformations wrought by the industrial revolution), began to dissipate after the passing of the first Reform Act. It was evident that there were still profound grievances held by working people when confronted with the apparent 'treachery' of the Whig politicians at Westminster and their middle class supporters in the provinces. These were underscored when it became clear what the nature of Whig 'reforms' would entail. Yet this did not explain why sections of the working class whilst still expressing radical sentiments did not fully endorse the militant radical and republican factions. In fact as the period moved closer to the inception of Chartism some working people were being drawn towards the established political parties specifically the Conservatives. This opened up the second line of enquiry. It appeared that as a result of the first elections called under the terms of the Reform Act the Conservatives were a party in full retreat with their very survival being openly questioned. Within two years the Conservatives were recovering but intriguingly they had begun to make overtures towards attracting the industrial working class who overwhelmingly did not possess the franchise. Why should they do this at such a moment when clearly their main aim was to re-establish themselves as an electorally viable political party? These two apparent anomalies run through the investigation which follows. A major subtext to this was the role played by political parties in the first half of the nineteenth century. A major transformation was taking place in how political parties functioned and what their role was in a rapidly changing social and economic Britain. Did these changes amount to what could be viewed as the onset of the modern political system?

Introduction

The essential area of discussion in this book is that during the period between the Reform Acts of 1832 and 1867 the working class of industrial north-west England and the Conservative party underwent a process of profound political change. From being a loosely organized coalition of sectional interest groups bound together by religion and tradition, the Conservatives after 1833 began to adapt their organization and principles to accommodate changes inherent in the industrial capitalist system. This had far reaching effects, as we shall see, on the party political system at the local and national levels, on social relations between classes and on the political culture of the nation. With regard to the working class it was a political transformation which affected both the way they themselves perceived politics and the way they were perceived by the brokers of power. For the Conservative party it was a process of relatively rapid adaptation forced by the pace of political change after the 1832 Reform Act and the social and economic consequences of industrialization, which forced the party to react to change in order to defend their principles, and, indeed, to survive. This book therefore is an exercise of investigation into aspects of political change, involving class behaviour and attitudes, and of institutions (like political parties) that contributed to these developments.

The emerging working class of the north-west can be viewed as the forerunners of a social group which after 1850 rapidly increased throughout British society. To examine the political changes which affected the behaviour and attitudes of this important social grouping in these formative years may go some way to explaining why the working class after 1867 appears to be so politically heterogeneous. What was happening in the north west of England between 1832 and 1867 in social, economic and political terms can be viewed as a precursor for what happened in other parts of the country as industrial capitalism advanced. It does not necessarily follow that social class is inevitably a pre-determinant for political affiliation. However, there is a belief among political scientists, especially those who have studied the working class, and among Marxist social scientists, that the social position of a group or class may determine political orientation, interest demands and representation.[1] When placed under the microscope of historical investigation however, this does not always follow. Hence a central feature through this book is the examination and explanation of the variations of political allegiances among the working class of the north-west in the aforementioned period.

One suggestion regarding working-class political heterogeneity is that in an objective sense the working class was undergoing major changes in the middle decades of the nineteenth century. However, of equal importance was that political institutions in Britain were undergoing major changes during these years. These changes included the nature of political representation, both in local and national politics, changes in the powers of the various branches of the legislature and the role and functions of the executive and the monarch, and, importantly for our purposes, in the development of political parties. It is the consideration of the changing features and functions of the political party, specifically the Conservatives, which takes up the bulk of the opening chapters.

Chapter one opens with an historiographical account of the emergence of the modern political party, including a discussion of how the approaches developed by political science is used to shed light on the debate. This chapter also advances the contention that it was only after the Reform Act of 1832 that we can meaningfully begin to plot the central elements of political change leading to the modern party system. This is exemplified in the way that the Conservative party in particular began

---

1   For example, E. Nordlinger, *Working Class Tories*, (London 1968) or R. Mackenzie and A. Silver, *Angels in Marble*, (London 1968).

to integrate sections of the working class into their party structure in the 1830s, something which before this period they had never attempted. In order to give these post-1832 changes significance we need to examine the situation in the immediate decades before 1832. Chapter one further describes the effects of change within the Tory/Conservative party, specifically the transformation of Toryism into Peelite Conservatism. Here the linkages are traced between the Toryism of the late eighteenth century, through to the coalition of the conservative Whigs in the early nineteenth century, the guiding ideological principles of Conservatism in the years immediately following 1832 and the attempts to retain elements of traditional Tory attitudes of paternalism in the face of the challenge mounted by Liberal notions of political economy and *laissez-faire*.

Chapter two deals with the relationship between the Tories/Conservatives and the other key element of our discussion: the industrial working class before 1832. The social and economic position of the working class coloured their developing political views and importantly, how they were perceived by the national and local Tory elites. Working class lurches towards extreme radicalism in the later eighteenth and early nineteenth centuries will be examined as will why they sought political citizenship. Also considered is the bitter acrimony that existed between the Tories and sections of the emerging working class between 1790 and 1832.

At this point the concept of class consciousness is introduced and as the term will feature throughout the book, it will be useful to make clear what the concept denotes from the very start. The term used to denote a subjective awareness on the part of urban proletarians of their objective economic and political position in society. Class, as a concept, suggests an objective relationship between the wage labourer and the owners and managers of capitalistic production. This may be said to be the objective reality of an individual or group's class position. However, the subjective awareness of the 'objective reality' on the part of those involved to a significant extent determines class consciousness. The recognition of this subjective awareness determines both individual class consciousness and the existence of a collective consciousness: that many others are experiencing the same or similar objective reality. Within this subjective awareness there may also be a political dimension. It is the existence and detection of the political dimension that denotes class consciousness is at a high level of intensity. When the political element is absent class consciousness is low and status differentiation within the class is high. However, when the mass of working people seek to radically change the existing social, economic and political order, with an alternative political structure of their own design and one which ensures at least equal political representation with other groups or classes, then levels of class consciousness can be deemed high. Conventionally within Marxist historiography, a worker who affiliates with the Conservative Party, especially at a time of mass radical working class political activity can be said to have low levels of class consciousness. Conversely high levels can be seen in the worker who supports a political group seeking to advance the interest of the working class as a whole over those of another class and of a bourgeois political party.

It is important, however, to examine the nature of class and community relationships and the societal influences which the working class were subjected to (like that of integration into either the Liberal or Conservative parties) in the light of the historical events and period of the time. What the historian must not do is attempt to place *a priori* theories and concepts (such as Marxian Socialism or modern Conservatism) onto the motivations and actions of people who had no knowledge of such concepts. The agreement here is there were valid reasons (in the sense that we do not require a theory of false consciousness to explain them) and that why some working people supported Conservatism, just as there were why some advocated physical force Chartism. However, the overall effect of political sectionalization was it lowered the levels of class consciousness of the working class as a whole and significantly reduced their potentiality for effective collective political action. A central purpose of this book is to explain why, in the first half of the nineteenth century, working class political sectionalization occurred by examining some of the space between objective 'social being' and the apparently fluid nature of working class consciousness.

Essentially the first two chapters are contextual preliminaries to what will be the central themes of the book. After these initial chapters the reader should be aware that when seen from the perspective of the Conservatives and significant sections of the working-class instrumental changes were acting upon the very foundations of British politics. What was being transformed was the fabric of Britain's political culture. Political culture is used here to describe the traditions, style, attitudes and behaviour of the governed, the governors and the subtle effects these have on the existing constitution and its institutions. In subsequent chapters this change will be detailed from the standpoint of the Conservative Party and sections of the working class in the north-west region.

The third chapter plots how the central state influenced the working class away from the perceived dangers of extreme radicalism at a time of national crisis. In the 1790s it became manifest that working people were becoming increasingly dissatisfied with the existing political elites by displaying disturbing signs of a shift towards extreme radicalism. Spurred on by developments in revolutionary France, the polemics of Thomas Paine and the attempts at organization by the Correspondence Societies, working people, especially in the industrial areas, were seen as a threat to civil authority at the moment the country faced an escalating and potentially disastrous war. One attempt to contain the problem was to form Loyalist Associations. The actions of the state at this time are important to the present study for two reasons. First, it affords an opportunity to judge the attempts of the local and central state to direct working-class opinion and, second, it offers an insight into the nature of those opinions. This chapter serves as a historical point of reference and comparison with developments to be detailed later.

Chapter three also looks at the reorganization of the Conservative Party in aftermath of the Reform Act. Changes to the party at the centre are examined but also the effect the organizational changes in the localities. The reasons why the Conservatives began to alter their organizational structure will be discussed and an assessment made of the effect these changes had on the immediate development of British political culture. One of the central reasons for change was forced by the terms of the Reform Act itself. One of the clauses of the Act was the annual registration of electors. This process was of particular relevance in the boroughs where, for the first time, local political parties were organized on a permanent footing. Here fresh evidence will be produced, from the very centre of the Conservative party, which suggests that the leadership were becoming concerned as to ramifications which the Reform Act brought with it and of the need to re-organize the party as a consequence.

The main theme of chapter four is how the Conservative Party after 1832 immediately began to attract wider membership through the setting up of local Operative Associations. Particularly relevant are the attempts of the Conservatives to direct working class opinion in the 1830s compared to the actions of the state in the 1790s, considering also the role of the urban middle classes, their attitudes and leadership. This chapter details the Operative Conservative Associations of the north-west, especially their organizational structure and, importantly, what their middle-class initiators intended their effect to be on the working class of the north-west. The contention being that as a process this led to working class political divisions and effectively reduced overall working class consciousness.

In chapter four the theme of working-class political integration is developed with the examination of the issues which directly affected working people and the involvement of local Conservatives. The idiomatic models of the politics of influence, the market and opinion are utilised in order to clarify the political relationships and organization existing after 1832. The concept of deference will be considered in relation to operative Conservatism as will the nature of paternalism in the light of changing patterns of urban industrial society.

Chapters five and six place the discussions of the foregoing in the light of evidence drawn from three case studies which reflect and refract the differing political and economic make-up of the region as a whole. These chapters compare political change, working class politics and Conservative party development in different parts of the region: in the market and county towns, the industrial boroughs possessing the franchise before 1832 and the new boroughs created by the Act of 1832. Chapter five is initially concerned with developments in the market and county towns of the north-west. The discussion focuses chiefly on the small borough of Clitheroe and the county towns of Chester and Lancaster. The pattern will be to subject the evidence to analysis around the considerations detailed in the preceding chapters: namely the various idioms of politics, and the relevance (or otherwise) of such features as religion, welfare considerations, the maintenance of civil authority, working class issues, deference and middle class traits of paternalism.

The old industrial borough of Preston is the next main subject of study. Preston is interesting as it was a traditional market centre but was also a substantial industrial centre. However, its key importance for this book is that the town possessed a householder franchise under the pre-1832 political system, which meant the working class of Preston made up the majority of electors both before and after 1832. This offers us an ideal opportunity to examine working class political development and the attempts of the political parties to influence them in a town where they possessed political and numerical importance. Again the findings will be subjected for signs of change in the form and features of the Conservative party, looking at how they organized their political actions in relation to the working class, key issues, patterns of leadership and electoral contests in both spheres of local and parliamentary politics.

Chapter six investigates the new boroughs, those granted parliamentary representation as a result of the Act of 1832. The cotton town of Blackburn provides the bulk of the evidence, but developments here will be compared with Bolton, a town of similar demographic and economic structure. These new boroughs, unfettered as they were by long-standing political traditions and customs, provide useful evidence as to working class political integration after 1832, offering an opportunity to analyse the political sectionalization taking place within the working class and the various manifestations of class consciousness. Issues directly affecting the working class will be of especial interest, as will the development and success of the Operative Associations and the Conservative Party. Here it will be seen that not only did these local working-class based political associations act as parties of social and political integration, but also as agencies of social conditioning, containment and control. They were also agencies of opinion dissemination and generation in ways that organized political groups had never attempted with working people before 1832.

The Reform Act of 1832 will crop up throughout this study for two essential reasons. First, it was around this time that working class political consciousness was, in a mass sense, arguably at its highest level in the period under discussion. It will be shown that levels of working class political consciousness among urban industrial workers had been rising steadily since the 1790s. However, it was the ramifications associated with their organizations promoting the Reform Bill which left the impression on the local and national elites of a potentially dangerous, indeed, threatening situation developing in the industrial regions of Britain. Second, the effect of the terms of the Act itself and its implementation forced the pace of political change and led to the emergence of the modern party structure.

The final chapter offers an analytical overview that highlights and draws together the key themes developed in the preceding chapters. Much of the discussion here will centre on the effects and the consequences of the points raised in relation to working class political development in the 1850s and 1860s. Also considered are the nuances involved in the changes of party political structures and the evolving political culture. Full democracy, as defined as the right of all adult citizens to select their political governors, was not achieved by 1870, but great advances were made in the spheres of both local and national government. This was especially so in the application of outside pressure on parties and political institutions, organized political action and the open acceptance of the political legitimacy of social groups, like the working class, who, in 1800, were not considered capable of forming rational political arguments or equipped to engage in representation. The seven or eight decades from the 1790s to the end of the 1870s witnessed a transformation in British politics and what follows is an attempt to show how part of the process took place.

1

The Emergence of Political Parties and the Transformation of Toryism

The intention here is to outline the main historiographical arguments surrounding the emergence and importance of political parties in Britain from the eighteenth century into the nineteenth. The chief reason for a re-appraisal is that from the 1830s the working class began to play an increasingly important role in party politics and this contributed significantly to the historical development of both. The relevance of such a development must therefore be contrasted with the evolution of both the working class and the political party as key ingredients in the examination of political change at this time. With regard to this latter point the second half of the chapter examines how Toryism was transformed into Conservatism and became more politically relevant to members of the working class.

Whigs and Namierites

The debate on the emergence of modern British political parties began in the nineteenth century and was dominated by the Whig view of rational progress expounded most elegantly by T. B. Macaulay's *History of England*. Macaulay began his narration just prior to 1688 and the Glorious Revolution and ended with the final Whig triumph over the forces of Tory ignorance: the 1832 Reform Act. In essence it was an account of the transition of the Whig faction (or factions) into early Victorian progressive Liberalism and as such is narrowly one-dimensional and teleological. However, Macaulay's *History* was for many years the accepted view that the modern (nineteenth century) political party came into being as a result of the Whigs' successful political and religious emancipation from the absolutist tendencies of James II (1682-1688). Secondly, their triumph over his Tory supporters during the Hanoverian succession and the three decades which immediately followed it, (1714-1746). And thirdly, the re-assertion of the Tories with the accession of George III and his attempts to apply the brake to progress with his opposition to the Whigs throughout his years of reasonable health. This struggle set the tone for the opposing factions, of Whig liberty and Tory reaction, up until the 1870s. Macaulay's 'History' sat well with central ethos of late-Victorian Liberalism based as it was on the necessity to reform and to advance deterministically located solutions to virtually every social and political problem. Furthermore, his *History* was a celebration of the winners in the battle between progress and reaction. Macaulay was at pains to remind the reader that it was the great Whig party that eventually ushered in the new dawn of political representation with the Reform Act of 1832. This was the ultimate achievement in the struggle to re-assert British liberties as championed from the 1780s by Charles James Fox.

It was not until the publication of Sir Lewis Namier's *The Structure of Politics at the Accession of George III* in 1929 that the crude thesis propounded by Macaulay was seriously challenged. Namier demolished the notion offered by Macaulay that the two party system could be traced back unbroken, to the last two decades of the seventeenth century. For Namier, such a system could not begin to be considered at any time prior to 1832 and the passing of the Reform Act. The historians of the nineteenth century who formulated the 'Whig interpretation', which Namier rejected, were mistaken in thinking that the political and constitutional norms of their day had been a constant feature of political development since 1688. Indeed, it could be argued that a 'pure' two party system has never existed for any significant period. Furthermore, the alternation of the two major parties which was so much a feature of Macaulay's age after 1832 finds few parallels in the eighteenth century except possibly from 1689 to 1714. It is thus misleading to think of a modern system of the alternation of party political power. However, in terms of historical development, Namier went too far in totally denying the existence 'in the modern sense'[1] of political party principles and ideological bindings before 1832. It is on this point that much of the criticism of the Namierite thesis has focused.[2]

Eighteenth-Century Gradualists

What seems to have occurred was that the reluctance displayed by Namierite historiography to admit the importance of the developmental type of political parties in the eighteenth century came about as a (Tory) reaction against the earlier (Whig) writers. In a sense overstatement produced overstatement, and the structure of post-1688 and Hanoverian politics went from being assumed to be the Victorian type of progressive constitutionalism to being a continuance of the seventeenth century court/country type. Here the constitutional role of the monarch was not subordinated to the ineluctable rise of party, but given equal emphasis with the (often corrupt) political machinations of an aristocratic oligarchical clique. What came under attack most fiercely in recent decades was Namier's assertion that the elemental parts of the old Whig and Tory parties fell away in the 1760s. John Cannon for example, in *The Fox/North Coalition*, contends his study of years 1782-84 "could not have been written except in party terms."[3] Thus amongst some historians there has been a tendency to return to a modified Whig view of events in the eighteenth century, not as a guiding methodology but as a means of historical explanation. This is so especially in relation to the descriptive utility of the term 'political party' rather than 'political faction' or mere groups of opposing aristocrats, which has been accompanied by a gradual erosion of the credibility of Namier on points of scholarship and detail. Recent historians[4] have pointed to Namier's lack of detail regarding the conduct of elections and his pessimistic view of human motivation. Also of his excessive attention to political patronage as a political motivator rather than issues and a failure to give due weight to the impact of foreign affairs and his lack of perspective.[5] His critics however, also point out that the most inherent weaknesses of Namier's position are to be found in admissions made within his own writings. For example, he conceded that the names and creeds of Whig and Tory: "which covered enduring types moulded by

---

1   L. B. Namier, *Crossroads of Power: Essays in Eighteenth Century England*, (London 1962).

2   See for example J. Cannon, *The Fox/North Coalition, Crisis of the Constitution 1782-4*, (Cambridge, 1969).

3   Ibid., p. 240.

4   The modern anti-Namierites would include, as well as Professor Cannon, Frank O'Gorman, in *The Rise of Party in England, The Rockingham Whigs, 1760-1782*, (London 1975) or his *The Emergence of the British Two Party System*, (London, 1982) and most recently *Voters, Parties and Patrons*, (London, 1989), L. G. Mitchell, *Holland House*, (London, 1980), J. Brewer, *Party Ideology and popular politics at the accession of George III*, (Cambridge, 1976). More traditional anti-Namierites would include H. Butterfield, 'George III and the Constitution', *History*, 43, (1958) pp. 14-33, K. G. Feiling, *The Second Tory Party*, (Oxford, 1938), G. M. Trevelyan, *Lord Grey of the Reform Bill*, (London 1952, ed.)

5   See for example T. W. Perry, *Public Opinion, Propaganda and Politics*, (Cambridge, Mass. 1962) pp. 191-2.

deeply ingrained differences and temperament and outlook",[6] did in fact exist. Also, and importantly, he conceded "in a good many constituencies the names of Whig and Tory still corresponded to real divisions."[7] The apparent contradiction, that party names could exist in Parliament and that real divisions continued in certain constituencies, but notwithstanding parties in a modern sense did not exist in reality, was never adequately explained by Namier. What later followers of Namier have maintained is the 1740s to the 1770s were the high point of the era of 'personal parties' associated with differing cliques, who retained the names and even some of the principles of Toryism and Whiggery. But they did not possess the disciplines, functions and features of political parties either between the periods 1688-1714 or after 1832.[8]

One of the most important recent critiques of the Namierite position has come from Frank O'Gorman, whose chief purpose is to stress the elements of continuity between the pre-1832 political world and that which followed the Reform Act and to emphasise the gradual nature of change.[9] In *The Emergence of the British Two Party System*, the book that addresses the subject most directly, he writes that, "The interpretation offered in this book conflicts with the accepted or orthodox view that a two party system was created by the 1832 Reform Act."[10] According to O'Gorman the lineage of the two party system can be traced back fifty years before the Reform Act. The years between 1806 and 1830 saw the development of a recognisable system of party with tight discipline, wide organization, and ideological distinctiveness and multivariate social/political functions.

O'Gorman tells us that the two-party system evolved as a result of realignments during periods of profound instability. Such periods were the early 1760s and the active political involvement of the monarch, between 1779 and 1784 and the crises surrounding the American colonies, parliamentary sovereignty and electoral reform. Again between 1792 and 1794 the effects of the French Revolution revived, on the one hand, popular radicalism, and on the other, popular patriotism and traditionalism. The political role of the monarch, religious toleration and war policy was the focus of political controversy between 1806 and 1812; and finally between 1827 and 1832, where the issues of religious and constitutional reform served again to divide groupings and forge realignment.

At the beginning of the 1760s, according to O'Gorman, the three groupings of ministerial Whigs, opposition Whigs and independents existed fairly harmoniously together, without, as we noted above, the trappings of party or political ideologies. He also tells us that seventy years on, even after the passing of the Reform Act:

> The central party institutions of the 1830s do not represent a new departure in the evolution of the two-party system: rather they represent the accommodation of that system to the particular circumstances of politics after the First Reform Act.[11]

The key motivating force for party political change in the second half of the eighteenth and early

---

6   Namier, *Crossroads*, pp. 229-30.

7   Ibid., p. 192.

8   Some examples are J. Brooke (ed. with Lewis Namier) *The History of Parliament*, 3 Vols., (London, 1964), or I. R. Christie, *Myth and Reality in late-Eighteenth Century British Politics*, (London, 1970), J. C. D. Clark, 'A general theory of Party, Opposition and Government, 1688-1832', in *Historical Journal*, vol. 23, no. 2 (1980).

9   Especially in *The Emergence of the British Two Party System*, and *The Rise of Party in England, The Rockingham Whigs, 1760-82*, and 'Party Politics in the Early Nineteenth Century', in the *English Historical Review*, January, 1987, *Voters, Patrons and Parties*, (Oxford, 1989), and more recently, *The Long Eighteenth Century: British Political and Social History 1688-1832*, (London 1997).

10   O'Gorman, *Emergence*, p. 126.

11   Ibid., p. 121, see also his 'Party Politics in the Early Nineteenth Century', p. 84.

nineteenth centuries for O'Gorman was the ability of the British political system to adapt or accommodate the prevailing winds of 'circumstances'. Hence, "the custom of thinking of politics instinctively in two-party terms had become securely established by 1832."[12] This was so firstly in the manner of conducting government business and in providing an opposition to the Ministry. Secondly, by establishing areas of organization both at the centre and on the peripheries. Thirdly, by mobilizing channels of communications via the medium of the written word, and fourthly, by the development of distinctive sets of political ideologies. O'Gorman contends that as each successive crisis unfolded between 1760 and 1832 it became possible to talk meaningfully of 'parties'. By 1812, and the start of Lord Liverpool's administration, the Whig politicians in office, backed by a 'covert administration group' and by the independents, had effectively fused to form a 'Tory Party'. The guiding credo of this group was the philosophy of Edmund Burke, especially his *Appeal from the New to the Old Whigs*.[13] They were opposed by the Foxite Whigs (led by Lord Grey and George Tierney) and by a loosely organized set of Radicals. The 'Tory' grouping, according to O'Gorman, became identified with loyalty to the Anglican Church and the crown, the preservation of the rights of property, especially political rights, the security of the country and the maintenance of law and order. It was this identification with basic principles that formed the basis of the rapid development of parties up to the last period of crisis between 1827-32. O'Gorman tells us,

> The events of the Revolutionary and Napoleonic years had infused them [the principles noted above] with a new relevance, and any government dedicated to these objectives, especially one which was continuously faced with an opposition which boasted of its pure Whiggism, was likely to find itself tarred with the brush of Toryism.[14]

However, O'Gorman is careful not to identify the administration of Lord Liverpool too closely with a hard or inflexibly doctrinaire political ideology. He says,

> The ethics of executive Toryism, the defence of the country, the landed interest, property, the established Church, and resistance to radicalism may have been so generalized that they scarcely amounted to a specific party programme. Indeed, the Whigs agreed with much of it. It would be unhistorical to depict the ministries of Pitt and his successors as reactionary governments confronted by a liberal and progressive Whig opposition. Opinions on Parliamentary Reform, Catholic Emancipation and the Slave Trade sometimes cut across political loyalties. At the same time, the government's frequently negative approach to such questions before the mid-1820s, its identification with political reaction and its self-proclaimed purpose of maintaining the countries institutions amounted to an identifiable Tory mentality.[15]

Thus, for O'Gorman, the nomenclature of political parties was effectively in place well before the Reform struggle. So too was a crude and embryonic form of party organization, both at the centre of political affairs, the legislative and executive, and in the localities. Although conceding that Pitt the younger was an a opponent of party political organization,[16] as indeed was George III, O'Gorman invokes Cannon's argument that in opposing party organizations the supporters of Pitt and the King became an organized party:

---

12   O'Gorman, *Emergence*, p. 121.

13   Edmund Burke, *Appeal from the New to the Old Whigs*, (London, 1791).

14   O'Gorman, *Emergence*, p. 59.

15   Ibid.

16   Ibid., p. 57.

... in his [George III's] anti-party crusade, his supporters had been forced to adopt the techniques of party itself — letters of attendance, pairing arrangements, co-ordinated tactics, organized propaganda and electoral planning.[17]

If this situation was true of the emerging Tory party, O'Gorman suggests it was an even more identifiable trait of the Foxite Whigs. He tells us this grouping had the rudiments of party organization dating back to 1782 and the relationship between Charles James Fox and his electoral organizer William Adam. With the assistance of Adam, the Foxite Whigs built up a powerful organization by 1790. They had a network of provincial supporters and organizers, a subscription fund for electoral purposes, the control of an influential section of the press and a tightening of the control and discipline of Fox's supporters in Parliament, with Adam functioning as Chief Whip in the Commons.[18]

It would seem that much depends on the interpretation of the term 'party' and what connotations the historian places upon it. As we have seen for Cannon and O'Gorman, political groups before 1832 were gradually assuming the roles and functions of political parties both at the centre and in the localities. However, Namier was fairly precise as to what was occurring in British politics up to 1832. What the historians following the Whig interpretation and, to an extent the revisionists, called parties were mere factions, located primarily at the national centres of political power, the court, the executive and parliament. Namier wrote.

> Parliamentary struggles for office necessarily produce a dichotomy of 'ins' and 'outs'; and the two party names were current since the last quarter of the seventeenth century: hence in retrospect the appearances of a two party system. In reality three broad divisions, based on type and not on party, can be distinguished in the eighteenth-century House of Commons; on the one side were the followers of the Court and Administration, the 'Placemen', par excellence, a group of permanent 'ins'; on the opposite side, the independent country gentlemen, of their own choice, permanent 'outs', and in between occupying as it were the centre of the arena, and focusing upon themselves the attention of the public and of history, stood the political factions contending for power, the forerunners of parliamentary government based on a party system.[19]

The key idea which marks Namier off from historians such as O'Gorman and Cannon is that parties were but 'appearances' and those political divisions were based on where the politician was placed, which again were not parties but differential 'types'. It would seem at first sight that Namier's three broad divisions, especially those who were the Ministerialist and Court Administrators, broadly correspond to O'Gorman's Tory party-in-the-making throughout the 1790s and the first decade of the nineteenth century. Indeed in a sense they do; the difference is one of emphasis. For Cannon and O'Gorman these groupings were to a greater or lesser extent parties developing historically the characteristics of recognizable political parties from the 1760s to the 1830s. For Namier they were merely appearances of parties, not actual parties, until the changes wrought by the reform crisis and

---

17 Cannon, *The Fox/North Coalition*, pp. 235-6.

18 O'Gorman, *Emergence*, p.47. See also James Vernon, *Politics and the People: A Study in English Political Culture, 1815-1867*, (Cambridge, 1993). Vernon suggests that the 'reforms' wrought by the various statutes, (but most importantly the Reform Act of 1832), in the nineteenth century had the effect of stifling the radical libertarian tradition and popular participation in politics which appear in the eighteenth century. This is a highly debatable point but the fact was that at no time in the eighteenth century was there a political 'party' or group that catered to the needs of the plebeian or working class. From 1832, all attempted to do so.

19 Namier, *Crossroads*, p. 220.

the Act itself made them so. This notion of the 'appearance' of party is a vitally important contextual and definitional point. What is needed is a means of differentiating between 'party' and 'faction' in the historical context. O'Gorman tells us that:

> Parties are to be distinguished from factions [a] in the scope of their legislative ambitions, (b) in the size of their parliamentary membership and the range of their popular support, (c) in their possession of an ideology of wide-ranging application.[20]

This is an admirable attempt at definitional accuracy, but it is one that is applicable only to the post-1832 period rather than that eighteenth or early nineteenth centuries. The fact was that in the eighteenth century the term party could at best be seen as a concept that was freely inter-changed with that of faction. As early 1754 it was suggested to the Duke of Newcastle that a new 'party' be established which would enjoin the conservative Whigs with the loyalist Tories.

> I would propose a new party be formed, consisting of Church Whigs and Hanover Tories. These together would make the best party for the Nation and I believe would be forever the most powerful party in it, able to crush all other factions and abolish the distinction of Whig and Tory, which has been so long destructive to the Peace and Quiet in this Kingdom. In truth Whigs and Tories are become at length two factions struggling now only for profit and power.[21]

It is important to note the political language but what is also relevant is that the writer was advocating an alliance of the conservative factions almost half a century before the momentous events of the French Revolution, which, according to O'Gorman achieved that end. Moreover, Johnson's English Dictionary, an important contemporaneous definitional source, makes no mention of 'party' but describes 'faction' as "tumult; discord; dissension" and dismisses the term 'Whig' simply as "the name of a faction".[22] With regard to O'Gorman's phrase that people had become accustomed to "thinking of politics instinctively in two-party terms". This exemplifies the chief problem with the O'Gorman thesis. While it addresses some of the peripheral areas it does not locate a series of definable points as to when it becomes historically meaningful to discuss the emergence of the modern two-party system, especially so in the light of O'Gorman's own distinction between 'party' and 'faction'. The factional nature of politics in the pre-1832 period can be clearly seen during O'Gorman's periods of crisis. In the 1790s, for example, the term 'Tory' takes on a more salient meaning in the light of opposition to the French Revolution and, importantly, those Foxite Whigs who appear to condone its principles. However, there is no evidence of a Tory 'party' organised along lines of the Conservatives in the 1830s. What was occurring in the 1790s and 1800s was the splitting apart of the old Whig factions with the conservative side fusing with Tory elements. Indeed as a process this had begun in the 1750s when Hardwicke began disassembling the barriers to Tory advancement and was maintained in the intervening period. For the most part the names of Whig and Tory mean little in the eighteenth and early nineteenth century contexts when contrasted with the structural and functional changes which were ushered in by the first Reform Act, as will be seen in due course. As John Phillips noted, when assessing the impact of the 1832 Reform Act. "It (the Reform Act) not only took the necessary first step towards more comprehensive reforms, it also

20 O'Gorman, *Emergence*, p.*viii*.
21 State Papers Domestic, SP 36/125, ff 28-29, Unknown to Newcastle, 4 January, 1754.
22 *Johnson's Dictionary: a modern selection*. Eds. E. L. McAdam and George Milne, (London, 1982 ed.) Johnson defines 'Tory' as "a cant term, derived I suppose from the Irish word signifying a savage. One who adheres to the ancient constitution of the state, and the apostolical hierarchy of the Church of England. Opposed to a Whig."

politicized much of the electorate to a degree not possible or imaginable before."[23] O'Gorman has taken a detailed look at the work of the late John Phillips and conceded some ground on the role played by the 1832 Reform Act. He suggests the Act "… had significant political and symbolic consequencies. Unquestionably among these must be included an immense politicizing effect and an unmistakable rise in electoral uncertainty and electoral participation."[24]

However, he does not go back on what he maintained in *Voters, Patrons and Parties*:

> I am not concerned here to speculate on the enormity of the changes ushered in by the Reform Act of 1832 nor to ruminate on the collapse of the old regime in England between 1828 and 1832.

Yet when he examines Phillips's claim that the 1832 Act "… as an issue or as a statute reshaped electoral behaviour in many boroughs, however politically or physically diverse", but importantly "the notable shift to partisanship found in some of these boroughs did not survive the 1840s, and the very altered circumstances of the 1850s must have reshaped some constituencies beyond recognition." [25] O'Gorman includes the caveat, "That to make undue claims for the Reform Act of 1832 entirely neglects these fundamental characteristics of political and electoral fluctuations between the first two Reform Acts."[26] The point is that the Act both introduced and accelerated change. Political parties had to be transformed in order to accommodate the new electoral and ideological circumstances wrought by the Act of 1832 and, as we shall see below, this was especially so for the Conservatives.

The Defenders of Orthodoxy

There are historians who not only defend the Namierite position regarding the slow emergence of the political party in the modern sense but also arguably go further. One such historian, Professor Ian Christie wrote in a review of O'Gorman's *Emergence* that, "The term 'Whig', on O'Gorman's showing, does not provide a good distinctive party definition of the early nineteenth century. 'Tory' is a misnomer for any politician of that period. The term 'Liberal Tory' is a monstrosity, and the sooner it can be buried the better."[27] J. C. D. Clark is even more forthright when he says: "The history of the Tory party in parliament between the early 1760s and the late 1820s may be simply written: it did not exist."[28]

J. C. D. Clark is the one of the latest and most determined pro-Namierite historians of party development. Following Ian Christie and Derek Beales, he disputes the notion that the political party of the mid to late nineteenth-century had a lineage which can be traced back to the mid-eighteenth century. Hence, he is opposed, on historical and intellectual grounds, to the position adopted by the anti-Namierites. He endorses the position of Derek Beales, who holds that it was the 1830s that was the crucial decade in the development of political parties. It was in this decade, Clark tells us, that parties completed their conquest of the House of Commons and became accepted as the organizations

23 J. A. Phillips, *The Great Reform Bill in the Boroughs: English Electoral Behaviour, 1818-1841*, (Oxford, 1992), p. 303.

24 F. O'Gorman, 'The Electorate Before and After 1832', *Parliamentary History*, Vol. 12, pt. 2, 1993, p. 175.

25 J. Phillips, *The Great Reform Act in the Boroughs*, p. 303.

26 F. O'Gorman, 'The Electorate Before and After 1832', p. 183.

27 I. R. Christie, Review of F. O'Gorman's 'The Emergence of the British Two Party System', in *History*, (Vol. 68, No. 223, June 1983).

28 J. C. D. Clark, 'A General Theory of Party, Opposition and Government, 1688-1832', *Historical Journal* (Vol. 23, No. 2, 1980), p. 305.

whose relative strength should determine the complexion of the government.[29]

According to Clark the political factions of both government and opposition were coalitions for most of the eighteenth century and certainly after 1760. He argues that the ministries from 1714 to 1760 gained power because their leaders had battled their way to the top of the Whig party. The ministries who enjoyed long periods of office between 1760 and 1827 did so only because they had initially been chosen by, and enjoyed the continued support of, the King. Support in the House of Commons came as a result of this royal favour. Not necessarily because there existed a large 'King's party' but rather, in critical moments, the ministries were able to claim the support of the independent members and managed to poach votes from the opposition by offering places and venal influence. This position is a justification of Namier's 'ins' and 'outs' scenario of political change and continuity. Clark explains that,

> At first sight the latter part of the [eighteenth] century displays a bewildering list of ministries. In fact successful governments had a common basis. In the years 1757-1827, power was held for over 74 per cent of the time by only four: the Newcastle-Pitt coalition; North's; the younger Pitt's and Liverpool's. They conformed to a type. They were non-party coalitions, coalitions in the sense that the party identity of the participating groups had been submerged on a basis of loyal support of the King's government and non-party in the late seventeenth century sense of party, since they were all Whig in the old sense, vis-a-vis the question of the succession.[30]

Clark further suggests that formal party organisation, both inside and especially outside parliament was lacking also. It was through the Treasury and not the organisation of party that government support inside parliament was rallied, and outside through the use of secret service money at elections.[31] For Clark political coherence came as a result of a tradition of an administrative ethic rather than one of party.[32] Clark tells us that the long Liverpool ministry was again only an 'appearance' of party. The long continuance of that administration gave it, eventually, the appearance of being opposite to the Whig *party* [Clark's emphasis] opposition; of being the other element in the ancient antithesis. It was an appearance only. Liverpool's cabinet was conducted on assumptions different from those incorporated in the party systems of 1832-46, 1846-68 or 1868-86. In the 1820s the issues of parliamentary reform and Catholic Emancipation, in particular, cut across party lines; when they ceased to do so, in 1827-32, the parties were torn apart.[33]

This 'appearance' of party is what has confused many of the historians who maintain that the features of party can be traced back to the mid-eighteenth century. Part of this confusion, argues Clark, is that modern historians have taken the language and popular idioms of the time too literally. As he says, "Too frequently the language is accepted as authentic, and inferences drawn from it to what the party structure must have been — *in order* [Clark's emphasis] for that language to have been accurate. But an argument in the contrary direction is necessary to show the senses in which, by contrast to reality, the language was used for political advantage."[34] Again the implied point is that party terminologies

---

29   D. Beales, *The Political Parties of Nineteenth-Century Britain*, (London, 1971), p. 11.

30   Clark, *General Theory*, p. 307.

31   Ibid., p. 308.

32   F. Bamford to the Duke of Wellington, in *The Journal of Mrs Arbuthnot, 1820-1832*, Vol. II, p. 337, (London, 1950 ed.) letter dated, 19 February, 1830.

33   Clark, *General Theory*, p. 310.

34   Ibid., p. 312.

merely corresponded to 'ins', 'outs' and 'independents' as convenient tags but not linked directly to parliamentary groups, nor, indeed, "to identities derived from the parliamentary stances of such groups."[35] In this way for Clark the position of the gradualists is refuted and the Namierite stance preserved. Clark also berates historians writing in the 1930s and 40s[36] (and more recently) those who contend that from 1807 to 1827 the government of Britain was conducted by the Tories. "Finding the word 'tory' in the contemporary political language," says Clark, "historians assumed that because there was an organized whig party, a tory party existed also"[37] Clark contests this saying that the political composition of the ministry of Lord Liverpool's "conformed to the pattern of North's and the younger Pitt's."[38]

A problem facing the Clark thesis when it is placed alongside that of the anti-Namierite gradualists is the latter's assertion that party alignments came about as a result of deep rooted and far-reaching political crises. The crisis most often cited as the one which re-galvanized Tory principles was the stance adopted by the Foxite Whigs in the aftermath of the French Revolution. As O'Gorman tells us,

> There can be no serious doubt … that the French Revolution provoked a vigorous debate in Britain between those already suspicious of reform and those captivated by the libertarian principles of the French Revolution. The writings of Burke together with the dislike felt by the middling and landed orders for the anti-religious drift of the Revolution after the Civil Constitution of the Clergy in July 1790 turned British opinion against reform.[39]

O'Gorman further suggests that the climate of opinion, indeed, a political culture created in Britain by the Revolution, can be depicted as "an upsurge of patriotism, as a religious (evangelical) revival, as a crusade in defence of Church and King — the historian is tempted to speak the language of party. A government pursuing 'Tory' policies over law and order, enthusiastically sustained by 'Tory' public opinion may be seen to possess a Burkean set of 'Conservative' values."[40] Clark, however, maintains it was the adaptability of the leadership of Portland, Perceval and Liverpool which allowed them to lead coalition ministries. They were helped, however, by the rivalries of the Foxite/Grevillite opposition coupled with weak inflexible leadership that prevented their becoming a serious political force until the reform crisis. Again the stress is on non-party coalition; its successful implementation by the political forces of the ruling executive and the lack of success on the part of the opponents of the ministry. Ian Christie sums up the position of the pro-Namierites thus:

> The correct label for those sceptical of change is 'Conservative'. Conservatism was evolving within the Whig tradition as part of the Whig tradition from the 1790s onwards and thus a gradual bifurcation of Whiggism helped to give birth to both the mid-nineteenth century political parties. In the 1830s Peel's choice of a party name was a formal recognition of this fact.[41]

---

35 Ibid.

36 Such as A. Aspinall, *Brougham and the Whig Party*, (London, 1927), M. Roberts, *The Whig Party 1807-1812*, (London, 1939), but also A. Mitchell, *The Whigs in Opposition*, (London, 1967).

37 Clark, *General Theory*, p. 314.

38 Ibid.

39 O'Gorman, *Emergence*, p. 46.

40 Ibid., p. 51.

41 Christie, *Review of Emergence*, p. 341.

Nineteenth-Century Gradualists

The picture described so far of the emergence of the modern political party is confused and the scene of intense academic debate with advocates on both sides of the Namier line of argument. However, unsurprisingly with increases in the scope and variety of sources in the mid-Victorian period there are some historians who go even further arguing that it is spurious to designate the 1790s or the early 1830s as watershed period at all. They suggest that the true date we can safely discuss the emergence of the modern political party be after the Second Reform Act of 1867 and the Ballot Act of 1872, with the advent of household suffrage and the secret ballot. The combined implications of these events, it is argued, meant that political parties had to become truly organized and develop the features and functions of modernity, especially with regard to competitively managing, for the first time in British politics, a truly mass electorate comprising often of conflicting interests and values.

But even these 'post-1867' historians of party cannot agree precisely when it is proper to speak of the emergence a recognisably modern political party. Nevertheless, Norman Gash, John Vincent, H. J. Hanham, J. B. Conacher, Maurice Cowling, E. J. Feuchtwanger, J. P. Cornford, E. F. Biagini, A. J. Reid, Robert Blake and Angus Hawkins[42] all, to a greater or lesser extent contend that the modern party system was slow in development. H. J. Hanham for example has said, "...the break in English political life ... came not in 1867 but in the years between 1880 and 1886."[43] He stressed changes in the machinery of politics that accompanied adjustments in the nature of the political parties. Hanham writes, "The Corrupt Practices Act of 1883 which linked election expenditure and made it easier and cheaper to get into parliament and gave a new importance to party organization."[44] He concludes the old system of parties and politics ended in the mid-1880s and that, "The chapter of political history that opened with the general election of 1885 was, in short, a completely new one. Leaders, parties, constituencies, were all different from those of 1867..."[45]

Norman Gash, in a slightly different vein, stresses the continuity of political change from the pre-Reform era to that of after 1832. He says, "The first Reform Act was both a landmark and a turning point, but it would be wrong to assume that the political scene in the succeeding generation differed essentially from that of the preceding one."[46] Elaborating further Gash writes,

> In fact the pre-1832 period contained many new features which it transmitted to the future; and the post-1832 period contained many old features which it inherited from the past. Between the two there is indeed a strong organic resemblance ... the continuity of political fibre was tough enough to withstand the not very murderous instrument of 2 Wm.IV., C.45 ... there was

---

42 N. Gash, *Politics in the Age of Peel*, (London, 1953), and *Aristocracy and the People*, (London, 1979), H. J. Hanham, *Elections and Party Management*, (London, 1959), J. B. Conacher, *The Peelites and the Party System*, (Newton Abbot, 1972), John Vincent, *The Formation of the British Liberal Party*, (London, 1966), Maurice Cowling, *Disraeli, Gladstone and Revolution*, (Cambridge, 1967), E. J. Feuchtwanger, *Disraeli, Democracy and the Tory Party*, (Oxford, 1968), J. P. Cornford, 'The transformation of conservatism in the late nineteenth-century', *Victorian Studies*, No. 7, (1963-64) pp. 35-66, E. F. Biagini, *Liberty, Retrenchment and Reform: Popular Liberalism in the age of Gladstone, 1860-1880*, (Cambridge, 1992), E. F. Biagini and A. J. Reid (eds.), *Currents in Radicalism, Organized Labour and Party Politics in Britain, 1850-1914*, (Cambridge, 1991), Robert (Lord) Blake, *The Conservative Party from Peel to Thatcher*, (London, 1983), Angus Hawkins, 'Parliamentary Government and Victorian Political Parties, 1830-1880', in *English Historical Review*, Vol. 104, (1989).

43 Hanham, *Elections*, introduction, p. xxx.

44 Ibid., p. xxxi.

45 Ibid.

46 Gash, *Politics in the Age of Peel*, introduction, p. x.

scarcely a feature of the old unreformed system that could not be found still in existence after 1832.[47]

Gash points to the maintenance of the system after 1832 through the nomination of members of Parliament by aristocratic influence, widespread corruption, and the continued domination in national politics by the greater and lesser aristocracy, especially in the social make-up of the legislature.[48] J. B. Conacher appears more cautious. "It is difficult to say when political parties in the modern sense first emerged."[49] However, he seems to favour the position of the anti-Namierites when he says the various parties that existed in the 1830s and 40s were "a coalition of sub-groups and subject to various tensions".[50] This was a situation that existed, suggests Conacher, until the two great political parties re-aligned after the fluidity of party affiliation in the years following the Conservative split of 1846. Robert Blake maintains that the Conservative Party was a product of the confusion of 1846 and less the product of Peel and his advisers in the 1830s.[51] Still with the Conservatives E. J. Feuchtwanger asserts that the combination of improved organization and the need to appease electors after 1867 marked off the post-1867 period from that which preceded it,[52] whilst J. P. Cornford examines in detail how the Conservatives coped with the structural forces of change in the 1870s and 80s.[53] For the Liberals, John Vincent is also inclined to the later date, he writes,

> The creation of a (predominantly Liberal) cheap daily press outside London, the action of organized labour and militant nonconformity, the Reform agitation of the 1860s and the chief representative significance of Gladstone, were the chief influences in the changing context of the Liberal Party. Up to 1865, that party had been the expression of personal rivalries and political differences within the aristocracy, broadly defined. After 1865 the Liberals, without important changes in their parliamentary personnel, came to represent great and dynamic social forces in the country, by reason of their vitalizing connection with their rank and file.[54]

Biagini and Reid maintain that the long transition of working class radicalism found its natural home in the Gladstonian Liberal party in the second half of the nineteenth century. This by implication suggests that mass participation in politics and its concomitant acceptance by the party leadership marked the turning point between the pre and post-1867 eras.[55] Angus Hawkins suggests that 1832 may indeed have been some sort of 'watershed' in that it redrew "the lines of political configuration". However, he argues that in the 1870s there emerged the "formation of parties different in nature, because (they were) different in their essential constitutional function, from the parties of the 1830s."[56]

---

47 Ibid.

48 Gash, *Aristocracy and the People*, p. 152.

49 Conacher, *Peel and the Peelites*, p. 10.

50 Ibid., p. 11.

51 Blake, *Conservative Party*, Ch. 1.

52 E. J. Feuchtwanger, *Disraeli, Democracy*, Introduction, p. xiv, and p. 268. See also by the same author, 'J. E. Gorst and the central organization of the Conservative Party, 1870-1882', *Bulletin of the Institute of Historical Research*, No. 37, (1959), and 'The Conservative Party under the impact of the Second Reform Act', in *Victorian Studies*, No. 2, (1958-59), pp. 289-304.

53 J. P. Cornford, 'The transformation of conservatism in the late nineteenth-century', *Victorian Studies*, No. 7, (1963-64), pp. 35-66.

54 Vincent, *Formation*, Introduction, p. xvii.

55 Biagini, *Liberty, Retrenchment*, and Biagini and Reid, *Currents of Radicalism*.

56 Hawkins, *Parliamentary Government*, pp. 638-639.

The Inter-disciplinary Approach

This then is the somewhat confusing and at times contradictory picture regarding the emergence and importance of the political party in the late eighteenth and early nineteenth centuries. Part of the problem is that the various positions adopted by historians have been arrived at because political change was viewed in a narrow context. Studies were compartmentalised around the political party or a specific event the Reform Act of 1832 or 1867, or a specific event at a specific period, the Reform Crises of 1830-32 or 1866-67, or the Secret Ballot Act of 1872, and so on. However, none of the historians noted above mention working class or plebeian involvement in party politics before 1832 largely because there virtually was no involvement. Yet, as will be seen below, there was working class involvement after 1832 and it is this feature coupled with changes occurring in organizational structures which points to fundamental changes taking place after 1832.

With regard to the problem of the emergence of the modern political party, it appears logical to utilize some of the approaches used by political scientists and political sociologists. The former are usually concerned with the detailed examination of the functions and features of political institutions and the latter with the effects the various institutions, such as the legislature or the executive or the political party, have on political behaviour. An example of how useful these approaches can be is to attempt to offer a definition of the functions of the nineteenth century political party as detailed by historians[57] building on the work of political scientists.[58] It seems that most historians and political scientists would agree that by 1914 most of the numerous features and functions of the modern British political parties were in position. The intention here is to re-examine the historical transition of these features and functions from the late eighteenth century. For if it can be shown what party features are on display and what functions are being performed, and, importantly, what attitudes and patterns of behaviour are apparent, then an advance will have been achieved.

By utilizing the term 'functions' of political parties the intention is not to subscribe to the methodology of structural functionalism in an absolute sense. The term is used here to describe the various changes in the post-1832 political parties had on both local political society and on the parties themselves. Briefly the main features and functions are that modern political parties are agencies of selection and recruitment by which the local and national elites are built up and maintained. In the contemporary world there are other methods and agencies of political recruitment such as trade unions, but the political party is by far the most effective agency. Political parties also play a vital part in coordinating the organizing of electoral activity. Similarly parties perform the function of disseminating and, indeed, generating both governmental and opposition programmes and policies. There is a problem as to precisely how much the rank and file determine actual policies, which are usually selected and initiated by the political elites. However, there is a process of consultation and consideration with various interested groupings, and one of those groups integral to the consultative process are the party's members and supporters if only as a sounding board and vehicle of political feedback. This function is linked to the important role which political parties have in politically coordinating governmental actions and the actions of the opposition. Importantly parties act as agencies of political integration of diverse sectional interests by acting as vehicles for the articulation

---

57 See for example J. A. Garrard, *Leadership and Power in Victorian Industrial Towns, 1830-80*, (Manchester, 1983) and by the same author, 'Parties, Members and Voters after 1867: A local study', *Historical Journal*, Vol. 20, No. 1 (1977), or D. Fraser, *Urban Politics in Victorian England*, (Leicester, 1978).

58 S. Neumann, *Modern Political Parties*, (Chicago, 1967).

and possibly satisfaction of political demands. This point regarding political integration provides parties with a related function in that they are agencies that allow individuals a platform for political activity and also are a useful device in political education, socialization and proselytization. A further feature is that they articulate ideas and organizations alternative to governments.[59] Political parties also act as disseminators of basic political principles, of conservatism or social democracy or Liberalism, and in their most extreme form can act as vehicles for the transmission of ideological doctrines. This is closely linked to the very basic function that political parties are instruments of marshalling and disciplining their political supporters. Political parties in the modern world tend to give legitimation to political activities so long as their members and supporters abide by the principles and structure of the particular party. Finally modern political parties to a significant degree determine the limits of not only the political agenda through policy initiatives, but also set the limits of political action, of what is allowable and what is not, especially with regard to its own supporters, but also on occasions other party's officials in both the local and national arenas.

Most of the features and functions outlined above can be said to be in place by the outbreak of the First World War, but their development had been slow. The argument here is that their origins can be traced as far back as the first decades after 1832. This guide should help in clearing a way through the somewhat confused and at times contradictory historiographical path we have outlined above. With regard to a verdict, it would seem that Messrs Clark, Beales and Christie are on solid ground. In the course of this book the aim will be to show there were qualitative changes in the functions of political parties after 1832 which were a direct result of the Reform Bill. There is little evidence that political parties acted as agencies for any of the aforementioned functions prior to 1832. Lines of party demarcation regarding fixed principles can be detected from the 1790s. But it was only in the late 1820s that the notion of broad cross-party coalitions with their inclusive assumptions, both at the centre of political activity and on the peripheries, that one party constituted the ministry and the other the opposition. This does not mean that the anti-Namierites are totally wrong. O'Gorman and others are right to point out the growing tendencies towards organized political activities from the 1790s. Precedents were set in organizing opposition to the Jacobins and Whig radicals, and, in the work of electoral organization, by William Adam for the Foxite Whigs. Nor are those historians completely wrong who argue that it is only meaningful to speak of the modern political party after 1867 and the advent of a mass electorate, but the changes wrought by the first Reform Act were so markedly different from what was the norm previously. The intention is to show in the chapters which follow that not all of the functions outlined were set into place in the years immediately following 1832, nor indeed by 1867. But sufficient evidence exists to suggest, with regard to the operation of parties, party politics and the integration of the working class, the Reform Bill was an important watershed, not only at the centre of political activity but also in the localities. As John Phillips, a scholar of constituency politics in the reform era has said,

> The Great Reform Bill as an issue or a statute reshaped electoral behaviour in many boroughs, however politically or physically diverse... The size of a parliamentary borough, the size of its electorate, its electoral composition before 1832, and its location, all had little to do with the impact of the Reform Bill, it transcended parochial concerns and conditions.[60]

For many of the areas of functional activity of political parties the 1830s was the crucial decade. It

---

59   See Garrard, 'Parties, Members and Voters'.

60   Phillips, *The Great Reform Bill in the Boroughs*, p. 294.

was here, as Derek Beales has rightly pointed out, parties "completed their conquest of the House of Commons and became accepted as the organizations whose relative strength should determine the complexion of government."[61] Caution however, must be shown in endeavouring not to read back our understanding of the parties of today to that period when the parties were merely developing the initial signs of modernity. The task below is to point out when the traits of the changing nature of parties first became apparent and meaningful, but vigilance must be taken regarding historical anachronism. Political and social change must be considered in the context of the past and not the ideas of the present. It must be stressed, political modernity did not dawn the morning after the passing of the Reform Bill. But on the other hand, the pace of political change did quicken appreciably in the 1830s and '40s in many areas of the political culture of Britain.

One of the crucial changes was that the political party ceased to be confined to the centre of political activity, in Parliament or at Court. Increasingly after 1832 political activity was to be found in the localities.[62] It was in the localities that the struggle for the Reform Act was begun, in places such as Bristol, Nottingham, Birmingham, Leeds, Sheffield and Manchester. This raising of the political consciousness of different social groups did not disappear with the Bill's enactment. A significant reason for its maintenance was that political parties, Conservatives, Whig-Liberals, Radicals and Chartists, operated effectively in these localities and part of the reason why they did so was due to the terms of the Reform Act and subsequently the 1835 Municipal Reform Act.

In subsequent chapters it will be argued that, when these developmental changes in the features and functions of political parties are broken down and analysed, the comparisons between the pre-1832 party political system and the one which followed the Reform Act are very revealing. This is especially so when they are exposed in their operation as institutions and their impact on the changing patterns of political behaviour and attitudes of wider society. Political parties are therefore, a major influence on political culture. This method of examining a political party and the changing political culture by using some of the techniques of political science will set the debate surrounding the emergence of the political party into sharper focus and allow points of contention to be explained more adequately. In order to illustrate some of the points noted above what is needed is the description of a political party in transition, in this case the Conservative Party.

The Transformation of Toryism

An initial task is to place the changes taking place into historical context and offer an understanding as to what Conservatism was in the 1830s. To do this we need to examine the traits of similarity and of difference between the Toryism and conservative Whiggery of the later eighteenth century and the Conservatism of Peel and his followers in the 1830s. The argument being that at the level of principles and ideology the party was transformed by Peel very quickly after 1832 in a bid to make the Conservatives a truly national party which could include sections of the working class as members and supporters. This, as will be seen in due course, was complimented by organisational change, at local and national levels. But first the guiding principles of the party need to be looked at comparing the Conservatism of Peel with that of eighteenth-century Toryism.

Traditionally the Tories were the group who defended the rights of succession of Charles II and

---

61 D. E. D. Beales, *The Political Parties of Nineteenth-Century Britain*, (London, 1971), p. 11.

62 See Phillips, *The Great Reform Bill, passim,* see also John A. Phillips and Charles Wetherall, 'The Great Reform Act of 1832 and the Political Modernization of England', in *The American Historical Review,* Vol. 100, No. 2, (April 1995).

James II in the 1660s and 1680s. However, James's insistence on closer ties with Rome in 1687 forced the Tories to chose between their King and the Church. At this point they opted for the Church.[63] The Tories joined with the Whigs in bringing about the Revolution Settlement on the basis of a compact between the sovereign and the people. Henceforth Tories still believed in Church and King but their loyalty was to the crown as an institution rather than to the monarch as a person. When Queen Ann failed to leave any direct heir, the conflict of loyalties between the King on the throne and the King over the water drastically reduced the Tory party in Parliament.[64] However, substantial elements among the clergy and the greater and lesser gentry preserved Tory feelings and principles as well as the Tory name in the localities. This is an important point. Even though for much of the eighteenth century the Tory party (as far as it existed) was denied office and power, Tory principles and ideas regarding patriotism and traditional practices and customs were popular among a wide section of social groupings. Among, for example, tenant farmers, yeomen and artisans of several kinds. Thus historically, when seeking the lineage for popular Toryism, political traditionalism, practices based on common law and the preservation of long-held customs, the line goes back at least to the seventeenth century. The apparent totality of the Whig triumph during the Hanoverian succession and their complete hold on political power at the centre, at least up to 1760, should not confuse the fact that in the localities Toryism still possessed areas of influence. This was so in the various Court Leets, the Tory-controlled Corporations, Vestries and, if their names had not been removed by Hardicke and Walpole, among the magistracy. Though numerically reduced there remained a significant Tory element among the 'independent' members who sat in the House of Commons and, when they joined with the factions of disaffected Whigs, were a thorn in the side of the parasitic Whig oligarchy. Thus the long tenure of Walpole's term of office was not completely unchallenged. Henry St John (first Viscount Bolingbroke) made it his aim to unite the Tories. Bolingbroke founded the *Craftsman* as a political magazine with a view to breaking the grip of the dominant Whig families with a call to governing the nation with talented men drawn from all factions and not exclusively by an oligarchy of the same political caste.

The advent of George III, cultivating, unlike his grandfather and great grandfather, patriotic sentiment, educated in the principles of Bolingbroke, reconciled the Tories once more to the person as well as the title of the monarch, and again Tories began to be seen as court. In fact the process of gradually ending the political proscription of the Tories had begun in 1757 by the elder Pitt at the outset of the Seven Years War. After 1760, however, and the accession of George III, the distinction of 'Court' and 'Country' was abolished as the new King endeavoured to construct an executive devoid of old party influences and the personal rule of the great Whig families. As the King said some years later, his intention was,

> to put an end to those unhappy distinctions of party called Whigs and Tories by declaring I would countenance every Man that supported my administration and concurred in that form of Government which had been so wisely established by the Revolution.[65]

---

63 The Declarations of Indulgences of James II. "We cannot but heartily wish, as it will be easily believed, that all the peoples of out dominions were members of the Catholic Church." In A. Browning (ed.) *English Historical Documents, 1660-1714*, (London, 1953), pp. 395-6.

64 The Tory membership of the House of Commons dropped from 358 in 1714 to 113 in 1761 and by the 1780s they had virtually disappeared. See Romney Sedgwick, (ed.) *The History of Parliament. The House of Commons, 1715-1754*, (2 Vols. HMSO, 1971), i, p. 19, or A. S. Foorde, *His Majesty's Opposition, 1714-1830*, (Oxford, 1964), pp. 335-8, or, again, I. R. Christie, *The End of Lord North's Ministry, 1780-1782*, (London, 1958).

65 Printed in H. Butterfield, *George III, Lord North and the People, 1779-1780*, (London, 1949), p. 3.

The Old Corps Whig leadership (Newcastle, Devonshire and Rockingham) now found themselves in opposition. As a means of holding their ranks together, it served their purpose to highlight their impeccable Whig credentials by pointing out that any ministry that allowed the personal rule of the monarch, in the fashion of the seventeenth century Stuarts, was Tory.

The 1760s saw some of the most contentious and momentous issues of the century initiated by Government: the Peace of Paris, the widening of the Excise Act, the Stamp Acts, the General Warrants and the Wilkes agitation. But it is indicative of the lack of party that the opposition Whigs were unable to maintain any lasting sense of united organization inside or outside Westminster. The Whig's attempt at maintaining their personal rule had failed. The Tories, however, increasingly found their principles of monarchical and patriotic loyalty, adherence to the Settlement of 1688, national security and law and order advanced. This was due to the policies pursued during peace and war by the younger Pitt, and after his death the conservative Whigs like Portland, Perceval and Liverpool.

Throughout the eighteenth century Tory policy evolved largely by adaptation to changing circumstances, but there remained certain guiding principles. First was the unbroken attachment to the Church of England. Part of the reason for this was political expediency and part was, as the Catholics and Nonconformists claimed, to maintain the privileges of the Established Church as laid down in the Revolution Settlement of 1688. Although Catholics were still regarded as suspect and were denied full political rights many nonconformists, while not allowed the full privileges of the Anglicans were admitted to positions of power in local politics, and were allowed to vote in elections. If the Whigs thought of themselves as defenders of religious toleration, especially of nonconformity, the Tories saw themselves as the defenders of the Established Church. Because defence of the Established Church of England equated with loyalty to the King and the Constitution, the Tories defended the abuses of patronage and privileges enjoyed by the Anglican Church, which lost them support amongst sections of the local non-Anglican clergy and local gentry.

Secondly, the Tories became closely attached to the landed interest, in opposition to many urban Whigs who favoured the rights of trade and commerce. This is not to say that the Whigs looked upon the land with disfavour. The ruling Whig oligarchy were amongst the greatest landowners in Britain but the question was one of giving priority to that interest which the two groups believed would best serve the national interest. In the case of the Tories this emphasis was on the capacity of the nation to be self-sufficient in as many areas of economic life as possible, but especially in agriculture; in the case of the Whigs it was an emphasis on trade and commerce. For much of the eighteenth century the Whig view prevailed, but again a sizeable amount of popular public opinion was in sympathy with the Tory view. Up to the 1760s at least, and possibly into the 1780s, this was especially revealed in expressions of a deep-rooted hatred of the House of Hanover and their Whig supporters. In 1755 for example an apprentice from Taunton somewhat injudiciously gave voice his opinions in verse:

> Come noble Britons once more your courage rise
> or to Hanover be a sacrifice.
> Whilst Hanover with Plenty is perfect
> With heavy Taxes we are prospect...
> Was Pelham here I'd shite in his face
> I'd do the same with Newcastle's Grace.[66]

---

66 Public Records Office, State Papers Domestic, 36/132, ff 24-25, John Sharp to Mr Amyand, 9 November, 1755. For aspects of popular Toryism see L.Colley, *In Defiance of Oligarchy: The Tory Party, 1714-1760*, (Cambridge, 1982) and by the same author, *Britons: Forging the Nation State*, (Yale, 1992). For other studies see. F. O'Gorman, *The Emergence of the British Two-party System*, (London, 1982), or John

Closely allied to the self-sufficiency argument of many Tories was the need to protect all types of domestic production for the benefit of the national good and of the maintenance of customary practices. This tended to mean that Tory magistrates were rather more sympathetic to plebeian grievances surrounding food shortages and contractual negotiations with employers.[67] The significance of this important point was not lost on the embryonic working class.

Thirdly, and finally, throughout the eighteenth century the basic political psychology of the Tory was of an individual who was adverse to change unless the need for it was proved completely. This habit of mind made many Tories feel ill at ease with the Settlement of 1688, though their leaders had helped bring it about; but as the years passed and the Revolution Settlement became the established order of things, Tories regarded themselves as its special guardians. This dedication to the established order, accentuated by revolution and war abroad and unrest at home, created a Tory image. In the years immediately after the conclusion of the Napoleonic wars in 1815, Tories were seen as hostile to the labouring masses and a brake on economic and political views of radicals. However, many sections of eighteenth century society could relate more to the homilies of Toryism than to aristocratic Whiggery.[68] This was largely why, with little or no organization inside Parliament and none whatsoever outside, Toryism as a loose set of political principles and policies managed to survive the eighteenth century. The call of Bolingbroke, and later George III, for non-party government was successful at the centre of power, especially in the administrations of the younger Pitt. But in the country at large Toryism still represented a political creed, even if, over the course of the eighteenth century this creed had become somewhat vague.

The Influence of Burke

Edmund Burke is regarded as the thinker that gave Conservatism its intellectual purchase.[69] In fact Burke was a Whig but increasingly, toward the end of his life, a conservative Whig or 'new' Whig as opposed to the 'old' Whigs led by Charles James Fox. But Burke remained a Whig until his death and always refuted the tag of Tory. Ian Christie is closer to the truth when he says that what Burke was outlining in his *Reflections on the Revolution in France*, and *Appeal from the New to the Old Whigs*,[70] was not Toryism at all as it was understood in the eighteenth century. It was the intellectual precursor of nineteenth century Conservatism. Nonetheless, the Tories of the late eighteenth and early nineteenth centuries found in Burke a close and comfortable ally. Nor is Burke important solely for his contribution to Toryism/Conservatism but is arguably more important for his intellectual justification of the political party as a legitimate and valuable institution.

Burke's first defence of the notion of party came in 1770 with the publication of his *Thoughts on*

Brewer, *Party, Ideology and Popular Politics at the Accession of George III*, (Cambridge, 1976), or Nicholas Rogers, *Whigs and Cities*, (Oxford, 1989). For the growth of popular patriotism and nationalism see, L.Colley, 'Whose Nation? Class and National Consciousness in Britain, 1750-1830', in *Past and Present*, No. 113, (November, 1986), or Hugh Cunningham, 'The Language of Patriotism, 1750-1914', in *History Workshop Journal*, Vol. xii, (1981), pp. 8-33.

67 For an example of Tory/Conservative attitudes towards authority and civil control see D. Eastwood, *Governing Rural England*, (Oxford, 1994).

68 O'Gorman, *Emergence*, Chapter 2, see also F. O',Gorman, *Voters, Parties and Patrons: The Unreformed Electoral System, 1734-1832*, (Cambridge, 1989), p. 322.

69 For an account of other early conservative theorists see H. T. Dickinson, *Liberty and Property*, (London, 1977), and for an alternative view see J. J. Slack, 'The Memory of Burke and the Memory of Pitt', in *Historical Journal*, Vol. 30, No. 3, (1987).

70 E. Burke, *Reflections of the Revolution in France and on the Proceedings of Certain Societies in London Relative to that Event*, (London, 1790), *An Appeal from the New to the Old Whigs*, (London, 1791).

the Cause of the Present Discontents.[71] This was a spirited attack on the increasingly successful attempt by those politicians close to the King to reduce Parliament to impotence. The traditional and essential role of the House of Commons was to check the power of the crown by having the facility to refuse funds. Burke argued a court clique had undermined this. This court faction had managed to persuade the King to buy the support of the House of Commons to vote — in extraordinary additions to the Crown's revenues. Such additions Burke and the Rockingham Whigs argued were not needed to uphold the dignity of the monarch, but were used to buy the support of sections of the House of Commons for dubious court policies. It was to stop this tendency that Burke initially pressed the idea of party. Only if the tenure of an administration was made to depend on the support of a declared party could this venal undermining of the traditional function of Parliament be curtailed. What was required, Burke argued, were honest men, publicly committed to stand or fall together, who could not be picked off by offers of place or office. As he himself put it, "Party is a body of men united, for promoting by their joint endeavours the national interest, upon some particular principle in which they are all agreed."[72]

As noted earlier to call a group of men a 'party' in eighteenth century (and continuing into the nineteenth) was to suggest that was something suspicious was afoot; the term was almost a pejorative one. Party was denounced as a conspiracy against the nation. Kings and politicians affected to be above party; to be, above all, patriots and non-party men. The King's ministers could not rule without support in parliament, which was often divided into parts; but these parts, as Namier noted were not parties as the term was used in either the late seventeenth century or mid-nineteenth century. They were loose collections, or groups of interests that could be influenced or swayed by place, privilege or money. There were opposers (the outs) of ministries, but this opposition was not organized in terms of party. This situation was tolerated up until Burke's blast, primarily on the pragmatic basis that it worked. There were other reasons. Tories did not organize themselves more fully because they believed that a closed cabal was just the form of pernicious practice used by the Walpolean and Pelhamite Whigs that they wished to counteract. Hence their calls for non-party coalitions to form administrations. For the Newcastle and Rockingham Whigs, once George III had taken up with the Tory view of 'broadbottom' ministries after 1760, it seemed the Tories would dominate office indefinitely and possibly do to the Whigs what they had done to the Tories since 1714. During that earlier period the Tories were open to the slur of Jacobitism and their opportunities for 'loyal' opposition limited. Here the Whigs' credentials were impeccable. Hence Burke's call for the unity of party, based around commonly held principles. What he expounded in *Thoughts on the Cause of the Present Discontents*, was a response to the threat posed by the Tories. Burke's views however, were strictly limited, as John Brewer tells us:

> Burke did not go so far as to argue that party should be co-terminus with government, i.e. he did not defend what we should think of as 'party government', nevertheless his conception of politics is one that envisages party as an enduring feature of politics.[73]

Burke's position, however, found little purchase with a monarch who was fervently anti-party and who for thirty years after 1760 surrounded himself with politicians of a similar persuasion.

---

71 E.Burke, *Thoughts on the Present Discontents*, (London, 1770).

72 Ibid., p. 335.

73 John Brewer, *Party Ideology and Popular Politics as the Accession of George III*, (Cambridge, 1976), p. 73.

After 1789, and the possibility that the French revolutionary experiment could spread across the Channel, Burke renewed his advocacy of the political party as a device necessary not only for responsible government but also as a defensive measure against organised Jacobinism. Burke was the first established political thinker and practising politician to advocate open and loyal opposition within parliament, indeed, suggesting that party government could be an instrument of freedom. He was the first modern politician to explain that organizations created for the capture of political power are not necessarily obstacles to good and responsible government, but on the contrary are a means to it, provided they work in the open and respect established conventions.

However, it must be stressed Burke was no democrat. He developed his theories of party and government precisely to offset the growing tendency of the early 1790s towards democracy among the mass of the population away for the centres of political power. He strongly held to the Lockean notion that only those with property or a viable stake in the political fortunes of the nation should be involved in the political contract. Only those with the most to lose, the gentry and aristocracy, were the natural governors and administrators of local and national government. For Burke, all revolutionaries and many radicals were socially and politically blind. They did not see the damage they caused or may cause before they act. They act regardless of the possible effects and ramifications, and this for Burke and for subsequent conservatives is inherently irrational behaviour.

Burke attacked egalitarianism and the natural 'rights of man', on the pragmatic grounds that those who advocated such ideas were deceiving their followers because they never could achieve their aims and objectives. He argued, as did many Conservatives in the nineteenth century, that differing talents exist among people as do different opportunities. It is this very difference which gave society its complex balance and structure. Especially important to Burke was the preservation of the prescriptive constitutional and political rights. Prescriptive rights were those which although customary and often not bound by legal or constitutional statute had proved their worth by standing the test of time and history, as such they should not be altered or reformed unless proved to be unequivocally defective. These features outlined by Burke proved to be a solid basis for the fusion of the old 'absolutist' Tories and conservative Whigs, especially so with the resurgence of English monarchy the after the summer of 1792 when the French King was executed. Loyal Associations and Reeves Societies sprung up nationwide (estimated at 2000 in 1795) which stimulated a jingoistic popular brand of Anglican Toryism and found a purchase among all grades in society. This swelling of support can be viewed as a reaction, but it was not a blind reaction, although at times it may have appeared so, especially during the Church and King riots. It was articulate, and the most eloquent presenter of this resurgent Toryism was, paradoxically, Edmund Burke.

Some commentators have portrayed the Toryism that developed in Britain after 1789 as a political creed opposed to all change, but this is not the case.[74] For Burke a specific and particular doctrine was being formulated and it was one which did not preclude the development of policies designed reform proven abuses. However, this was developed by politicians after Burke's death in 1797 and more relevantly after the death of the younger Pitt in 1806, a leader who, while he was in office, more than anyone adhered to George III's aversion to party. What makes Burke's view of party so novel and historically relevant was that he developed it as a means of preservation. Unlike the Country Tories or George III and the younger Pitt, or indeed, the radicals of the 1790s, Burke believed that the best way to ensure the maintenance of the existing political and social order was to maintain the traditional political system. Burke argued that parties were the best means of gaining unity and

---

74 Particularly the radical press during the reform crisis and Chartist years.

political alliances. He advocated party as a means of preserving the existing political system as well as preserving the Whigs. The Whigs were needed to provide political balance; their destruction would be dangerous to the preservation of the entire political fabric of the nation.[75]

Although Burke was unquestionably a conservative he did allow for reform and change. But only within the existing social and political structures: such change and reform must aim at the assured and gradual restoration of an institution to its original purpose of fulfilling its customary and prescriptive operation. Indeed on some questions Burke appears to be quite liberal, not too surprising given his Whig credentials. His liberal tendencies are evident in his discussion of the relief of Catholic disabilities, Irish affairs or the nationalist movements in Europe. But it was in his development and championing of political economy and free trade which revealed his liberal leanings and it was here that he had a significant influence on future politicians like Lord Liverpool, George Canning, William Huskisson, Lord Goodrich, Sir Robert Peel and William Gladstone.[76]

The Transition to Conservatism

The idea that society grows and develops like any other organism was not Burkean, it was the product of the 'organic' paternalistic Tories of the mid-nineteenth century, which owed much to the earlier writings of Coleridge and application of Disraeli. The transformation of old Toryism into Conservatism was of a slow transition and, indeed, after 1846 and the party's split over the Corn Laws, many of the older Tory principles of protectionism, the obligation for those with wealth and prestige to protect the less fortunate, again came to the fore. But the Conservatism of Peel was the foundation of Conservatism throughout the nineteenth century, and it is relevant to explain how it related and grew out of the amalgam of late eight century Toryism and conservative Whiggery.

Nineteenth-century Toryism and Peelite Conservatism owe much of their ideological principles to the conservative Whigs, led philosophically by Burke and politically by the Portland Whigs, in the loyalist climate of the 1790s and the first decade of the nineteenth century. It owed relatively little to the old Toryism of the first half of the eighteenth century. The new Toryism of the Duke of Portland, Henry Addington, Spencer Perceval, Lord Liverpool, George Canning and, ultimately, Sir Robert Peel stemmed directly out of the reactions to the possible spread of the French Revolution, the radicalism of the Foxite Whigs and the philosophical ideas of Edmund Burke. In the years prior to 1789, the traditional Tories denied office and actual power, offered support to various leaders, but never as a unified party. The principles that held them together spiritually were their total support of the Anglican Church and of the title and office of the Monarch. The old Tories remained a force in the House of Commons even though their leadership was dissipated after the early 1760s. This group were rarely placeholders, but were generally representatives of the country (or county) interest and sworn to its protection. They shunned office, scorned bribes and were essentially non-professional in their approach to politics, they enjoyed their status for its social prestige, usually in their locality, rather than for material gains. The support these old Tories gave the King was particularly effective because it was given voluntarily and expected no reward. Once the independent Tories turned against

75 E. Burke, *The Works of Edmund Burke*, 8 Vols, (London, 1854-89), i, pp. 373-74.

76 More will said of Burke's influence on Peel in due course but Gladstone writing in 1886 wrote of Burke, 'December 18. Read Burke; what a magazine of wisdom on Ireland and America. January 9. Made many extracts from Burke — sometimes almost divine'. The historian and Liberal politician T. B. Macauley, thought Burke, 'The greatest man since Milton.' Quoted in John Morley, *The Life of William Ewart Gladstone*, (London, 1908), p. 389.

a ministry it could not survive long. The independent Tories had survived throughout the eighteenth century but the 1790s and the first decades of the new century saw the beginnings of a cohesive party. What held them together was opposition to the radicalism of Foxite Whigs and all that it stood for, the comforting philosophy of Burke (often with the political economy left out) and the leadership of the conservative Whigs of Pitt, Portland, Addington, Perceval and Liverpool.

Although in political terms the amalgam of conservative Whigs and Tories was in the ascendancy as a basis of broad support (both inside and outside the legislature), and although this support was gathering momentum throughout the Napoleonic wars, there were few signs of party organization. It was essentially a cabinet coalition. The long ministry of the younger Pitt came to an end in 1801, and this served to fragment the coalition which had governed Britain in the 1780s and '90s into Pittites, Addingtonians, Grenvillites, Canningites, and the supporters of the Duke of Portland with the Foxite opposition outside power. The precise reasons and causes as to how and why the various groups came together is the subject of intense debate and is extraordinarily complex. But essentially there are two reasons. Firstly, the Pittite group, numbering about sixty members of Parliament, realized after their leader's death in 1806 that in order to maintain the political principles of Pitt they must act in a way that their leader never would have approved: to act and organize as a single unit. Secondly, Burke, one of the most respected thinkers and parliamentarians of the age, had given the theoretical justification of party based on sound constitutional propriety. Among electors the only extra-Parliamentary political organizations of any significance existing in the first three decades of the nineteenth century were the annual dinners held by the Whig Clubs in order to celebrate the memory of Charles James Fox, and the more permanent and widespread Pitt Clubs. Liverpool's administration of 1812 was broadly based but at its core were the old Pittites with places found for George Canning and Lord Sidmouth (formally Henry Addington). It united upon the basis of loyalty to the monarch, a sense of duty to the nation and the defence of the established (or prescriptive) institutions in Church and State. Added to these basic principles was the decidedly anti-Burkean belief in the need to protect agriculture, arguably excusable during wartime but maintained after 1815. However, it was because of the ministry's uncompromising stance on questions of law and order, but also because of its economic policies, that the opponents of Lord Liverpool's administration referred to it as a 'Tory' government.

In several respects the term 'Tory' is misleading. Firstly the government of Lord Liverpool never allowed the Prince Regent, or George IV after 1820, the range of prerogatives the old Tories allowed in his father; this limitation of the powers of the monarch was traditionally Whig in outlook. Secondly there were members of Liverpool's Cabinet who pursued a traditional Whig foreign policy, most notably George Canning, who believed in granting independent status to nations such as Poland and Greece. Thirdly there were ministers, again Canning but also Robinson and Palmerston, who were in favour of Catholic Emancipation in order to resolve the political problems of Ireland. Fourthly, in economic affairs, there were important elements within the Liverpool government who attempted to steer the Cabinet away from rigid protectionism as advocated by the old Tory faction, and towards giving manufacturing industry at least equal status to agriculture, most notable of this group was William Huskisson. Fifthly, although Liverpool's ministry had a reputation for a tough line on law and order it is unlikely that the 'reforming' Whigs of Tierney, Ponsonby and Grey would have done any differently. Especially given the seriousness of the outbreaks of Luddite violence and the almost paranoid sentiments of many of landed and middle classes in the wake of the French Revolution and war. Moreover, the Home Office, under the direction of Robert Peel made more legal reforms than any government for over a hundred years. The sixth and final point regarding Liverpool's government is that there were even those members, Peel, Croker, Goulbourn, who pressed for some concessionary measures of Parliamentary reform before the reforming Whigs put through a far more sweeping measure between 1830 and 1832.

On all points Burke and Pitt would have concurred, because the essential fabric of society on the basis of prescription and property was being conserved by moderate measures. It suited the backbench Tory traditionalists to forget what Pitt and Burke said and wrote in support of the above questions, and to push to the fore those aspects of their heroes' policies which suited the sentiments of traditional Toryism. To be sure the backbench Tories were significant numerically and their views could not be ignored but crucially the ministry of Lord Liverpool was a coalition of conservative Whigs and moderate Tories. It was in essence the penultimate stage in the development of Conservatism. The traditional Tories realized the transformative tendency and vented their anger on those ministers, such as Canning who they believed went too far, even to the point of withdrawing their support when Canning formed a government in 1827. At this point the coalition fell apart and Parliament began to divide along 'party' lines. The liberal supporters of 'Catholic' Canning (Huskisson, Melbourne, Palmerston and Landsdowne) joined the Whigs. Those who could not support Canning on the Catholic Question formed a separate group led by Wellington and Peel.[77] The two leaders were joined by the traditional or 'Ultra' Tories, men like Lord Londonderry, the Lowther family, Lord Salisbury, Lord Eldon, Lord Lyndhurst, Sir Richard Vyvyan, Edward Knatchbull and numerous backbenchers mainly drawn from the shires.

However, the Ultras never felt entirely confident with their new leaders, suspecting them of 'liberal' tendencies. These were confirmed when, in 1828, Wellington as Prime Minister repealed the Test and Corporation Acts and a year later gave in to the clamour and passed Catholic Emancipation, primarily to avert an insurrection in Ireland. At this point the Tories may have deserted Wellington had it not coincided with the first of the measures of the reform of parliament put forward by Earl Grey and the reforming Whigs. The sweeping nature of Grey's proposals provided a point around which the Tories/Conservatives could rally. But the Burkean nature of conservative Whiggery was maintained by Peel, Goulbourn, Aberdeen and others, and, in the early 1830s, became formally recognised as the term 'Tory' was replaced by 'Conservative'. Thus a direct line can be traced from the practical policies of Pitt and the theoretical or philosophical foundations laid by Burke, through to Portland, Liverpool, Canning and Peel. Many of the backbench 'Conservatives' were in reality old Tories under a new name. Support was given to Peel and the Conservatives firstly because it was widely understood that they genuinely believed in the preservation of the prescriptive and constitutional principles enshrined in Church and State, even though they found Peel's aloof and impersonal style unsupportive and were still suspicious of his policies. The second reason was that there was no one (in the House of Commons at least) equal in political stature to Peel; thus they were stuck with them and, to his occasional chagrin, he with them. The unity of the Peelite Conservatives and the old Tories was preserved because of what each perceived as the dangers posed by the reforming Whigs (influenced as they were by the radicals) to the Constitution. Such dangers included the independence of the two branches of legislature, the rights of the monarch, and the preservation of the Anglican religion as the national Church of England. The chief difference between the Peelite Conservatives and the Ultras or old Tories was one of temperament regarding not only specific issues

---

77 It was not only that Wellington and Peel could not support Canning's policies but also that they detested him personally. See for example L. Woodward, *The Age of Reform*, (Oxford, 1962 ed.), pp. 74-5.

but political change as such. If any group were resistant to change of any kind it was the Ultras. They were unshakeable in their defence of the Corn Laws, in their hostility to the factory system and the proponents of political economy. The Ultras or old Tories were totally opposed to parliamentary reform of any kind, and were vehemently (in some cases pathologically) anti-Catholic. On this last question the argument was crudely simple for the Ultras. It demanded how could a man or group of man swear a quasi-sacred allegiance to their King and country, when they have already sworn allegiance to the Pope in Rome? To the Ultras all Catholics were suspect, all potential traitors and all indolent ritual worshippers. In an attempt to prove their case they pointed to Ireland or to England's traditional enemy France. In the second example a revolution had already occurred, in the first it could happen at any time.

Although many Peelites felt affinity to the basic principles of the old Tories, especially on religious questions, they could not accept their dogmatic assertiveness regarding policy options. Peel, like Burke realized that national needs were in a state of rapid change and that the old Tory philosophy of political rigidity was impracticable to Britain in the 1830s. Peel at no time believed in pure *laissez-faire* as a doctrine, maintaining the state had a role in intervening in the national economy, but neither did he believe in blanket protectionism. Peel's moderation and quest for consensus similarly revealed itself on religious questions. He was an Anglican and not a supporter of Catholic Emancipation, but he recognised that the Catholics and nonconformists had reasonable grounds for complaint regarding abuses within the established church. This is why he set up the Ecclesiastical Commission in 1835 and gave the Irish Catholics a government grant towards the cost of training priests at Maynooth. While the Peelite Conservatives could agree with the old Tories on the need to protect and preserve the political constitution in Church and State, and further agree with Burke that rash political innovation was highly suspect, they did not agree that all reform was necessarily bad. If it proved to be needed then it should be considered; similarly the Conservatives under Peel did not believe that political groups or parties existed solely to protect the interests of a given section of society. This is why Peel mistrusted the sectional interests of the Anti-Corn Law League as much as he was disdainful of his old Tory backbenchers who advocated protection for domestic agriculture. The Peel fortune was built on the rapid economic expansion of the late eighteenth-century, thus he did not share the animosity felt by the old Tories to the factory system but, conversely, he was well aware of the unscrupulous and ruthless practices of some factory masters. As will be discussed in due course, this was a factor that was to emerge during his second ministry from 1841. For Peel the Conservative Party was a national party representative of all grades of society and their various interests. Peel was decidedly not a democrat. He believed like Burke that property and education were the best qualifications for political participation. He did, however, realize that differing political interests existed and that the Conservative Party had to cater for the popular will through its representation, not in extra-parliamentary activity but in the House of Commons. As he stated in 1838, "My object for some years past, that which I have most earnestly laboured to accomplish, has been to lay the foundation of a great party, (cheers) existing in the House of Commons, and deriving its strength from the popular will..."[78]

Perhaps, then, the key differences between Peelite Conservatism and old Toryism can be summarized thus. Firstly, old Toryism represented a sectional interest, albeit a wide one, Peel a national one. Secondly, the old Tories stood for extremes in policy and Peel for moderation and

---

78   Speech by Sir Robert Peel at the Merchant Taylors' Hall, 12 May 1838. From *The Authentic Report of the Conservative Festival at the Merchant Taylors' Hall*, Conservative Journal Office, (London, 1838). See also Robert Stewart, *Party and Politics, 1830-1852*, (Basingstoke, 1982), chapter 5, pp. 62-77.

consensus. Peel and the Conservatives were, however, treading a fine line. On the one hand Peel recognized he had to placate those Tory elements on which his majority in the House of Commons rested. As he showed in the Merchant Taylors' Hall speech of 1838.

> I will, in conclusion, briefly state what I mean by Conservative principles. By Conservative principles, I mean ... the maintenance of the Peerage and the Monarch — the continuance of the just powers and attributes of the King, Lords and Commons in this country... By Conservative principle I mean that, coexistent with equality of civil rights and privileges, there shall be an established religion and imperishable faith, and that established religion shall be of the Protestant Church... By Conservative principles I mean ... the maintenance, defence and continuance of those laws, those institutions ... and those habits and manners which have contributed to mould and form the character of Englishmen.[79]

On the other hand, Peel recognized the need to widen the social foundation of the Conservative Party to include all sections of society and that this would upset many of the old Tories. The problem was noted by Lady Palmerston in her journal in 1841, after Peel had made a speech at Tamworth Library in which he advocated the need to open up knowledge to all classes of society and to strengthen the bonds between them. She wrote, "tho' he (Peel) bids for popularity in all his speeches, he disobliges his followers thereby. They do not like ... a speech he made at Tamworth at some literary meeting, in which he said all classes were alike and that education should not be merely confined to the Church of England (very displeasing to his bigot followers)."[80]

It was Peel's wish to make the Conservatives a national and truly representational party and he realized this could not be achieved on the narrow basis of landed Toryism alone. These old Tories were, as Henry Goulbourn defined them in 1834, "deaf to all improvement which comprises change".[81] From 1833 Peel and the Conservative Party were remarkably successful in changing the direction of an outdated and outmoded political grouping. They further changed the perception of the wider public to the point that the Conservatives won a clear electoral victory within ten years. This led many to believe that the Tories were dead as a political force. But the old Tory elements did not disappear. In the later 1840s after Peel had repealed the Corn Laws, landed Toryism under the leadership of Lord George Bentinck, Benjamin Disraeli and Lord Stanley, came to the surface and over twenty years of sullen suspicion of Peel and his political views exploded into intense hatred. The Peelite leadership were split off from the main party, although many backbench supporters of Peel did remain, Conservatism began to re-trace its Tory antecedents. The problem in the following years was that the policies of free trade invoked by Peel actually worked, and Disraeli and Derby knew this. Protectionism was quietly removed as the central plank of the post-1846 Conservatives and Peel's central objective of strengthening the old institutions by means of controlled and moderate reform became acknowledged as the central tenet of Conservatism. However, at this point our emphasis changes to look at how the industrial working class emerged and how sections of them responded to traditional Toryism and, from the 1820s and '30s to Peelite Conservatism.

79   Peel, *Speech at the Merchant Taylors' Hall*, p. 99.
80   T. Lever, *The Letters of Lady Palmerston*, (London, 1957), p. 248.
81   Peel Papers, British Library, Ad Mss, 40333, ff 177, Goulbourn to Peel, 8 December 1834.

2

The Emergent Working Class and Political Relationships, 1800-1832

The discussion will now be broadened by examining the relationship between Toryism, Conservatism and the industrial working classes up until the elections of the first reformed Parliament of 1832. We need to examine the attitudes of the Tory and Conservative elites and the lower orders before the advent of a nationally organized political party. This is necessary to gauge the significance of the transformation of attitudes of sections of the industrial working class from that of apparent antagonism to the Toryism of governments up to 1833 to the acceptance and support of Conservatism in the later 1830s, '40s and '50s. The ultimate change worked in two ways. From being a group whose political outlook was antagonistic to the manufacturing and working classes, the Tories, as they developed into Conservatives, began to embrace some of those interests. Similarly sections of the working class, from being inherently hostile to the Toryism of the type epitomized by Sidmouth or Eldon, began to look more kindly on the Conservatism of Sir Robert Peel. However, the historical context needs to be examined by outlining the attitudes displayed by both sides in the decades before the 1830s.

Tory Attitudes

The lines of change bear out the themes that began to be developed in chapter one. In several key areas the essential functions of the political party were not performed before 1832. Included within the principles of traditional Toryism was the desire to preserve the constitution, a sense of patriotism and an attachment to the interests of agrarian and agricultural sectors of the economy. During the Napoleonic wars, patriotism gained a purchase on the consciousness of many working people, not least in Lancashire. This situation should have reinforced traditional Tory values and moreover given an economic boost to the skilled working class through increased government contracts. But the war also brought with it extreme hardships the form of high food prices and severe trade recessions, especially in the years when Napoleon enforced his blockade. The Tories demand for the protection of domestic agriculture was perceived as an overt act of political partiality in favour of the landed and propertied classes and against those who held no land or property. This, coupled with a harsh and rigid penal code and a deep mistrust of organized labour, served, in the years from 1790 to 1832, to make Ministerial Tories extremely unpopular among a large section of the emergent working class of the industrial north-west. As the migrants from the hamlets and villages moved into the rapidly increasing textile towns of Lancashire after 1800, some of these families may have felt an attachment to the Tory principles of the eighteenth century. However, loss of independence and severe cycles of trade depression, coupled with a growing perception that national government and politicians were inherently hostile to working class grievances, increasingly moved more and more working people toward popular radicalism.

The national and local political elites were much frightened by the possibility that the principles and the political ramifications of the French Revolution might find a purchase with the socially and politically disenchanted in Britain. In the 1790s the younger Pitt revoked his previous support for Parliamentary reform, and, indeed, passed, in 1799, the first of the Combination Acts, in an effort to prevent the workers of various trades from collective action in support of their grievances. The tendency was for both national and local government to pursue increasingly draconian policies of legal coercion and political reaction. This was necessary in order to isolate and eradicate what were primarily working class social and economic grievances regarding the loss of customary work practices and the imposition of new and more rigorous techniques of production. The Tory elites were traditionally not the group associated with the commercial and industrial interests of Britain and had few links with either the workers or manufacturers who suffered under the frequent cycles of booms and slumps of the late eighteenth and early nineteenth centuries. The conservative Whigs and Tories were concerned to secure domestic peace and order whilst maintaining a long and, at times, precarious war with France. France was traditionally a national enemy and therefore it is no surprise that, at a period of high patriotism, any sign of sympathy to republicanism, or political opposition to government policy during the war, would be labelled by those of a conservative disposition as being seditious. It is also understandable that this extremely defensive conservatism would continue for a considerable time after the national conflict itself had been resolved, in this case after 1815. It might appear to some historians, writing some hundred and eighty years after the events, that the actions and reactions of government and their conservative Whig and Tory supporters bordered on hysterical paranoia. At the time however, for the propertied and others in positions of influence, the French Revolution and the war that followed were attempts at the complete destruction of everything they valued. It is in this context the actions and reactions of those who perceived the situation to be threatening and dangerous must be considered. The war propaganda was intense and was carried to ludicrous lengths even twenty years after its conclusion. The French and Jacobins were portrayed as inhuman barbarians. For example, as late as 1834, the *Blackburn Alfred* compared the humane nature of the British mode of execution with that of the French, and ludicrously questioned the fact that decapitation produced instantaneous death. It wrote, "The head of a criminal named Tillier being submitted to examination after the guillotine, the head turned an every direction from whence it was called." Indeed reports of cannibalism among the French troops appeared as late as 1835.[1] With such speculation and general anti-Gallic feelings it is little wonder that among wide sections of Conservative opinion when they were told that the disputes and reforms demanded by the working class were Jacobin in origin, they were inclined to believe them. Such an atmosphere explains why the authorities were unwilling even to listen to the demands of groups possessing as much self-proclaimed probity as the Loyal Order of Mechanics or the Loyal Association of Weavers.

For the forces of government Pitt set the pattern in the 1790s. When, in 1795, the King on his way to the State Opening of Parliament was jeered and stones flung at his carriage, the response was immediate. A Royal Proclamation was issued against seditious assemblies, and in the House of Commons Pitt introduced Two Acts. These declared it to be treasonable to incite the people by the written word or by speech and banned all meetings of over fifty persons without first notifying a magistrate, who were given wide powers to ban meetings or stop speeches, arrest speakers and disperse smaller meetings. It became a capital offence to defy the orders of the magistrates. Habeas

---

1   *Blackburn Alfred*, 8 January 1834, *Morning Chronicle*, 1 February, 1835.

Corpus, or the right of trial before imprisonment, had been suspended since May 1794 in an effort to stem the rise of popular radicalism (especially in London) against the government of Pitt and in favour of Parliamentary reform. The culmination of this legislation was the Six Acts of 1819. Here Lord Castlereagh attempted firstly to prohibit drilling and military training amongst non-military personnel. The Acts allowed magistrates to enter and search houses without warrants, renewed the prohibition of meetings of over fifty persons and increased the stamp duty on periodicals making them unaffordable to working people. Once again, as a matter of course, Habeas Corpus was suspended. The government felt for much of the period between 1794 and 1831 that only by implementing such measures of legal coercion could law and order be maintained. The tone of an executive besieged was again set by Pitt who is reported to have said after the passage of the Acts of 1795 that: "My head would be off in six months, we're [sic] I to resign."[2]

The moderate Whig reformer, Sir Samuel Romilly, summed up the widening breach between the various groupings within society in 1807 when he said. "The influence which the French Revolution has had over this nation has been in every way unfavourable to them. Among the higher orders it has produced a horror of every kind of innovation: the lower, a desire to try the boldest political experiments, and a distrust and contempt of all moderate reforms."[3] This then was the perception of respectable opinion. The coalition of conservative Whigs and Tories under the direction of Lord Liverpool believed that the popular claim for reform, Parliamentary, economic, religious and social, were manifestations of a deeper conspiracy to undermine the very fabric of British society. Earlier it was outlined how the need to maintain law and order, preserve the rights of property, the monarchy, the Anglican Church, and the prescriptive rights of the constitution served to galvanise the union of conservative Whigs and old Tories. But so too did the elite's fears and suspicions of those members of society below them. As one member of the Lancashire magistracy, Ralph Fletcher of Bolton, wrote to the Home Secretary in 1802 in relation to the Cotton Arbitration Acts:

> In this neighbourhood [Bolton] the seditious seem to be mostly occupied about the intended application to Parliament for regulating the cotton manufacture. This application... certainly originates in the *Jacobin Societies* [Fletcher's emphasis] and is intended as a means to keep the minds of the Weavers in a continual Ferment and as a pretext to raise money for them which will probably be employed in part at least, to seditious purposes.[4]

These feelings continued after the end of the Napoleonic wars, not only in the manufacturing districts but in other economic sectors as well. Even in agricultural areas, still the largest single industrial sector in terms of output and employment, and protected by the Corn Laws of 1815, severe cycles of depression occurred in the years immediately following Waterloo. When the farmers complained, the Tory squires and county gentry were quick to demand further redress, not just for economic reasons but also to offset any political discontent among the farmers. At the General Election of 1818 William Huskisson reported to Lord Liverpool that the radicals were even beginning to sway the opinions of the yeomanry, usually the stoutest defenders of Toryism. He wrote, "They despise the Whigs; but they are no longer what they were ten years ago in their attachment to the old Tory interests and principles which are prevalent in the Nobility and Gentry."[5] A widening political gap appeared. On the one hand there were those who believed that government and its administration

---

2   Quoted in E. P. Thompson, *The Making of the English Working Class*, (Harmondsworth, 1978 ed.), p. 159.

3   Sir S. Romilly, *Memoirs of the Life of Romilly*, (London, 1840), p. 537.

4   Public Records Office (Kew), HO 42, Fletcher to Portland, 3 April, 1802.

5   Quoted in J. E. Cookson, *Lord Liverpool's Administration, 1815-1822*, (London, 1955), p. 143.

should be immune from outside pressures, and on the other there were those below the elites who contended that a closed political oligarchy, whose primary wish was to conserve the constitution, was politically static and detrimental to the nation's interest as a whole. Robert Peel noticed this when he returned to England after six years as Chief Secretary in Ireland. Writing to his friend Croker in March 1820 he said.

> Do you not think that the tone of England ... is more liberal, to use an odious but intelligible phrase, than the policy of the Government? Do you not think that there is a feeling becoming daily more general and more confirmed ... in favour of some undefined change in the mode of governing the country.[6]

A feeling that political change was in the air was apparent but the Tory elements of Liverpool's administration, Eldon, Sidmouth, Wellington and Castlereagh, were determined that no change in the political contract be considered, not at least while they remained in office. In justification for their intransigence on constitutional and parliamentary reforms they utilized the theories and concepts of Burke. This resistance to popular politics and those who expounded it served to galvanize the Tories and conservative Whigs into a party unit, but it also provoked significant hostility to those who "would leave everything as it is".

For many Tories and conservative Whigs the views of Peel, were symptomatic of the feeling that the post-war political world was changing. For this group a curious situation had developed in which public opinion, with more influence than it ever had previously, was becoming daily more dissatisfied with the share of actual power it possessed. Peel was writing in the wake of the Peterloo disturbance of 1819 and the Six Acts which had followed quickly after the depressing catalogue of alternate bouts of disorder and repression beginning in 1794. The list is long and it includes several outbreaks of Luddism, the riots in East Anglia, the march of the Blanketeers, the Pentrich rising, Peterloo, the Huddersfield rising, Spa Fields, and, arguably the most serious, the Cato Street Conspiracy. Then there were the consequent actions of the state in the form of Special Commissions, Orders in Council, the secret committees of enquiry, suspension of Habeas Corpus, and Seditious Meetings Acts. In purely parliamentary terms, but only in those, riots and disorders were the least of the ministry's problems. In this sense government was never stronger in the legislature than when there were plots and disturbances. However, in London and other centres of urban power events such as Peterloo only increased the widespread feeling that the country was in a state of crisis. The crisis indeed seemed worse than in the 1790s since it was not a matter of a specific danger to British society inculcated by ideas brought in from outside, but a more pervasive atmosphere of violence and disunion within. Tories, Whigs and Radicals, with some justice, could feel that these were symptoms of an unhappy and divided nation, even though they disagreed both on causes and remedies. Ministers, such as Huskisson and Canning, could reiterate the arguments of the increasingly influential political economists: that the laws of economics were inexorable and legislative intervention likely to do more harm than good. However, if the educated public was willing to accept this doctrine in the abstract, they also felt strongly, if somewhat illogically, that something was missing in practice. The discontent and distress in society, even if not directly the fault of the government, materially weakened its prestige and damaged its influence. To be seen to do nothing was to invite widespread unpopularity and worse. It can be argued that Ministers were not indifferent

---

6   Croker Papers, Vol. 2, Clements Library, University of Michigan, Ann Arbor, Peel to Croker, 18 March, 1820. For a discussion of the importance in the growth of the pressure of public opinion see, P. Hollis, *Pressure from Without*, (London, 1974).

to the problems of the economy and the hardships of the poor; nor indeed to the general dissatisfaction of the public with the conduct of the government. Their difficulty was to know what, if anything, they could do about it. Direct concession to political agitation, which meant in effect making substantial changes in the actual fabric of the constitution, was out of the question. In the immediate post-1815 period, there was no inclination for parliamentary reform in either Parliament or Cabinet. As Romilly observed, the effect of the revolutionary struggle had been to harden the resistance of the governing classes to any organic change.

Yet an alternative road did emerge for a ministry that wished to appear both moderately progressive and conservative. As well as utilizing the work of Burke there was also the eighteenth century school of economic reform, best represented in Britain by Adam Smith. This group (which in Liverpool's administration included Canning, Robinson, Huskisson and Palmerston) concerned themselves not with doctrinaire plans for ideal constitutions or attacks on established political institutions, but with an examination of the methods whereby enlightened legislators could improve the lot of society as a whole. The prime object of this new political science, was not to take power off the governing classes, which radicals as diverse as Paine or Bentham wished for, but to teach them how to promote the happiness of the people in their charge. In general terms this was the position of the conservative Whigs and moderate Tories in the first two decades of the nineteenth century. However, the perceptions of the working class themselves in the north-west (the most rapidly industrialising region in Britain) differed from those of the government to an alarmingly dangerous extent. To give balance to the picture of the relationship between the Tories and the emergent working class of the north-west we must also examine their grievances about the existing political society.

The Emergence of the Working Class in the Industrial North-West: An outline of the debate

The disputes engaged in by the emergent working class of the industrial north-west began in the 1760s and were concerned primarily with the introduction of new technology in cotton spinning. The interest is to trace the growing political awareness of this social grouping that evolved as a result of what were chiefly economic and social grievances, like the imposition of new work practices and the resultant loss of independence. This 'political' element in the attitudes and behaviour of the emergent working class is vital to understanding the development of a working class consciousness in the first half of the nineteenth century. But it is a question that has in the past, and still is producing a lively debate amongst social and political historians. It may be worthwhile at this stage to outline some of the most salient and relevant arguments before moving on to describe the events which illustrate the attitudes of the working class of the north-west from the 1790s to the struggle for the Reform Bill. The reason for this is to outline the attitudes of the elites and of the working class prior to the 1830s and to contrast this with the situation from the mid-1830s.

The first historians who systematically investigated the development of the industrial working class in the late eighteenth and early nineteenth centuries were John and Barbara Hammond.[7] The Hammonds worked within the tradition of Whig historiography stressing the progress of industrial labour to overcome obstacles placed in their way by the forces of capital and the state. In this they were in tune with the views of the Fabians and the progressive Liberals of the early twentieth century. According to the Hammonds the workmen of the 1760s had still a degree of independence

---

7   John and Barbara Hammond, *The Skilled Labourer*, (London, 1979 ed.), with an introduction by John Rule.

and freedom in their daily life. They drew on sources like Samuel Bamford's *Passages in the Life of a Radical* and his picture of the Lancashire weaver towards the end of the eighteenth century.[8] These essentially domestic workers possessed limited autonomy, they could leave off work when they pleased, to tend a smallholding or have a meal or take a smoke and a chat. This worker was not "disinherited from the old village economy in which a man did not merely sell his labour but had some kind of holding and independence of his own."[9] The industrial changes of the 1770s, argued the Hammonds, destroyed this social economy with its margin of freedom and choice for the worker. To some upper and middle class observers the new agencies of industrial change, such as the utilization of capital for the building and equipping of factories, promised a great saving of human labour but would also socially condition and morally uplift the lower orders.[10] That the majority of workers subjected to this transformation resisted was unsurprising considering the workers appeared to gain no financial compensation for this increased effort. They saw, in contrast, the owners of capital becoming enormously wealthy at the workers expense. Not only this but the lifestyle of the working class also underwent a transformation.

This was the crux of the Hammond's case. The working class of the late eighteenth and early nineteenth centuries resisted industrial change not only because they were materially worse off, domestic workers of the earlier eighteenth century were not affluent by any means, but because they saw on the one hand the visible signs of a maldistribution of the results of their labour and on the other the closing-in of a social and economic system which they likened to slavery.[11] The Hammonds were well aware of the fact that transition from a semi-feudal or corporate industrial system to a full blown capitalist mechanised system was a slow process. However, they were at times guilty of utilizing the language of 'golden age' sentimentalism. For example:

> Surely never since the days when populations were sold into slavery did a fate more sweeping overtake a people than the fate that covered the hills and valleys of Lancashire and the West Riding with factory towns that were to introduce a new social type for the world to follow.[12]

The Hammonds were right to point out that economic and industrial relations had been gradually changing from the late fifteenth century and the end of feudalism. The mechanization in the late eighteenth and early nineteenth centuries meant the removal of the 'last vestige' of initiative and choice in the daily lives of working people. Indeed they were at pains to show that it was the culmination of a long process. The last vestige, for so much had been lost already that the upper class came readily to think of the surviving elements as an anachronism. For two centuries there had been a steady concentration of economic power in the hands of a small class.[13]

The 'last vestige' was important. It distinguished between allowing a margin of freedom and choice, prevalent in the older type of social economy, and the conditioning agencies of new industrial society. They argued that so much attention had been given to the transitory nature of the development of capitalism before the industrial revolution that there was a marked tendency to underestimate the transformations on the emergent mass working class that came as a result of

---

8   *The Autobiography of Samuel Bamford*, Two Vols. Ed. W. H. Chaloner, (London, 1967 ed.)
9   Hammonds, *Skilled Labourer*, p. 2.
10 See for example P. Gaskell, *The Manufacturing Population of England*, (London, 1833).
11 Hammonds, *Skilled Labourer*, p. 3.
12 Ibid.
13 Ibid., p. 1.

industrialization. The Hammonds knew well that by the 1770s and '80s the majority of domestic workers were already dependent upon capitalist enterprise, but this did not mean that the changes induced by the latest phase of industrialization were unimportant. Indeed they were so important that when a weaver in Oldham or Blackburn or the cropper in Halifax or Huddersfield looked back in the 1820s or 1830s to the beginning of his life, he believed he could remember a time when the worker was in all senses a freer man.[14]

The social economy with its margin of choice and independence, its inherent belief in the fair and just price for labour as well as the widespread assumption that the forces of the state existed as a last recourse of arbitration. This was not a myth, as authoritative research of recent years has revealed.[15] There were of course trade depressions in the eighteenth century as well as in the nineteenth, most notably during times of foreign crises, but in these situations the hand workers had opportunities for the diversification of their labour. A picture is drawn from several trades, wool croppers and weavers, cotton spinners and weavers, framework knitters and so on, with such frequency for it to be dismissed as a romantic dream of an idyllic past. It was a world which was to disappear due to the regimentation and authority of the factory system itself and by hand workers who resisted the factory but worked long hours in order to mitigate the effects of falling piece rates in the early nineteenth century. The Hammonds were correct to point out that the reactions of such workers, as well as those employed in the factories, to conditions in the nineteenth century was intense and passionate because of the recent experience of better times. This led many of the working class to seek radical political solutions to their plight, but also maintained were aspects of a Tory tradition in terms of deferential attitudes to the elites and, importantly, respect for custom and prescriptive rights. The Conservatives drew on such feelings in the decade after 1832.

The main problems with the Hammonds are not their passages of description and explanation, which are both scholarly and copious in primary sources. Rather it is their failure to analyse the motivations of the working class in terms of contemporary politics as well as in the social and economic aspects. At one level the Hammonds did recognise the wider political context within which the industrialisation of early decades of the nineteenth century took place. Many political leaders, argued the Hammonds, saw the new work practices as a means of controlling the lower orders. As they wrote,

> From this spectacle [of the French Revolution] the rulers of England had derived one set and fixed idea: the idea that the art of government was the maintenance of discipline ... Hence their unquestioning welcome to an industrial system that seemed to answer their own purpose and to answer the purpose of nature as well: to reinforce at once the law of authority and the law of progress.[16]

However, the Hammonds were reluctant to admit that resistance to the factory system — especially Luddism — on the part of working people were in any meaningful sense political, and certainly not revolutionary. This fear on the part of the elites of working class insurrection was at best the machinations of paid informers intent on giving their employers reason for their continued employment. Or at worst the kind of information the government wished to put before Parliament in

---

14 S. Chapman, *The Lancashire Cotton Industry*, (Manchester, 1954 ed.), p. 46.

15 See for example, E. P. Thompson, 'Time, Work discipline and Industrial Capitalism', *Past and Present*, No. 38, (1967), or by the same author, *Customs in Common*, (London, 1991), especially chapters 4 and 5. See also A. J. Randall, 'The Industrial Moral Economy of the Gloucestershire Weavers in the Eighteenth Century', in John Rule (ed.) *British Trade Unionism, 1750-1850*, (London, 1988).

16 Hammonds, *Skilled Labourer*, p. 311.

support of their draconian measures of social and political coercion. Thus, for the Hammonds, the rumours of a general rising in Lancashire in 1812 were started "solely by spies".

The tale is an intricate one, and the material on which to base it disordered. Four main factors stand out. 1) A general discontent with power looms; 2) Deliberate but unsuccessful attempts to destroy the obnoxious looms fomented if not originated by spies; 3) Food riots, beginning in anger at high prices and ending in the destruction of power looms or buildings; 4) Rumours of a 'general rising' started as far as can be gathered solely by spies.[17]

Following the work of the Hammonds, F. O. Darvall wrote in 1934 that there was no evidence to support the claim that the Luddites of Yorkshire and Lancashire had any political motivation whatsoever. He concluded that, "despite the great efforts of the spies to prove such motives" the Luddites had no large-scale political designs.[18] For over a generation this view remained the orthodox position until the publication of E. P. Thompson's *The Making of the English Working Class*, where a very different interpretation of Luddism appeared, making the Hammond's analysis the subject of a rigorous and continuing debate.[19] Thompson believed he recognized in the work of the Hammonds a reformist/Fabian-like predisposition to minimize to the point of extinction the role of direct action, inter-class violence and high levels of class consciousness in the history of the development of the English working class. He wrote:

> The chapters on Luddism read at times like a brief prepared on behalf of the Whig opposition, and intended to discredit the exaggerated claims made by the authorities as to the conspiratorial and revolutionary aspects of the movement.[20]

This view of intense conflict between the working class and the forces of governmental authority is one of the keystones of Thompson's, and more broadly the Marxist, view of the development of a working class consciousness. Similarly, this theme of both political and class conflict is an area of interest to this book. Especially the attempts made by the local and national elites to utilize the vehicle of the political party as a means of resolving deep-rooted conflicts and steering sections of the working class away from extreme radicalism and towards respectable and legitimate (and safe) political involvement.

For Thompson the high levels of working class consciousness can be shown to be manifest if the overwhelming mass of the working class display a sophisticated and vigorous set of political aspirations on behalf of themselves as a class as opposed to the political aspirations and norms of other classes. It is therefore essential to show the emergent working class had this political dimension

---

17 Ibid., p. 223.

18 F. O. Darvall, *Popular Disturbances and Public Order in Regency England*, (London, 1934), p. 174.

19 E. P. Thompson *The Making of the English Working Class*, (Harmondsworth, 1978 ed.), especially chapter 14. With relevance to Luddism see also the following works: J. Stevenson, *Popular Disturbances in England*, (London, 1992), J. Dinwiddy, 'Luddism and Politics in the Northern Districts', in *Social History*, 4, 1 (January, 1979), by the same author, 'The 'Black Lamp' in Yorkshire', *Past and Present*, 101, (1974), and *From Luddism to the First Reform Bill*, (London, 1986), E. J. Hobsbawm, 'The Machine Breakers', in *Labouring Men*, (London, 1964), see also the introduction by E. P. Thompson to Frank Peel, *The Rising of the Luddites, Chartists and Plug-Drawers*, (London 1895, reprinted, London 1968), M. I. Thomis, *The Luddites, Machine Breakers in Regency England*, (Newton Abbot, 1970), L. Mumby *The Luddites*, (Edgware, 1971), the introduction by John Rule to J. and B. Hammond, *The Skilled Labourer*, (London, 1979 ed.), F. O. Darvall, *Public Popular Disturbances and Public Order in Regency England*, (Oxford, 1980 ed.), S. I. Mitchell, 'Food Shortage and Public Order in Cheshire, 1757-1812', in *Transactions of the Lancashire and Cheshire Antiquarian Society*, 81, (1982), V. C. Burton, 'Popular Unrest in South-east Lancashire and North-east Cheshire during the Luddite period', (M.A. thesis University of Lancaster, 1976) and D. Walsh, 'The Lancashire 'Rising' of 1826', in *Albion*, 26, 4, (Winter, 1994).

20 Thompson, *The Making*, p. 626.

in their subjective evaluation of their objective class position as industrial capitalism began to transform their lives. A major part of the problem lies in the treatment of evidence that consists to a great extent of the reports of paid spies and informers to receptively panic-stricken magistrates and government officials. Thompson argues that the Hammonds, by discounting all such evidence, present an unreal case that can only be sustained by a special pleading which exaggerates the stupidity, rancour, and provocative role of the authorities to the point of absurdity; or by an academic failure of imagination, which compartmentalises and disregards the whole weight of popular tradition. We end in a ridiculous position. We must suppose that the authorities through their agents actually created conspiratorial organizations and then instituted new capital offences (such as that for oath-taking) which existed only in the imagination or as a result of the provocations of their spies.[21]

What Thompson is suggesting requires elaboration. Lancashire machine breaking, beginning in the late 1760s, suppressed in the 1770s and re-lit in the early 1800s, where one is expected to disentangle the aspirations, (political or otherwise), of those involved is a particularly difficult area of study. The predisposition of the Hammonds was to believe *bona-fide* insurrectionary schemes on the part of working people were highly improbable or, alternatively, wrong, undeserving of sympathy and therefore to be attributed to a lunatic irresponsible fringe. Thompson examined why the working class held advanced radical political attitudes by 1812. War had continued for almost twenty years. Trade unions had been coerced and suppressed. The weavers had suffered a cataclysmic decline in living standards, hunger and food shortages were severe and widespread. Why, he asks, does it appear improbable that men (and women) in such circumstances should advocate widespread political change or even revolution? The only reason, argued Thompson, for believing reports on the revolutionary aspects were false was based on the assumption that such evidence derived from paid agents is bound to be false. Reading the same evidence without such an assumption Thompson produces a version suggesting that by May 1812 Luddism in Lancashire had largely given way to a heightened political awareness and a revolutionary organization.[22] He goes further and suggests that an identical form of oath to one found on an associate of Colonel Despard at the time of the 1802 insurrection is one of many pieces of evidence which links the revolutionary underground of 1802 with events ten years later. However, he is disinclined to believe rumours of a national organization or the involvement of genteel leaders; instead he stresses that Luddism was a movement formulated and organized by the working classes usually in the localized community. For Thompson the subjective awareness of their objective position during this phase of industrialization made the working class conscious not only of their own class in relation to other classes but politically aware of the exploitative nature of capitalism and of those in local and national government who condoned it. "Even while attacking these symbols of exploitation and of the factory system", he writes, " they became aware of larger objectives, and pockets of 'Tom Painers' existed who could direct them towards ulterior aims."[23] One way to assess the changes of plebeian attitudes and early working class consciousness is to contrast developments over time. Traditionally Toryism could count on a measure of popular support by practising paternalism, the opposition to arbitrary Whig government and its corrupt tendencies.[24] The depth of this support varied from place to place and over time but

---

21 Ibid., pp. 631-7.

22 Ibid., p. 647.

23 Ibid., p. 657.

24 See L. Colley, *In Defiance of Oligarchy: The Tory party, 1714-1760*, (Cambridge, 1982), chapter 6, also by the same author, *Britons: Forging the Nation, 1707-1837*, (New Haven, 1992).

essentially it was made up of several historical features. Firstly there was, as Colley has pointed out, a strong historical link between Anglicanism and patriotism that was attractive to many working people. As she writes,

> In the seventeenth and eighteenth centuries the power of tory-Anglicanism was socially far more widespread than is sometimes assumed, not least because Church of England loyalties were interwoven with popular patriotism... Few men and women had little to do with Whig bishops. For most of them the predominantly tory parsons were the most visible and accessible representatives of the Church, and in the first half of the eighteenth century these men evoked more respect than hostility.[25]

Also in parts of England Tory-Jacobitism found a purchase on plebeian consciousness (in Lancashire particularly). This was not necessarily because of deep-rooted religious or counter-revolutionary convictions (although aspects of this did exist). But because popular memory coupled with the arbitrary practices of the ruling Whig oligarchy fused to create a vision of a Tory/Stuart past in which fundamental devices of protection co-existed with a degree of latitude to work practices, pastimes, beliefs, customs and modes of plebeian enjoyment. The Whigs and their Puritan ancestors (as with the Liberal 'reformers' after 1832) appeared to be attempting to direct and control the practices and life-styles of working people. The record of the Whigs was not good in terms of policies that affected the daily lives of the labouring classes. There were the widespread powers of Excise officers; the indirect taxation policies of Walpole and the Pelhamite Whigs and the burdens of which fell disproportionately on plebeians. The seemingly ineluctable moves toward economic rationalism and its attendant 'improvements'; the widespread provision shortages and the blatant profiteering in periods of dearth; the harsh penal code, Laws of Settlement and a tightening of access to poor relief, all contributed negatively against the Whigs among many working people. Also contributing to a hardening of attitudes of plebeians against the Whigs were the relatively minor local examples of progress. Samuel Bamford, recollecting the Middleton of his youth in the 1790s, gave an insight into this lost world and the feelings evoked:

> On the other side of the church, the space which is now occupied as a burial-ground, was a large and excellent bowling-green, which was much frequented by the idle fellows of the village who preferred ale-bibbing in the sun before confinement on the loom or at the lap-stone. At last it was broken up and the games put a stop to, chiefly, it was said, because the late steward under the Suffields, could not ... overawe, or keep the rustic frequenters in such respectful bounds as he wished to.[26]

Here we see the end of a recreational custom that Middletonians had enjoyed since 1617 when James I gave his royal permission maintaining traditional sports against the attempts of the Puritans to suppress them.[27] It was around questions such as these that sectional plebeian and working class Toryism historically rested.

However, from the 1790s economic slump, the widespread dearth of provisions and the cultural cleavages wrought by industrialization, condoned as it was by Tories in government and among

---

25 Colley, *In Defiance*, pp. 153-4.

26 Samuel Bamford, *The Autobiography of Samuel Bamford, Vol. I, Early Days*, (ed. W. H. Chaloner, London, 1967 ed.), p. 26.

27 Godfrey Davies, *The Early Stuarts, 1603-1660*, (Oxford, 1985 ed.), p. 76. See also R. W. Malcolmson, *Popular Recreations in English Society, 1700-1850*, (Cambridge, 1973), Hugh Cunningham, *Leisure in the Industrial Revolution*, (London, 1980), E. P. Thompson, 'Patricians and Plebs', in *Customs in Common*, (London, 1991).

sections of the magistracy, lost the Tories much of their support, especially in the manufacturing districts of the north-west. For Thompson, therefore, Luddism was part of the transitional development of the working class, "one is struck not so much by its backwardness as by its maturity… One can see Luddism as a manifestation of a working class culture of greater independence and complexity than any known to the eighteenth century."[28] The Hammonds saw working class development between 1790 and the 1830s primarily in economic and social terms whilst for Edward Thompson it is conceived in economic, social and political terms.

From the early 1980s the entire position of class (and more specifically the working class) as an explanatory concept came under attack. In terms of British social history this was begun with the publication of Gareth Stedman Jones's *Languages of Class* in 1983.[29] Stedman Jones suggested firstly that historians of the working class should analyze with more empirical care what the working class were actually saying and, more particularly what was being said by their class representatives on their behalf. The language of their representatives, Stedman Jones assumed, was the language of political radicalism as it developed from the 1790s.[30] It is worth briefly outlining why language is so important to Stedman Jones. He rightly asserts that language, the manner through which experience is objectively expressed and transmitted, either orally or in a literary form, is a highly complex medium. The problem of language, he suggested, is particularly acute for social historians who rely almost exclusively on the languages of the past for primary evidence. According to Stedman Jones historians have been unaware or deliberately overlooked that language is itself part of the material of the objective reality of social existence (social being) in terms of its structure and modes of use. It is precisely because language is a material entity in its own right that it is virtually impossible to deduce from its use 'some primal anterior reality', or the 'social' experiences of the users.[31] The very structure of language determines the articulation of its use and thus the deep experiential meaning that the language is supposed to convey (and for social historians to abstract) is lost.[32] This argument has serious ramifications for the historian attempting to assess the levels of class consciousness merely by extrapolating key expressions of the language used, for we can never be sure that what was being said (or written) constituted the expression(s) or the manifestation(s) of the shared experiences of the person(s) making the statement, because of the complexity of the structure of language itself. Stedman Jones's solution is to apply a 'non-reverential' conception to language. By this he means analysing, in a very detailed manner, what terms and propositions the language actually contains and then setting this in the wider material context. According to Stedman Jones historians should attempt to explore, "the systematic relationship between terms and propositions within the language rather than setting particular propositions into direct relation to a punitive experiential reality of which they were assumed to be the expression."[33] It is not enough for historians to assume an interpretation of written sources as direct expressions of the working class experience. Rather, we should examine the nuances, in terms of morphology and phonology, of what the discourse *itself* is relating from the past.

This brings us to the second area in which the Stedman Jones thesis is of relevance when analysing

---

28   Thompson, *The Making*, pp. 657-8.

29   G. Stedman Jones, *Languages of Class: Studies in English Working Class History 1832-1982* (Cambridge, 1983)

30   Ibid., p. 105.

31   Ibid., p. 20.

32   Ibid., pp. 20-1.

33   Ibid., p. 21.

working class consciousness and class generally: the crucial area of politics. Stedman Jones argues that the working class did not develop class ideology or politics based on a class position but rather utilised an older form of radicalism which can be traced back to the 1760s and the days of John Wilkes and to writings of Tom Paine in the 1790s. This is highly contentious and, as will be demonstrated in due course, was not always the case. Certainly, the traditional political language of radical reform, based on notions of the free-born Englishmen, the historic role of equal justice and natural rights and calls for wider political citizenship held a wide constituency within the working class as was seen in 1816-19, 1831-34 or 1839-42. However, such views were also incorporated into a widening set of demands which reflected developing working class grievances. There was at no time a single ideological construct of radicalism. There were several radicalisms often operating simultaneously. Other political languages containing different political principles, such as Conservatism or Liberalism, also vied for an audience and, although less effective in years of high class consciousness, gained purchase in the periods of intra-class sectionalization. We must remember that political languages are mutable and change to fit circumstances, as do the interests and context of those to whom they were addressed. If Stedman Jones exaggerates the importance and continuity of older radical ideologies he is certainly correct in promoting the importance of the politics of a given age to the analysis and evaluation of nineteenth-century relationships. As Stedman Jones rightly asserts "… it was not consciousness (or ideology) that produced politics, but politics that consciousness."[34] As he says,

> What we must therefore do is to study the production of interests, identification, grievance and aspiration within political languages themselves. We need to map out the successive languages of radicalism, liberalism, socialism etc, both in relation to the political languages they replace and laterally in relation to the rival political languages with which they are in conflict.[35]

However, we must also be careful not to assume that on all or any occasions the overwhelming majority of working people were susceptible to a single given political language, or subscribed to the principles inherent within a single political language. The pioneering work of Stedman Jones has had a major impact among social historians, especially those terming themselves post-modernists, but their position is not one lending itself to easy definition. As one post-modernist admits,

> Post-modernism is a difficult area. Because post-modernists see nothing as fixed or solid this jeopardises the sorts of attempts they may make to define what they see themselves as part of, whilst some commentators have doubted (self described post-modernists notwithstanding) the very existence of the condition.[36]

Indeed, but the question remains just what does post-modernism represent? Post-modernists tend to find the grand theories and grand narratives of change redundant in the post-modern 'secularising, democratising, computerising and consumerising' world. Such products and discourses of the enlightenment on which liberalism, humanism or Marxism found purchase no linger applied as central explanatory concepts. For post-modernists 'de-centring' is the key to a new and vital approach to the study of social history.

This approach was illustrated in Stedman Jones's article 'Rethinking Chartism' in *Languages of*

---

34   Ibid., p. 19.

35   Ibid., p. 22.

36   K. Jenkins, *Re-Thinking History*, (London, 1991), p. 59.

Class.[37] Here Stedman Jones maintains that strict reading of Chartist texts and speeches testify to the lack of ideological sophistication inherent in the movement. Put simply, the Chartists were attacking the wrong enemy when they railed against the aristocrats and landed wealth. The real enemy were the capitalist employers but he says these remained largely unscathed by radical critiques before 1850. This suggested to Stedman Jones that political mobilization and consciousness was not created by an economic objective reality but by politics. Class consciousness did not lead to heightened political awareness among working people as the materialist position adopted by Edward Thompson suggests, but rather that the political awareness of the situation led to heightened consciousness. Indeed, the traditional view of class as presented by social historians is, according to Stedman Jones, flawed because it possesses no fixed meaning. As he says:

> ... the term 'class' is a word embedded in language and should thus be analyzed in its linguistic context; and secondly, that because there are different languages of class, one should not proceed upon the assumption that 'class' is an elementary counter of official social description, 'class' as an effect of theoretical discourse about distribution or production relations, 'class' as a summary of a cluster of culturally signifying practices or 'class' as species of political or ideological self-definition, all share a single reference point in an anterior social reality.[38]

In this scheme class possesses no permanent or rigid definition and is not capable of being understood as being objectively real. The multiple nuances of its application, according to Stedman Jones, give it various meanings within a society at any given time, and even more historically over time. Therefore it is impossible to utilize class as descriptive concept in the historical context because it is not and never was an objective reality. Apart from its use in contemporary communication, writing and speaking (discourse), class possesses no external reality or reference. What class-as-language, or indeed society-as-language, does is to convey through signs, symbols and coded meanings, understanding to ourselves and others. The world, therefore, is constructed or 'invented' according to our use of discourse. To be able to begin to understand the complexities of the past, post-modernists suggest that concepts like class, which have occupied the centre of the debate for so long, should be downgraded or 'de-centred' so that a far more comprehensive picture of the past can be seen.

The linguistic approach owes a great deal to the sociological methodology of phenomenology while its philosophy is derived from the social theory associated with hermeneutics. With phenomenology, society is not a thing with an existence of its own which controls us but rather is something we re-create every day thorough normal activities and routines. Crucial to this notion is the daily utilisation of common assumptions used to interact with others. Thus a key element in the construction of social reality and in communicating interpretations to others is language. This is a highly subjective, indeed idealist, conception of society and how it operates. Whilst conventional historiography sees the past as having been real, with a life of its own above and beyond the individual, post-modernists and phenomenologist see the past and society as something individuals create and re-create in their everyday routines and interactions. The creation of 'reality' is all in the mind of the individuals. This leads on to the proposition adopted by idealists that, whilst materialists portray individuals as beings whose behaviour is largely determined by external forces such as the economy and social environment, phenominologists and post-modernists view people as independent

---

37   G. Stedman Jones, *Languages of Class: Studies in English Working Class History 1832-1982*, (Cambridge, 1983).

38   Ibid., pp. 7-8.

and free agents. They have the power to determine their own future and are capable of structuring and controlling their own world. People in the present, as in the past, do not have to be manacled to their social responsibilities and roles; they have the power to break free. Human actions are not merely reactions to external or material forces; they are not instinctive but calculated and motivated. There is a link here with the older social philosophical tradition of hermeneutics which investigates and interprets human behaviour in terms of institutions, culture, semiotics and discourse as essentially intentional. In order for this to become meaningful, the investigator must attempt to unravel the logic of the situation by 're-living' the events from the point of view of the actors of the time. This re-enactment, termed *verstehen*, was primarily used as a systematic means for the social scientist to gain access to the subject matter. For social theorists utilising the hermeneutic method such as Gadamer, Habermas and Bauman, language is the public medium of social being and existence.[39]

An important methodological ingredient in the post-modernist view of history is that so-called scientific or correct historical research procedures do not reflect the way the past actually was but rather the way conventional historians want it to be. Thus there are in effect two discourses; the discourse of the actors actually present in the past (which are scattered and fragmented and are mere 'traces' of reality) and the discourse of historians which is impinged onto the past. The major problem is that, for all their insistence on the necessity of de-centring class as a concept central to power relationships in the past and on the need to further strip discourse of the teleology of the conventional historical accounts, post-modernists nevertheless still have recourse to the familiar practices. What they reject is the universality of modernistic notions of a 'meta' or master narrative based on some form of ideological 'world view' such as Marxism. For a time post-modernism or post-structuralism became the vogue in the writing of social and cultural history. Its adherents were strident in the belief of forging new ground in the study of these disciplines.

Part of the problem with the 'linguistic turn' is that some of its most vociferous proponents do not use language very well in attempts to portray what are some important areas of historical interpretation. As Geoff Eley and Keith Nield wrote in 1995, the tonality of the engagement (in this case more specifically with the work of Patrick Joyce) is the mode of address:

> One of the most striking features … is its peremptory, exhoratory timbre, its apocalyptic and apodictic tone. Historians *must* do this, they *cannot ignore* that, they had better get their act together. Joyce's commentary presents itself as the new, self-evidently persuasive, overpowering logic of the age, of contemporary enquiry, a truth that cannot be opposed, that somehow supercedes everything else, everything that comes before.[40]

As well as the tone, what is possibly even more problematic is the core of what post-modernists and post-structuralists are attempting to put forward in their condemnation of previous historical interpretations. It was as if the influence of French post-structuralists and deconstuctionists in the 1970s had opened up a new and tantalizingly fashionable form of intellectual truth. It became almost *de-rigueur* that this must be conveyed in form of vocabulary that was designed to express that maximum of opacity and imprecision. In fact Edward Thompson was (unlike his post-modernist critics) impressively rigid in pursuit of linguistic precision, both in his reading of contemporary sources and in his interpretation of their meaning. This indeed is conceded by one historian who has

---

39 Hans-Georg Gadamer, *Truth and Method*, (London 1975), Jurgen Habermas, *Knowledge and Human Interests*, (London 1972).

40 Geoff Eley and Keith Nield, 'Starting over: The Present, the Post-Modern and the Moment of Social History', *Social History*, Vol. 20, No. 3 (Oct., 1995), p. 335.

embraced the post-modernist methodology. As Marc Steinberg writes,

> ... the revisionist readings of Thompson's work miscast the vision of language in his cultural perspective ... the alternative narratives of Joyce and Vernon reify political language in ways quite contrary to the epistemology of the linguistic turn ... Thompson's cultural Marxism at times is truer to the revisionists proffered perspective than their own analysis.[41]

The contention here is that Thompson was correct in his assertion that the political dimension of working class consciousness was increasing from the 1780s, reaching its peak in 1831-3 and in certain places being maintained for the next two decades. However, after this passing of the First Reform Act, the political development of working class autonomic aims and objectives was curtailed by devices of containment and control imposed on sections of them from above. One of these, the political integration of sections of the working class by the Conservatives, will be subsequently discussed. But first the foundations must be laid by examining the antecedents that forced the elites to re-formulate their position towards the industrial working class.

Working Class Politics before 1820

Early in 1799 weavers of Lancashire were complaining of decrease in the price of labour and formed themselves into the Association for Mutual Protection, and for obtaining parliamentary relief. At the end of April a Wigan magistrate wrote to the Home Office saying a number of societies were being formed. He wrote that, "when the sum of five hundred pounds is collected by the grand central committee at Manchester ... they are to pay it into the hands of some great person in London who (they) hath engaged to procure them an Act of Parliament for an advance in wages."[42] On May 27 the same correspondent sent to the Home Office an address that had been issued to the public by the newly formed Association of Weavers. The address was to be printed and distributed in various towns in the name of the General Committee assembled at Bolton on 13 May 1799, John Seddon was President and James Holcroft was Secretary. The Committee was composed of representatives from Bolton, Manchester, Salford, Stockport, Oldham, Wigan, Warrington, Blackburn, Chorley, Newton, Bury, Whitefield, Leigh and Chowbent, in total there were 28 representatives on the General Committee. In their address they made a direct claim for political in intervention.

> The present existing laws that should protect weavers, etc from imposition, being trampled underfoot, for want of a union amongst them, they are come to a determination to support each other in their just and legal rights, and to apply to the Legislature of the country for further regulations, as it may in its wisdom deem fit to make, when the real state of the cotton manufactory shall have been laid before it.[43]

The correspondent, John Singleton of Wigan, sent the weavers' address to Home Secretary Portland, who denied the weavers had grounds for complaint. The labouring classes were, said Portland, "fully employed and very well paid for their labour and before these arts were used to disturb their peace

---

41   M. Steinberg, 'Culturally speaking: finding commons between post-structuralism and the Thompsonian perspective', *Social History*, Vol. 21, No. 2, May 1996.

42   PRO (Kew) HO 42-47, undated, John Singleton to Portland.

43   Ibid. As to the number of members involved the figures were high in the 1790s, see also Thompson, *The Making*, p. 460.

and make them discontented was both happy and contented."[44] The government, in whom the weavers had placed such faith, responded by passing the first Combination Act of July 1799. However, the passing of the Combination Act did not deter the weavers nor did it diminish their faith in Parliament as a council for the application of redress. At the end of February 1800, the journeymen weavers of Yorkshire, Derbyshire, Cheshire and Lancashire petitioned Parliament "praying for a more speedy and summary mode of regulating abuses and for the settling of wages, pay and price of labour from time to time."[45] It should be remembered that the Combination Act nominally prohibited combination amongst manufacturers as well as amongst wage labourers. Thus the weavers took the opportunity to point out their position was in part due to a powerful combination of the master weavers and manufacturers and that the Petitioners, scarcely earning a bare subsistence by their daily labour, are totally unable to seek the Suppression of Combinations of so much Secrecy, Wealth and Power, or any redress of their Grievances, by any existing Law.[46]

Indeed some masters and manufacturers sided with the workers. In May 1800 a petition arrived at the House of Commons from the master manufacturers of Cheshire, Yorkshire and Lancashire stating that many of their difficulties arose because there was no longer any power to settle wages. A Committee of the House of Commons was appointed to take evidence, the all too familiar outcome was that the weavers did not obtain their required regulation of a minimum wage, but instead were given an Act providing for arbitration in the cotton trade.[47] This Act provided that in all cases of dispute over wages and hours of work each party could name an arbitrator and, if the arbitrators could not agree, to submit the points in dispute to a Justice of the Peace, whose decision would be final. In the actions of working people at this time, we see a belief that their economic rights could, and should be protected by a direct political appeal to the national legislature. In presenting their arguments and producing evidence to support their petitions they were working within the existing political system. But it further reveals that they possessed a degree of political awareness, displaying a collective political consciousness in a class sense, albeit draped in the trappings of obeisance to the existing political institutions. This situation, however, did not last long.

The Arbitration Act had some success for a short time as a device for settling disputes and protecting workers from actual frauds. But inherent within what was, in reality, permissive legislation were two flaws that the manufacturers utilized quickly. Firstly the Act required masters to appoint an arbitrator, and made provision for cases of disagreement between arbitrators, but it contained no provision to compel arbitrators to act. The manufacturers, discovering this flaw, simply appointed an arbitrator living in a distant place who in reality had no intention of acting, with the result that the arbitration went no further. Similarly, when the arbitration went to a magistrate as a final test, on the few occasions that it did, it was often discovered that the magistrate had some indirect link (e.g. financial) with manufacturing, and was biased. The argument the magistrates produced was that the demands made by workers were an attempt to fix wages, which, they argued, the Act was not empowered to do. In such a situation, compounded as it was by wartime food shortages and high prices, the emergent working class lost faith in the forces of local and national political power and began to develop a more militant attitude to their distress. As for the elites, they were becoming

44   PRO HO 42/47, Singleton to Portland.
45   *House of Commons Journal*, 5 March, 1800.
46   Ibid.
47   39 and 40. George III, C90.

increasingly uneasy regarding the political attitudes of the industrial working classes.

By 1803 the judge in charge of the Northern Districts wrote to the Home Office that "much of sedition has mixed itself with the Weavers Petition and Bill ... cavalry should be stationed near Bolton and an eye kept on the whole quarter."[48] The magistrates and judges were alarmed at the lack of respect towards authority shown by the working class, so were the manufacturers. In 1800, the Bolton manufacturer, Thomas Ainsworth, told the first Sir Robert Peel, "There is nothing to fear from Jacobinism."[49] By 1801 the same correspondent was writing of the possibility of a general rising. "If ever there is an invasion or other commotion to employ the regular force of the country I make no doubt but that opportunity will be seized."[50] At Bury, William Yates, Peel's partner, was similarly alarmed. "I am sorry to say that what I have seen and heard today, convince me that the country is ripe for rebellion and in a most dangerous situation and I firmly believe that if provisions continue at the present high prices, a Revolution will be the consequence."[51] A measure of the frustration felt on both side can be gauged from the attempts of the local state to enforce the sedition laws against expressions of working class verbal frustration and political sentiments. In 1795 John Bower, a Bristol cooper, was imprisoned for saying

> in the presence of divers liege subjects, 'Here's to Tom Paine's good health and that he may plant the tree of Liberty in the centre of England, the Garden of England before the first day of May next. Damn the Duke of York and all his family.'

At Salford in 1801, a working man named Dyson was sent to the house of correction for uttering "Damn the King and Country." When told he would be informed against his anger spilled over into "damn the magistrates, damn the volunteers as a set of damned fools", and that it was "time to take Billy Pitt's head off."[52] However, more dangerous than such displays of verbal disaffection with the Government was that doctrines subversive of the existing order were being formulated and circulated in the cotton districts. This was certainly the belief of Colonel Fletcher of Bolton. He informed the Home Office that he had "encouraged several loyal masters who employ great numbers of servants in different branches of cotton manufacture, to examine into the political opinions of their workmen, and discharge such (who) are known to be Jacobin from their employ."[53]

Such was the fear of the authorities of their growing unpopularity throughout the manufacturing districts that in 1801 the Home Office began the procedure of employing informants which was to last for over thirty years. The clerical magistrate, Rev. Hay of Manchester, was overjoyed when he told the Duke of Portland he had secured the services of an informer.[54] Similarly Col. Fletcher also began to use the services of a Mr Bent to infiltrate meetings of the working class of Bolton.[55]

In 1803 an amendment was made to the Arbitration Act which empowered the magistrate to choose a panel of not less than four and no more than six persons, half representative of the manufacturers and half of the workmen. This amended version again proved ineffective although it served to split the Weavers Association into those, such as Richard Needham of Bolton, who were

---

48 PRO (Kew) HO 42/50, undated, Justice Bayley to Portland.

49 Ibid., undated, Ainsworth to Peel.

50 Ibid., 12 March, 1803, Ainsworth to Peel.

51 PRO (Kew) HO 42/61, 14 March, 1803, Yates to Peel.

52 PRO (Chancery Lane) Assi/4/22, Gloucestershire Lent Assize, 1 April, 1795, and PRO (Kew) 42/62, undated and unsigned.

53 PRO (Kew) 42/62 undated, Fletcher to Portland.

54 Ibid., undated, Hay to Portland.

55 Ibid., HO 42/62 and 42/65, Fletcher to Portland.

regarded as loyal weavers and those like John Knight of Oldham or Samuel Bayley of Rochdale who became convinced that appeals to an unreformed Parliament useless. An example of this view can be found in a petition from the weavers of Bolton who, in 1813, complained that the Act of 1803 was "unavailing inasmuch as not one conviction before a magistrate under this law has ever been confirmed at any Quarter Sessions of the Peace."[56] To many working people it was another example of the continued and unremitting erosion of their rights in favour of the masters which had been gathering pace since the 1750s in the latter's appeal to statute law over common law ending the customary practices of the former. The effect was to remove the mediatory powers of the Justices of the Peace and place sole power in the hands of the manufacturers, with the resultant loss in worker independence and paternalistic protection. This clearly demonstrated that the traditional rights vested in an open access to common law were no longer viable. But growing disillusionment with the forces of authority did not prevent the moves to obtain a minimum wage for cotton workers in 1807-8, and the 'loyal' branch led by Needham carried this agitation forward. The local elites and large manufacturers of Manchester, Chorley, Preston, Bolton and Stockport supported these loyal weavers. Some of the employers even raised a subscription in order that the workers representatives could travel to London to present their case to the President of the Board of Trade, Earl Bathurst, and his Commons Committee.[57] Once again this was greeted with deaf ears in London. The arguments against the measure of a fixed minimum wage included the problem of different skills required for different qualities of cuts and the numbers of workmen who would be discharged as a result of its possible enactment. It was also argued that the problem was not that wages were too low but that they were too high, and thereby attracting an abnormal supply of labour to the trade. The news of the defeat in May 1808 gave rise to serious rioting in Manchester, which left one man dead and several injured.[58] A strike followed with looms idle in Rochdale, Wigan, Bolton, Stockport, Bury and Chorley, and by early June in Manchester alone it was estimated that there were 60,000 looms idle.[59] The strikers demanded an increase of 33.3 per cent on present wages. The masters almost at once agreed to increases of 20 per cent, Needham and the 'loyal' weavers supported the Master's offer, but the strikers held out drawing on funds held by the Friendly Societies. The strike lasted until mid June and the extremists appear to have won further concessions from the manufacturers, but even in what was primarily an economic dispute political elements can be detected. Firstly the strike came about because appeals to the conservative Whig/Tory government failed. Secondly, and more explicitly, some strike leaders were urging the men not to return to work but, instead, to direct their energies towards attacking the government and its war policies which, they argued, were the true sources of their distress.[60] The local and national authorities attempted to control this display of economic (and political) insubordination by overt coercion. A Wigan magistrate, Col. Silvester, suggested the taking away of shuttles by the strikers be made a capital felony. The Mayor of Wigan recognised the duplicity of such a course but wished to use the terror of law as means of exerting social control. He reported to the Home Secretary, "The case was considered by me to be barely a felony — but I wished to give it that construction, conceiving that such an interpretation of the offence would have

---

56 *House of Commons Journal*, 25 February, 1813.

57 *Parliamentary Papers*, (1834), Select Committee on Handloom Weaver's Petitions, evidence of Philip Halliwell, p. 447. In total £477.1s.6d was raised, the larger donations came from Ainsworth, (Bolton), £75 0s 0d, Horrocks, (Stockport) £31 0s 0d, J. B. Spencer, £10 10s 0d, and Sir Robert Peel. £31 10s 0d.

58 *The Times*, 28 May, 1808.

59 *Annual Register*, (1808), p. 63, (Chronicle).

60 PRO (Kew) HO 42/95, Handbill, enclosed in an unsigned letter dated 2 June, 1808.

great effect on the Minds of the People."[61] The striking weavers were undeterred, with women in the forefront of the dispute, as *The Times* bore witness:

> The women, it was said, are, if possible, more turbulent and mischievous than the men. Their insolence to the soldiers and special constables is intolerable, and they seem to be confident of deriving impunity from their sex.[62]

In 1809/10 a brief upsurge in trade occurred but the cotton industry again entered into serious slump in August 1810, with the consequent reduction in wages. At Blackburn a 'Manifesto' was printed by the weavers, elaborating a strategy of economic stability. The basis of their plan was,

> Simply this: Reduce the quantity of goods when the market is overstocked, and their value will undoubtedly increase with the scarcity. Gentlemen, the whole body of weavers have come to a determination not to submit to a Reduction in Prices, but will rather be limited in the Quantity of their Work, and will, in conjunction with their Masters, bear every privation for a few weeks or months, until a change takes place in the Markets.[63]

This manifesto created such alarm among the magistrates they asked for troops to be sent to the town, a precaution necessary because the local militia was composed mostly of weavers.[64] Another manifestation of the discontent felt by working people towards the government of Spencer Perceval was that although petitions continued to be sent to parliament they were no longer addressed to Ministers of the Crown but to members of the reforming Whig opposition, most notably to the radical Samuel Whitbread.[65] Petitions of 17,000 from Bolton and of 40,000 from Manchester were sent to the House of Commons not just from weavers, but signed by mechanics, spinners, printers, tailors and others.[66]

At Manchester a Committee of Working Men was formed to gather and forward the petition. Richard Taylor and John Knight were the chief organizers, Knight in particular was to remain active in working class politics for decades. When the Commons again prevaricated on the claims of the workers of the north-west, Knight wrote a remarkable paper, which signals unavowedly the rise in the political consciousness of the working-class leadership. He argued the evidence produced by the Working Men's Committee on behalf of working people in the north-west was irrefutable, but the Commons Committee could not suggest any single expedient to remedy the complaints of the working class. Knight argued the mood of the Common's Committee "tended to circumscribe matters which ought to be left to their own operation, and which like water would find their own level." He pointed out the hypocrisy of why some "measures are frequently opposed at one time, by the same arguments by which at other times they vindicated and supported."[67] In his paper Knight displayed a considerable level of political sophistication, but it also contained a thinly veiled threat suggesting

---

61 Ibid., 15 June, 1808.

62 *The Times*, 25 June, 1808.

63 PRO (Kew) HO 42/108, handbill.

64 Ibid.

65 PRO (Kew), HO 42/197.

66 PRO (Kew) HO 42/117, and *Hansard*, 254 June 1811.

67 Knight's paper was forwarded to the Home Office by Ralph Fletcher. PRO (Kew) HO 42/117, Fletcher to Ryder, 21 November 1811. For more on the activities of John Knight, see John Foster, *Class Struggle and the Industrial Revolution*, (London 1974), see also the *Diaries of Edmund Butterworth* in Oldham Reference Library.

that the government should consider the "number of petitioners involved and the extent of their sufferings". He went on,

> But when we consider likewise, that the legislature has already interfered in matters of apparently less moment — has enacted laws for regulating the price of *corn* [Knight's emphasis], for the assize of bread, for fixing the price of labour in the case of the Spitalfields Weavers, and Journeymen Tailors of London; for augmenting the salaries of judges and clergymen; for regulating commerce, ... This Committee are utterly at a loss to conceive on what fair ground legislative interference can be improper under circumstances so necessary ... If laws can be made to regulate the necessaries of life, laws should be enacted for regulating the wages by which such provisions must be purchased, especially when (as in our case) such wages have lost all reasonable balance and proportion... The moral to be drawn from these events is that the House of Commons, as is at present constituted or appointed, is unfit to manage your affairs... Had you possessed 70,000 votes to elect members to sit in that House, would your application have been treated with such indifference, not to say inattention? We believe not. You are urged to exert yourselves to recover the right of electing representatives and extending the franchise.[68]

Knight's message makes it clear that the workers of the north knew their recent history. But most important was his call for agitation surrounding the electoral franchise which showed that among the radical working class the mood had changed from one of agitation of a pressure group type to one demanding wholesale political reform. The arrogance of the political and manufacturing elites in ruthlessly pursuing the tenets of political economy was about to explode, such was the anger and desperation of working people.

The disturbances which swept through the manufacturing districts of the East Midlands, Yorkshire and Lancashire have been well documented,[69] but it is essential that they be seen in the context of Knight's call for political action on the part of working people to attain political representation and citizenship. That they were unsuccessful matters little in this context. What is important is that early in the emergence of the working class of the industrial north-west a political side to their class consciousness was developing. Older forms of civil control were no longer effective and the question remained just how the elites could contain the mounting pressure emanating from the industrial working class. Tension was high on both sides with deep divisions appearing between the classes, but the actions of the working class show they were rapidly loosing patience with the existing social and political order. The situation would be dangerous at any time, but in wartime precarious indeed.

We are fortunate in that a piece of evidence survives which details the process in which the working class decided their actions in the Luddite period. In April 1812 a meeting of weavers was called at Dean Moor, near Bolton. The meeting opened with a discussion of the old Elizabethan Statutes that gave magistrates the right to fix wages linked to the price of provisions. The talk turned to the bad government of Bolton particularly in relation to the Overseers who often kept the poor waiting twenty or thirty hours a week for their allowances. The Orders in Council were attacked as were several local manufactures, the price of food was discussed and the prospects of trade in the immediate future. At this point the 'Blacks' entered:

---

68 PRO (Kew) HO 42/117.
69 See note 19 above.

On the arrival of the Blacks or persons with their faces blackened, the whole were formed into a Circle and one of the Blacks addressed the Meeting, asking what was to be done, recommending good order, wishing all to speak freely but only one at a time. When he ended a man with a clean face began describing the situation in the Country, the Hardships and Miseries of the industrious Weavers and Mechanics, which he attributed to the War, the Orders in Council were reprobated, and also the system of reducing Wages instead of diminishing the quantity of work in a given time, he recommended likewise a Subscription to apply to Lord Ellenborough [the Lord Chancellor] for a Mandamus to compel Magistrates to do their duty. He was answered by one who was disfigured who said it was all damned nonsense to talk of Law as no Justice would be done except they did it themselves.[70]

This is a remarkable document for it indicates not only the mood of the Luddites but offers evidence of splits within their ranks as to the best course of action. One group wished to return to the traditional forms of redress by applying to mediatory powers of the magistrate. Conversely the hard-liners had lost all faith in the fair arbitration of the Justices and called for direct action by the working class to hammer home to the elites their anger and grievances. The split regarding tactics is important, but of more relevance to the points detailed here is the homogeneity of the Lancashire working people acting as a class in the pursuance of political redress. What working people demanded was the same kind of protective devices that were enshrined in common law and had been protected by the state since the sixteenth century. However, from the mid-eighteenth century the tenets of political economy gradually began to replace the traditional customs and practices of working people. These changes had developed most rapidly in the north-west after the introduction of the factory system. Traditionally the various roles of the magistrates were pivotal to the smooth running of the local community. When, as happened in the north-west from the 1770s, the magistrates began to relinquish their powers of mediation in terms of apprenticeship entry, working practices, wages and industrial contracts generally, working people were forced to seek redress against arbitrary work practices on their own. The changes in contract and statute law and the traditional role of the magistracy created the situation within which working people were forced to seek political solutions.[71] It provided the political culture for the generation of class consciousness amongst the working class because they now had to fend for themselves. Some sought to convince the state to return to its former practices by peaceful petitions and memorials. Others, however, attempted more direct and violent ways of nudging the state to face up to the plight of the industrial working class. But the actions of the conservative Whigs and Tories was to enforce the rule of law with vigour and suppress all attempts of working people to organise and protect themselves.

These actions by the authorities, both local and national, in attempting to curb this growth of working class resentment only served to highlight to the mass of the working class the apparent disdain which the conservative Whigs and Tories held them. Indeed many moderate members of the middle classes felt angered at the excessively harsh treatment which the forces of the state handed out to Luddites and political activists. One example must suffice. When, in 1812, the mill at Westhoughton was attacked by Luddites, a local doctor, Robert Taylor, protested at the severity of the sentences passed on those convicted. His letter picked out the reasons for the actions of the authorities and the lengths the state was prepared to go to suppress working class anger. He wrote,

---

70 PRO (Kew) HO 42/128, Depositions, April 1812.

71 See Paul Langford, 'Just Authority', in *Public Life and the Propertied Englishman, 1689-1798*, (Oxford, 1994 ed.), E. P. Thompson, 'Custom Law and Common Right', in *Customs in Common*, (London, 1991), and Douglas Hay, 'Property, Authority and the Criminal Law', in D. Hay, P. Linebaugh and E. P. Thompson, *Albion's Fatal Tree*, (London, 1975).

We are told of members of revolutionary principles which have been smouldering for years: and which ... are revived by the fancied grievances of improved machinery ... we are told that all Jacobins ought to be *swept into oblivion* [Taylor's emphases] ... He (Fletcher) then expresses a doubt whether the *mildness of these punishments* did not operate as an encouragement to the disaffected in the Northern Counties ... At Lancaster none of these qualms of compassion were allowed to interfere with the steady march of the law. There only eight were capitally convicted, but even-handed justice consigned the whole eight to the hands of the executioner... It will be recollected that one was a boy (of 13 years of age) so young and so childish, that he called out for his mother at the time of his execution thinking she had the power to save him.[72]

It is little wonder that the authorities, especially the government, were held in contempt by the mass of working people. The sentences noted above were carried out in April 1812; in May Prime Minister Perceval was assassinated in the House of Commons and it occasioned a display of elation among working people nationally. At Bolton, Colonel Fletcher complained "the *mob* expressed *joy* (Fletcher's emphases) at the News."[73] In the Potteries a witness heard the news when "A man came running down the street, leaping into the air, waving his hat around his head, and shouting with frantic joy 'Perceval is shot, hurrah! Perceval is shot, hurrah!'"[74] A crowd in Nottingham celebrated and "paraded the town with drums beating and flags flying in triumph." Outside the House of Commons when Bellingham, the deranged assassin, was taken away "there were repeated shouts of applause."[75] It is apparent that the conservative Whigs and Tories were not at all popular in the final years of the Napoleonic wars. Nor, were they when the war was successfully concluded. Even the great hero, Wellington, one of their own ilk, failed to raise the fortunes of the Tories with the masses.

The end of the Napoleonic Wars resulted in a brief resurgence of economic activity. However, working class calls for constitutional reform continued and were spread nationally. We get an impression of the means by which the message of reform was transmitted from the following report from Bristol in 1816:

A short time ago a man arrived in the town of Frome, blowing a horn, and wearing blue ribbons in his hat, emblazoned with "petition for reform etc," and offering the Nottingham, Stockport and Liverpool resolutions, printed together, for sale at twopence each, and of whom he stated he had sold a great number at Calne, Chippenham, and other places. He had sold about forty at Frome.[76]

A dangerous manifestation of the rise in working-class political awareness and consciousness was an open spirit of hostility to employers and social elites, even when they attempted benevolence. Under the influence of the political reformers many out of work labourers and weavers began to look with ridicule at the efforts of private charity undertaken by the local elites. "What do the poor want", ran one Bolton pamphlet, "Wages not alms: Work not charity."[77] At Wigan the attitude of the working class was even more direct and uncompromising, declining to receive the local charitable

72 Bolton Reference Library, B323-Z Blac, Letters of Dr. Robert Taylor.

73 A. Prentice, *Historical Sketches of Manchester*, (Manchester, 1851), p. 46.

74 Frank Peel, *The Rising of the Luddites, Chartists and Plug-Drawers*, (London, 1895, reprinted, London, 1968), pp. 156-7.

75 A. Briggs, *The Age of Improvement*, (London, 1959), p. 157.

76 *Bristol Gazette and Public Advertiser*, 12 December, 1816.

77 PRO (Kew) HO 42/154, dated 26 October, 1816.

subscription, "using very impious language and observing they would have reform not relief."[78]

What is noteworthy in the north-west is the development of an intra-class leadership among working people at this time, a phenomenon which the local middle classes were to exploit with vigour in the 1830s. However, in these years after the end of the Napoleonic wars the national political leadership of conservative Whigs and Tories had no understanding of the possible political advantage gestures of involvement and interest might procure. This again is in marked contrast to the situation that came about after the 1832 Reform Act was operational. An example of the national leaders' ignorance of the political advantages of at least listening and encouraging anti-Reform sentiments among working class-leaders came in 1816. In Bolton the anti-Reform working class leadership was Richard Needham, Thomas Ainsworth and Thomas Thorp. Ainsworth recalled in a letter to the Home Secretary, Lord Sidmouth, an interview he had with him in 1816. At this time he presented to Sidmouth, at the Home Secretary's request for "a statement of the fair average price of labour paid to weavers", adding his own suggestions for relief.[79] At the time of the interview, Ainsworth reminded Sidmouth that,

> a petition lay upon the table signed by 20,000 weavers to the Prince Regent. I hope your Lordship will pardon my being plain. I did feel most intensely the slight and cursory manner in which your Lordship overlooked the paper, and the few minutes you took to give a decisive answer to what concerned near a million of souls. Seeing the weekly earnings you said, "poor things! can nothing be done for them." I replied (feeling as I did, rather too warmly, for which afterwards I was very sorry), "It is as easy as for your Lordship to wind up your watch." After a very few words, laying your hands upon the Weavers Petition you said, "You may tell the Petitioners, I will present their petition the Prince Regent at the Levee on Monday next." Then obeying your Lordships motion, I bowed and left the room. Week after week I was enquired of, if any answer was received? No, No, No, was answer often repeated.[80]

After this display of ministerial intolerance, indeed indifference, the 'Loyalist' triumvirate of Bolton became supporters of parliamentary reform. All three loyalists spoke in favour of reform, as well as the minimum wage, at a meeting calling for parliamentary reform held at Bolton in late September 1816.[81] The lack of awareness of the potential importance of political support among sections of the working class, indeed the apparent indifference which leaders like Sidmouth attached to it, illustrates the point made in chapter one. Prior to 1832 the notion of 'party' and what modern political scientists have seen as a prerequisite of party, *i.e.* a wide political basis of support, was not present. This served to alienate those moderate members of the working class and drew them nearer to the entrenched opponents of the conservative Whigs and old Tories. As one noted Tory reformer, Richard Watson, perceived with discomfort at the end of the Napoleonic Wars, "The common people were, in every village, talking about liberty and equality without understanding the terms."[82] Elite and working class attitudes were undergoing a transformation. This environment of attitudinal change affected the urban groups of the industrial north-west profoundly in the years between 1790 and 1832. The Act of 1832 can be seen as a catalyst to changes in British political culture, in that parties became stronger. Furthermore they also began to integrate social groups into their orbit and it forced the elites to take

---

78 PRO (Kew) HO 42/153, Byng to Sidmouth, 15 October, 1816.

79 PRO HO 42/197.

80 Ibid.

81 PRO HO 42/154, Fletcher to Sidmouth, 7 October, 1816.

82 *Anecdotes of the Life of Richard Watson, Bishop of Llandaff*, (London, 1817), p. 270.

notice of the interests and orientations of groups the system had previously ignored, or had been unable to integrate, primarily because of their diffuse nature. Increasingly, however, in the first four decades of the nineteenth century working people were articulating their demands and grievances as a class that made attempts to accommodate their interests and direct their opinions much easier than had been the case in the eighteenth century.[83] But before describing the activities of the national political leaders during the reform crisis and the effect the Act had on subsequent party organization, the continuing development of the political dimension of working class consciousness needs further consideration.

Working Class Developments in the 1820s

Initially many working-class leaders were reluctant to embrace the 'Jacobin' views of Painite radicalism in the years between 1790 and 1815, primarily because of the anti-patriotic taint such views engendered. However, after the conclusion of the war such expressions became widespread amongst the working class of the industrial north. The working class were developing a political strategy to apply pressure in an attempt to redress their grievances. Significant here was the lead offered by Hunt at the Spa Fields meetings of 1816-17. In his speeches Hunt encouraged the working class to throw off the lead given by the 'Gentleman' radicals and organize themselves, he also demonstrated the power of the pressure exerted by the mass platform.[84] However this expression of working class discontent manifested itself, either by violent forms of direct action levelled against the 'progressive' mill owners and other local elites, or by the elaboration and widespread articulation of Painite/Huntite social and political reforms, is of less importance to this book than the fact that it existed, and served to politically unite the industrial working class of the north.

The united political front of the working class, the development of their own radicalism and the serious political threat posed to the local and national elites through the initiation of the mass platform, can be clearly seen in the developments from 1817 to 1832. At Blackburn, for example, in 1819, working class women organized their Reform Society to compliment the towns' male version.[85] At a meeting of 30,000 working class reformers held on 5 July the Blackburn Female Reform Society carried the banner 'Liberty or Death.'[86] In her speech, Alice Kitchen called for all men in the country to join the general union and called for universal suffrage, election by ballot and annual Parliaments.[87] The point that working people would only attain redress for their grievances once they had representatives in the House of Commons elected by the working class was reiterated by John Knight. He further called for a minimum wage and legislation to back it up, repeal of the Corn Laws and other restrictions of products of common use. He continued,

> As long as our laws are made by men whose interests are so different, if not opposed to the general good, there is very little room to hope for any improvement in our situation, any diminution of our extreme and unprecedented sufferings … nothing less than a radical reform of the Commons House of Parliament will ever produce any considerable diminution of your

83 See Langford, *Public Life*, pp. 476-7.

84 See J. Belchem, *'Orator' Hunt, passim*, (Oxford 1985); J. Belchem, 'Henry Hunt and the evolution of the Mass Platform', *English Historical Review*, (October 1978).

85 *Manchester Observer*, 10 July, 1819.

86 Ibid., the journalist reporting the meeting estimated that "between 30,000 and 40,000 were present."

87 Ibid. There were also Female Reform Societies at Ashton-Under-Lyne, Bolton and Stockport. See *Manchester Observer*, 17 July, 1819.

sufferings or procure any permanent relief.[88]

In August 1819 occurred the event that was to serve as a lasting influence upon the British political tradition, especially concerning the politics of the working class. On August 16 there assembled between 60,000 and 100,000 people at St Peter's Fields, Manchester, to peacefully demonstrate in favour of parliamentary reform. The demonstration had been planned for weeks in advance and the authorities both in Manchester and London were well informed. Yet Sidmouth ordered the arrest of the main speaker, Henry Hunt, at the meeting. All the fear and contempt which the authorities felt towards the working class reformers was unleashed on that day. They charged as Hunt was about to speak, in the ensuing confusion the yeomanry killed eleven and over five hundred were injured. A description by Francis Place to John Cam Hobhouse offers an insight into the attitude of sections of society to working class social, economic and political demands:

> These Manchester yeoman and magistrates are a greater set of brutes than you can form a conception. I know one of these fellows who swears "Damn his eyes, seven shillings a week is plenty for them"; and when he goes round to see how much work his weavers have in their looms, he takes a well fed dog with him… He said some time ago that "The sons of bitches had eaten up all the stinging nettles for ten miles around Manchester, and now they have no greens to their broth." Upon my expressing indignation, he said, "Damn their eyes, what need you care about them? How could I sell you goods so cheap if I cared anything about them."[89]

The charge by the Yeomanry at St Peter's Fields undoubtedly left a lasting impression on the working class of the north-west, but its immediate aftermath had a greater effect on working class radicalism than the authorities could have considered. The incident served to split the already fragmentary radical leadership and their supporters into Constitutionalists (Hunt, Sir Francis Burdett, J. T. Saxton and others) and 'Ultras' or extremists, (Arthur Thistlewood, Richard Carlile, James Watson, etc.). The extremists were in the majority in Bolton, Blackburn, Wigan, Oldham and Burnley. The Constitutionalists were in the majority in Manchester, Bury, Liverpool and Preston. But this split was rendered less significant by the fact that throughout this development of working class radicalism national leadership had been poor. If sections of the middle classes had sympathy for the plight of the working class, (especially so after Peterloo), agreed with their claims that the political system was unrepresentative, and condemned the use of Government spies and 'agents provocateurs', such feelings were dissipated over the Cato Street Conspiracy, when Thistlewood and his colleagues attempted to assassinate the cabinet at dinner early in 1820.

Following the débâcle of Cato Street, for most of the 1820s working-class radicalism was effectively leaderless. Yet the political element of working class consciousness continued to grow in many parts of the north-west. In the years between 1790 and 1820 the emerging working class and their leaders devoted their energies to harnessing their grievances and industrial claims to wider political mobilization. In a sense this was a knee-jerk reaction to the new work processes and the intolerance and injustice they perceived emanating from classes above them. This was in the tradition of the eighteenth century, and indeed the even earlier perception of the just or fair price of, in essence, the moral economy.[90] What we can see from 1811, and Knight's manifesto, is the awakening

---

88   *Manchester Observer*, 10 July, 1819.
89   Quoted in Thompson, *The Making of the English Working Class*, p. 751.
90   See Thompson, *Customs in Common*, chapters 3, 4 and 5, see also, for the political implications of plebeian customary practices, A. Wood,
     'The place of custom in plebeian political culture: England, 1550-1800', *Social History*, Vol. 22, No. 1, (January 1997).

of the working class leadership to other, more subtle and sophisticated strategies. It involved politically educating the mass of the working class as to their real economic position and the exploitative relationship under the capitalist factory system. This manifested itself at the time in insurrectionary displays of violence, but it was not revolutionary, these leaders in the main did not wish to destroy the existing political system but merely to be citizens within it. Government coercion was savage, and it forced the lid on a barrel of rising discontent, but working class resentment for the pre-Reform political elites was widespread. What was notable about this period was that throughout the north-west the working class were united in their solidarity, which cut across status and trade boundaries, to defend their living standards. This more than anything else gave the local radicals their positions of leadership.

The 1820s, up to the reform crisis of 1831/2, consolidated this educative process. The growth of unstamped radical tracts, generally pursuing a republican democratic line on the basis of Paine's writing, was most notable between 1819 and 1833. There was Cobbett's *Political Register*, Wooler's *Black Dwarf*, Doherty's *Voice of the People*, others like *The Red Publican*, *The Destructive*, *The Pioneer*, the *Poor Man's Guardian* and many more. Added to this was the growth of working-class literacy and political education associated with the Sunday schools, especially those of the Primitive Methodists. There was the development of a fiercely independent form of trade union consciousness, informed with a strong sense of working-class independence and political radicalism. At Stockport, for example, the radical leader Joseph Mitchell reported that the Primitive Methodist chapel was used on the Monday night as a meeting point for working class leaders, on Tuesday for "moral and political readings"; on Wednesdays, "a conversation or debate"; Thursday, "Grammar, Arithmetic etc" was taught. Saturday was a social evening; while Sunday was a school day for both adults and children.[91] This work of education was also being carried on in the home.[92] As Edward Thompson noted, the Female Reform Society of Blackburn pledged themselves "to use our utmost endeavour to instil into the minds of our children a deep and rooted hatred of our corrupt and tyrannical rulers."[93] Throughout the 1820s, therefore, class consciousness was developing and maturing in a variety of ways amongst the industrial class of the north.

It has been argued that the 1820s as a decade was relatively peaceful compared to the previous two decades.[94] In the north-west, however, this was not the case. Although there were variations in the intensity of feeling in different parts of the region, attributed to the 'constitutional' or extreme nature of the radical leadership in a particular place, working class leaders shared an intense mistrust, not to say hatred, of the national political elite. Throughout the 1820s in east and central Lancashire, (the towns around Blackburn, Burnley, Colne, Whalley, Accrington, Chorley), the working class displayed tendencies of extreme radicalism, direct action against the local elites in positions of power and local manufacturers. A dispute began at Blackburn in 1823 when the masters reneged on their promise to keep to the price lists agreed to in 1812 and 1818. By 1826 the situation in Lancashire had deteriorated further and in the spring of that year the *Gentleman's Magazine* reported that, "the unparalleled stagnation of trade in Lancashire and Yorkshire" had been closely monitored in London

---

91 Quoted in Thompson, ibid., p. 788.

92 Most if not all of the Sunday Schools in Lancashire before 1832 were 'radical' or nonconformist, the Anglican Church did begin Sunday Schools for working class children until the later 1830s. For examples see Samuel Bamford, *Early Days*, pp. 23-38, also G. I. T. Machin, *Politics and the Churches in Great Britain, 1832-1868*, (Oxford, 1977).

93 Ibid., p. 788.

94 See Thompson, *The Making*, pp. 781-2.

and "apprehensions were long entertained of some serious disturbance."[95] The details of the events in 1826 have been dealt with elsewhere, but the political content that informed, at least in part, the actions of the working class need highlighting.[96] At a meeting of the Blackburn weavers in late March it was announced that in the calico trade there were 2,807 in full employment, 6,412 were unemployed and the rest, 1,467 on half-time.[97] It was further noted that the poor rates were exhausted, as was the subscription fund. As to the blame for this situation the working class leaders pointed to the unregulated use of power looms; the lack of a minimum wage and of a uniform price list for cotton cuts. But finally, (and importantly, for here we have the overtly political element), they blamed the government for the Corn Laws. Indeed one source suggested that the disturbances of 1826 in the North were triggered when "on the rejection of Mr Whitemore's Motion for repealing the Corn Bill, all hopes of amelioration were abandoned. The unemployed and starving workmen were driven to despair, and they broke out into open riot."[98] These events, therefore, were yet another stress point in relations between capital and labour, the working class and the state and the inexorable rise of political economy.

On April 18 a group of financiers were stoned as their coach arrived at Sykes power loom factory in Accrington and the First Dragoon Guards were dispatched from Blackburn.[99] On Monday 24 April a mass meeting was held at Enfield, a place of convenience where the four roads leading to Accrington, Burnley, Whalley and Blackburn met. Afterwards 10,000 marched to Blackburn as a display of unity and strength and began destroying only the new looms. The effect of these demonstrations of working class force on the psychology of the middle classes and the authorities should not be underestimated. What they were witnessing were 10,000 people, armed to the teeth, openly defying the civil and military power of the district. The disputes spread rapidly across the region and into Yorkshire, and funds for fellow workers came from places near and far; from Liverpool, Bristol and Yeovil in Somerset.[100] It is little wonder that the local elites felt threatened, for this was not merely a demonstration against food shortages, but against the power of mill-owners. Indeed, the events of 1826 lingered long in the memories of the elites. For example, when a military barracks was to be built in East Lancashire in 1842, the elites of Blackburn sent a memorial to Prime Minister Peel calling on him to situate the military permanently in their town. As evidence they cited not the numerous electoral disturbances, the bitter industrial disputes, nor the serious threat posed by the Chartists, but the 'rising', as they termed it, of 1826.[101] The rioters of 1826 only gained one of the demands they placed before the manufacturers, the fixing of a uniform price list, but they did gain a small victory at national level. Their demand for an opening up of the ports to put foreign wheat in Lancashire markets was granted by Canning in a special enabling bill.[102]

There existed among the working people of the north-west a perception, dating from at least 1811, that political rights were required if they were to enhance their class position. This is a sign of rising

---

95 *Gentleman's Magazine*, May 1826, p. 458.

96 D. Walsh, 'The Lancashire 'Rising' of 1826', in *Albion*, Vol. 26, No. 4, Winter (1994).

97 *Preston Chronicle*, 25 March 1826. For a fuller account of the disturbances of 1826 see D. Walsh, 'The Lancashire Rising of 1826', in *Albion*, vol. 26, no. 4, Winter (1994).

98 *Gentleman's Magazine*, May 1826, p. 458.

99 *The Times*, 22 April 1826, *Preston Chronicle*, 23 April 1826.

100 See Walsh, 'The Lancashire 'Rising' of 1826', L. Mumby, *The Luddites and other essays*, pp. 46-7, (London 1971), *The Bristol Gazette*, 4 May 1826.

101 British Library, Peel Papers Ad. Mss. 40501, Hornby to Peel, 21 January 1842.

102 *The Times*, 2 May 1826.

levels of working class consciousness. Some historians might dispute this. It could be argued that there is a great deal of evidence about pressure group demands, rather less for actual political rights. The violent disputes of 1826 were essentially a form of loosely organized pressure group activity centred on primarily economic grievances. But the political element was just under the surface, as the *Blackburn Mail* bore witness when it referred to those involved in the 1826 dispute as "the disciples of Paine and the blasphemies of Carlile."[103] The logic of the situation also suggests that a political element was present. For here were a large section of the regions population suffering appalling privations due to trade recession and industrial rationalization and the government appeared not to be acting in their interests. The Government appeared to be acting in the interests of those groups the working class believed were the cause of their problems, the aristocratic idlers, the place and fund holders, but also importantly the industrial manufacturers of nascent capitalism. This was a classic period of economic boom and slump. Workers throughout the textile regions were being forced to accept reduced wages, suffering short time, or unemployment, yet at the same time workers witnessed a massive expansion of capital outlay by leading manufacturers who extended their factories and increased the use of power loom. From the perspective of the working class this appeared contradictory. On the one hand, mill-owners were reducing wages and hours, giving the reduction of orders and profits as the primary cause, yet on the other, the factory masters were spending huge amounts of funds on the very objects which would reduce the workforce and wages even further. Not only this but the Government seemed unwilling, indeed hostile to combating high food prices by allowing cheaper foreign grain onto the market and sticking rigidly to the 1815 Corn Laws was protecting one group in society at the expense of another. Yet in the industrial sector the state was apparently following the 'laws' of political economy and legislating on behalf of the manufacturers. It is only a short step from being able to recognise one's objective class position in economic terms, to forming a political consciousness that identifies the source of the problem. In this case, that of the inability or unwillingness of the state to act or legislate on behalf of those who feel they are being repressed. The obvious solution for industrial workers, which became apparent from 1811, was to gain working-class representation within the institutions of local and national political control. In the local sense this was focused on those ancient institutions of local politics: the Open Vestry and the Select Vestry, and, in the national sense, on the growing realization of the necessity of the reform of parliament, to include representatives of the working-class interest.

The 1826 disturbances in the north were eventually put down by a massive influx of military power that left ten people dead and scores injured. But what needs reiterating about working-class development at this time, in contrast to the subsequent events after 1832, was the homogeneous nature of the working class response. Evidence for this comes from the development of general unionism and in the way the various trades were able to co-operate with each other. We have shown how, in various parts of the region, the handloom weavers, power loom weavers and spinners were able to work together on equal terms, but also other trades were involved in working class politics before 1832: shoemakers, hatters, tailors, mechanics, builders, joiners, all of high status in occupational terms and mixing freely with those of lesser status, such as power loom or, (as was increasingly the case), handloom weavers.

Nor was this interaction without its traditional symbolism and ironic humour in the displays of collective grievance. During a dispute in the silk weaving town of Macclesfield in 1829, for example, 3,000 workers marched through the district. The *Macclesfield Courier* described the scene as the

---

103 At the time the disputes were regarded as possessing a political element, see letter in the *Blackburn Mail*, 14 June 1826.

crowd, some dressed as mourners and carrying black flags, marched through the town. Amongst these were a small loaf at the end of a pole trimmed with black crepe, another pole had several teeth suspended at its top with the inscription "to let, the owners having no further use for them." But again the message was serious. Other flags carried the inscriptions "we only want to live by our labour", and "cursed is he who grindeth the face of the poor."[104]

Some idea of the level of working class consciousness and their disaffection with the political elites can be gained by examining the responses of those social groups who were directly affected by the increased levels of working class activism, namely, the manufactures and middle classes. It is apparent that the traditional methods of controlling and containing the activities of the emergent working class were not functioning well, given the problems the working class posed to the authorities from at least the 1790s. However, this varied geographically and within regions. If we take the problem of the vacuum left by the magistracy in the industrial districts abrogating their former roles of mediator, juror and local government officer, the problems of social control and containment of the working class confronting the authorities was daunting. In the north this was largely the manufacturers' own doing, given that they demanded no interference whatever in the relationship between worker and master. The result was that social and community harmony began to be strained as authority ceased to be respected by many working people. However, as will be seen in due course, some Conservatives and many old Tories understood the nature of working class feelings and possessed a certain sympathy for their situation to a far greater extent than Liberals, besotted as they were by political economy and the principles of *laissez-faire*. Lord Francis Egerton, for example, the Conservative MP for south Lancashire, wrote to Sir Robert Peel saying that he would not be able to join him at Drayton because he was saddled with the task of calming both sides in a dispute surrounding the Ten Hours agitation. Egerton complained the county magistracy had been over zealous in their treatment of the workers demonstrating in favour of the Ten Hours Bill. He therefore had to remain in Worsley in order "to prevent the magistrates from making my quiet little village the Botany Bay of Lancashire."[105] Such attitudes, when combined with structural changes in party organization and wider political integration were important in securing a basis of working-class support for the Conservatives.

The overall effect of the working class struggles from the 1790s through the 1820s was to induce fear and shock among the middle class. If they had contrived to dismiss the Jacobin 'cranks' and demagogues in the past, towards the end of the 1820s they took their threats seriously and lobbied local and national political leaders for effective powers of civil control. If anything, the relationship between the forces of authority (and the manufacturers and middle classes of the industrial areas) and those opposed to them (an increasingly politically articulate and frustrated working class) were not improving but deteriorating as industrial capitalism was consolidating. Working people were openly displaying their frustration and anger in vast numbers. By resorting to direct action and destroying power looms working people were sending out a message both to the employers and the forces of national and local authority. The message was that they suffer to a point, and that their economic and political interests had be considered as well as those groups places socially above them. The power loom was both a real and symbolic manifestation of the loss of the weavers' independence and perceived rights, as well as a threat to their living. Importantly, the ease with which the working class could destroy the mills suggests that the system of order and social control were being stretched to

---

104 *Macclesfield Courier*, 2 May 1829.

105 British Library, Peel Papers, Ad. Ms. 40425, ff 400-402, Egerton to Peel, 28 December 1836.

dangerous levels. Apart from sending in military force or arming the mill-owners, which was unwelcome, unpopular and might provoke further trouble, there was little the state could do to protect property against a the crowd.[106] There was virtually no regular police and, as shall be shown in subsequent chapters, the propertied middle classes and manufacturers felt threatened in the 1820s and early 1830s by what they perceived as an increasingly violent and 'revolutionary' working class. The middle classes felt helpless and confused, and blamed the government for its apparent inability to protect property adequately.[107]

The Working-Class and the Reform Bill

Increasingly, the indications were that the working class of the industrial north-west had abandoned their attitude of social deference and were developing a radical set of political solutions. It has been suggested by some historians that nationally the working class did not manifest a recognizable class consciousness in the early nineteenth century, let alone a revolutionary consciousness. They point out that they had no advanced political theory or strategy.[108] Indeed, some have suggested that they had no political aspirations at all.[109] In the same vein, the agitation surrounding parliamentary reform in the early years of the 1830s, the involvement of the working class is portrayed as merely the tale of a middle class inspired strategy.

Firstly, the argument that the working class had no political edge to their agitation in the period from 1810 to 1830. During the early phase of the struggles from 1810 to 1820s, although the primary aim was the removal of the statutory impediments to working class independence exercised by manufacturers and the forces of authority, a political edge did develop. The formation of Parliamentary Reform Associations throughout the manufacturing districts is evidence of this. Indeed, these associations included branches formed by women, arguably the most disadvantaged group of all. Although the mass involvement in these associations may have waned and been re-ignited, this does not necessarily mean that working people lost interest in political solutions to their collective predicament. It merely means that probably they were engaged in other things, most notably the attempt to earn a living. However, in most of the larger demonstrations of working-class grievances, both locally and at a region-wide level, working class political symbols were to be found. Such symbols included the *tricolour*, the symbol of the French Revolution of 1789; the blue cockade, the symbol of popular liberty; and the white scarf, the symbol of universal suffrage.[110] More often

---

106 As noted above, a strong military force was quickly moved to the north to augment those already in position. The clearance was also given from London to provide rifles and other weapons to the mill-owners and their servants for the defence of their property, see *The Times*, 1 May, 2 May, 3 May, 4 May 1826.

107 See 'Ministers, Magistrates and Reformers: The Genesis of the Rural Constabulary Act of 1839', in *Parliamentary History*, Vol. 5, (1986), E. C. Midwinter, *Social Administration in Lancashire, 1830-1860: Poor Law, Public Health and Police*, (Manchester, 1969), L. Radzinowicz, *A History of English Law and its Administration from 1750*, (4 Vols. 1948-68). See also the memorials and addresses to Sir Robert Peel, British Library Ad. Ms. 40401, Hornby to Peel, 21 January, 1842; and for a working class perspective, Ad. Ms. 40491, J. A. Stewart to Peel, 5 October, 1841.

108 See for example H. Pelling, *The History of British Trade Unions*, (London, 1963), or A. E. Musson, *British Trade Unions, 1800-1875*, (London, 1977).

109 Musson, *British Trade Unions*, or M. I. Thomis and P. Holton, *Threats of Revolution in Britain, 1789-1848*, (London, 1977).

110 See J. R. M. Butler, *The Passing of the Great Reform Bill*, (London, 1914), Asa Briggs, 'The Background of the Parliamentary Reform Movement in Three English Cities', *Cambridge Historical Journal*, (1952), James Epstein, 'Understanding the Cap of Liberty: Symbolic Practices and Social Conflict in Early Nineteenth-century England', in *Past and Present*, No. 22 (February, 1989). See also D. Walsh, A. J. Randall, R. Sheldon and A. Charlesworth, 'The Cider Tax, Popular Symbolism and Opposition in Mid-Hanovarian England', in A. J. Randall

than not the speeches delivered on such occasions would include references to political matters, be it parliamentary Reform, or the unjust nature of the Corn Laws and other forms of indirect taxation, or the various acts of repression carried out by local and national governmental bodies. To suggest therefore that during this period the working class had no political aspirations is highly misleading.

As to the claim that working-class politics had not developed any sense of political strategy or theory, this is more difficult to disprove. But there are signs that an abstract form of political thought based on popular democracy was being articulated and developed among wide sections of working people before 1832.[111] This took various forms, from the historical base of the seventeenth century Leveller tradition to the revolutionary thought of Spence. But if a single work or works by a single author which had the effect of proselytizing the idea of popular democracy amongst the working class, and encapsulated their feelings during this early stage (and indeed beyond), then it would probably be the writings of Tom Paine. Paine's *Rights of Man* and *The Age of Reason* (especially the former) both of which date from the last years of the eighteenth century. Not a great deal of Paine's works rank as first class examples of political thought, (Burke got much the better of the battle between the two), however, at the level of popularizing a series of ideas regarding the abuses inherent within the British political system at that time, coupled with his blatant disregard for the social and political conventions of the day, he was extremely successful. Paine's call was essentially one in which Britons should be given definable and legitimate rights based upon common justice and fairness. In short, a call for a Bill of Rights comparable with that of the U.S.A. Simultaneously, the legislature had to be purged of the place-hunting, fund-holding, sinecurists, and the corrupt hangers-on of the aristocracy. Once these had been swept away a popular legislature would be formed based on the mandate of universal suffrage. At the time of Paine's political activities in the 1790s, his ideas received a direct attack from the conservative Whig, Burke. Burke had the misfortune to utter two words that inflamed the passions of working people and contributed to their increasing dislike of conservative Whiggery and Toryism, when he described the lower orders as the 'swineish multitude', such pejorative language did not endear the starving industrial workers to Paine's opponents. But probably the most important feature of Paine's work was that he provided a popular political manifesto that supported basic working class claims for citizenship. Over the years this grew in significance and was something which the elites, (Conservative or Liberal), no matter how much they vilified Paine personally, could not ignore.

Paine's works are radical, but they are essentially reformist, albeit couched in the language of republicanism. Nowhere does he speak of economic levelling, or the termination of the basically subordinate relationship between labour and capital; indeed, he extols the virtues of commercial and industrial enterprise. If, therefore, we are to trace the thread of reformism in the political thought and actions of the British working class in the nineteenth century, Painite radicalism takes us back a very long way. This leads to a further argument, that the middle class reformers, to gain them a greater involvement in parliamentary politics, used the working class. This view suggests that all working class political activity was merely the tail of middle class led organizations for parliamentary reform and that the working class actions during the reform crisis of the early 1830s were never revolutionary. Again the evidence here is contradictory. Some areas were more active than others and the activities took on different forms depending on the area. The examination of the politics of

and A. Charlesworth, (eds.) *Markets, Market Culture and Popular Protest in Eighteenth-century England and Ireland*, (Liverpool, 1996).

111 See J. Belchem, 'Republicanism, popular constitutionalism and the radical platform in early nineteenth-century England', *Social History*, Vol. 6. No. 1 (January 1981), N. Kirk, 'In defence of class', *International Review of Social History*, Vol. 32, (1987).

Birmingham, for example, during this period clearly shows that the calls for reform and its subsequent organization were firmly in the control of the middle class and the lower middle class.[112] But a look at developments in Bolton or Manchester, or Blackburn or Oldham, one sees the same political unions based on the Birmingham model, but firmly under the control of the factory based working class.[113] A significant reason why this situation would not be found in Birmingham was that the structure of capitalistic development differed from that of the north-west. Birmingham certainly had industry in the early 1830s, but there was not a large-scale factory population; it was based mainly a network of small workshops and 'little masters', unlike the factory populations in the mill towns and cities of the north-west.

The conventional argument is that the national leaders of the Parliamentary reform movement, Place, Attwood, Brougham and Parks, merely used the threat of working class resistance, and even rebellion, as a means of negotiating a settlement suitable for all but the most die-hard defenders of the old system. The problem is that the Tory and conservative Whig resisters to reform, Lyndhurst, Wellington, Peel and Croker, were well aware of the blackmailing efforts of Brougham and the reform leaders. However, they quickly realized that once the rebellion or revolutionary threat had been put in train the chances of the middle class leadership being able to contain it were very slim. The working class leaders also knew this. As the *Poor Man's Guardian* pointed out in October 1831 during the height of the first phase of the reform crisis:

> … violent revolution is not beyond the means of those who threaten it, but it is also to them their greatest object of alarm; for they know that such a revolution can only be affected by the poor and despised millions, who, if excited to the step, might use for their own advantage … who would thus [then] have their clear rights and property endangered; be assured that a violent revolution is their greatest dread.[114]

The reforming Whig ministry was well aware of the mood of rising expectations of many working class radicals on the one hand, and, on the other, the taunts of the Tories, that they were giving too much away in their scheme of reform. This is why they drew a precise line at who was to receive the vote and who denied it. The Prime Minister, Lord Grey, in an attempt to forestall any leaps in the expectations of the extreme radicals, categorically stated that, "If any persons suppose that this reform will lead to ulterior measures, they are mistaken; for there is no one more decided against annual Parliaments, universal suffrage and the ballot than I am. My object is not to favour, but to put an end to such hopes."[115] In the immediate aftermath of this statement many of the aspirations of the radicals were dampened. But many of the working class in the manufacturing towns still clung to the idea of radical reform, even after Grey's speech, and began to take over the organization of the movement from the middle class reformers. As Francis Place noted,

> The systematic way in which the people proceed, their steady perseverance, the activity and skill astounded the enemies of reform. Meetings of almost every description of persons were held in cities, towns and parishes, by journeymen tradesmen in their clubs and by common

112 Briggs, *The Background of the Parliamentary Reform Movement*.
113 See *Blackburn Alfred*, 22 October 1832, or W. Brimelow, *A Parliamentary History of Bolton*, (Bolton 1880), see also the 'The Butterworth Manuscripts', Oldham Reference Library.
114 *Poor Man's Guardian*, 15 October 1831.
115 Cited in Thompson, *The Making*, p. 892.

workmen who had no trade clubs or associations of any kind.[116]

In all the major manufacturing towns of the north-west political unions were formed, and, as noted above, by 1832, the majority were in the hands of the working classes. Just how this was achieved is interesting, and offers an example of the political attitudes that informed working class actions. At Bolton the local Political Union was formed in the autumn of 1830 and was made up predominantly of the lower middle class (shopocracy), small manufacturers and skilled working men. By December 1831 however, its committee of 25 persons was made up overwhelmingly by what a contemporary source described as "chiefly working men".[117] What happened was that the more extreme working class radicals had ousted the politically moderate lower middle class. The split occurred in October 1831 when the Lords threw out the Reform Bill after much wrecking and prevarication. In Bolton, a public meeting was called for but refused by the Boroughreeve on the specious grounds of the cost to the ratepayers. The situation deteriorated and reached a potentially dangerous point in November when the King issued a Royal Proclamation outlawing Political Unions and banning all political meetings. On November 27 a meeting of the Bolton Political Union was held and attended by the entire committee. Votes were taken and resolutions passed calling for universal suffrage, vote by ballot and annual parliaments without either property qualification for the electors or the elected.[118] At this meeting the shopkeepers and moderate radicals led by William Naisby walked out when a call came to hold an open-air public meeting in defiance of the Royal Proclamation. The council of the Political Union was firmly in the hands of the working class radicals. On the 28 December (a workday) the public meeting was held in Bradford Square. In the chair, Thomas Smith, a weaver, opened the meeting by calling for a Painite Bill of Rights, and again reiterated the call for a radical reform of parliament, whilst at the same time conceding "that all property honestly acquired be sacred and inviolate."[119] But the cry was also "down with the Bishops" and "No Peers", underscoring once again the Painite influence.[120] At this time the Bolton Union claimed a membership in excess of 4,000. All the members paid a regular membership fee of $2d$ per month; its total funds by the end of 1831 were put at over £1,000. By the standards of the 1820s and 1830s this level of working class political organization is impressive, and it was to become mobilized to an even greater extent in 1832 when Lord Grey's government resigned and created the so called 'days of May' crisis.

The working class of the north-west believed that the Reform Bill of 1832 was but the first step in a series of reforms which would restore their political, social and economic rights, giving them citizenship within the existing political contract. It had to be supported at all costs even in the face of discouraging statements made by Grey, Landsdowne and Russell. The Tory opposition to the bill believed in roughly the same kind of scenario. They heard Grey's denunciation of extremists and how he would preserve the rights of property at all costs and, further, how relatively moderate the claims of the Reform Bill were in comparison with the demands of the extremists. But the prevailing Conservative and Tory fear was that, allow one crack in the dam of the Constitution and the "revolutionary flood would rush in", as the Tory editor of a Blackburn newspaper so graphically put it.[121] These factors are evident in a letter sent by John Wilson Croker, the Tory and former Admiralty

116 British Library, Place Papers, Ad. Ms. 35148, October, 1831, Place to Grote.

117 W. Brimelow, *Political and Parliamentary History of Bolton*, (Bolton, 1880).

118 *Bolton Chronicle*, 5 December 1831.

119 *Bolton Chronicle*, 5 December 1831.

120 Ibid., speech of Walter O'Carol.

121 *Blackburn Alfred*, 21 January 1832.

chief, to Home Secretary Melbourne. The most important point to note is that it is clear from Croker's letter that sections of the working class of the north had been mobilized, and that some of them had began a to march to London "to carry the bill":

> ... there arrived today in this little village some workmen from Manchester, who, under the pretence of offering some cotton yarn for sale, were strong and sturdy beggars ... they told me they had left Manchester in a *considerable body* [Croker's emphases] ... The article they had for sale could be of no value to the villagers and it is clearly a pretence. After some conversation ... they said they would not go back to Manchester until they had carried the *Reform Bill* with them and that there were thousands and thousands resolved upon that.[122]

In Gloucestershire workers were also combining, in this case woollen workers and agricultural labourers, to press for their political rights and in so doing instilling fear in the middle classes as this letter from a member of the gentry makes clear:

> I hope that the Unions among the lower orders are not extending near you as they are in this neighbourhood — some of our day labourers of worthless character joined the procession of woolcombers and wore the distinguishing medal — What have we not to dread from such combinations.[123]

Comments by later historians confirm that at this moment, working class consciousness was sufficiently high to bring about an open rebellion, if not an actual revolution. Raymond Postgate and G. D. H. Cole said, in *The Common People*, "Never since 1688 had Great Britain been so near an actual revolution; never in all the troubles of the next two decades was she to come so near it again."[124] According to Edward Thompson, "In the autumn of 1831 and in the 'days of May' Britain was within an ace of revolution which once commenced might well (if we consider the simultaneous advance in co-operative and trade union theory) have prefigured in its rapid radicalization, the revolutions of 1848 and the Paris Commune."[125] Thompson bases his assessment on the power of the middle-class/working-class radical alliance, suggesting that the working class response had a strength that had not been seen before. In fact, as had been shown above, working-class political development in parts of the north was in advance of this. As witnessed by the way their leadership dispensed with the lower middle class dominated Political Unions and took over their organizations, advocating a much more working class orientated set of aims and objectives.

The Tory and Conservative opposition certainly expected trouble. The Duke of Wellington personally supervised the preparations against the attempted seizures of Strathfieldsaye, his country home.[126] Croker arranged for ships for his family and friends to flee the country, and even the unflappable Peel began to arrange his own private army at Drayton.[127] The usually taciturn Francis Place, one of the leaders of reform but no friend of revolution or radical working class politics, noted

---

122 Croker Papers, William Clements Library, University of Michigan, Ann Arbor, Croker's Letter Book, Vol. 26, Croker to Melbourne, 18 May 1832.

123 Gloucestershire Record Office, Winchcombe/Clifford Papers, D149/F52, George Cooke to Nathaniel Clifford, 13 June 1832.

124 G. D. H. Cole and R. Postgate, *The Common People*, (London, 1976 edition), p. 255.

125 Thompson, *The Making*, pp. 898-9.

126 *The Times*, 18 May 1832.

127 Croker Papers, Clements Library, University of Michigan, Ann Arbor, Croker's Letter Book, Croker to Hertford, 18 May 1832, and Croker to Peel, 11 November 1831.

in May 1832 in a private letter:

> We were within a moment of a general rebellion, and had it been possible for the Duke of Wellington to form an administration the thing and the people would have been at issue ... Barricades of the principal towns — stopping the circulation of paper money ... (in short) it would have been an act of the whole people to a greater extent than any which had ever before been accomplished.[128]

Rebellion or revolution was prevented on the one hand by the reformers' moderate national leadership being able to convince the working class that the Reform was merely the first stage in a series of reforms designed to rectify social and political imbalances. On the other hand this process was assisted by the statements of national leaders like William Cobbett saying that half a loaf was better than none. Also it should be noted that violent revolution was not what the majority of the working class actually wanted. What they did want was those placed socially above them to witness their plight and to see their point of view. In this sense revolt could only occur as a last resort, but the situation was very serious, as incidents at Derby, Nottingham and Bristol revealed. The latter being potentially the most serious, given the suggestion of fraternisation between the military leaders called to quell the riots and the rioters themselves.[129] However, in the final analysis it is probable that a general insurrection would only have to have been forced on the working class by the intransigence of the 'diehards' and Ultra Tories. Basically, even at this high level of consciousness, the working class wished, if possible, to follow the reformist path. This reluctance to sweep away the existing political tradition was a feature that ran deep in the British radical tradition.

Nonetheless, working class consciousness was operating at a very high level in the pre-Reform period. There also appears a strong sense of intra-class political unity coupled with a developed sense of political awareness in a class sense; further there was a will to advance the interests of the class in a political sense and there was a will to act on behalf of those interests. Here we see the beginnings of a working class based programme for political and social change based on a crude, but effective form of political theory linked to popular democracy and an economic theory based on cooperation. Finally there was a sense of mass unity without the sectionalization associated with intra-class status differentiation. In the five or so years after 1831-2, however, the high level of working class consciousness began to fragment, never reaching a comparable level of intensity for the next fifty years. Class consciousness did rise during the first phase of the Chartist years, from 1838 to 1842, but changes in the structural relations between capital and labour, coupled with the subtle changes in the nations political culture in the years between 1832 and 1842, meant that Chartism never looked likely to succeed in a radically changing society. This interpretation gains value when the Chartist phase is compared to the potential threat the working class displayed in 1831-32. This distinction between the two phases of activity is based on comparing, on the one hand, the perceptible fears manifested by those social groups above the working class in the early 1830s with those of the early 1840s, and, on the other hand, the relative inability of the authorities to control a dangerous situation in 1831-2, and their ability to control Chartism between 1838 and 1842. The next area of consideration is how the situation began to change after 1833, examining how interclass relationships began to improve and, importantly, how the initiative was seized by the middle classes. The nature of the relationship between the elites and the working class was deteriorating as the Reform Act received the Royal seal

---

128 British Library, Place Papers, Ad. Ms. 27295, ff 26/27.

129 *Bristol Gazette and Public Advertiser*, 12 January 1832.

in June 1832, and the purpose of this chapter has been to plot this worsening relationship. The power of the working class was feared by many of the elites, but in some Tory circles it was understood. Many old Tories lamented the passing of the old customs and values as much as working people and they too decried the age of machinery. This was to manifest itself in support for the Short Time Movement and Radical Toryism. But others recognised that the working class had become more politically conscious during this period, especially in relation to the hated tenets of political economy. For us this was a feature of their rising levels of class consciousness, but to some Tories and Conservatives, this was something that they could turn to their advantage if their party was organizationally reformed. It is this latter feature which now needs examination. In the 1830s the Conservatives particularly began to radically reformulate their attitudes towards the industrial working class of the north and this had ramifications not only for the working-class but also for the Conservative Party.

3

The Re-organization of the Conservative Party after 1832

The archaic and essentially loose organization and structure of the old Tory/conservative Whig coalition, as outlined earlier, cannot in organizational and functional terms, be defined as a party according to the set of criteria described in chapter one. The intention here is to show how this situation changed at the national level in the wake of the Reform Act, and more specifically how these changes allowed for wider political integration. Initially however, a description must be given of the basic structure of political groups in the 1820s. This was based around groupings in parliament with very loose organization in the country outside.

Political Organization before 1832

Essentially the reason why the Tories had no organization outside parliament, and very little inside it, was that as the group associated with Ministry of the Crown they had no need of formal organization. The method of managing elections, not to mention public opinion, in the pre-Reform political world was by personal influence. This personal influence would have the national policies pursued by the government (or opposition) as its basis, but the influence itself was located at the local level. This usually took three forms: the greater or lesser aristocratic and gentry families of a given constituency; a dominant economic or commercial interest, (for example merchant influence at Bristol or the City of London); or by closed or oligarchical borough corporation. It was therefore rare, but not unknown, for elections to be decided on the presentation of the difference of opinions of the competing candidates over political issues. The norm was for those intent on becoming an MP to reach an agreement before the election to avoid the disruption and expense of a contest. In case a contest was called between two rival political groupings, the government always had the advantage of being in possession of office and of the 'Treasury Chest', of which more will be said later.

In fact constituency representation before 1832 was grossly unrepresentative of population density and differing centres of interest orientation, especially the 'new' manufactures of textiles and engineering.[1] More than half of the English boroughs before 1832 were situated in Wiltshire and the coastal counties south of the line from Norfolk to Gloucestershire. This gave the maritime and agricultural interests predominant influence in the House of Commons. The franchise in these boroughs was varied and haphazard. In certain places, such as Preston, there was the Scot and Lot franchise, open to all males who paid local rates. Elsewhere the vast majority of boroughs were made up of electors of the holders of certain privileges, handed down in primogeniture. Most electorates were small and their registration was unnecessary because imposters would quickly have been detected. In the counties and Scot and Lot boroughs, voters could prove their qualifications by producing receipts for the land tax or local rates. In boroughs with small electorates the patron could use money or territorial power to secure the return of candidates according to his wishes. Croker

---

1   See Paul Langford, 'Property and 'Virtual Representation' in Eighteenth-Century England', in *Historical Journal*, 31, 1, (1988).

(Chief Secretary to the Admiralty in the Liverpool ministry) estimated in 1827 that 42 per cent of the House of Commons was directly at the disposal of landed patrons and that 73 per cent of these were under Tory control; eight peers alone controlled 27 per cent of seats.[2] The existence of the nomination boroughs, and of the patron, gave an especial character to English politics before 1832. Since political power nationally had become centred on the House of Commons and power in that assembly depended on votes, political groupings or individuals could buy votes or seats on the open market. The nomination boroughs thus became, as one historian put it, "the instrument by which the Government of the day maintained its majority."[3] This was necessary because the authority and discipline associated with the modern political parties was lacking before 1832. The price the government paid to the patron was occasionally in money, but more often in the form of political advancement and jobs in the public services for the patron's relatives and dependants. When George III attempted to build up a political grouping of his own he too was forced to become "the first of the borough-mongering electioneering gentlemen of England."[4]

The nomination boroughs existing in the north-west before 1832 were Chester, under the control of the Grosvenor family, a seat at Preston held in the interest of Lord Derby, one of Clitheroe's seats was controlled by the Earl of Brownlow and the other by Viscount Dunstanville, and one of Lancaster's seats was held by the Earl of Longsdale. In the south of Lancashire one seat at Newton was owned by the Leigh family, whilst the seats at Wigan were shared jointly by Sir Robert Holt Leigh and the coal owner Hodson. In the twelve borough seats in Lancashire before 1832 only one seat from Lancaster and the two Liverpool seats were open to contest. Of the nine closed seats the Tories held five to the Whigs four.[5] It was in the open boroughs that much of the money was spent to bribe, 'treat' or influence electors and non-electors. A Tory argument against the Reform bill was that it would have the effect of increasing both venal activities and expense. The Liverpool election of 1830 serves as an illustration as Charles Greville, the Whig diarist, revealed:

> The Liverpool election is just over... It is said to have cost near £100,000 to the two parties, and to have exhibited a scene of bribery and corruption perfectly unparalleled; no concealment or even semblance of decency were observed; the price of tallies and votes rose, like stock, as the demand increased, and single votes fetched £15 to £100 a piece.

"Here comes the difficulty of reform," continued Greville, "for how is it possible to reform the electors?"[6]

According to the prevailing theory of electoral representation before 1832, variations in the franchise allowed the representation of different sections of the community. Thus the interest of the town could be declared in the open boroughs, and the county members usually represented the agricultural influence. Therefore manufacturing interests were 'virtually' represented in the boroughs controlled by rich manufacturers and merchants. It was believed that representation was, and should continue to be based on property and wealth and not on numbers.[7] Given such a basis of representation the government had no need of any formal organizational structure in the country

---

2   E. L. Jennings (ed.) *The Croker Papers*, vol. 1, pp. 368-72, (London, 1884). The figures are 276 out of the 658 seats in the House of Commons were at the disposal of landed patrons, and that of these 203 were Tory controlled with Peers possessing 57 seats.

3   C. R. Fay, *Huskisson and his Age*, (London, 1951), pp. 46-7.

4   Quoted in L. Namier, *England in the Age of the American Revolution*, (London, 1950), p. 4.

5   T. H. B. Oldfield, *Representative History of Great Britain and Ireland*, Vol. IV, (London, 1816), pp. 285-96.

6   *Greville Memoirs*, Vol. II, 2 December 1830, (London, 1938).

7   See 'Observations on the British Constitution', (Anonymous pamphlet, 1831), p. 12.

because they had such a large advantage in the nomination boroughs and in the counties. One example of the influence they pressed on their supporters is given in a letter from Lord Liverpool to the Earl of Longsdale, a prodigious collector of boroughs in Cumberland and north Lancashire, one of whose nominees, Sir James Graham, sat for Cumberland.

> The conduct of Sir James Graham unfortunately produces the worst effect, for he seems to have a satisfaction in showing his resentment to the government, not less by the manner of his opposition than by the opposition itself... If your feelings and opinions concur with ours... may I request of you to use your influence with those who are connected with you...[8]

The ability of newspapers to guide and influence political opinion, individual parties, as distinct from Governments, was not great before 1832. One of the most important aspects of the political history of Britain in the early nineteenth century was the growth in the power and political influence of the press. Both Whigs and Tories complained of their inability to direct the press to their satisfaction. Indeed, Wellington was openly contemptuous of the press, as Lord Ellenborough noted in his diary in 1830. "We have neglected the press too much. The duke relies on the support of 'respectable people' and despises the rabble; but the rabble read newspapers."[9] This, however, began to change after 1832. Having noted that formal organization in terms of party was minimal before 1832, this needs contrasting with an account of the struggle for the Reform Act and its subsequent effects on British political culture after 1832.

The Conservatives and the First Reform Act

One of the most important functions of the political party and of the press is to inform, educate and influence the public. Before 1832 there had been examples of pressure being brought to bear on a ministry from outside Parliament, the most striking being the campaign against slavery and the question of the removal of Catholic disabilities. But issues, even though mobilized largely from outside, only began to apply real pressure on the government when they were debated inside the House of Commons. Even then these issues did not become 'party' issues but attracted widespread cross-bench support and opposition. The proposed Reform Bills of 1831-2 were more serious for the Conservatives and Ultra Tories because they served to galvanize the Whigs and Liberals into a serious party and the Conservatives into what appeared to be an entrenched party opposed to any reform whatsoever. Further, the vast majority of those in the country held this impression. Toryism, as was the case between 1800-1820, was once again being seen as the party of knee-jerk reactionary opposition to what many regarded as a long overdue reform.

The outside pressure which the agitation for reform built up in the country, and especially in the manufacturing districts, was unlike anything seen previously. What was especially disturbing was the apparent alliance between the middle class reformers and the working-class radicals. The agitation began in early 1830. In January, Attwood founded the Birmingham Political Union, the example being quickly followed in other urban areas. By November, Greville was recording the scenes in London:

> It was expected last night that there would be a great riot, and preparations were made to meet

---

8   British Library, Liverpool Papers, Ad. Ms. 38262, ff 323, undated, Liverpool to Longdale.

9   Ibid., p. 405.

it. Troops were called up to London, and large body of civil power put in motion…The Duke of Wellington expected Apsley House to be attacked and made preparations accordingly, at Temple Bar a body of weavers with iron crows had been dispersed.[10]

Later in November 1830, Greville stated the situation was becoming desperate, and, most alarmingly for the elites, more of the working class were becoming involved.

> The state of the country is dreadful; every post brings fresh accounts of conflagrations, destruction of machinery, [and] association of labourers … Cobbett and Carlile write and harangue to inflame the minds of the people … Distress is certainly not the cause of these commotions, for the people have patiently supported far greater privatations than they have been exposed to before these riots.[11]

In November 1830 Wellington resigned and the Whigs under Lord Grey formed a ministry pledged to Parliamentary Reform. The new Ministry formed a committee made up of Lords Russell, Duncannon, Durham and Sir James Graham, to examine reform proposals and to submit a scheme to the Cabinet. On 1 March 1831 Russell laid the ministerial proposals before the House of Commons. They proved to be more drastic than even the most sanguine of Radicals had dared to hope. The first feature of the Bill was the disenfranchisement of sixty boroughs of less than 2000 inhabitants, who returned in total eighty members. The net reduction of the House of Commons was to be 62 seats. Also there was to be a drastic simplification of the voting qualification (£10 rateable value) and the introduction of annual registration of electors. It is worth briefly considering the Conservative/Tory arguments against the Bill before expanding on the effects it had on them as a party. The most basic argument was that the Reform Bill would destroy the political harmony and stability that had existed throughout most of the eighteenth century. For many Conservatives and Tories the Bill that gained the Royal Assent in June 1832 was seen as a great betrayal. To a significant extent this attitude rested upon certain assumptions about the possible changes the Bill might produce. Peel's main argument was that despite the protestations of the Whigs, that the measure was final and irrevocable, it would be merely the first stage of a series of reforms. It could not be a final settlement because the precedent had been set. Importantly, the working class radicals also held this view. Many Conservatives were willing to redress some anomalies inherent in the old system, especially in the large urban areas. However, many Tories believed they had been betrayed by political leaders who had pledged themselves to maintain the fundamental nature of English constitutionalism as laid out by the settlement of 1688. The thing that kept the Conservatives united, for Peel had no liking for the Ultras, was the sheer scope of the Whig Bill. Many Tories blamed the "base and bloody Whigs", but also the pressure exerted by the rising middle classes in the manufacturing districts. Many, including Peel, saw in the passing of the Bill not only the dismantling of the old constitutional system, but the dawn of a new political era. This would be an era in which it was believed intense political struggles would be manifest; bitter divisions would occur between political parties, between classes and between differing religious and economic interests. The latter included the agricultural as opposed to the manufacturing interest, the urban versus the rural, Protestantism versus Catholicism. Conservatives and Tories argued that the constitution had remained intact even though there had been occasions of political conflict in the eighteenth century. This was so because of the placatory and

---

10   *Greville Memoirs*, 10 November, 1830. Charles Greville was a particularly useful source as his position of Clerk to the Privy Council made him conversant with all shades of political opinion.

11   Ibid.

consensual effects of the political settlement of 1688 with each branch of the legislature and executive: Monarch, Lords and Commons, each independent and able to check the possible excesses of the others. The Reform Act, they argued, would wreck the old order, and to a significant degree their prognostications were correct. Less committed observers held similar opinions. Writing in 1831, John Stuart Mill, who could never be described as a conservative, said England was in a 'transitional condition'. He believed that there were no persons to whom "the mass of the uninstructed habitually defer; ... the ancient bonds no longer unite, nor do the ancient boundaries confine."[12] No group understood this more than the Conservatives. For the Conservatives and Tories the situation was serious, even though in the long run-in to the first General Election under the terms of the Reform Act, the Tories at least attempted to enter the contest with a certain sense of bravado, as the diarist Greville noted:

> The Tories evidently expect that they shall re-appear in very formidable strength ... it would be for the better to erect a Conservative party upon a new and broader basis, than try to bolster up this worn-out, prejudiced, obstinate faction.[13]

It is interesting to note Greville's referring to the Tories as a 'faction' but in order to plot the remarkable recovery of the Conservative party after 1832 we need to understand the perceptions of those who genuinely believed that England was on the very brink of disaster, indeed revolution. Conservatives believed this because of what the tenets of the Reform Act exemplified. The Bill was perceived as being merely the first stage in a range of sweeping reforms which would destroy the very foundations of British political stability, and to a certain extent they were correct. Most damaging of all was the apparent dismantling of the three planks upon which the British Constitution rested: the prescriptive rights of the Monarch; the independence of the House of Lords and Commons; and thirdly, the predominance of the Established Church of England. It was the threat of the eradication of these constitutional prerogatives that, after Reform, served to weld the Conservative Party into what was essentially a new and viable political opposition, both inside and outside Parliament. The Tories became part of the Conservative Party, though they did retain their identity, not from any great admiration of Peel as a leader (they regarded his policies with deep suspicion) but because there was nowhere else for them to go. This coupled with a profound hatred and fear of reforming Whiggery forced them to take the Conservative Whip. It is one of the paradoxes of British political development that, in seeking above all else to maintain the existing political system, the Tories and Conservatives created a fundamentally new and far reaching political dimension; the effective political integration of the working class into the party structure. One of the main contentions of this book is that the re-structuring of the Conservatives after 1832 was a major contributory factor not only in the development of the modern political party, but also in the shaping of Britain's emerging political culture.

---

12 Quoted in G. Himmelfarb, (ed.), *The Spirit of the Age: Essays in Politics and Culture*, (New York, 1963), p. 36.

13 Greville, *Memoirs*, 25 July, 1832. In a similar vein see the letter from Lord Granville Somerset to his father, the sixth Duke of Beaufort, in September, 1831. Drawer 10/2, the Beaufort Archive, Badminton, Gloucestershire. See also the memorandum from the leading Conservative and ally of Peel, Sir Henry Hardinge. "The Tories must withdraw their opposition and by some compromise save the creation of Peers ... so long as Peel and Croker and Goulburn, Herries, Inglis, Dawson etc, hold back, it is impossible to do anything in the Commons. We only break up the Conservative Party and prolong the inevitable *revolution*. (Hardinge's emphasis) Nothing can save us but union." Hardinge to Londonderry, 15 May 1832, C2, File 11, McGill University Library, Montreal, Canada

The Conservatives Organizational Response

When viewed from the perspectives of the political scientist and the political sociologist, which is rare for this period, the 1832 Reform Act stands as a watershed in British political development. The 1830s saw the consolidation of the organized parliamentary party with its attendant disciplines and controls, and the widespread recognition that political parties could be the vehicles of legitimate political opposition to the Ministry of the Crown. But the period also saw the dramatic growth of political organization in the localities to include groups never before involved in the party. For the Conservatives in the localities as well as the centre, the actions of the reforming Whig government and the progressive Liberals acted as a spur for improved organization in the localities and saw a heightened sense of party political rivalry in the area of local government. As Derek Fraser, a historian of urban politics during this period, has pointed out, local politics were used by the major parties as merely a pawn in the wider political game of attracting support and gaining power, as a means to an end in the wider political world.[14] It should not be forgotten that local politics often provided bitter contests, and, as Fraser tells us, divided down party lines for the exercise and pursuit of power "... from the 1830s onwards."[15] But the terms of the Reform Act itself and, indeed, the Municipal Reform Act of 1835, forced the Conservative party to organize itself on a permanent basis in the localities in ways that had never been necessary in the past. Many local and national political leaders continued to demur as to the disruption, cost and agitation such contests would produce. Doubts were raised as to the ability of groups to mobilize their forces and take advantage of the annual process of registering of electors, which meant that a local party caucus had to be operational at all times. In a politico-cultural sense the concern was political attitudes became hardened and most local institutions, from the Court Leet, Corporation, Vestry, Improvement or Police Commissions to the election of Churchwardens and Poor Law Officials, became politicized.

It is important to consider the organization of the Conservative party at the centre immediately after Reform because it was the changes enacted here which complimented changes taking place in the localities, particularly in relation to the inclusion of sections of the working classes into the party. The party at the centre felt it necessary to organize opinion against what they regarded as the dangerous tendencies displayed by the Radicals and the more extreme Whigs. In order to mobilize opinion in a hostile political environment immediately after 1832, supporters had to be convinced and rallied to the conservative side. Supporters, drawn from all grades in society and comprising of both electors and non-electors, were needed in order to capture (or re-capture) a newly municipalized borough, or Improvement Commission or Board of Guardians, as a necessary first step to eventual parliamentary control. In order that this might be achieved, the various types of supporters had to be galvanized into presenting arguments and answers in favour of Conservative thinking. This last point was again significantly new in that for the first time a party was attempting to present its general ideological principles as applicable not only to those in positions of social, educational, or political status, but to the nation as a whole.

It was vital for the Conservatives of the post-Reform years to show their opponents, as well as those of moderate political opinion, that Conservatism (unlike Toryism) was representative of the nation as a whole. Of all interests and sections of society, not just of the privileged elites, agriculturalists or the county squirearchy. The editors of the provincial press in the manufacturing

14 D. Fraser, *Urban Politics in Victorian Britain*, (Leicester, 1976).

15 Ibid., p. 10.

districts gave publicity to various social groups, especially the working-class, who supported the Conservatives, partly to embarrass the so called 'popular' parties of the Liberals and radicals, but also for the reasons outlined above. The editor of a Lancashire paper noted in 1837,

> There is no surer sign of the advance of constitutional opinions, than the increase of Conservative societies, and particularly among the operatives. How potent an answer it is to those contemptible charges which are so fondly and fervently directed against us, and how fatal to the assertion that we possess no hold over the affections of the people.[16]

The question was how to win over the affections of the people for a party who were seen as the resisters of reform and whose recent record toward the working class was not good. In July 1832, after the Act of Reform had received the Royal Assent, Alfred Mallalieu, the editor of the London based *Public Ledger and Guardian*, suggested to Lord Aberdeen, a leading Conservative, that the new situation created by the Reform Act required new tactics and techniques of electioneering.[17] He argued that this was especially important in the boroughs, which, with the concentration of the middle-class vote, presented the Conservatives with their most serious threat. This was in line with what most leading conservatives believed. The argument was that the replacement of the old nomination boroughs by the representatives of commerce and manufacturing would eventually swamp the House of Commons, rendering the lower house a delegatory assembly dictated to by the burgeoning forces of the Midlands and North. This would benefit the Whig/Liberals, and, in the words of the Duke of Wellington, keep "their rivals the Tories out of power *for ever*." (Wellington's emphasis.)[18] It was believed that the landed interests in the county constituencies would still be predominant in the House of Commons, at least for the first few years after Reform. Of the 165 seats re-allocated under the terms of the Reform Act, only 62 were to be allotted to the new boroughs, which proved the judgement correct. However, Mallalieu went on to argue that the landed predominance would in the long-term be challenged by "the superior shrewdness, tact, intelligence and untiring activity of the trading representatives." Mallalieu compared various groups and was "struck on the one hand with the great activity displayed in various parts of the country by the reforming Whigs and the revolutionary parties, and on the other by the listlessness and sluggish waiting upon providence displayed by the Conservatives." He argued that, "The slow and easy process of county and borough electioneering ought not to be applied to these new interests", suggesting the traditional means of managing elections in the localities were now useless. What was needed, argued Mallalieu, were men representative of the interests of the electorate existing in the boroughs, able to match the Reformers and broaden the basis of Conservatism and the Conservative Party,

> Men who by their connexions [*sic*] and well judged combinations would enable the party powerfully to influence the town elections; who by their ultimate acquaintance with the habits, prejudices, opinions and wants of particular places and districts would be able to point out the fitting sort of candidates, willing to undergo the expense and labour requisite, supported as they would be by a skilful arrangement and bringing to bear all the elements of Conservative and aristocratic influence existing in and about the towns, in aid of their own resource among the

---

16   *Blackburn Standard*, 8 November, 1837.

17   British Library, Herries Papers, Ad. Ms. 57420, ff 104, Mallalieu to Aberdeen, 3 July 1832.

18   Clements Library, University of Michigan, Ann Arbor, Croker Papers, Wellington to Croker, 30 September, 1833.

more independent portion of the community.[19]

In the case of Bolton, Blackburn, Bury, Clitheroe, Lancaster, Preston, Rochdale, Warrington, and Wigan this is precisely what happened. Mallalieu suggested that a permanent organizing committee be formed of twenty-four persons with an ex-cabinet minister as chairman, to supervise the elections from London.[20] Half of the committee was to be made up of Conservative members of parliament, and half to be representative of the commercial, shipping, distributive and manufacturing interests. He further suggested that:

> the committee would of course sub-divide themselves according to the portions of the Empire where each could operate most effectively. Active and extensive correspondence would be opened... Candidates on the spot would be assisted and encouraged. Where these were wanting, candidates possessing the requisite qualifications would be provided from the metropolis, in some instances at their own cost entirely, in others with some small aid from the common fund.[21]

The members of the committee, argued Mallalieu, should not be treated as inferiors, remembering that, under the working of the new Act, "The middle and lower classes have acquired so tremendous an accession of power as can only be comprehended and managed by and through parts and portions of themselves. This is the new blood of which I speak."[22] The committee members should be given ready and confidential access to the party leadership. He suggested it was only by drawing together the bonds of common interest between the lower classes, the middle classes and the aristocracy that the Conservative party could perform its duty and recover from the effects of the Reform Bill. This, he argued, was especially important in the urban areas not normally associated with Conservative principles. "The most dangerous portion of the new constituency will undoubtedly be that of the towns, it will also be the most difficult to manage."[23]

Mallalieu had previously been of service to the party, in 1831 it was on his suggestion to Lord Stuart De Rothesay and Wellington that the Carlton Club be formed in order "to invite the Conservative party to reconcile the ultra and liberal sections."[24] It was at the Carlton that the organizing committee operated after the disastrous results of the first elections under the terms of the Reform Act in January 1833. Mallalieu's memorandum was remarkable because it detailed the means by which the Conservative Party must transform itself in order to survive, and, significantly, the failure of the Conservatives at these first elections (less than 150 seats) proved the point. Mallalieu was correct in his assessment of the changing nature of Britain's political culture after Reform. He foresaw the need of a large political party able to integrate differing social groups, regardless of their social station and interests, into the party's structure. This point was not lost on Sir Robert Peel, the leader of the party. He wrote to Lord Harrowby early in 1833 "...the vast mass of mankind of the highest as well as the lowest station, cannot be disregarded in politics."[25] Mallalieu also saw the need for the party to direct opinion purposefully and to control and influence members and supporters in a

---

19 British Library, Herries Papers Ad Ms 57420, ff 104.

20 Mallalieu suggested John Charles Herries, hence why the memorandum is in the Herries papers.

21 Ibid.

22 Ibid.

23 Ibid.

24 British Library, Aberdeen Papers, Ad. Ms. 43243, ff 126.

25 British Library, Peel Papers, Ad. Ms. 40402, ff 231-33, Peel to Harrowby, 5 February 1832.

new and original way. Mallalieu was editor of the party *Public Ledger and Guardian*, but also acted as leader writer for several newspapers including, *United Services Gazette*, and the *Surrey Standard*, whose articles served for newspapers at Leicester, Blackburn and Dover.[26] This tells us much about the party's gradual moves towards centralizing the distribution of information to the localities after 1832, and also, importantly, how it began to control the provincial press.

In deference to Professor Gash and other historians who argue the continuity of the political order after 1832, it must be clearly stated that the old system was not eradicated immediately after the Reform Act.[27] The social make-up of the House of Commons remained essentially the same and there still existed nomination boroughs, corrupt candidates and electors. However, it was the politics of opinion as well as influence and the offering of treats that rapidly gained importance in the urban setting.[28] In several ways the post-Reform political system was still archaic but attitudes were changing, and, in terms of plotting the process of modernization of the political party, Mallalieu's memorandum to Aberdeen is central because in it we see the beginning, the germ, of the modern political party. Indeed, Mallalieu himself believed his work to have been important. Writing some twelve years later to Lord Aberdeen he indulged himself in unashamed self-promotion:

> May I be pardoned for telling Sir Robert [Peel] that, when the history of those times comes to be written, the truth will not be told if it be not stated that I was virtually the sole-founder of the party under its present title of Conservative and not Sir Robert as assumed... Your Lordship did me the honour to approve, and to bear to the Duke of Wellington, my memoir on the necessity of re-constructing and re-uniting the party, still unreconciled from the Emancipation question, with the means and applicancy [*sic*] suggested to the end, which led to the... establishment of the Carlton Club with other measures.[29]

Put into effect immediately after Reform, these measures require closer examination. By 1833 the Organizing Committee of the Conservative Party was meeting (usually) weekly at the Carlton Club. The original committee had been formed the previous year. It comprised of John Charles Herries, Charles Arbuthnot, William Holmes, Sir Henry Hardinge, Sir John Beckett and Lord Lowther and it met at the house of the former Chief Whip, Joseph Planta, in Charles Street, hence the somewhat derogatorily name of the 'Charles Street Gang'. By the summer of 1833 the committee at the Carlton had undergone a change of personnel in the wake of the disastrous Conservative results of 1832-33. The Chairman of the Committee was Lord Granville Somerset, the party's treasurer was Sir Henry Hardinge, but the most significant new appointment was that of Francis Robert Bonham, acting, as Professor Gash has noted, as the first full-time 'political secretary' of the Conservative party.[30] Bonham was effectively the first national party agent. His primary task was to collect and collate information from all localities, and, importantly, keep the national party leadership informed as to the state of party feelings away from Westminster, and also the level of party strength and organization.[31] Bonham, it must be stressed, did not seek to interfere in local party autonomy, this would have been a

---

26   British Library, Aberdeen Papers, Ad. Ms. 43243, ff 125.

27   See N. Gash, *Reaction and Reconstruction in English Politics*, (Oxford, 1965), chapter one, or his *Politics in the Age of Peel*, (London, 1953), especially the introduction.

28   T. Nossiter, *Influence, Opinion and Political Idioms in Reformed England*, (Brighton, 1975).

29   British Library, Aberdeen Papers, Ad. Ms. 43246, Mallalieu to Aberdeen, 17 April 1846.

30   N. Gash, 'F. R. Bonham, Conservative Party Secretary', in *English Historical Review*, (October 1848).

31   Bonham was in daily contact with Peel and weekly contact with the other party leaders. Reports to the constituencies were sent out regularly, the frequency increasing during periods of parliamentary elections. See British Library, Peel Papers, Ad. Ms. 40615 *passim*.

mistake, but he did send out regular information sheets, points of advice and, on occasions, specific directives in the form of gentle prods to the organizers in the localities. There are several examples of the type of information Bonham received and dispensed. For example, in 1837 when the elections were pending he wrote to Peel:

> Lincoln is in fact I believe to be quite safe, at least for Stott-Ellis, but it will certainly require some money, at most I hear £1000 ... Mahon, who is now at Strathfieldsaye would easily ascertain the feelings of the committee at Finsbury which is cheaply organized.[32]

Or again, another example of information being conveyed from the localities to the leadership in London, this time from the Member for Liverpool, Lord Sandon, to the chairman of the Organizing Committee, Lord Granville Somerset:

> I understand that you are collecting information from all parts of the country as to the feelings of the electoral bodies and the chances of the elections... In Liverpool itself, my opponent Thornley has implied that he will not come forward again, and if no other Conservative candidate were proposed it is clear, that there would be no contest... There is certainly an improved feeling in the town ... the vileness of Lord Durham has alarmed men of property; and the squabbles and unsteadiness of the late government has disgusted and alienated men of all parties... Francis Egerton is considered quite safe for South Lancashire: if two tories are not proposed even then the chances would still be in his favour, and two tories are possible but not likely. Of Warrington and Wigan you will have heard... [The Earl of] Wilton told me again of four... might be reckoned on in Lancashire in case of a dissolution.[33]

In October 1840, Sir James Graham wrote to Bonham simply to say that: "I have no news for you except that the reports of the Registration in North Lancashire is excellent and makes *both* (Graham's emphasis) seats quite secure."[34] Finally a letter from a Mr Sydney in 1839 gives an illustration of the kind of assistance Bonham and the committee was asked to provide.

> Can you tell me the politics of Sir Hy. Maud?, and can he be got at in any way. He has taken the brewing interest of one Thompson... which will give him great influence especially over the public houses in that district, which heretofore have been used against us, and if it could be turned in our favour would make considerable difference in the county election (they say 30 votes) and probably in the town also: Sir John Reid is Maud's partner, perhaps it might be managed through him.[35]

Sydney seems to have been an agent of Bonham's for two days after the above letter he writes, "What are the state of politics at Reading? I have been asked whether there would be a good opening for a Conservative there."[36]

We see in the activities of Bonham, Granville Somerset and the party Organizing Committee the beginnings of a central organizing body. Admittedly, it was not until 1867-8 and the work of John Gorst that the Central Office was officially created and the various Conservative associations centralized into the National Union. However, it can be clearly seen that from 1833 and the formation

32 British Library, Peel Papers, Ad. Ms. 40422, ff 289, Bonham to Peel, 8 December 1836.
33 British Library, Peel Papers, Ad. Ms. 40404, ff 318-21, Sandon to Somerset, 8 December 1834.
34 British Library, Peel Papers, Ad. Ms. 40616, ff 162, Graham to Peel, 29 October 1840.
35 British Library, Peel Papers, Ad. Ms. 40617, ff 76, Sydney to Bonham, 27 November 1839.
36 British Library, Ad. Ms. 40617, ff 77, Sydney to Bonham, 29 November 1839.

of the various clubs (of which more will be detailed subsequently) and the Organizing Committee at the Carlton, that the Conservatives had embarked upon the first stages of a modern party in an organizational sense. The work of Bonham in transforming the organization of the Party was significant and was recognised at the time. Writing just after the elections of 1841 that saw the Conservatives under Peel returned with a majority of 76, Charles Arbuthnot wrote to Bonham extolling his effort of the previous eight years. "You have laboured well and satisfactorily and you ought to be proud."[37]

Another element regarded by political scientists as essential in the organizational structure of the modern political party is a central fund to be used for matters relating to elections and the publicizing the party's principles and policy positions. Modern parties (of government and official opposition) receive funds from the state, but this merely covers cost at a general election. For the period between elections these parties rely on subscriptions from the broader membership, but also from key individuals and groups who feel the need to forge closer affiliation with the party they believe best represents their interests. In the early decades of the nineteenth century, as was the case in the eighteenth century, the finance of elections was usually left to the individual candidates in the various localities. They would either expend the money out of their own pockets, or would be supported, in the case of a nomination borough, by the local patron sympathetic to the principles of the party, or would raise funds by subscriptions donated by the party's local supporters. Similarly, election petitions, brought by the aggrieved losing candidates in a bid to prove electoral malpractice, would be financed locally. However, by far the most normal method was for candidates to fund themselves. This ensured that those with the most property at stake, that is to say the wealthiest, maintained their political interest and representation in the House of Commons.

The outlay could be enormous. For example, Lord Francis Egerton, the member for South Lancashire, (a largely industrial area which made it a target seat for both Whigs and Conservatives), complained to Sir Robert Peel in 1837, "Having spent some £10,000 on two elections and having a majority to show ... I should be sorry to see one or two Whigs ship into such a representation from the mere want of candidates on our side."[38] Arthur Aspinall, an historian of early nineteenth-century politics, denied the existence of the party chest.[39] However, evidence exists which suggests a central fund was available for various political purposes after 1832. In the run-up to the first Reform elections, Alfred Mallalieu wrote to Lord Aberdeen of the need to mobilize the press in order to make it clear to the public precisely what Conservative principles were, as opposed to the intransigence of the Ultras and Old Tories. He wrote, "The rumours were that two or three millions were subscribed by the Conservative Party for the press and the forthcoming elections. I was encouraged by the late Lord Frank to search for money which would be used to begin a newspaper which would press for moderate Conservative principles."[40] The party utilized its election fund in prestige constituencies singled out for special effort, if only in order to show their opponents and supporters alike the strength of the party. South Lancashire was one such prize, but in this instance, as Egerton was the inheritor of the Bridgewater millions, the party fund was seldom needed. Other places were different, one such prize was Dublin, the headquarters of the Irish repealer, Joseph O'Connell. So too was traditionally radical Westminster. In 1837, the party's treasurer, Sir Henry Hardinge, wrote to Peel that the party had allocated "£2,400 for Dublin City and £3,300 for Westminster — the candidates

---

37 British Library, Peel Papers, Ad. Ms. 40617, ff 101, Arbuthnot to Bonham, 23 July 1841.

38 British Library, Peel Papers, Ad. Ms. 40426, ff 411, Egerton to Peel, 14 May 1839.

39 A. Aspinall, 'English Party Organization in the Early Nineteenth-Century', in *English Historical Review*, Vol. XLI, (1926), pp. 400-3.

40 British Library, Aberdeen Papers, Ad. Ms. 43243, ff 226, Mallalieu to Aberdeen, 4 August 1844.

and their committees must do the rest."[41] After the elections were over, (successfully in the case of Westminster), Hardinge sent Peel his personal assessment of the places which had received special attention and funds. At Westminster, where, in 1837, the former radical, Sir Francis Burdett was standing as a Conservative, Hardinge wrote,

> ... our young men of the Carlton, about 120 divided into districts, were at their posts before 7 o'clock, urging the voters who had promised to the poll, and before the result could be known, the great mass had voted to Burdett... What a strange situation is politics — Palmerston voting for a radical — Burdett seated amongst the Tories — and democratic Westminster... concurring with Burdett that the Constitution, Parliament and Church are in danger.[42]

Of the targeted seats probably the most expensive, paid entirely out of party funds, was the Dorset by-election during the height of the Reform when, it was estimated that £30,000 was spent on getting an opponent of the Reform Bill, Lord Ashley, elected.[43] Although a central fund existed, only very few of the party's leaders knew of its existence. The reasons for the secrecy were two-fold. Firstly, it was unwise to allow the opposition the opportunity of casting aspersions about the uses of such a fund, and secondly, in reality no party could undertake to assist, still less totally maintain, candidates in every contested constituency.

Hardinge, as treasurer, sent out circulars for subscriptions to the party's wealthy elites. The decision on how the money should be spent was left to a sub-committee of the Organizing Committee: the Finance Committee. It comprised Hardinge, Sir Thomas Fremantle, (the party's Chief Whip) Lord Rosslyn (who looked after Scottish interests), Viscount Stormont (who looked after Irish interests), Lord Redesdale (the chief Whip in the Lords), and Sir George Clerk, the leading Whip in the Commons. All large withdrawals would need the authorization of the party's two leaders, Wellington and Peel.[44] A list of the fund subscribers in the House of Lords for the elections of 1837 serves to show the amounts individuals were willing to subscribe. The Duke of Newcastle headed the list with £2,000, the Duke of Wellington and Lord Lonsdale each subscribed £1,000, the others were Lord Brownlow with £300, Earl Howe, £300, Lord Ripon with £100 and Lord Ashley, £10.[45] Indeed some contributors appear to have paid their subscriptions or pledges by instalments. For example, Sir Benjamin Durban paid a total of £2,400 in such a manner in 1833.[46] So did a Dr J. Erik in 1835.[47] In the same year at the election at Windsor, Hardinge wrote a memorandum that proves that the Carlton committees did have funds available for electoral purposes.

> An agreement was made upon that Sir J Gully should undertake the contest for Windsor and to incur an expenditure of £500. Beyond that amount the necessary aid (pecuniary) was to be afforded by the Carlton Club, Sir J G has fulfilled his part of the contract, and more than

41 British Library, Peel Papers, Ad. Ms. 40314, ff 177, Hardinge to Peel, 12 May 1837.

42 British Library, Peel Papers, Ad. Ms. 40314, ff 178-9, Hardinge to Peel, 12 May 1837.

43 British Library, Aberdeen Papers, Ad. Ms. 43243, ff 125, Mallalieu to Aberdeen, 4 August 1844. See also Croker Papers, Clements Library, University of Michigan, Ann Arbor, Letter Book Vol. 25, Croker to Lord Hertford, 19 September 1831. "Even old Eldon has offered £1000 ... they may have all the money in a few days, but in a few days the opportunity may be lost ... the only chance I see of stopping the revolution is by success in Dorset."

44 British Library, Peel Papers, Ad. Ms. 40409, Rosslyn to Peel ff 114-15, 146-7, (1835).

45 Quoted in N. Gash, 'Organization and the Conservative Party, 1832-1836', in *Parliamentary History*, part II, (London, 1983), p. 138. See also McGill University, Hardinge Papers, Box C2, Files 2-21.

46 McGill University, Hardinge Papers, Box C2, File 14.

47 Mcgill University, Hardinge Papers, Box C2, File 10, see also, C2, File 15, C2, File 16.

doubled the expenses above stated; and therefore claims the fulfilment of the other part; so must many demands arising out of the election.[48]

The election fund was used to assist a limited number of candidates who, from their personal circumstances or official position, deserved exceptional support. In 1837, for example, the Conservatives of Manchester, unable to find a suitable local candidate, sent a deputation to the Carlton Club to meet Sir Henry Hardinge, to find a strong candidate and some finance to break the hold of the Manchester Liberals.[49] Hardinge advised W. E. Gladstone, but Gladstone would only stand 'in absentia' having already agreed to fight Newark for the Duke of Newcastle. However, even with Gladstone unwilling to visit Manchester, he still polled well over 2,000 votes, thanks to the liberality of funds made available both locally and from London.[50]

Part of the money used on elections would be for the bestowing of treats on electors and non-electors, arranging for voters travel expenses, the canvass, publicity and, of course, the local and national agents. Bonham had his own team of agents who he sent out at periods of electoral activity. In 1837 he wrote to Peel that the west-midlands were being supervised by one Forster, in the north-west his agent was an unsuccessful barrister, Charles Wilkins, whose activities will be described in more detail later.[51] In Ireland, Bonham and Hardinge also had a team of agents, Enius McDonnell, David O'Croly and Edward Fitzgerald.[52] The party also used local agents, for example, Richard Backhouse at Blackburn, Thomas Yates at Preston, Robert Sowler at Manchester, and so on. Bonham liaised with local agents controlled by other leading members of the Conservative Party. For example a Mr Lawrence, who acted for Lord Ellenborough in North Gloucestershire and Worcestershire;[53] in Wiltshire, Joseph Neald; in West Gloucestershire and in Monmouthshire a Mr Wyatt acted for Lord Granville Somerset;[54] for North Lancashire and the Borders a Mr Lamond acted for Sir James Graham.[55] All this was useful in gaining valuable information regarding the state of the register and of political feelings generally. However, these men acted also as local party organizers before an election, during the course of an election and, if required, afterwards with the petition. This required money, and, in certain circumstances, if this was lacking locally as we have seen, the central fund could be utilized. There were also the various local associations and clubs that existed not just at election times but permanently, these too required organization, and again supplied Bonham with information. The growth in support for Conservatism after 1836 needed the use of initiatives covering a range of activities. In the area of propaganda, for example, the use of pamphlets written in the Conservative interest enabling supporters to rebuff the arguments of the opposition and inducing a sense of camaraderie among the party faithful.

Most of the subscription lists drawn up by Hardinge were used to pay for the writing of propaganda and publicity pamphlets. It was believed that the Anti-Corn Law League first utilized the power of the personalized printed message, but the Conservatives were operating in a similar fashion several years previously. In 1837, for example, they spent £384 9s 4d for 46,000 circulars and

48   McGill University, Hardinge papers, C2, File 16, memorandum dated 6 February 1836.

49   *Manchester Guardian*, 20 July 1837.

50   McGill University, Hardinge Papers, Box C6, File 1.

51   For the west midlands see British Library, Peel Papers, Ad. Ms. 40424, ff 263. In the north-west see Peel Papers, Ad. Ms. 40416, ff 328; see also *Manchester Guardian*, 2 June 1841.

52   McGill University, Hardinge papers, Box C2, File 15, (1835).

53   Gash *op. cit.*, p. 140.

54   The Beaufort Papers, Badminton, Gloucestershire, Somerset to Beaufort, 12 February 1836.

55   British Library, Peel Papers, Ad. Ms. 40616, ff 109, Graham to Bonham, 10 November 1839.

£10,000 in total for the Westminster election in 1838, £410 10s 7d for 51,000 circulars and 65,000 lithographed enclosures.[56]

Widening the Conservative Appeal

By far the most important and urgent area for action by the Conservative leadership immediately after Reform was to present the Conservative message, both nationally and locally, through the newspapers. Before 1832, the Liverpool government utilized part of the Secret Service fund to purchase newspapers in Ireland to control and direct public opinion. But the experiment does not seem to have been attempted on mainland Britain. During the reform crisis itself not a single major London newspaper supported the Tories.[57] Even as late as 1834 Croker was complaining to Peel that the London papers were in the main hostile and asked the new Prime Minister, "Who is to manage the press (for) managed it must be; and by a Cabinet Minister too. I think Herries is your best man for this."[58] However, Croker was probably unaware that Herries, a former Cabinet Minister under Wellington, had attempted to establish Tory/Conservative influence over the London press a year earlier through buying the influence McEntagart, an unscrupulous former editor. This had proved a disaster, with the party losing over £3,000 to silence McEntagart, who threatened tell all of how the Organizing Committee had, since 1830, attempted to buy off editors and reporters.[59] Nor was this disastrous attempt the first or only occasion the party had attempted to control a section of press and laid itself open with dealings with men like McEntagart.[60] In Herries's words such men had "hugely inflated power as to the intimate workings of the party." Writing to Charles Arbuthnot (a former Chief Whip) in November 1834, he lamented,

> You know the whole story and can judge as well as I can what this scoundrel has it in his power to do … all that this fellow may chose to say, truly and falsely, of the doings of Charles St.[61]

However, Conservative relations with the press did improve and this was a result of good fortune and hard work, rather than nefarious intrigue. Peel won over many journalists, behaving with frankness and candour during his 'Hundred Days' ministry in 1834-5. It was also due to Wellington and Lyndhurst who, by late 1834, recognized the error of their former views. In November 1834, when the Conservatives formed their ministry, Wellington and Lyndhurst approached the editor of *The Times*, Thomas Barnes, in an attempt of securing the support of the paper. On 19 November Barnes signalled the terms on which he would assist the ministry. The Reform Act was to be allowed to stand unaltered, as were the other measures of reform passed by the Whigs, and there was to be no change in foreign policy. But Wellington, believing *The Times* could not be influenced, declined to pledge himself to such a policy, especially in view of the fact that Peel, the incumbent Prime Minister, was abroad at the time and unaware of the negotiations.[62] Even though no treaty was

---

56 Buckinghamshire Record Office, Fremantle Papers, Ms. 80/50, undated, Fremantle to Redesdale.

57 C. S. Parker, *Sir Robert Peel from his Private Papers*, (London, 1899), Vol. I, pp. 115-16.

58 Clements Library, University of Michigan, Ann Arbor, Croker Papers, Vol. 27, pp. 345-6, Croker to Peel, 17 December 1834.

59 British Library, Herries Papers, Ad. Ms. 57371, ff 18-22.

60 McGill University Library, Hardinge Papers, Box C2, File 9. This refers to dealings with a William Jordan of the *Morning Herald*, which, in 1831 had cost the party £1,000.

61 British Library, Herries Papers, Ad. Ms 57371, Herries to Arbuthnot, 7 November 1833.

62 For a more detailed account of the relations between the political parties and the press see, S. Koss, *The Rise and Fall of the Political Press*, (London, 1978).

actually entered into, *The Times* did give its cordial support to the ministry in its short existence. Another factor which swayed *The Times* over to the side of Peel's moderate conservatism was the secession of Lord Stanley and Sir James Graham from the Whigs. Barnes was a close ally of Stanley's, and, when the latter pledged his support for Peel's ministry, Barnes followed them.

In the provinces, as we noted from Mallalieu's memorandum, the Conservatives made major inroads in their attempt to influence moderate opinion. In the north-west there were several Conservative newspapers, two in Manchester, the *Courier* and the *Chronicle*, and the *Bolton Chronicle*, the *Blackburn Standard*, the *Preston Pilot*, and the *Wigan Gazette*. Most of the newspapers took their editorials direct from London, written by men like Mallalieu, James Fullerton and Enius McDonnell and others, and financed partly out of funds supplied by the Carlton.[63] The working classes were singled out for special attention. After the Conservative Party took office in 1841 negotiations took place between Sir Thomas Fremantle and William Painter, the editor of the *Church of England Review*. Discussions focused on a new weekly paper called *The Journal of the Working Class*, designed to cater to popular taste and expressly to counteract radical influence. Fremantle suggested to Peel that the paper was likely to do good and that they could give Painter £2,000 to meet initial expenses.[64] Little came of the initiative, but the fact the party at the highest level was considering the idea reveals just how much the Conservatives had changed.

However, it should not be forgotten that despite the efforts of the central organization in drawing together the threads of the party, the main conduit of political affairs in the localities were local men. It was inevitable that this should be so given the very recent nature of political organization after 1832. Local knowledge, local opinion and influence, and local support and subscriptions were indispensable for electioneering in the distant counties and boroughs. In their efforts to mobilize the press, especially the local press, the Conservative leadership realized this. One manifestation of the situation was the way in which the party leadership attempted to address themselves to the lower classes, pandering to popular tastes and emotion. One example was Peel's 'Tamworth Manifesto' but another, and equally relevant, was his speech at the Merchant Taylors' Hall in May 1835. Not only was this a party rallying speech but also a subtle change can be detected, from the overtly aristocratic Tory party of pre-1832 to a more middle class orientated party of post-1832. Peel said,

> We deny that we are separated by any line or by separate interests from the middle classes. Why, who are we? If we are not the middle classes ... it is because we owe our elevation to those ... principles of moral conduct that we have a right to say that our interests, and theirs are united... Why the very charge brought against myself disproves such an insinuation. What was the charge? That the son of a cotton spinner (great cheering) that the son of a cotton spinner had been sent for to Rome to make him Prime Minister of England.[65]

This view held by the highest in the party, that Conservatism should address itself to those social groups who previously had been known as zealous opponents of the Tories, was based on two complimentary factors. Firstly, the precarious position of the parliamentary Conservative Party in the wake of the General Election of 1832-3 necessitated the broadening of the party's appeal, becoming more flexible in the presentation of policy arguments to different social groups. This meant it needed a more expansive organizational structure. Secondly, the perception of many Conservatives was that

---

63   See British Library, Aberdeen Papers, Ad. Ms. 43243, ff 125.

64   British Library, Peel Papers, Ad. Ms. 40476, ff 70-73.

65   Speech re-printed in the *Preston Pilot*, 16 May 1835.

the great cities and the manufacturing districts were the seedbeds of extreme radicalism and democracy. In the language of the time this was termed the revolutionary 'Movement', the objects of which Conservatism was pledged to oppose. One method of countering the effects of popular radicalism was to construct a form of popular Conservatism, and this could best be achieved through the local press.

In July 1835, these factors were drawn together in an influential article in the Conservative journal *Blackwood's Edinburgh Magazine*, entitled 'Conservative Associations', written by Sir Archibald Alison.[66] The article called for the formation of Conservative Associations to act as "a barrier against the forces of anarchy."[67] It called on prominent Conservatives in the industrial areas to embark on a programme of political education among the working class.

> How is this information to be conveyed to these classes? How is the truth or political knowledge to pierce the dense and cloudy atmosphere of our great manufacturing cities… It is here that Conservative Associations might operate efficaciously in aiding the cause of truth. The part they have to perform is to organize the means of sound constitutional journals among men of moderate principles, and thereby confirm those already gained and make converts among the disaffected.[68]

Alison suggested local Conservatives should purchase the local journals and newspapers, "with a view to their diffusion, at an under-price, among the persons of an inferior grade."[69] At the same time however, he warned local Conservative leaders not to underestimate the political sophistication of the working classes.

> And, in making the selection, let them avoid the common error of supposing the working classes can understand nothing but works expressly intended for their illumination. There never was a greater mistake; they should be addressed by the same arguments as are deemed fit for their superiors; and, if only they can be got to read them, truth in the end will work its way in the humblest class as well as in the most elevated.[70]

At all levels the Conservatives were attempting to organize their party and wider public opinion in the years immediately following the Reform Act, and in ways which had never been attempted before. They had, for example, become aware of the need for recruitment of local as well as national political leaders, enveloping them in the central tenets of the party creed; and began both locally and nationally to play a far larger role in organizing elections than previously. A further departure from pre-1832 politics was that national leaders gave public speeches outlining policies alternative to those of the Whig government and, along with Peel, began to rally party support among disparate social groups. They began to disseminate their basic political principles on a far wider scale through the press than had occurred previously, they also attempted to impose a more disciplined aspect to the marshalling of their supporters and members. Finally, they gave a sense of legitimacy to groups who they politically integrated into the orbit of Conservatism, in contrast to the politically and socially unacceptable principles and actions of the radicals.

---

66   *Blackwood's Endinburgh Magazine*, (July 1835). More on Alison's contribution to *Blackwood's*, see the *Wellesley Index of Victorian Periodicals*.

67   Ibid., p. 9.

68   Ibid., p. 8.

69   Ibid.

70   Ibid.

There were three reasons why this activity was vitally important to the Conservative Party. Firstly, the sweeping nature of the reforms of the Whigs and the Liberal progressives, secondly the loose nature of the Conservative Party's organizational structure, and, finally, the perceived growth of extreme radicalism in the working classes. In the mid-1830s there was a widespread fear among sections of the elites that the Whig reformers were going too far in their attachment to progress. From 1829 and their defeat over the question of Catholic Emancipation, the Tories and Conservatives felt the Whigs and Liberals were not only out to destroy them as a political force but were seriously endangering the constitution. According to the view of Conservatives in the 1830s, the Reform Act was a final and irrevocable act of appeasement to the clamour for reform. Similarly, many Conservatives believed that any further drastic changes in the political constitution, especially in relation to the independence of the House of Lords and the position of the Established Church, should be resisted at all costs. Increasingly throughout the 1830s, Peel and the Conservative front bench opposition sought to gain political advantage, both in Parliament and outside, at the expense of the Whig ministry. In the years 1834-1836 the front line of this attack was in the House of Lords, and it was to Peel's credit that he imposed the discipline of the party on the fiercely independent Ultras in the House of Lords.

Although the fear of Whig extremism was a very real threat and served to weld the conservative forces together, the reality was that in the immediate aftermath of Reform the party was very loosely bound together in a formal structural sense. There were still factions sitting on the conservative side of both the Commons and the Lords. There were, as noted above, Ultra Tories, who, by varying degrees, opposed all efforts of political innovation. There were more moderate Tories who had a faintly Liberal tinge and looked to the revered memory of the younger Pitt for solace and guidance. There were radical Tories who wished to formally ally the party to the radical working classes in an effort to halt the 'pushy' commercial and manufacturing middle classes, and of course there were the Peelite Conservatives who advocated moderate reform whilst still preserving the tenets of the Constitution. This latter group was, in the mid-to-late 1830s, the rising force in conventional politics and it is to Peel's credit that he gave their views credence, coherence and widespread appeal. This potency of this middle path appeal is encapsulated in a letter from Nathaniel Clifford, one of the Gloucestershire gentry, to Sir John Guise, a Knight of the Shire. Writing in 1838 he said,

> The Conservatives have become more ready to reform real abuses than the Tories ever were, and the reformers are endeavouring to retain power by existing agitation on the Corn Laws and other measures which will probably not be so easily controlled as the agitation on the Reform Bill was, and that — it has since been admitted — occasioned the imminent danger of a Revolution ... I put it to be a weakness not to declare myself a Conservative though not a Tory.[71]

Similarly, the improved nature of the organization, allied to the work of Lord Granville Somerset, Sir Thomas Fremantle and others in the Whip's office, plus the fear of Whig reforms, held these varying forces together. So too did the success of the organizational changes outside Parliament that seemed to be pulling the party around from facing virtual extinction in 1833, to a party of minority Government in 1835. Moreover they were gaining electoral support in the most unexpected of places, such as the manufacturing districts of the north-west.

The final reason for necessitating a change in the organizational structure was concern on the part

---

71   Gloucestershire Record Office, Winchcomb/Clifford Papers, D149/F52, Clifford to Guise, 23 June 1838.

of the middle classes, as well as of Conservatives, about the growth of extreme and dangerous radicalism. This was an especial concern among the urban working classes, (though not solely as the Swing riots of the agricultural labourers in 1831 testified). Peel summed up the situation in a speech in 1838 and it is worthy of extended quotation:

> My object for some years past … has been to lay the foundation of a great party (Cheers) … deriving its strength from the popular will … Gentlemen I was deeply impressed with a conviction … of forming such a party from the period when a great change was made in the representative system of the country … that conviction led me to the conclusion that it was necessary … by assuming a new position, by the rejection of the old tactics. … it was desirable to form a party whose bond of connexion should be the maintenance of that particular measure of reform, but determination to resist further constitutional changes … Our own party had been reduced by the Reform Act to little more than one hundred members … but I did not despair … I looked forward ultimately to the formation of a party as now exists. I did believe that the good sense of the country would at length place confidence in a party which did not profess hostility to improvement, but which manifested a determination to abide by the leading principles of the British Constitution.[72]

Popular Political Organization: Loyalist Associations

While change was taking place to the party at its centre there were important developments occurring in the localities. Essentially the same kind of reasons applied chiefly; the defence of the constitution in Church and State, the fear of progressive Liberalism, of extreme radicalism and the desperate need to keep the Conservative party afloat in the wake of the rising tide of radical reform. The intention now is to look at these organizational attempts to assert the Conservative Party and its principles from the viewpoint of the geographical locality of the north-west. An area, because of its advanced industrial structure, not regarded at the time as being a natural constituency for Conservative success. Nevertheless, the Conservative Party was successful in large parts of this region between 1832 and 1870. However, in order to assess the historical significance of the Conservative Associations after 1832, it is necessary to look, by way of contrast and comparison, at the earlier form of political societies dating from the 1790s, termed Loyalist Associations.

The political cleavage wrought by the French Revolution served to polarize opinion in Britain into those who initially welcomed the events in France and those who feared that a dangerous precedent had been set in 1789. Those reformers, such as Thomas Paine, who proposed improving or perfecting the constitution on theoretical grounds, could be viewed, however mild or moderate their proposed changes, as advocating the English should embark on the same path as the French. If anyone required propaganda to argue against change, the French supplied them daily. Burke, for example, argued that not only did incompetents allowed into power under a weak constitution mishandle the government of France, but the very points and basic principles of the revolution were themselves endangered by the limitations of governmental authority designed to protect them. The English constitution, in contrast, served in practice the purposes of government and protected individuals within the state.

In the middle of May 1792 George III issued a Royal Proclamation calling for an end of the circulation of 'seditious' literature. The Home Office gave out instructions that the Proclamation be

---

72 Sir Robert Peel's Banquet Speech at the Merchant Taylors' Hall, (1838), cited in Frank O'Gorman, *British Conservatism*, (Harlow, 1986).

read aloud in all parishes and, further, that local parochial officials should call meetings for the purpose of drafting addresses of loyalty. Similarly, the Proclamation was printed in most of the newspapers of the day, with an editorial urging the formation of societies and clubs for the purpose of organising the addresses. This was the beginning of the loyalist movement, and throughout the nation 71 counties and 315 towns and cities reported favourably to the Proclamation and addresses of loyalty. The Proclamation had asked that subjects of the crown should "avoid and discourage" tendencies toward social disorder, but in reality every address was a pledge by a section of the local community to the existing constitution. The focus of this loyalty by the associations was the King, the symbol of their patriotic sentiments. The English Loyalists first appeared as the result of the theoretical and conceptual challenge made to the constitution by the radicals, the practical demonstration of the fruits of these theories was the situation unfolding in revolutionary France. Their significance at this stage was not only the abstract response to Painite sentiments by Burke but that thousands of ordinary citizens gave a vote of confidence in the existing political constitution when it appeared to be under attack, displaying their loyalty openly and visibly.

The horror felt by the elites at the 'September Massacres' in Paris and at the subsequent emigration to England of the supporters of the monarchy heightened the tensions between the Ministry and the reformers. Also of concern were the location, number and intended use of privately acquired arms and the links between radicals in Britain and France. But most worrying of all was the Proclamation of the General Convention of November 19, which declared the assistance of the French armies to all peoples wishing to follow the example of French republicanism. This was the crux of the crisis of 1792. The English radicals took new inspiration from this second Revolution which served to stimulate an increase in the activities of the various reform societies. The domestic tranquillity created by the May Proclamation vanished, replaced by anxiety that the determined revolutionary principles operating in France could be exported to Britain. After three months of rising tensions, Pitt and his ministers, seemingly supported by wider political opinion, concluded that a revolution was indeed possible in England and issued a Proclamation for all areas to prepare to form defensive militias:

> We have received information that in breach of the laws, and notwithstanding our royal proclamation of the 21st day of May, the upmost industry is still employed by evil disposed persons within this kingdom acting in concert with persons in foreign parts, with a view to subvert the laws and established constitution of this realm, and to destroy all order and government therein; and that a spirit of tumult and disorder, thereby existed, has lately shewn itself in riots and insurrections.[73]

Domestic subversives, acting in concert with foreigners, were seen as attempting to overthrow the state, and it was believed their efforts were at least partially successful. The Loyalist Associations were regarded at the highest level of the state, as being essential to the mobilizing of propaganda against all forms of radicalism and the collecting of information on radical activities, but also to the actual defence of the nation. The impetus for the initiation of Loyalist Associations came from central government, albeit covertly.[74] Grenville, Foreign Secretary in Pitt's Ministry, wrote to his

---

73 *Annual Register*, (1792), p. 166.

74 See R. R. Dozier, *For King, Constitution and Country*, (Kentucky, 1983), pp. 61-4. For the literature on this subject see Harry T. Dickinson, 'Popular Loyalism in Britain in the 1790s', in Eckhart Hellmuth (ed.) *The Transformation of Political Culture: England and Germany in the Late Eighteenth Century*, (Oxford, 1990), A. Mitchell, 'The Association Movement of 1792-3', in *Historical Journal*, 4, (1961), D. E. Ginter, 'The Loyalist Association Movement of 1792-93 and British Public Opinion', in *Historical Journal*, 9, (1966), E. C. Black, *The Association*,

brother, the Duke of Buckingham, in November 1792 about the necessity of mobilizing loyalist support. "The hands of the government must be strengthened if the country is to be saved; but above all, the work must not be left to the hands of the government, but every man must put his shoulder to it, according to his rank or station in life, or it will not be done."[75] Grenville, on behalf of the government, understood that what was needed was more than force or the threat of force against the radicals and reformers, but a seemingly spontaneous demonstration by ordinary Englishmen in support of the existing constitution. The underlying motive was one in which those attempting to cultivate dissatisfaction with the existing state of society and politics would be shown the hopelessness of their endeavours, though it is doubtful Grenville had any clear notion of how this might be achieved.

The original idea for the formation of Loyalist Associations came from the ultra-conservative Whig, John Reeves, who towards the end of November formed the Association for the Preservation of Liberty and Property against Republicans and Levellers. The first advertisement appeared in *The Star*, a firm supporter of the Ministry, on November 23. Another government newspaper, *The Sun*, must have been appraised of the developments, for on the same morning suggested:

> The better order of Britons are at length roused by the boldness of domestic enemies, are forming themselves into Associations, for the purpose of repressing and defeating the pernicious doctrines now afloat in this country.[76]

Similar advertisements followed in *The Times* and the *Morning Chronicle*. However, the important link, that there was some form of governmental involvement, comes from the fact that Reeves was a close friend of the Under-secretary of State at the Home Office, Evan Nepean. Even if he did not know the precise nature of the plans of the government, he would be aware of their general desires and aims. Moreover, Reeves was not a wealthy man, but he somehow found the money to finance one and a half columns of space in the expensive London newspapers. There is also the sheer improbability of a former high ranking civil servant doing exactly what the government wanted without having some sort of nod in the right direction. Each Loyalist Association performed two important functions. By advertising its existence it sent a message to all reformers that there also existed a group dedicated to the preservation of the constitution. The propaganda value of the thousands of groups that were formed to counter the relatively few radical organizations may in itself have been decisive in reducing the threat of internal disturbances. The second function was more practical. The standing committee chosen at the formative meetings of the Associations ranged from ten to upwards of one hundred. Not including all other associations and counting only those actively involved, this meant that the peace-keeping and monitoring capability of the government had been increased by at least 15,000 individuals and probably many more. Crucially, this was not motivated from a narrow political stance, but was one in which the ministry of the day drummed up support to offset a possible political revolution and to maintain constitutional government.

The rapidity with which the Loyal Associations were formed was remarkable, and it affected all regions of the country.[77] Religious boundaries were overcome as at least sixteen dissenting

---

(Cambridge, Mass., 1963), A. Booth, 'Popular Loyalism and Public Violence in the north-west of England, 1790-1800', in *Social History*, 8, (1983), and his 'Reform, Repression and Revolution: Radicalism and Loyalism in the North-West of England, 1789-1803', Ph.D. thesis, (Lancaster, 1979), Roger Wells, *Insurrection: The British Experience, 1795-1803*, (Gloucester, 1983).

75   William Grenville, *Memoirs of the Courts and Cabinets of George III*, 2 Vols., (London, 1855), II, pp. 227-28, 14 November, 1792.

76   *The Sun*, 23 November, 1792.

77   British Library, Reeves Papers, Ad. Mss. 16930-31.

congregations made their loyalty known either by advertising in the local paper or by joining as a group.[78] The great majority of the lower middle classes and emergent working class who joined the Loyalist Associations were involved in the various trades or services who had direct contact with the public: the Worshipful Company of Butlers of London, the London Bakers and the Billingsgate porters.[79]

In the north-west eight towns sent in Addresses of Loyalty, and although in a few towns Associations of Volunteers were formed there is little evidence that the mass of working people flocked to join them.[80] There are several reasons why the region as a whole was relatively reluctant to join in the government-inspired loyalty movement. If we assume firstly that the impetus in the localities to form Loyalist Associations came from the middle ranks of society in Lancashire, such men were in the main involved in commerce and industry. The chief industry of the region was cotton textiles which was dependent on overseas trade both for its raw materials and the bulk of the sales of its finished product. A war on the seas therefore would result in the curtailing of trade, manufacturers would be initially unwilling to support a potentially long and damaging war, until, that is, the government contracts began to fill their order books. Secondly, labourers and skilled workers would similarly be unlikely to support the government for the same reasons, or, importantly, because these groups were becoming increasingly radical as the factory system eroded the independence of workers. Nevertheless, as the war with France developed and the taint of Jacobinism became widespread, men like Hulton and Fletcher of Bolton did not find it difficult to fan the flames of reaction and draw-in some support from sections of the emergent working class. The most usual method employed by the Associations to gain adherents was to place copies of the *Addresses* at various centres, to be signed by those who were unable to attend the initial meeting of the Declaration of Loyalty. For Associations representing large areas, such as counties, divisions or hundreds, this was the practical and logical step to take. However, some of the Associations took a more direct approach. At Bolton, and at Wakefield, Yorkshire, not only did the leading members solicit every house for a signature or mark of agreement, they also made a list of those who would not sign, with their reasons for not doing so appended and sent to the Home Office.[81]

Recenlty Katrina Navickas has looked in detail at loyalism and radicalism in Lancashire between 1798 and the end of the Napoleonic Wars.[82] The author suggests that,

> Britishness was a conglomeration of local and religious affiliations, which could be transcended or connected by supra-national allegiances of religious, philosophical, or political beliefs. Popular politics in Lancashire revealed all these allegiances expressed within the form of 'Lancashire Britishness' shared by loyalists and radicals alike.

The author then moves on, but here is, in several respects, the crux of the book. Regionality is a crucial aspect of the forming of historical identity. It needs to be considered in the long and short

---

78 British Library, Reeves Papers, Ad. Ms. 16929.

79 It is apparently surprising to one historian that the workers of Robert Pickering, a paper-hanging manufacturer, were "arduous in our loyalty and approbation to the constitution of King, Lords and Commons, as those of a superior order." It made sense in such a climate of mass nervousness to be publicly ingratiating, especially if one's livelihood was at stake. This said, there was a genuine and widespread outpouring of loyalty to the state and the predicament facing the country. Dickinson, *Popular Loyalty*, p. 521.

80 Booth, thesis.

81 British Library, Reeves Papers, Ad. Ms. 16929.

82 K. Navickas, *Loyalism and Radicalism in Lancashire 1798-1815*, (Oxford, 2009)

term across a range of factors, social, economic and, of course, political.[83]

The Loyalist Associations were important because they were the first organized movement of conservative, constitutional bodies that attempted to draw the support from all grades in society. However, they differed from the Conservative Associations of forty years later in three important aspects. Firstly, they were primarily government inspired, and not *party* political inasmuch as, though they opposed radicalism or Jacobinism, they did not support a set of political principles and policies inspired by one party and seeking to attract political support at the expense of another. Secondly, and following on from this, they were formed in an atmosphere of high tension, of war or the immanency of war. Hence the main factor which bound them together was not just loyalty to the constitution, although this aspect was to be of lasting significance in some cases, but loyalty to the nation; in short, of overt patriotism. This leads to a third distinction with later developments in that they did not feature for long after 1794. This is compounded by the fact that in Lancashire and other parts of the country the volunteer movement found it difficult to muster or maintain support among the working class. However, it should not be forgotten that the Loyalist Associations broke all precedents. Here, for a time, was a genuinely mass movement expressing conservative sentiments that did much to subsequently revitalize the dormant principles of Toryism. For the historian it is normally the voices of the disaffected and of those who demand change which catch the attention. The working people who supported the Loyalist associations were proclaiming in favour of the political situation as it existed and most decidedly against sudden dramatic changes of the constitution. It was this feature which was the important historical precedent for the Conservative Associations of the 1830s and 1840s.

The chief activators and organizers of the Loyalist Associations were the lesser aristocracy or those of middling sort, not surprising when one considers that as property holders they had most to lose from the success of revolutionary Jacobinism. As was the case with the Conservative Associations some forty years later, it was 'respectable' individuals who were usually elected to the committees, and the members were expected to spread the message to the lower orders.[84] The Loyalist Movement was based, (as was the impetus to form Conservative Associations in the 1830s), upon something broader than mere status or property, although such factors were of course important. It was primarily based upon emotion, a deeply felt relationship between the individual and his nation. In some respects this can be described as romantic conservatism. Patriotic sentiment was reflected in a form of romantic atavism. This was given legitimacy by Burke in his veneration of history and prescription, but it become an inspirational reality during this early period of the war when the nations past became a treasure house of inspiration for the present.[85] The adventures of great and patriotic heroes became subjects for novels, poems and works of art. Nostalgia for medievalism, for chivalry, knights and ladies, heroism and mystery, honour and armour, gripped the emotions of many sections of society from the 1790s until well into the nineteenth century.

Part of the reason for this creation of a chivalrous utopia was the war and the threat posed for the nation, but part was also concerned with impact of industrialization and urbanization. This was felt most keenly by those who had first hand experience of the forces of modernity, such as sections of the working classes in the rapidly changing industrial north, or the agricultural wage labourers whose livelihood was under constant threat by enclosures and agrarian rationalization. These people looked

---

83 Ibid., pp. 10-11

84 For the social composition see Dozier, *For, King, Constitution*, *passim*.

85 See Linda Colley, *Britons: Forging the Nation, 1707-1737*, (New Haven and London, 1992), especially chapter 7.

back to a past that appeared idyllic, uncomplicated and just. In this sense, the deep attachment to medievalism or the distant past was a direct repudiation of the values of industrial society, a rejection of economic and social rationalism associated with the proponents of progressive reason. Also there was a yearning for imagination as opposed to reality and for religion over atheism. This idealization of a past society with its stable community and the inter-meshing of its social groupings remained one of the most compelling political and social visions of the nineteenth century. As will be seen, Tory Radicalism in the 1830s and '40s was also imbued with such sentiments and attracted widespread support among sections of working people in the north of England. However, the starting point of the institutionalization of such sentiments began to flourish in the dark days of the 1790s and the formation of the Loyalist Associations. Romantic Toryism began to grow in an environment in which love of the nation became of greater importance than concepts of reason, liberty, equality and fraternity imported from across the Channel. With perception one can begin to understand why such diverse groups as Friendly Societies, Dissenting Congregations of Methodists or Quakers, liveried companies, innkeepers and even inmates of prisons sent in Loyal Addresses. At a time of national stress, they were expressing emotions that would prevail in the next century. Such emotions knew no class boundaries. These early Loyalists were the overt nationalists of England, made up of all ranks of society, whose political legacy lasted much longer than the living memory of the tumult and eventual war that initially gave them life. The prime motivation that awakened patriotism was a perception of a threat to the constitution. Whether appraised of the threat by the newspapers, official proclamations or by their own experiences of radicalism, the loyalists met the threat directly. Political attitudes were being cleaved apart, between reformers/radicals and loyalists/conservatives, or, at its most acute, between the extremes of radical republicanism on the one hand and Church and King zealots on the other.

In February 1793, France declared war on England and the influence of Loyalist Associations were at once lessened. Englishmen of all political persuasions now focused their attention on winning the war, thus the efforts of the Loyalists was merged into the larger stream of activities. This had the effect of broadening the specialised political message of Loyalism; namely that of defending the constitution. Many of the Loyal Associations became local centres for recruitment and raising subscriptions for the war effort. At Manchester, for example, the Association decided to raise a corps of marines and subscribed £5,000 on the spot. By May, the associators were collecting to assist those rendered unemployed because of the war and had already subscribed "upwards of £1,000."[86] Collections for this purpose were raised in Manchester churches, where £94 1s was donated at one meeting. These funds were given to the unemployed upon application in the form of checks that could be exchanged for food. Also the Manchester Association attracted 1,700 enlisted volunteers.[87] They showed that radical reform of the constitution could be halted, and, indeed, was so for almost forty years.

Local Political Organization in the Early Nineteenth-Century

A form of Loyalist Association was maintained during the early years of the nineteenth century. This chiefly comprised societies formed to honour the memory of William Pitt. These 'Pitt Clubs', as they were known, were composed mainly of a town's Tory and conservative Whig elite. The annual

---

86   PRO (Kew) HO 42/28 Lodge to Nepean, also *York Courant* 4 March 1793, 20 May 1793, 27 May 1793.

87   *The Times*, 28 January 1793.

subscription varying between £2 and £5 ensured this was so. Pitt Clubs were formed in most of the major urban centres of the north-west: at Stockport, Manchester, Salford, Oldham, Rochdale, Bolton, Blackburn and Preston.[88] Some were known simply as 'The Bolton Pitt Club', but others varied their names, thus we have the Liverpool 'True Blue Club' or the Lancaster 'Heart of Oak' club. This was a continuation of the organized loyalist sentiment of the early 1790s, and, in some cases, of older forms of local political organization. However, in the early nineteenth century although such societies may have assisted the Tory or conservative Whig candidates during elections on an informal basis this was not their chief function. Their main object was to dine and eulogize upon some great event in the nations recent history: Trafalgar Day or the acknowledgement of "the pilot who weathered the storm" on the anniversary of Pitt's death.

These societies were little more than annual or bi-annual gatherings of local elites who shared a similar set of political principles. It was right that this should be the case for, although occasionally a political celebrity may deign to honour the assembly with his company, generally the government discouraged displays of overt partisanship. The Loyalist Associations were justified in the early 1790s because there appeared a possibility that the constitution and the nation could be threatened by a surge of radicalism and a union between the French and English Jacobins. During the war such external organizations were not as important. Their usefulness had been served; they had shown that the overwhelming majority of Englishmen were loyal. However, given that the associations of reformers, radicals and the disaffected working class were closely monitored, local elite political associations were not. Such bodies working outside and beyond the control of political leaders in London could be a profound embarrassment, and give the opposition opportunities for pointing to ministerial double standards. Also, the Liverpool ministry claimed to be a broad based coalition of political interests, such overt display of uncontrolled and unsanctioned partisanship could not be officially sanctioned.

The Pitt Clubs were, however, maintained throughout the 1820s even though they were little more than middle class based debating and dining societies. The attitude of the Conservative Party's national leadership regarding these harmless (and only marginally useful) gatherings was reflected in a letter from Lord Granville Somerset to his brother, the Duke of Beaufort:

> I received 3 or 4 days back an invitation to belong to a club of gentlemen ... and inviting a subscription of £5 per annum: the objects ... appear limited to dining 4 times yearly ... how I shall have the power of dining at Devizes unless I am at Badminton, and when there, I shall much prefer your dinner... On the other hand if you wish to support this club and if its funds are to be applied to hustings objects and not to culinary ones, I shall give you my subscription: but I have no mind to pay £5 for Petty House gastronomists.[89]

As stated above, the Liverpool administration was based upon a broad coalition of the conservative sentiments and principles of Britain's body politic. The attitude of these conservative Whigs and Tories toward the electorate and the wider general public was one of detachment. To be sure the electors were important, and the gentlemen of the counties were relied upon to keep the local peace and run the county government, but the running of the nation and the formulation of policy were the domain of the cabinet, executive and legislative. Outside interference from political societies, whether loyal or otherwise, was discouraged.

---

88 For example, see Bolton Reference Library for a subscription list of the Bolton Pitt Club, DDHU 52/82/11.

89 Beaufort Papers, Badminton, Gloucestershire, Somerset to Beaufort, 28 September 1837.

The Middle Classes and Early Political Organization

To the middle classes the growth of working class radicalism was disturbing. Tory attitudes and perceptions, coupled with a recent history of savage hostility to the working class, widened the gulf between the governed and the governors. Earlier it was outlined how even in the 1790s and at the height of patriotism, the Loyalist Associations were weakest in several industrial districts. Throughout the 1820s working class levels of political consciousness were maintained and, after 1829, received greater encouragement when influential members of the middle classes also began to call for parliamentary reform. Political Unions began to be formed throughout the industrial districts, especially in those areas such as Manchester, Sheffield, Birmingham and Leeds that had no parliamentary representation. In the crucial year of 1829 Prime Minister Wellington bowed to increasing outside pressure and granted Catholic Emancipation. Joseph O'Connell's Catholic Association had manipulated much of this outside pressure. It was formed in 1815 in order not only to gain Irish Catholics their educational and political rights, but ultimately to repeal the Acts of Union of 1800. In 1823 O'Connell began the Catholic Rent, a mass subscription of a penny a month, and gave the movement the impetus and resources to mount a truly national campaign. This mobilization of the Catholic interest produced, in turn, a protestant reaction in the form of Brunswick Clubs and Protestant Associations. These organizations also raised money by subscription but were only intended to be effective in Ireland in opposition to O'Connell. They were also not overtly party political, although many Tories and Conservatives of national standing gave them tacit support. The Brunswick Clubs received no official sanction, and indeed many, including Peel, regarded these groupings (as was the case with the Orange Orders) as extremely unsettling and damaging to moderate opinion. Also of concern was the effect extra-Parliamentary activity and uncontrolled political mobilisation might have on the national public peace on all political sides. But the fact remains that the Catholic Association was an extremely successful early form of pressure group and both it and the Protestant Association showed the way forward in terms of organising a mass of supporters.

Even more dangerous and threatening were the Political Unions who, like the various types of religious/political associations, operated mainly in secret and outside the pale of 'respectable' and legitimate politics. The involvement of the working class of the north-west in the Political Unions has been noted earlier, but for the Conservatives what made these organizations doubly dangerous was that they seemed not only to be tightly organized and well-disciplined but also (initially at least) led by the respectable middle classes. Indeed, just the groups who Canning, and later Peel, wished to attract to the socially broader-based principles and policies of Conservatism. Tory and Conservative intransigence over the Reform question, although arguably based on sound political logic, had the effect of alienating many groups of the middling sort who, in normal circumstances, could be expected to rally to their cause.

This point was underscored by the results of the first general election held under the terms of the Reform Act. We have seen how the Conservative Party at the centre began to reorganise itself after the dreadful defeat of 1832-3. But in the localities Tory and Conservative middle class activists took the lead in attempting to place their party back on a stable footing. The initial phase of these attempts was, firstly, to consolidate existing Conservative support and, secondly, to woo those naturally conservative middle classes back to the side of the party and away from the radicalism and reformism of the Liberals and progressive Whigs. This was seen as being of immediate necessity for two reasons. Firstly, to halt the disaffection to basic constitutional principles in the wake of the victory of Reform and, secondly, because of the structural working of the Reform Act itself, especially the registration process. With this latter point it was crucial that the local party be organized permanently in order to be able to attend to the annual register of electors. This was an essential organisational function forced upon the political parties as a direct result of the Reform Act itself.

In January 1833, as news of the elections of the first Reform Parliament spread, Conservative Associations began to be formed. On January 19 associations were formed in Gloucestershire, Berkshire, and societies at Bath and Bristol. The Tory newspaper, *John Bull*, reported the formation of the Bath society:

> The inhabitants of Bath have followed the example of those of Bristol, and have formed a large and highly respectable Conservative body, the first object of which is to … make arrangements to secure, at the next election men of totally different politics, and who are likely to stand forward in defence of the Constitution — the avowed enemies of innovation and destruction.[90]

From their inception the aim of these associations were primarily political (as opposed to the social functions of the Pitt Clubs), their object being to oppose radical reformism and secure Conservative representatives. Later, in January 1833, Conservative Associations were reportedly being formed in the counties of Durham, Essex, Suffolk, Hampshire, Worcestershire, Warwickshire, Cumberland, and Sussex.[91] The South Lancashire Conservative Association was also formed in January 1833, at the Bay Horse Inn in the small town of Newton-le-Willows. Later in the 1830s the Bolton landowner William Hulton recalled its beginnings:

> When the men of Lancashire were borne down by the unfortunate result of Sir Thomas Hesketh's election, a few despondent individuals sat in the window of a common pothouse in Newton. It occurred to them that it was their duty to call upon every friend of the Monarch and the Church to counteract the machinations of the enemies to both.[92]

By August 1833 the South Lancashire Conservative Association had formed itself into branch districts covering the southern part of the region and the various representatives came together to hold a conference and a celebratory dinner. Two hundred attended, mostly middle class, but the aristocratic elements of the party's hierarchy were present to legitimise the proceedings. These included the Marquis of Salisbury, the Earl of Balcarres, Lord Kenyon and Lord Skelmersdale. Hulton spoke, and it is interesting to note that, even at this early date, the middle class Conservatives were turning their attentions to the lower orders. He said that the Conservatives

> wanted that which would make the poor man happy and contented in his cottage, and would teach him a reverence for the laws which every man ought to feel … By disseminating Conservative principles amongst their equals — by kindliness to all those who had just claims on their wealth — and by sheltering the poor from oppression they would secure the honour of the King, the prosperity of the country and, he trusted the true faith in which they had been brought up.[93]

---

90 Reprinted in the *Preston Pilot*, 19 January 1833.

91 *Preston Pilot*, 26 January 1833, 13 April 1833.

92 *Bolton Chronicle*, 15 July 1837.

93 *Preston Pilot*, 13 August 1833.

The above passage conveys the initial aims of the Associations. Firstly, that middle class Conservatives should show concern for the working class and steer them away from radical tendencies, a response which differed totally from the brutality and inveterate hostility these same men had shown during the earlier years of the century. Also law, order, property and the constitution must be preserved from rampant reformism. Furthermore, middle class Conservatives must evangelize the principles of moderate Conservatism. These feelings were reiterated the following year at the second anniversary dinner when 703 attended in the company of the parliamentary party's chief whip, Sir Thomas Fremantle. The chairman, the Earl of Wilton, again revived the theme to proselytize wider society of the need to promote Conservative principles, pointing out the dangers of radicalism.

> It ... was his honest conviction, that by the timely exertion of his friends, and societies such as this, the country might at no distant day be restored to that wholesome state in which it had once been the glory of all English breasts to behold her. They must endeavour to show the people the delusion which it had been the practice to contaminate them with. They must convince them of their kindly feelings which the Conservatives held towards them, and to show them that instead of their being their enemies ... they were their friends.[94]

This call to a romantic and idealized view of the past has been noted earlier, but it must be reiterated that to many social groups it was a powerful psychological tool. The past was painted as being comfortable and secure, the present, progressive, dangerous and insecure. This was a ploy local Conservatives were to perfect and use over and over again in the three decades which followed 1832. This conference also marked out the distinction between the genteel and gentlemanly nature of the dining and debating Pitt Clubs of pre-1832, and the harsh reality of the post-Reform political world. John Roby, leader of the Rochdale Conservatives, pointed this out in no uncertain terms:

> Their meeting was not assuredly for the purpose of merely eating and drinking and making speeches; no, their objects were to strengthen themselves against the great struggle which was inevitably approaching; in fact to review their troops before the battle... It was not only as a body, but individually they must work, as each man might do something to combat the Whig-ridden monster begotten by French malice on English credulity.[95]

There were of course objections raised by the opponents of the Conservatives to their new-found zeal to organise. Among the leaders of this reaction was the Liberal *Manchester Guardian*. As the first Associations began to be formed in early 1833, the *Guardian*, in an editorial, pointed out the contradictions of the Conservative position:

> This is capital. A parcel of people who have almost made themselves hoarse by declaiming against political unions, are proposing, not only to establish a political union of their own, but to establish one having *branch societies*, [*Manchester Guardian*'s emphasis] and therefore directly in the teeth of the Delegations Act.[96]

There was also opposition from within Conservative ranks when the North Lancashire Conservative Association was formed in June 1835. Lord Stanley, one of the MPs for North Lancashire and a

---

94   Ibid., 13 September 1834.

95   Ibid.

96   *Manchester Guardian*, 23 February 1833.

recent convert to Conservatism, engaged in a lengthy public correspondence with the Association's President, Sir Thomas Hesketh, in an effort to dissuade him. Stanley depreciated the need to form societies and associations: "You may say that you are numerous, strong and united; that your opponents, even if numerous, are disunited among themselves and comparatively unimportant in wealth and station. If it is so, you have little to fear, and little need of an organization to oppose them."[97] But Stanley's main criticism was the political breach and possible consequences of embittered conflict that political societies might engender, and, further, that the role of such societies might even undermine the functions of Parliament itself. His outburst demonstrates that the lessons of the Revolutions in France were still paramount in the minds of the political elites.

> But if extending your views beyond local objects, you seek to form part of a general organization throughout the empire, of country clubs, and local clubs, and District Associations, acting in concert, usurping, in fact the power of government, and combining to carry on the affairs of the country through their instrumentality, I can conceive nothing more dangerous to public liberty, no more injurious to a stable or rational Administration, than such a state of affairs. Power vested in clubs acting in concert for national objects, was one of the most dangerous ... symptoms of the early stage of the French Revolution ... if there be a course calculated first to control the House of Commons, next to call in question and put in jeopardy the House of Lords, the Church and the Throne, and in the progress of the operation to destroy the public peace, private happiness and national confidence.[98]

In the localities this was a risk worth taking for the sake of Conservative principles and to stem the seemingly inexorable rise of extreme radicalism. The editor of the *Preston Pilot* jumped to the defence of the NLCA and, in an illuminating passage, said that political cleavage had already occurred, and if the principles of Conservatism were not put before moderate opinion in an organized and systematic fashion "those of another might." Hesketh in his own defence replied:

> ...I believe I speak for the sentiments of all those who were present at the meeting in question, when I say, that they all felt and feel that such associations have been *necessarily* and *unavoidably forced* [Hesketh's emphases] upon the country; first, by the baneful effects of the Reform Bill, ... and secondly, by the measures of the present administration as now proposed, to despoil the rights of property both of church and State, in addition to those encroachments already effected by that administration...[99]

Thus for the first time in Britain a network of organisations had come into existence to actively promote a political party, not just a wide ranging set of political principles or, as noted in chapter one, of a political faction.[100]

Hesketh's point about association being forced by the effects of the Reform Bill refers primarily to the registration clauses, and, because of their importance, we need to outline them. Both the Reform Acts of 1832 and 1867 required qualified voters to fulfil certain registration requirements. In rural constituencies the law made the parish overseer the responsible official for the electoral register, and required all persons possessing the required qualification (40 shilling freeholders and £50 tenants at will) to make out a formal claim to be registered. The annual list of claims, together with the

97 *Preston Pilot*, 13 June 1835.
98 Ibid.
99 Ibid.
100 O'Gorman, *Emergence of the British Two Party System*, p. 18, see also chapter one above.

94

existing list of voters, was required to be exhibited in public and any voter or claimant had the right to challenge any name on the list, while it was within the right of the overseer to reject a claim. This, incidentally, reflects the political importance of the parish overseer, and explains the fierce political battles to secure the election of overseers. Those with disputed claims could appeal to the revising barristers court, and were entitled to costs (at the barristers discretion) against an objector whose objection was deemed frivolous. The objector on his part was required to give notice of objection both to the overseer and to the person whose qualification he took exception to. The nature of the objections were numerous; failure to give adequate notification of a change of address, failure to pay rates on time, receiving of parochial relief, or simple ineligibility.

The system in the boroughs was somewhat different.[101] Here, as in the counties, the overseer was the official chiefly responsible for the register, but the responsibility for the list of freemen voters, whose rights were preserved by both the Acts of 1832 and 1867, devolved upon the town clerk. As the parish overseer and his officials were responsible for collecting the poor rate, the names of all occupiers of houses would, in theory, be entered in the occupiers' column of the rate book. The overseer simply constructed his list of voters by transcribing the names that appeared in the occupiers' column. There was thus no need for persons qualified either as occupiers under the terms of the 1832 Act, or as residents under the Act of 1867, to make formal claims. The roll of the freemen or burgesses was in the possession of the town clerk, who made up his list from the existing electoral roll of freemen. But if, for any reason, the name of the person qualified for the franchise was omitted from the lists, he had the right to send in a claim for registration. Similarly any voter had the right to object to another voter under the terms of borough £10 rateable value qualification.

Efficient organization of the local party was crucial. If a local party could get more names of their supporters on to the register, or strike off more of their opponents' supporters, they would win elections. Especially in the boroughs, annual registration battles not only served to force the pace of constituency organizations, but also acted as a stimulus to party feeling, enhancing the self-identification of the supporter to the party. Indeed the process helped to sustain such feelings in a way that was not necessary before 1832. The different nature of the various types of registration and qualification explains, in part, the need of the Conservative Associations and Societies to organise themselves according to the locality, for one of the primary functions was to marshal their forces in the battle for the registrations. The north and south Lancashire Conservative Associations were responsible for their respective county divisions; they divided themselves into the branches in accordance with the various parish boundaries and reported directly back to their headquarters in Preston and Newton. It was here that the party's registration records were kept and sent forward to Bonham at the Carlton. The various County Associations paid for all the registration expenses of their supporters out of funds subscribed for that purpose. The borough associations were more autonomous, being solely in control of their own finances and records. Each borough was peculiar to itself and only those with direct local experience could be expected to supervise its organization. For the registration, the borough was divided into branches or ward districts and branch societies were set up. The various ward branches met regularly ensuring that party political organization was operating on a permanent basis, information was exchanged, tactics discussed and information forwarded to Bonham in London.[102]

101 For a detailed account of the registration process see J. Alun Thomas, 'The System of Registration and the development of party organization', in *History*, (1950), pp. 81-98.

102 For the importance of this aspect of permanency to political scientists see, for example, M. Duverger, 'Basis of Parties', in J. Blondel, (ed.) *Comparative Government*, (London, 1975 ed.), p. 100.

The county associations acted as an executive body in overall control of all the various affiliated societies throughout the region. In the summer all the Societies sent representatives to the annual county conference held at Preston or Newton. Thus all the various branches fell ultimately under the influence of the regions two central bodies. Article seven of the general rules of the north Lancashire association explains the procedure,

> Where any town or local district within the division shall have 30 or more members may [*sic*] form themselves into a branch or district association... That such branch or district association shall have the power ... [to] act generally in their own affairs, admit and hold local meetings; such branch and district associations shall ... report their proceedings to the secretaries of the general associations ...but that no public proceedings shall act without the sanction of a subsequent general meeting.[103]

Actual membership figures of the various societies at this early stage of development are difficult to assess as no documents have survived. However, given the size of the various delegates annual conference and General Meetings, in south Lancashire over 1,000 in 1836,[104] and in north Lancashire over 400,[105] the overall membership was substantial. By the end of 1836 Conservative Associations existed at Stockport, Ashton, Manchester, Salford, Rochdale, Middleton, Oldham, Bury, Bolton, Warrington, Wigan, Leigh, Chorley, Liverpool, Preston, Lancaster, Clitheroe, Blackburn and Darwen. In Scotland the Conservatives formed a branch exclusively for women,[106] and at Warrington a branch for juveniles was formed.[107] It must be stressed that the initial impetus for the organization of the Conservatives of Lancashire (and elsewhere) came from the professional and manufacturing middle classes, and from landed gentry of the counties. This reflected a broadening of the political representation of Conservatism and the rising power of the new bourgeoisie in this region. It was realized that the Reform Act was not only a triumph for this class, but that its very operation required a new approach to politics. Many 'respectable' members of the politically moderate middle classes had allied themselves with reform during the years 1830-32: it was vital that the Conservatives make an attempt to win back these sections to political moderation, and not let them drift into radicalism or progressive Liberalism. This meant that the party had to be flexible and approachable. As noted earlier, Peel's Merchant Taylors' Hall speech of 1835 recognized this. But he also realized the need of borough and county party organization in order to give the Conservatives a permanent presence and to accommodate the new factor of the register. In 1838 he wrote to the former Tory chief whip, Charles Arbuthnot, on the widespread changes in political affairs following the Reform Act.

> There is a perfectly new element of political power — namely, the registration of voters, a more powerful one than either the Sovereign or the House of Commons. That party is strongest ... which has the existing registration in its favour. It is a dormant instrument, but a most powerful one in its tacit and preventative operation ... what use is the prerogative of dissolution to the Crown, with an unfavourable registry, and the fact of its being unfavourable known to all the world. Then it is almost impossible to make any promotion, or vacate any office, for fear of sustaining a defeat. The registration will govern the disposal of offices, and determine the

---

103 Resolutions 6 and 7 from the 'General Rules of the North Lancashire Conservative Association', *Preston Pilot*, 6 June 1835.

104 *Preston Pilot*, 10 September 1836.

105 Ibid., 22 November 1836.

106 *The Times*, 23 April 1838.

107 *Preston Pilot*, 14 February 1835.

policy of party attacks, the power of this new element will go on increasing ... and there the contest will be determined.[108]

It was vital that the Conservatives make a vigorous attempt to attract the support of the middle class electorate of the north-west boroughs and of other industrial regions. In organizing the party after 1832, the Conservatives embarked on a significantly new era of the development of the political party.

These middle-class Conservatives corresponded in form and practice to the type of political organization a noted political scientist termed the party of 'individual representation'.[109] According to Sigmund Neumann, the party of individual representation is characteristic of a society with a restrictive franchise and limited political participation. Its organization is permanent and the chief functions of its members are canvassing, proselytising and, importantly, the recruitment of both supporters and political leaders in local and national areas of political activity. The importance of the Conservative success in recruiting new political talent from their associations in the north-west is most striking in the period after 1832 when many commentators believed the Conservatives were on the edge of extinction.[110] But in the years after 1832 they had remarkable success among the local manufacturing middle classes in the industrial north-west, a region that had for decades one of the most hostile areas for Toryism. Many local middle class manufacturers became Conservative members of Parliament. At Stockport there was T. Marsland, at Blackburn there was a succession of Conservative members, W. Feilden, J. Hornby and his brother W. H. Hornby. Indeed this seat returned two Conservative mill owners to Parliament on three occasions, 1841, 1865 and 1868, and from the period from 1832 to 1862 never failed to return at least one. At Preston there was Robert Townley Parker and at Bolton, William Bolling. At Rochdale there was J. Entwistle and later C. Royds. At Warrington the local Conservative member for many years was the brewer G. Greenall, at Wigan the mine-owner J. H. Kearsley. Even radical Oldham returned a Conservative, J. F. Lees, in 1835. Many of these 'new' men were recruited from the ranks of their local Conservative Association.

Neumann explains that the party of individual representation allows the supporters much freedom to issues of conscience and policy option, whilst retaining a limited form of party discipline. Also, although permanently constituted, its members tended to meet less frequently in the periods between elections only reforming at the approach of a contest. In the case of the Conservatives of the 1830s this is only partially true. The need to attend to the annual register and local governmental elections meant that the organization was on a more permanent basis than Neumann suggests. But they were certainly tailored to the needs of the specific locality. The Conservative Associations formed in the north-west after 1832 were an important development in the history of the modern political party.[111] From this time Conservatives in the localities began to use the party as a means of attempting to change working class political opinions and allegiances. It is the nature of these attempts that is the subject of the next chapter.

---

108 Cited in C. S. Parker, *Peel Correspondence*, vol. 2, (London, 1899) p. 368.

109 S. Neumann, *Modern Political Parties*, (Chicago, 1967).

110 See for example *Greville Memoirs, op. cit.*

111 See Appendix 1 for the full text of the national Conservative Institution formed in April 1836.

4

Operative Conservatism: Its Development, Structure, Role and Function

It became important for committed Conservatives to attempt to attract a wider basis of support in order to combat the ascendency of the progressive reformers and Liberals. This chapter will develop this theme by considering the reasons why the middle class Conservatives of the north-west attempted to attract industrial working class support. We need to plot the course of Operative Conservatism in the north-west, the geographic spread of the working class branches, the financial basis, the functions and roles the local bodies performed, especially regarding issues affecting working people. Once the reasons why the middle classes tried to attract working-class support has been established it is important to consider what working people got out of the relationship. The various idioms of politics need to be discussed in relation to the spread of 'opinion' politics among working people, a feature indicative of pluralist political system and the factors supporting these developments.

The Middle Classes and Operative Conservatism

By the middle of the 1830s much middle-class support was returning to the Conservatives as the Parliamentary election results of 1835 and 1837 bore witness, partly due to the unpopularity of the Whigs, but also because of the greater flexibility of Peelite Conservatism. It was recognised that after 1832 differing social and economic groups required specifically different approaches in order to placate their various interests. This was the central theme of Peel's speech at the Merchant Taylors' Hall and the Tamworth Manifesto of 1835. This was a major reason for Conservatives organizing themselves in the localities. The operation of interest and pressure grouping will be detailed in due course, but it should be noted at the outset that it was in the 1830s and 1840s that interest and pressure groups began to be associated and assimilated into the existing political parties. Many, but not all, were exclusively middle-class organizations; some were led by the middle-classes seeking to place the plight of a disadvantaged group before a wider audience; others attempted to steer the masses away from profligacy, or drunkenness, or ignorance. All, however, sought public support and attempted to push their demands upon established political parties

In chapter three it was noted that from the 1790s rising levels of working class consciousness was most concentrated and advanced in the industrial districts of the north-west. This high level of class consciousness continued to develop in the 1820s and early 1830s, years after the extreme xenophobia of the Napoleonic wars had raised widespread alarm among the political elites. The crisis of Reform saw the high point of working-class political consciousness. Many middle-class reformers allied themselves to the grievances expressed by working people, using the latter's discontent and numerical strength as potential weapons against those opposed to Reform. Two important points must be reiterated. Firstly, beleaguered Conservatives were uneasy of the continued union of moderate middle-class reformers with the mass of the working class. The prospects of the survival of not only the party but also the existing constitution were in serious jeopardy should such a union be maintained after 1832. The assurances of moderate Whigs that the constitution would be safe did little to allay Conservative fears. In the counties and towns of the south and midlands this was a primary reason for the formation of Conservative Associations in order to consolidate the middle class traditionalist and propertied sentiments against reformist alliances and initiatives. In the north-west a second factor was important in the formation of the middle-class Associations. This was not so much a concern of a strong political alliance between the middle-class reformers and working-class radicals as the increasingly alarming tendency for the radical extremists among the lower middle classes and working classes to operate independently of the elites. By the early 1830s industrial Lancashire possessed a political society which was sharply designated into three broad sectors. Firstly, there was the progressive and economically dynamic Liberals epitomized by Manchester Liberalism. This group was nonconformist in religion, orientated towards reform in politics and made up the majority of the regions' men of commerce and manufacturers. Secondly, there were a substantial body of moderate, generally middle-class, Conservatives, overwhelmingly Anglican in religion, believing in measured reform of proven abuses, even to the extent of supporting the 1832 Reform Act. They were drawn chiefly from the borough/county divide, but included several Anglican manufacturers. The political principles of one such man, John Fowden Hindle of Woldfold Park near Darwen, exemplify this group. As a prospective candidate for Blackburn in 1832, he made clear his political views:

> Entertaining ... a warm affection for every useful Institution, I am fully sensible of the duty of redressing grievances, and removing abuses, wherever they may exist, and I trust I shall always be found among the advocates of every constitutional Reform, having for its object the happiness of the community, and the extension of our Agricultural and Commercial interests.[1]

In addition to these two conventional political groups there were the radicals. This group was made up of small tradesmen, shopkeepers, and, importantly, many working-class activists. They operated most effectively in the arena of local politics, the Vestry and Select Vestry, the Police and Improvement Commissions and, in certain places, like Preston, in municipal politics. Up to 1835, and in certain cases beyond that date, the local politics of Blackburn, Ashton, Oldham, Bolton and Rochdale were under the control of a radical grouping supported, as they were, by sections of the politically committed working class. In the main they had little truck with the two main political groupings, preferring instead their own independent position. To many of working people the progressive Whigs and Liberals were despised because they tended to be intractable adherents of the 'laws' of political economy as masters and as national governors implemented 'reforming' legislation, further reducing the independence and constraining working people. Set against this general context, the aims of the local Conservative Associations were two-fold. The first was to influence as many working people as possible against the unsound and constitutionally dangerous views of the extreme radicals. The second was to use the widely unpopular 'reforms' and general principles of the progressive Whigs and Liberals to widen the social basis of their support. These were the primary reasons why the Conservative Associations in the north-west formed operative or working-class based branches of their societies.

---

1   Blackburn Reference Library, Local Studies Collection, *The Election Address of John Fowden Hindle*, 29 June 1832.

The distinction of being the first Operative Conservative Association belonged to the Conservatives of Leeds, who, in February 1835, "met together for the purpose of discussing the propriety of forming a society." In early March an Address was issued which set down the reasons of forming a society designed for working people:

> As we are jealous of being enslaved by the proud boasters of a mock liberty, we will at all times secure ourselves against the undue exercise of authority; our liberties which are our glory ... shall be sacredly transmitted to our children... Our design forming ourselves into a society is to secure these blessings, to resist the machinations and violence of those whose conduct leads ... to anarchy and confusion; and to furnish our minds by means of newspapers and other publications ... to furnish an antidote to those publications of a dangerous tendency... and to unite with our follow townsmen and fellow-subjects in whatever would advance the national welfare... We invite persons of true Conservative principles to unite with us: especially ... the Operatives. We ask them to aid us in our efforts to defend the rights of 'THE ALTAR, THE THRONE AND THE COTTAGE.'[2]

The idea of steering the working classes away from the dangers of extreme radicalism by socializing them in constitutional politics was one of the initial functions of Operative Conservatism and was a chief motivation of middle-class involvement. The role of the written word, as a means of combating the emotive language of radicalism was something that was actively pursued by the leading national Conservative journals. In 1835 *Blackwood's Edinburgh Magazine* ran an article entitled 'Conservative Associations', written by the historian Sir Archibald Alison, outlining the state of the manufacturing districts in no uncertain terms, "It is in vain to conceal that in the present political condition of Great Britain, it is in the highest degree dangerous. The manufacturing class, the natural depository in every age of republican opinions, have more than tripled in the last half century."[3] He argued that Conservatives must waste no time in coming to grips with this situation, but warned it would be a long-term project, "As the democratic tendency of the great majority of the public press, and almost all that is addressed to the lower orders in the great cities ... [it is] by long and painful efforts, that the poison is to be expelled, from its social body, or an antidote provided for its malignity." Above all, the means for spreading of constitutional political information had to be extended to the working class. What worried Conservatives was that the overwhelming majority of the most populous group in society might be forever lost to radicalism. Alison provided he readers with some solutions:

> How is information to be conveyed to these classes? How is truth or political knowledge to pierce the dense and cloudy atmosphere of our great manufacturing cities... Some part of the funds of every Conservative Association should be devoted to the purchase of the ablest journals and periodicals of the day, with a view to their diffusion, at an under price, to persons of an inferior grade, whom it is practicable to win over to safe and constitutional principles. By doing so a double object is gained. Talent is encouraged to devote itself to such undertakings, and numbers, who never otherwise would get a glimpse of the truth, have the means of illuminating their minds afforded them.[4]

At the core of Alison's article lay the double purpose of encouraging wider activism among the

---

2   W. M. Paul, *A Brief History of the Operative Conservative Societies of the United Kingdom*, (Leeds, 1838).

3   'Conservative Associations', in *Blackwood's Edinburgh Magazine*, (July 1835), p. 6.

4   Ibid., p. 8.

educated middle classes and proselytising sections of the working classes. Of this second group, Alison warned that their intelligence should not be underestimated, "In making their selection, let them avoid the common error of supposing the working classes can understand nothing but works expressly intended for their illumination. There never was a greater mistake." He said that they should be addressed by the same arguments as their superiors, "and if they can only be got to read them, truth will in the end work its way in the humblest class as well as in the most elevated."[5]

In the same year (1835) a prominent Conservative mill owner told Peel during his 'Hundred Days' ministry of the potential support among the working class, this time from Blackburn:

> Permit me to state that I do, and must, believe that, if the truly sound portion of the operative classes would be united together, they would form a tower of strength to the present government: they are tired and disgusted with the Whig's oppression and naturally direct their attentions to their genuine patrons and friends.[6]

Other sections of the party's national leadership were also in favour of attempting to influence the working classes, especially through the written word. A letter from Charles Arbuthnot, (a close friend of Wellington), to Herries, the former Treasury Secretary, reported that the Duke had been told of Herries's attempts to mobilise the press and that he thought his plans 'judicious', suggesting the party should be doing a great deal more and very quickly. Wellington stressed that the party should specifically address itself to regional press, especially in the industrial regions.

> …there are papers at Leeds and Manchester that exercise influence in these manufacturing districts and I have thought too we might publish cheap penny pamphlets… I confess I would try to muzzle Cobbett who I believe is always able to be bought, and is certainly a most able writer… I think the country is [in] so critical a situation, and yet one in which a strong effort might be so successful.[7]

As well as the power of the press the Conservatives of Lancashire employed other means of political influence. From 1836 the Conservatives employed Charles Wilkins, a former barrister, as regional organizer and election agent. In the former capacity he toured the north-west advising Operative Associations of the latest national policy positions and suggesting how the Conservatives would remedy their local grievances. He advised them in organizational strategies, the registration and how they might legitimately influence the electors. In Preston in July 1836, where the majority of electors were still the working class under the old Scot and Lot franchise, he told the Operative Conservatives to recruit the women of Preston to their cause, a brilliant tactic well in advance of its time. He said,

> Make the women of Preston your allies in this glorious fight, and take my word for it, victory will be yours … when your radical neighbours wives see the fruits of Conservatism so displayed, they will not content themselves till they have forced their husbands into your ranks.[8]

He was also active in his capacity as local or regional electoral organizer. In 1845 a Liverpool merchant, Joseph Saunders, pacified Sir James Graham on the prospects of the forthcoming contest by saying, "I should be glad to confer with Mr Bonham on the question of organization, I am told

---

5   Ibid.

6   British Library, Peel Papers, Ad. Mss. 40418, ff 172, Feilden to Peel, 16 March 1835.

7   British Library, Herries Papers, Ad. Mss. 57371, ff 98, Arbuthnot to Herries, undated.

8   *Preston Pilot*, 16 July 1836.

Wilkins is going there with £12,000 in his pocket."[9] It can be seen therefore that from the mid-1830s the national and regional Conservatives were completely re-thinking and re-defining their party's organizational structure, and sections of the working class were an important part of their plans. It was argued earlier that a new political culture was rapidly developing in Britain during the 1830s one that now embraced all sections of society in politics. There was even a transformation in the vocabulary and language of party politics. The political and social outlook of the old Tory, part self-satisfied optimism, part pride and self-importance, gradually turned to a new forthright approach, more dynamic and appealing. The old Tory catchwords indicating the Church and King loyalty of the eighteenth century, "Lord George Gordon and the Protestant Succession", now gave way to phrases and idioms better suited to the times. Indeed, in certain cases, these were directed at specific classes. For example, "the Throne, the Altar and the Cottage", reinforcing the importance of working people to the constitution. The phrase, "When bad men combine, good men must unite", which emphasised the need for Conservatives of all classes to join together in defence of their principles against attack by progressive Whigs, Liberals and Radicals. Indeed one newspaper in the north-west produced its own "Conservative Catechism"

Q. What do you mean by Conservatism?

A. Loyalty and Honesty, or an attachment to our form of Government, as settled in 1688, for securing civil rights and liberties.

Q. What is an Ultra Tory?

A. A fool.

Q. What is an Ultra Whig?

A. A rogue.

Q. What is a Radical?

A. Both: that is to say, as a rogue having no money in his own pockets, he wants to help himself out of yours and mine; and being a fool, he thinks we shall let him do so without resistance.

Q. What is a Liberal?

A. A selfish, greedy, discontented, overbearing, tyrannical fellow.

Q. What is meant by Reform?

A. Correction of abuses, and progressive movement by separating evil from good.[10]

Also important in the mid 1830s, as will be seen later, was the trend towards a heightened sense of respectability and political legitimacy which vitiated against the older forms of influence and corruption and more towards the politics of opinion. Crucial to this development was the utilization of issues, especially in the local context. The role of issues will also be detailed later, but it will be useful here to briefly outline how they were used by the Conservative middle classes to capture the support of sections of the working class. From the mid-1830s, a significant section of the working class found Conservative principles in general, and Operative Conservatism in particular, appealing. This was especially the case for two types of working men who found Conservatism influential. They did so for reasons that had little to do with social or political deference, but more to do with political and social pragmatism. One type of working class Conservative was concerned with questions which affected his daily existence, another with the need to maintain traditional values and customs of the working class and, importantly, with religious questions.

---

9   British Library, Peel Papers, Ad. Mss. 40616, ff 328, Saunders to Graham, 22 January 1845.

10   *Preston Pilot*, 1 December 1838.

The first type of operative Conservative was persuaded that the new Conservatism of Peel and his followers in the country committed itself to issues which directly affected working people in the manufacturing districts. These included resistance to the harsher elements within the 1834 Poor Law Amendment Act. Indeed, in certain places, like Bury, Rochdale and Oldham, the Tory Radicals opposed the Acts introduction altogether, and did so with the support of the local middle-class Conservatives.[11] Another issue that attracted broad working-class support was the factory reform movement. This first type of worker may not have been committed to Conservatism as such, but rather to the issues which Conservatism allied itself in the manufacturing districts, and this secured the support of this politically moderate working man. They saw in the rhetoric of Conservatism a viable alternative to the apparent unfeeling self-righteousness of progressive Liberalism and political economy so favoured by many employers in the manufacturing districts. Another type of working man was firmly committed to Conservatism. This person was typically Anglican or Presbyterian, imbued with ambitions of upward social mobility and natural Conservative or traditionalist proclivities. They saw Operative Conservatism as a respectable way of opposing radicalism and the Liberals, defending his religious convictions, gaining legitimate involvement in politics, coupled with active citizenship and possibly developing a route to social advancement. The majority of the members of the operative associations appear to have been literate and politically articulate, and, although they did not possess the parliamentary franchise, they were encouraged to engage in political activities.[12] In Blackburn, for example, Henry Kenyon was typical. He was originally a power loom operative, later he became a solicitors' clerk, and for many years was Secretary of his town's Operative Association, eventually becoming its President. He was also an active Vestry member, so too were other members of the Blackburn Operative Conservative committee; Charles Tiplady, a bookbinder; Thomas Dewhurst, a joiner; Richard Caldwell, an operative spinner; Thomas Bennett, a dyer and cloth finisher. These men were also members of the non-electors committee of John Hornby, a local mill-owner and the successful Conservative candidate at the parliamentary election of 1841. An illustration of their social mobility can be seen when one looks at those who gained the electoral franchise. Of the members of the 1837 Committee of the Blackburn branch, only the bookbinder Tiplady had the vote in the elections of that year. Ten years later, although some names had changed on the twenty-man committee, fourteen appeared on the electoral roll.[13] This supports that active and loyal membership of the Operative Association could be a means of social advancement for some of the working class. The political sociologists, Butler and Stokes, and David Lockwood, all maintained that working class political pragmatism has been a feature of their support for Conservatism since 1945. It could well be that it has a history that stretches back considerably further.[14] Added to these groups of pragmatic Conservatives were those of the working class who were overtly deferential to the elites and their religious and political offices. The Operative Conservatives of Leeds give us an example of this attitude when they offered:

---

11 It should be noted that so did the radical Liberals, especially at Oldham and Rochdale. However, at Bury, throughout the whole of 1837, the Conservatives refused to implement the new law. When the Poor Law Commission tried to impose the law, they were advised that no Conservatives would either vote for or sit on the Board of Guardians, rendering the Act virtually inoperable. See *Manchester Guardian*, 10 May 1837.

12 See for example the second annual report of the Blackburn Operative Conservative Association in *Blackburn Standard*, 2 November 1837. "The signatures of the Declaration (of intent) show the members to be literate, and by availing themselves of the means the Society affords, they must direct their education into a channel that will tend to their own welfare and add to the honour and prosperity of their native country."

13 Blackburn Reference Library, Poll Books for 1837 and 1847 and appendix four.

14 See D. Butler and D. Stokes, *Political Change in Britain*, (London, 1974, second edition),

reverence [*sic*] the King and all in authority, we pay due deference to all who are in high stations ... while we exalt them, we raise ourselves; as we should depress them, we proportionally lower ourselves. While we maintain their rights, we secure our own, and while we defend their privileges we increase our own.[15]

The Development and Structure of Operative Conservatism

Before enlarging on the motivations and active roles carried forward by the national Conservatives and the middle classes in the localities, it will be useful to examine how these working class institutions came into existence and briefly look at their organizational structure. It is clear that the Conservatives of the north-west were influenced by the way the Political Unions had in galvanizing working-class opinion between 1830 and 1834. However, a great deal will be missed if Operative Conservatism is viewed as a simple reaction against radical political unionism. It is true the initial object of middle-class Conservatives in attempting to involve sections of the working class in Conservatism was to deflect them from the harmful effects of extreme radicalism. Importantly however, it also conveyed to working people their entrance into the formal party structure, which in turn gave them a sense of citizenship; of belonging to the polity even if, at this stage, they did not possess the formal franchise. Crucially this not only began to transform the working class Conservatives, but also the political outlook of the middle-class Conservatives and the party itself. By incorporating sections of the working class into the party, and accepting their interests and their limited demands with regard to policy, the party leaders in the region forged a tenuous, but perceptible link with the working class's political needs and aspirations. This is most notable in the localities, for in most cases the party's national leadership, specifically Peel, attempted to remain aloof from sectional interests. Even he, however, in regard to economic and fiscal policy, agreed with his Home Secretary, Sir James Graham, that "we must endeavour to redress the wrongs of the labourer."[16] This growing understanding of the situation faced by working people, coupled with the experience of the local associations, led Conservatives to gradually believe that they were fit to exercise their legitimate political rights. This process began in the 1830s and increased noticeably after the decline of Chartism until, in the mid-1860s, a Conservative government conceded the franchise on millions of working men with the removal of the property qualification.

Returning, however, to the 1830s and how the Conservative Party and Conservatism was changing political attitudes. From their inception the operative associations were designed to fit into the organizational network of the Conservative Party at county and borough levels. They may have been intended to be outlets of working class political participation but were seldom wholly made up of working men, and there was never any intention that they were to be solely controlled by working men. Conversely, and the distinction is important, many Political Unions and trades associations after 1832 were controlled by working men for working men. This was the case at Bolton, as it was at Blackburn and Oldham.[17] The social, political and economic aims and objectives of Political Unions were centred on working class advancement and stressed the separate and premier importance of the

---

15 W. M. Paul, *Operative Conservative Societies, op. cit.*, p. 9.

16 Bodleian Library, Oxford, Graham Papers, Graham to Peel, 2 September 1842, see also John Foster, 'The Declassing of Language', in *New Left Review*, (March/April 1985), p. 33.

17 For Bolton see W. Brimelow, *A Parliamentary History of Bolton*, (Bolton, 1880), for Blackburn, W. A. Abram, *A History of Blackburn*, (Blackburn, 1879), for Oldham, see Oldham Reference Library, The Butterworth Manuscripts.

working class. In contrast the Conservatives (and the reforming Liberals) stressed the inter-connectedness and plurality of society, and it was they who laid down the terms of the established political order. Anyone, or any groups, who did not accept this was not a friend of constitutional politics as seen through Conservative eyes. One of the essential aims, therefore, of the operative political clubs was convincing the members of the correctness of legitimate constitutional politics as opposed to the illegitimacy and danger of radical politics. The language used at this time is an important indicator of the type of working-class supporter the Conservatives were seeking to attract. The slurs on the 'destructive classes', Papist republicans, or the 'unpatriotic' Jacobin radicals, suggested disreputability typical of organizations existing beyond the pale of politically respectability. This is in marked contrast to the 'loyal' and 'constitutional' Conservative Associations. The words of William Simpson, the editor of a leading Conservative newspaper in the region and himself a future honorary member of an operative association, illustrate the idioms conveyed by the language used:

> If, in times like these, it is necessary that all constitutional men should combine in order to resist the ... disloyal and destructive, it is impossible that we can too earnestly urge the formation of such [Operative Conservative] societies or too highly applaud their objects and principles... How potent an answer it is to these contemptible charges ... that we possess no hold over the affection of the people.[18]

From the mid 1830s Operative Conservative Associations were designed to appeal to the hardworking, church attending, usually Protestant, self-respecting, working man. A man who had little time for organizations disdainful to rank or wealth, of the 'seditious' or 'infidel' combinations, which trades unions, secular Owenites and republicans were often portrayed. Even as late as the 1840s Conservatives of the north-west were hanging effigies of Tom Paine and publicly burning his 'Rights of Man' in the streets.[19] During this early phase, respect for property, deference to the Anglican Church and education, were constantly pressed as imperatives and signs of respectability which working people should be encouraged to emulate.[20] Importantly however, Conservatives allowed working people far more recreational latitude than did the progressive Liberals. For example, although Conservatives frowned upon excessive self-indulgence of any kind, they poured scorn on those who would deny working people their pleasures and recreations in an attempt to morally 'reform' them. This is why at times they mocked the Temperance Movement as this passage from Preston illustrates:

> The water worshippers assembled in considerable numbers as before; and, as before their arch-enemies and relentless tormentors, the anti-hypocriticals, took up their position in still greater force. Accordingly, on the one side the air was rent [sic] with the loud bellowings of the fanatics, and on the other was to be heard the continued shouts of holiday mirth mingled with the incessant sound of escaping corks.[21]

This toleration of minor indulgences was another reason why sections of the working class found Conservatism more appealing than the rigidity of progressive Liberalism. However, the Operative

---

18 *Blackburn Standard*, 8 November 1837.

19 Ibid., 11 November 1840.

20 The manifestations of such attitudes are numerous, see, for example, *Preston Pilot*, 7 October 1837, *Manchester Courier*, 11 June 1836, *Blackburn Standard*, 21 April 1841, for the views of Henry Kenyon, former secretary of the B.O.C.A.

21 *Preston Pilot*, 27 June 1833.

Conservatives, whilst embracing constitutionalism, strongly urged the Conservative Party to take up their grievances. In 1835 an Operative Conservative from Manchester (an operative spinner named Longton) gently prodded the third South Lancashire Association Conference when he said that he felt:

> the sentiments of no ordinary class flowing in my mind. It may be said that you are interested in the spread of Conservative associations throughout the Kingdom, I know, gentlemen, you are deeply interested; but ... is not the operative deeply interested ... we wish to have reform in the true sense of reformation, that is in removing the evil and preserving the good.[22]

Operative conservatives, whilst suggesting measures for the redressing of working-class grievance, had to remain subservient to rank and social station. Indeed, as noted above, working people were encouraged to impress these traits on others, especially children. An example of this aspect of Operative Conservatism came in 1841, when, at a ceremony of presentation to the secretary of the Blackburn Operative Association, Henry Kenyon was asked how he became a Conservative, when, in his own words, he was "surrounded by radicals". He replied that he, "attributed his not becoming a radical to an early Church of England education, fear of God and of the King ... and respect of his superiors. He mentioned these matters merely to impress on those gentlemen present who had children of their own, the necessity of giving them early, such an education."[23] In the mid 1830s and 1840s, the major difference between local radical associations and the Operative Conservative or Reform Associations, in terms of organization, aims and objectives, was that the former were controlled by working people themselves and it was they who dictated the political terms of reference. The organizations designed by the two main political parties for working people were, on the other hand, never wholly constituted of working people, nor were they ever controlled by them, and, quite clearly, the political terms of reference were set by the middle classes.

If an essential purpose of Operative Conservative Associations was to redirect sections of the working class away from the dangers of extreme radicalism, then the alternatives had to be amenable and affordable to working people. Support for this came in the subscription fees charged and the benefits of membership. By early 1835 the Conservatives realized that if they were to attract working men they had to reduce their entry fees and subscriptions. For example, in February 1835 the Blackburn Conservative Association, the parent body of the future Operative Association, reduced its annual subscription from one guinea to five shillings. This was in order, they said, "to afford an opportunity for such of the working classes who are disposed to stem the progress of revolutionary doctrines to become members of the association."[24] Those working men who did enrol complained that five shillings was still too high and, when the operative branch was formed soon after, the annual subscription was reduced to two shillings. Once the opportunities existed for working people to join, the speed at which the operative branches were formed and their geographical spread was remarkable. As noted, the working men of Leeds formed the first Operative Association in February 1835. Immediately afterwards Operative Associations were formed at Bradford, Barnsley, Sheffield, Ripon, Wakefield, Huddersfield and on the other side of the Pennines in Salford. In July 1835 the Manchester Operative Conservative Association held its inaugural dinner. In August workers in Bolton formed their Conservative Society; the South Lancashire Conservatives formed an operative

---

22 Ibid., 17 October 1835.

23 *Blackburn Standard*, 21 April 1841.

24 *Blackburn Standard*, 8 February 1835.

branch at Wigan in October, and, in November 1835, the Blackburn and Darwen branches were formed. In December, the Liverpool Operative Conservative Association was initiated and in early 1836 Preston, Chorley, Middleton, Ashton, Oldham, Rochdale, Bury, Stockport and Warrington began societies. Throughout 1836 over 100 Operative Conservative Associations were holding their first inaugural conferences.[25]

By 1837 places as geographically distant as Leicester, Salford, Nottingham, and Preston had Operative Conservative Committees in every ward, as well as central governing bodies.[26] The numbers of working people who were attracted to these associations could be large. For example, at Salford in 1838, the veteran, former radical, Sir Francis Burdett, now acclaimed as a "perfect specimen of the English country gentleman" by the Tory press, attended the third anniversary dinner of the association along with 2,000 others.[27] Again at Salford in 1838, a witness reported "that Operative Conservatives held a tea-party and ball, to which more than 3,000 persons attended, nine-tenths of them ladies."[28] These attendances show the popularity of Operative Conservatism and compare favourably with anything the Liberals or Radicals could muster, and this at the beginning of the rise of Chartism. Indeed on the eve of the Sacred Month of 1839, the Operative Conservatives of Preston claimed a membership higher than that of the Chartists.[29] There were, however, other features of the operative societies that attracted working people and served the party in the 1830s and '40s.

Aims, Objectives and Financial Basis of Operative Conservatism

An important function of these operative associations was the prudential one of sick care and burial. The majority of the local associations copied the example of the purely profit orientated Sick and Burial Clubs already in existence. These were formed several years before the 1830s, in the manufacturing districts and acted as assurance organizations maintaining club funds for the relief of sickness, unemployment and death of their members. The importance of the Sick and Burial Clubs to the working class should not be underestimated. Very often they were the only means by which a working person could obtain medical treatment and subsequently receive a non-pauper, Christian burial. The Operative Conservatives of the north-west enthusiastically utilized this facility and others, in 1836, for example, the Preston branch of the Operative Association ran a building society for the benefit of their members.[30] It is likely these benefits were a source of new membership to the associations and the dividends realized were a useful bonus for working people on low incomes or experiencing lay-offs.

A working-class member of the Sick and Burial Club run by Operative Conservatives paid between 2s and 2s 3d per month. This was within the budgets of most working people in full time work.[31] If an operative was disabled he was allowed 1 guinea per week, if his wife died he received

---

25 See *The Times*, 5 January 1835, and *passim*, W. M. Paul, *Operative Conservative Societies*, *Blackburn Standard*, 4 February 1835 and *passim*, *Preston Pilot*, 24 January 1835 and *passim*, *Manchester Guardian*, 2 May 1835 and *passim*, *Manchester Chronicle*, 18 April 1835 and *passim*, *Bolton Chronicle*, 21 November 1835 and *passim*, Oldham Reference Library, The Butterworth Manuscripts, 1 January 1836 and *passim*.

26 *The Times*, 5 January 1837.

27 Ibid., 20 April 1838.

28 Ibid., 20 April 1838, and *Preston Pilot*, 21 April 1838.

29 British Library, Ad. Mss. 34245B, Vol. 2, ff 119, Walton and Halton to Lovett, July 1839.

30 *Preston Pilot*, 26 March 1836.

31 The average weekly wages of power loom weavers (usually women) were approximately 8s 6d at this time, operative spinners 9s per week, an engineer 15s per week and an overlooker 40s per week.

£5 to bury her, if he died she received £7. Surpluses, if any, were divided equally amongst all the members, and there was usually a subsidised annual dinner.[32] Given that the premiums were slightly higher than for other, non-political societies, and also that there were large differentials in wage rates, it would appear that the Operative Conservative Associations were seeking to attract the better off type of working-class members. Societies with the larger memberships, Salford, Manchester, Bolton, Wigan and Liverpool, would have realized a small profit from these Sick and Burial Clubs, which would be utilized for political purposes, but it is difficult to see how societies with only moderate membership could realize a profit. In these associations the venture was operated solely for the benefit of the membership, probably at a loss.

Most of the money used to operate the working class-based associations came from the middle classes; richer Conservatives and honorary members contributed significantly to the funds of the operative associations. All the parent bodies held annual balls and the monies raised were given to the upkeep of the various subsidiary associations. The stocking of libraries and newsrooms were from donations from richer Conservatives. All the various Conservative Associations throughout the north-west were financially autonomous, there is little evidence of any national funds used to bail out a branch in financial difficulties. As well as individual donations of money and gifts, there were fêtes, tea-parties, whist drives, dinners and balls, all organized to raise money as well as entertainment to keep the operative associations afloat. They provided therefore a dual benefit: one of entertainment, amusement and education of the members, and secondly, keeping the various associations financially viable. Throughout the 1830s up until the split of 1846, there is no evidence that any of the Conservative Associations folded through lack of financial support. The question as to the use of the party's national funds in assisting regional associations is uncertain. There is little evidence, in the periods between elections, of funds sent from London to aid local associations. However, during election periods, certain societies were assisted directly from London secretly and quietly. This secrecy was necessary to ensure that the Carlton was not inundated with requests for help that its funds could not possibly meet. Nor could their opponents cry bribery if such acts of financial assistance were kept secret and selective. But assistance was given, as this letter marked 'very private' from Bonham to Peel reveals:

> Sussex seats winnable. At all counts it will require the whole conservative strength to be organized and put forward with will and energy to ensure success … the previous victory was achieved solely by the good management of the Conservative Association which was formed here two years ago. You will not be surprised that this Association is now on the wane and requires our very intensive support.[33]

Furthermore, it seems clear that the Carlton did keep a special fund for just this purpose as this piece from the *Metropolitan Conservative Journal* reveals:

> A lamentable mistake in which Conservatives in remote districts fall, is in trusting to the metropolis for candidates and to the Carlton Club for funds. In the first instance, the London appointed members are the very worst, and in the second the Carlton Club rarely subscribes anything from the joint-stock purse but in very peculiar and urgent cases.[34]

---

32 *The Times*, 8 January 1838.

33 British Library, Peel Papers, Ad. Mss. 40424, ff 140, Bonham to Peel, 23 September 1837.

34 *Metropolitan Conservative Journal*, 26 June 1837.

Also it is probable, judging from the general feeling of Conservative politics in the constituencies, that any systematic payment by the Carlton would have been regarded as an intrusion in local authority by the national organization and been bitterly resented. In the localities it was believed that local political patronage began at home, and indeed it could have meant defeat if the party's political opponents became aware that political finance was lacking and had to be propped up by outside influence. The pattern was that the local gentry, industrialists and men of commerce found the money. This is not to say of course that Bonham and the Carlton had no influence. Their task, however, was gathering and sending out political information, intelligence and the organizing of elections.

The influence of the middle classes in the setting up of Operative Conservative Associations was considerable. However, by the end of the 1830s middle-class involvement had undergone a subtle change. In 1833-4 when Conservative Associations were originated it was committed middle-class conservative activists, like Hulton of Bolton, who were in the forefront of both their organization and the dissemination of party principles. By the later 1830s most Conservatives held the view that all the middle classes, not just the activists, had a responsibility to politically educate those of a lower social station, and, furthermore, the working class Conservatives should attempt a similar role within their class. Thus one of the central objectives of Operative Conservatism was the influence and political containment of the local community. John Bennett, the headmaster of Blackburn Grammar School and acting President of the Operative Association, exemplified these features. Speaking in 1839, on the eve of the Chartist disturbances, he offered a perceptive insight into the social and political forces operating in the industrial districts:

> A great portion of the lower classes are democratic... Now if we take into view the constant influx of new population ... the breaking up of the old framework of society, the dispersion of domestic circles, everyone left to his own resources, the consequent overflow of operatives, the reduction in wages, the poverty and discontent, the innumerable temptation to improvidence and vice which they are beset, we need seek no further for the facility of political excitement presented to every agitator among these classes... Now sir for improving the perilous situation of this class it is the duty of every wealthy Conservative to contribute by his wealth and influence to the diffusion of Conservative principles... It is the duty of every Operative Conservative to invite and encourage his poorer neighbour to become a member of our Association, to attend our reading room ... he would thereby arm himself against the poisonous principles which are promulgated by those rabid and fanatical revolutionists who would raise themselves on the ruin of our altars and our houses.[35]

This statement epitomises the fears, very real in 1839 that the working class, if left uncontrolled, would turn to the Radicals *en mass*. It was made when the Blackburn Conservative Association was reaching the height of its influence. East Lancashire were peculiar as compared to other parts of the region in that physical force Chartism did not become a mass movement, Blackburn remained relatively quiet throughout the agitated summer of 1839. This was a situation that the local Conservatives were quick to take credit for, attributing it to their 'missionary work' among the working class. In the next two years, the Operative Associations throughout the north-west continued to grow and attract members. 1841 was the high point. Nationally Peel was elected with a large majority and in Lancashire the Conservatives split the seats with the Liberals with each party returning thirteen members to the House of Commons. Local Conservatives applauded themselves;

---

35 *Blackburn Standard*, 27 November 1839.

they had unity over most political questions and in the majority of boroughs for the first time since 1832 they had a favourable registration. In the space of ten years a remarkable organisational transformation had taken place both at the centre and in the localities. The threatened flooding of the House of Commons by the extreme Radicals from the new boroughs had not happened, not even during the height of the Chartist agitation did it look likely. Operative Conservatism, the political integration of a key section of the industrial working class, was a small but significant part of this transformation of political attitudes.

Operative Conservatism and Political Science

At this stage it will be useful to assess the significance of Operative Conservatism from the perspective of political science. Significantly, Operative Conservatism was the forerunner of what later became, in the 1870s, the Conservative Working Men's Associations and Clubs, and was a primitive form of the party of 'social integration'. This term was utilised by the political scientist, Sigmund Neumann, to describe what he believed to be a relatively modern type of political party, dating from the era of the mass European socialist parties in the 1880s. As noted earlier, the middle-class dominated county and borough Conservative Associations, corresponded to Neumann's party of individual representation, catering for the individual who allies himself to it because it corresponds ideologically to his personal political credo and policy initiatives. This type of party is loosely organized for most of the time, coming together as a potent political force only at the approach of elections. For the rest of the time contact between the member and the party are minimal. In contrast, during the 1830s the Conservative Party of the north-west developed the traits and functions similar to the party of social integration. This type of party seeks to attract a mass membership and to organize the supporter not just politically, but in a variety of ways which directly affect his day-to-day existence. The party will take care of his wife and children in case of accident or death; informally educating him; politically socializing him to what the party regarded as legitimate political activities, but also offering regular social functions for the members. The great benefit for the party was that it possessed an army of political activists in the field and was operational at all times.

John Garrard, a historian who has investigated Neumann's thesis, tells us that, "None of the literature appears to regard the old middle-class parties as capable of producing a party social integration."[36] He presents a conclusive case that both of the main political parties operating in Salford after 1867 came very close to being parties of social integration. From the evidence outlined here, this line of analysis can be taken back to the period before the 1867 Reform Act and the advent of a mass electorate.[37] Garrard's tentative conclusions of the immediate post-1867 period are sound and based on historical precedent. The Conservatives of the north-west were acting as a party of social integration for a section of the working class as early as 1835-6. The two important ingredients which were lacking at this time from the Neumann's model were a truly mass membership and the electoral power of a politically organized working class, although in the case of Preston, with its Scot and Lot franchise, the evidence is interesting, as will be seen below. Compared to the post-1867 situation, Operative Conservatism never attracted a truly mass membership in the 1830s and '40s. At

---

36   J. A. Garrard, 'Parties, Members and Voters after 1867: A local study', in *Historical Journal*, 20, I, (1977), p. 146.

37   J. Garrard, 'Parties, Members and Voters after 1867', in T. R. Gourvish and Alan O'Day, (eds.) *Later Victorian Britain*, (Basingstoke, 1988), p. 145.

Preston in 1839 Operative Conservatives had a membership of over 600.[38] But this figure was still higher than the 400 members attributed to the Chartists on the eve of the Sacred Month.[39] What is notable is that for the first time a section of the industrial working class were permanently organized by a mainstream national political party, and this was a significant change in the political culture of the period.

It is doubtful if the instigators and organizers of Operative Conservatism ever wanted a mass membership. They appear to have been seeking to attract a certain type of working class member: respectable, self-improving, religious and a social leader within his class, but without the rigid morality of the Liberal activists. It was vital to the party that they attract respectable supporters, if only to offset accusations of fostering the type of mob mentality associated with Church and King bigotry.[40] For the Conservatives voting power was of little consequence, for the primary aims were political enlightenment, political socialization and the ability to direct working people away from extreme radicalism, as well as the ability to canvass and put pressure on electors. The evidence for Lancashire and the north-west suggests the agitation in which the working class had been engaged from the 1790s to the 1830s had a profound effect on middle class perceptions of an organized radical working class. Operative Conservative and Operative Reformist attempts to politically integrate key groups into moderate legitimized politics were just one of their responses. Others included the organization of formal education, the relief of poverty, the discipline of the factory and control of other social necessities such as housing. It was crucial to the manufacturers particularly and the propertied middle class generally, after the consolidation of industrial capitalism in the 1830s, that the radical nature of working class consciousness be reduced and nullified. By the 1860s this had taken place and was probably a source of satisfaction to many of the middle class and the state authorities. But the process of political sectionalization was by no means complete by the mid-1830s. Nor was it a phenomenon that occurred evenly throughout Lancashire. The working class of east Lancashire, for example, were politically sectionalized relatively early. However, the working class of radical Oldham and Rochdale remained politically united into the 1850s. Eventually, even here working class consciousness did fragment and political sectionalization was a major factor. Even during the years of Chartist activity there were working class Chartists who supported the Conservatives and Liberals as well as the Six Points. Operative Conservatism aimed its pitch at the literate, politically articulate, usually skilled working class men who would probably command respect from their peers, and who, throughout the years of high class consciousness, may have been in positions of trades union or political leadership.[41]

A central theme of this book is that working class political sectionalization can be traced back to the middle years of the 1830s. Class solidarity in east Lancashire began to fragment early because the middle class manufacturers produced a network of social constraints relatively quickly. Our contention is that Operative Conservatism was an important part of this network of containment. Middle class Conservatives of Lancashire and the north-west were acting as political conciliators by allowing the working class into their party, a party whose leading members only a short time before had acted so harshly toward working-class political aspirations. As a process, this changed not only those of the working class who became involved in Conservatism, but the class as a whole as they

---

38 *Preston Pilot*, 20 July 1839.

39 British Library, Ad. Mss., 34245B, ff 119, Walton and Halton to Lovett, July 1839.

40 British Library, Peel Papers, Ad. Mss. 40424, ff 277, Bonham to Peel, (1838). Also 40420, f. 74, Wynn to Peel, 17 April 1835.

41 For more on this see the activities surrounding the career of W. H. Hornby of Blackburn, detailed below in the case-study section on Blackburn.

became politically sectionalized. It also changed the middle-class Conservatives, because they had to be seen to take up the cause of working-class interests and demands, and the party nationally, because it had to accommodate, through policy initiatives, measures which appealed to a wide social basis of political support. In some parts of the region the high levels of class consciousness displayed by the workers of Oldham and the 'popular' style of Rochdale's politics was retained for longer. This was primarily because the radical leadership dominated politics in those towns not the Conservatives who gained the upper hand in much of east Lancashire or the Liberals, so numerically strong at Manchester. Thus the question became one of political leadership, something discussed in due course.

For the members of the operative associations, the personal benefits were very similar to those described by Garrard in the 1870s and 1880s. There were trips and picnics, literary and social facilities, guest speakers, contact with the party's hierarchy, the encouragement of legitimate political involvement and finally the sick and benefit facilities that were, at certain times, of crucial importance to the very existence of working-class members. The members, on the other hand, were expected to go out and argue the Conservative case and inform others of its benefits. The reason why the national party allowed the localities to set up the various types of Conservative Associations, for it would not be true to suggest that the national leadership were directly involved initially, was that they greatly improved party organization in the constituencies. Once the leadership at the Carlton realized that the various types of associations were politically respectable they utilized their benefits to the full, especially with regard to the registration of electors. Some working class members were drawn towards Operative Conservatism out of a sense of social deference to the local elites, others out of political deference to the office and officers of power. Some because of their extreme opinions and their hatred of Catholics or the Irish migrants, there was always a racist and bigoted element within the various associations which some of the local middle class leadership attempted to exploit. However, many working class members were attracted to Conservatism because their opinions on certain key issues coincided with the policies being expounded by the local and national Conservative leadership. It is to these questions of deference, traditionalism and, most notably, the role of policies and issues within Operative Conservatism and the wider working class in the north-west that now require discussion.

The Idioms of Politics and the Role of Issues within Operative Conservatism

So far we have engaged in the detailed examination of Operative Conservatism, concentrating on the basic structure and functions of these societies and focusing mainly on the impact they had in the north-west region. The focus now is to look in more detail at the wider political behaviour among the working class, examining specifically why some working people began to find Conservatism amenable from the mid-1830s to the second Reform Act and beyond. We need to look at both the expectations of those traditionalistic and conservative members of the working class, and also the placatory policy initiatives produced by local and national Conservatives for working people.

Earlier it was suggested that a major function of modern political party was the articulation of the wishes and aggregated demands of its members and supporters in the form of policy initiatives. Policies are important in swaying those not committed to a party, but at the beginning of the nineteenth century, however, things were rather different. Before 1832 ministries were primarily concerned with the maintenance and defence of the state, internal law and order and of the raising of revenues. Policies enacted by ministries were, therefore, mainly reactions to constantly changing events set in the context of 'high politics'. It could be argued that in the eighteenth-century Whig ministers were, in general terms, more sympathetic to commerce and to religious dissent than Tories. But if this was their traditional posture it was widely challenged in the last quarter of the eighteenth century. Whig economic policy was attacked most famously in Adam Smith's *Wealth of Nations* and, at the social level, in the fact that no dissenter could send his son to an English university nor any Catholic to Parliament. There were of course great popular movements in the eighteenth century and early nineteenth century, for example the Wilkesite agitation of the 1760s, anti-excise demonstrations, parliamentary reform and the Association Movement, the question of slavery and Catholic Emancipation. However, the overwhelming view of politicians was crusades conducted outside Parliament should not be allowed to influence policy inside branches of the legislature. Agitating the political passions of the masses was regarded as extremely dangerous and tantamount to infusing revolutionary feelings. Policy at all costs must be decided in Parliament by members acting independently of pledges given to sectional interests in the constituencies.

The justification for this position was twofold. Firstly, political leaders believed the general public, informed as they were by the dubious financial scruples of the press, could never be adequately appraised as to the ramifications of a given policy as a Minister of State or the member of Commons or Lords Committee. Thus, on the eve of 1832, the prevailing view was that agitation 'out of doors' was at worst a dangerous, and at best a mischievous, form of meddling. The Prime Minister made most policy decisions in close consultation with his Cabinet colleagues and the Monarch. In the case of the Conservatives, the aloofness of Peel and his propensity for deafness when addressed by his backbenchers, was for many years notorious.[42] Arguably, Peel was maintaining a long tradition of leaving policy decisions to those in the highest positions of ministerial office. Eventually even he had to bend to outside pressure, and the feelings of his backbenchers can be interpreted as a sign of the rejection of the old system and a feature of party politics.

The second justification of policies solely being the concern of the legislature was the traditional independence of both of the Houses and the members. One of the great fears of the Conservatives over the 1832 Reform Act, and one of the central foundations of their opposition to it, was that the House of Commons would become more important than the House of Lords. Also, that the Lower House would be swamped by the radical members of the boroughs brought in by their courting of popular measures and pledges. Again, a major reason for organizing the party, both at the centre and in the localities, was to prevent just such an eventuality. Post-reform electorates differed in two main areas from pre-reform. First, and most obviously, they were usually larger, and secondly, in areas of industrialization and urbanization the local society was more complex and thus more productive of political pressures. There was an increasing tendency for the more numerous sections of the electorate to seriously argue the merits and demerits of policies and alternative policies. There was, in short, a greater propensity amongst the public to express opinions based on the considered examination of policy and to express their own sectional interests in the form of political demands.

An important work by Tom Nossiter, *Influence, Opinion and Political Idioms in Reformed England*, elaborated an argument on the idioms or expressions of politics between 1832 and 1874. The relevance of Nossiter's work is that it offers a model for the type of politics engaged in by working people generally and working-class conservatives in particular. For Nossiter, there were three kinds of political relationship.[43] First there were the politics of influence. This rested on an

---

42   See N. Gash, *Peel*, (London, 1976), p. 141.

43   T. J. Nossiter, *Influence, Opinion and Political Idioms in Reformed England: Case Studies from the North-East*, (Hassocks 1975), pp. 5-8.

organic notion of society whereby the societal gradations of a community were reflected in the disposal of patronage and political power. This type of political community was a remnant from the eighteenth-century type of social organization, based on the large estate having its use, duties and reciprocal responsibilities. According to Nossiter, the politics of influence were not purely a rural or market-town phenomenon but one which could be "transferred with greater or lesser incongruity to the city or the company town alike."[44] There were occasions when influence was brought to bear, not necessarily as a crude form of coercion or of irresistible pressures at periods of elections, but rather as an assiduous realisation on the part of an elector to take pragmatic account of his total situation within the network of influences that made up his day to day existence.

Nossiter's second idiom or political variable was that of the politics of the market. Here the vote or political participation was seen as an "economic asset to be bought or sold according to the laws of political supply and demand."[45] Again, Nossiter stresses this may not have been the crude and selling of votes, but often the paying of expenses, or the paying for lost time, or tipping for a service rendered or the giving of treats: food, travel, drinks etc. Nor was this type of politics to be found solely during periods of elections. It was expected that an MP or local politician should give generously to local charities and reward local activists, either as individuals or collectively through contributions to the annual dinner of the local association, or other gifts and treats. Finally there was the politics of opinion and interest. Contemporaneously, he suggests, this was known as 'agitation' immediately after the passing of 1832 Act, and as 'conscience' during the 1850s and '60s, and finally, in the early 1870s, gained full expression with the final success in carrying the Secret Ballot Act in 1872.[46] Nossiter tells us that few constituencies could be described as fitting exactly one or other of these three conceptions of nineteenth-century politics, but he suggests that his model helps to clarify a very confusing pattern of political development. His study is based on research of the north-east of England, a region which Nossiter admits was 'unique' in its especial attachment to Liberal politics.[47] This points to the problem of Nossiter's three typologies. All regions were different, indeed areas within regions were different. What might have been common practice in one was different in another. This is something to bear in mind later in this book, but it is worth making the point here that in the north-west the trend was towards opinion politics among working people and a more diffused pattern of leadership than that found in the north-east. Derek Fraser has pointed out that the north-east region was unique. Although it contained that mix of agriculture and industry so typical of Britain during the consolidation of the industrial revolution, in political terms, it was still locked into the single interest type of political orientation. This was more akin to the political environment of the eighteenth-century.[48] Fraser's work on the large cities of the north and midlands suggests, (as does the research here), that it was opinion which, after 1832, was the salient feature of local politics in these types of urban area.[49] Fraser cites *The Times* as evidence for his case:

> What *The Times* said of the West Riding to a greater or lesser extent applied to the larger cities: 'with its 30,000 voting men and its unequalled concentration of interests [it] is beyond the reaches of all influences but those which appeal to the conscience of man. No threats, no

44 Ibid., p. 6.

45 Ibid.

46 Ibid., p. 7.

47 Ibid., p. 2.

48 D. Fraser, *Urban Politics in Victorian England*, (Leicester, 1976), p. 185.

49 Ibid., chapters 8 and 9.

frowns, no quarter day … Here if anywhere is a free election'.[50]

Although influence (especially patronage) and the politics of the market are to be found in the north-west, increasingly the trend after 1832 was towards opinion politics, based upon social groups either with purely political issues or with social, economic and religious questions which became political issues. Fraser is right to assert that Nossiter's study is based on a narrow conception of nineteenth-century politics.[51] For although Nossiter has devised these three conceptualizations of political activity, this activity itself is primarily concerned with the formal participation in politics encapsulated in the act of voting. Thus, for Nossiter, the 1872 Secret Ballot Act attains a huge significance, because it was harder to influence or buy votes for those attempting to influence or corrupt no longer had any guarantee that the client voter had stuck to his pledge. When looking at nineteenth century politics purely from the standpoint of casting votes then this is a plausible argument. However, in this study the contention is that post-1832 politics must be understood in a far wider context, one that embraces the changing nature of the political party, the political attitudes of the non-electors as well as the electors. The vote was merely the culmination of a process of political stance formation in which opinion and bargaining played a part irrespective of whether, in an immediate sense, the outcome is categorised as influence or opinion based. The benefits accruing to the members of Operative Conservative Associations (sick and benefit provisions, education, etc.) gives support to this point.

Taken individually, Nossiter's three categories impinge too exclusively on the separate nature and explanatory context of the given idiom. Various inter-linking factors came into play in different places at different times in the political world of Britain after 1832. Increasingly, in the north-west, local politicians attempted to gain support and power on the basis of issues which directly affected the working class. As will be seen in due course on the Conservative side, examples of this can be found in the agitation surrounding the imposition of the New Poor Law after 1836 or the Factory Question. Also from the 1830s onwards in religious questions linked directly to Irish migration. Of course there were occasions when local landed or industrial magnates attempted to influence electors and non-electors, but this was part of a wider network of social controls which the elites operated after 1832. There were episodes of corruption after the first Reform Act, but even here the growing tendency is towards political respectability, which, coupled with the increasing size of electorates in the constituencies of the north-west, rendered this idiom of Nossiter's, though still significant, increasingly marginal. The tendency of parties and politicians at the local and national level was, in the north-west, to appeal for support on the basis of principles, policies and issues and, importantly, leadership.

Operative Conservatives, Radical Tories and Paternalism

As noted earlier, those initially involved in the active membership of the Lancashire Operative Conservatives were the 'respectable' working men. However, there were occasions when the mass of working people was called upon to support Conservatism. This brings us to the role which issues played in the 1830s, 1840s and 1850s, and how they were utilised by the local conservatives. So far the suggestion has been that the role of Operative Conservatism as a political institution was one of political socialisation and proselytization. Also that local and national Conservative leaders supported

---

50 Ibid., p. 185.

51 Ibid., pp. 184-5.

the Conservative Associations as being not only useful organizational bodies but also fulfilling the role of explaining the essential Conservative principles and importantly, in the case of the Operative Associations, of steering sections of the working class away from dangerous radicalism. Initially, at a general level, Operative Conservative Associations resembled a form of Conservative Mechanics Institute. They were places where discussions and debates could be held, where Conservative newspapers and literature could be read and absorbed. Two points are important here. Firstly, for the Conservative leadership, this explanatory function was important because it re-directed the worker away from the influences of radicals and republicans in the public house or the place of work, and placed him in an informal, educational environment with his like-minded peers. The workplace and the public house were important once the operative was fully committed and conversant with the arguments of Conservatism. Then he could influence and persuade his fellow workers, but the initiation and instruction had to take place in a less disruptive atmosphere. Secondly, the worker, for his part, was displaying to his superiors that he was at least willing to be improved and to be regarded as a respectable and legitimate citizen of his class and party. This differed from the politics of influence in that this was a voluntary activity on the part of the individual, based on an appeal made by the political party to gain his support.

The situation worked well for both sides. The Conservative leadership knew precisely who it could rely on and encouraged the converted to bring more into the fold, so they too could defend the constitution against the encroachments of the 'Destructives': the Reformers, the Radicals, the republicans and others advocating wholesale changes in society. The Operative Conservative, on the other hand, was not just a passive member of political society like other non-electors, but was displaying a desire for respectable political citizenship in his open support for the Conservative cause, and, importantly, within the mainstream of legitimate politics. Eventually the working class Conservative might attain the right to vote and full citizenship by gaining better employment opportunities and a higher rated home. Once he could vote, the Association would take care of his annual registration fees. These functions were not, of course, peculiar to the Conservatives, the Liberals did the same things, especially with the faggot votes created by the Anti-Corn Law League in the early 1840s. However, in the 1830s the first aim of the local Conservatives was to instil into a section of the working class the basic Conservative opinions. Dr Nossiter wishes to call this 'agitation', as he terms opinion based politics at this time, then the local Conservatives of Lancashire gloried in the term, as a Mr Cheetham, a local schoolmaster, told a meeting of Chorley Operatives in November 1836:

> At the commencement of the Association our opponents charged us with agitation. It was said that our design was to cause masters to be against their servants, fathers against their sons; but he would say that if to endeavour to instil right views and implement sound constitutional principles in the hearts and minds of the working classes, if to endeavour to create a kind and good feeling amongst our fellow townsmen by showing them the duties they owe to each other, be agitation, then he would say we glory in agitation.[52]

Without doubt, however, Conservative Associations were of most practical national benefit to the party organizationally when, during periods of parliamentary elections, committed working class Conservatives would be on hand to canvass electors and argue the Conservative case. However, Operative Association membership fluctuated across the region. The Preston branch, formed in

---

52 *Preston Pilot*, 26 November 1836. The First Annual Report of the Chorley Operative Conservative Association, 21 November 1836.

December 1835, began with inaugural membership of 60 persons, by the end of October 1836 the branch had increased its membership to 450.[53] In December 1836 the Warrington Operative Conservative Association claimed a relatively large membership of 500,[54] and in 1838 they boasted 740 members and, as well as the usual social amenities, plus an Operative Conservative Brass Band.[55] At Wigan the membership of the Operative Conservative Association was 850 in the summer of 1836.[56] At Liverpool the membership was said to be in excess of 1,000, with a branch in every ward in the city, and in November 1836 the Tradesmen's branch attracted 120 new members in the course of a single meeting.[57] By July 1837 the Bolton branch had a membership of 1,500 with an additional 200 female members.[58] In April 1838 the membership of Salford Operative Conservative Association was put at 1,700,[59] and Manchester claimed 900 members for its Operative Association.[60] The initial membership of the Blackburn Operative Association was 40 in November 1835, but by 1838 it was over 400. According to the annual reports of the BOA, membership for the town (not the parish) never rose higher than 600 in 1844.[61] Blackburn ranks, therefore, as the kind of town with an association of middling membership compared to its larger neighbours at Manchester, Liverpool, Salford and Bolton. But there were also smaller associations at Rochdale with 400 members,[62] Heywood with 350 in 1837,[63] Chorley 300 in 1836,[64] and others with no recorded membership at all at Burnley, Poulton-le-Fylde or Upholland and many, many more.

The periods, however, when the Operative Associations of the north-west did increase coincided to periods when the issues linked to regional Conservatism were at their strongest. At periods of high social tension, political issues, strong leadership and organization acted as conduits, bringing previously apathetic members of society into the political arena. This was the case in the north-west especially with issues concerning the relief of poverty, the Ten Hours Movement, the Corn Laws, Parliamentary reform and Church reform associated with the Church rates question and education. Added to these were those which affected working people only indirectly or intermittently, such as public health, temperance and, of course, trades unionism. These issues will be examined in more detail in the next chapter when Operative Conservatism is discussed comparatively across the region. It may be of use, however, to explain the value of issues to Conservative activists. This brings into the discussion another facet of the relations between the working class and the Conservative Party in the 1830s and '40s. This concerns a group known, somewhat confusedly, by the apparently contradictory term of Tory-Radicals or Radical Tories. The *Manchester Guardian*, writing in May 1837, attempted to clarify this seemingly contradictory political terminology. It said,

Tory Radicals are those persons who, by professing the most extreme radical opinions in

53 Ibid., 19 November 1836.

54 Ibid., 3 December 1836.

55 *Manchester Guardian*, 26 May 1838.

56 *Preston Pilot*, 16 July 1836.

57 Ibid., 12 November 1836.

58 Ibid., 22 July 1837.

59 *Manchester Guardian*, 18 April 1838.

60 *Manchester Courier*, 21 April 1838.

61 The Annual Reports of the Blackburn Operative Conservative Association for, 1836, 1837, 1838, 1839, 1840, 1841, 1842, 1843, 1844, 1852, 1853. In the *Blackburn Standard* of those years.

62 *Preston Pilot*, 13 August 1838.

63 *Manchester Guardian*, 14 January 1837.

64 *Preston Pilot*, 19 November 1836.

politics, are yet always ready to play into the hands of the Tory Party. The Radical-Tories are those who, calling themselves Conservatives, and pretending the highest veneration of the constitution, are nevertheless always ready to preach resistance to the law, and to support any incendiary whom they may consider likely to annoy their political opponents.[65]

Although tinged with the usual sarcasm, there is a grain of truth in these definitions. An example of this can be found in the reform crisis itself and immediately after. Historians have noted an informal union of the Ultra Tories and the Ultra Radicals, their common bond being an intense hatred of the factory system supported philosophically by political economy, which many associated with social disruption and injustice. The 'reforming' bourgeoisie typified these new forms of manufacturing and its attendant doctrine. The Ultra-Tories feared the House of Commons would be deluged with these new men of the industrial boroughs; the Ultra Radicals argued that such men were blatant exploiters of labour and, once in Parliament, would gain enough political power to increase exploitation. Both groups also shared a form of romantic atavism that was becoming culturally popular as the effects of industrialisation became more widely appreciated and as the 'Condition of England' debate gained publicity. D. C. Moore has written a detailed analysis of this strange union.[66] He suggests that, politically, both groups found themselves on the same side in their detestation of Wellington, the Tory/Conservative leader from 1828 to 1833.[67] The Ultra-Tories were incensed at Wellington's capitulation over the Catholic Question, the Radicals for his hostile attitude towards the labouring classes. In fact, the *Manchester Guardian* maintained throughout the parliamentary contests of the 1830s and early '40s that collusion existed between the Tory section of the Conservative Party and sections of the extreme radicals, and with some justification. However, its distinction between 'Tory-Radicals' and 'Radical Tories' was rather cosmetic and, for our purposes, confusing, as the terms were interchangeable at the time. One of the major factors that drove many of the radically inclined working classes into the arms of the Conservatives was the way the reforming Whigs and Liberals dealt with salient issues of the day which directly impinged on working class existence. However, before examining these issues in detail the context must be set by outlining the basic theoretical stances adopted by the Tory-inclined Conservatives and the radically-inclined working class in the industrial north-west after 1832.

We noted earlier the atavism surrounding past-directed and often romantic perceptions held by the remnants of the old Tory party in the second half of the eighteenth and early nineteenth centuries: the so-called 'Romantic Tories'. Many radicals in the industrial north-west shared this highly effective illusion of the past. The key for both was the natural justice, responsibilities and rights apparently available to all groups in a bye-gone age. For the Tories this was based on prescriptive property rights and social responsibilities relating to a theory of paternalism. That is to say the elites had a responsibility to the needs of those below them when the lower orders fell upon distressed times. For the Radicals it was mediated through a perceived view of the protective role of the state and the enshrined natural rights and justice of a former age. The affinity of interest was the need for security felt by both groups in a period of profound insecurity, given the rising power of thrusting entrepreneurs and progressive reformers, and the alliance appears less contradictory than at first sight. During the 1830s, '40s and '50s many impoverished members of the working class began to accept the leadership of the local and national Conservatives for three basic reasons. Firstly, many

---

65 *Manchester Guardian*, 10 May 1837.

66 D. C. Moore, 'The Other face of Reform', in *Victorian Studies*, (September 1961).

67 Ibid., p. 7.

Conservatives of the Tory variety and sections of the working class were unwilling to passively accept the changing nature of society as envisaged by the progressive Liberal middle classes. For the working class, as the new devices of social organization, constraint and control were introduced by the Whig/Liberals, such as the New Poor Law, or changes in the old forms of local government in the 1830s, so the political conflict increased, in an attempt to resist their implementation. Secondly, north-west (and many Yorkshire) Conservatives of the traditional Tory strain developed a social theory, which attempted to guarantee the security of labour through a reformulation of paternalistic responsibilities, natural rights and justice. Thirdly, these northern Conservatives attempted to give practical effect to their social philosophy by advocating issues and policies which reflected their concern for the working class, and, of course, to gain adherents. These issues included advocating factory reform, opposition to the New Poor Law, non-political trades unionism and, in certain cases in the 1840s, allying themselves with the rural utopianism which many workers of the north-west associated with independence and security, especially those relatively new to the urban situation.

An important factor drawing sections of industrial workers and traditionally inclined Conservatives together was their common resentment of the middle-class Liberal progressives.[68] The vast acceleration of daily life and the changes in the centres of political power which industrialisation brought to the industrial districts left some Conservatives and many members of the working class (especially the unskilled and semi-skilled) feeling bereft of power, or even the opportunity of expressing their grievances. Rural Tories and the Conservatives of the market and county towns, as well as the lesser skilled working class, took a long time to be convinced that industrialisation in any sense improved the quality of their lives. Or that the dreaded 'laws' of political economy would be a solution to individual and social problems. The unstable social and, especially, economic conditions in the north-west demonstrated to working people that they should reject the theories of linear progress so fervently insisted upon by the Liberal middle classes. Working men found that they were a limited and dispensable part of the industrial process, a mere factor of production. Instead of the promised long-range progress of the Liberals, many unskilled and semi-skilled workers demanded an immediate remedy for the iniquities of industrialisation. Of those who migrated to the towns prior to the mass influx of Irish men and women attempting to escape the famine of the mid-1840s, substantial numbers came from the rural or semi-rural villages situated five to ten miles from the urban areas.[69] These people preferred the predictable life typical in a rural society because of the lack of economic security and independence witnessed first hand in the towns. Such groups were reluctant to believe that industrial progress would include them, beset as it was from an endless succession of booms and slumps. Given their recent history and experiences, it was asking a great deal of this section of the working class that they should accept the unknown direction of 'progress' in which they had only a very partial share. Increasingly, these workers responded to leaders who promised simple political solutions to the complex problems raised by industrial life.

There were occasions from 1838 when semi- and unskilled workers of the north-west turned to Chartism, but they did not automatically accept the leadership of skilled working class, as had been the case in the 1820s and, indeed, continued to be the case among the more independently situated workers of Birmingham or London. One of the most popular Chartist leaders in the north (including

68 At this point the description is referring to the radical Tories and Conservatives and not sections of the mainstream Radicals who, in general terms saw the idle classes and aristocrats as the real enemy. However, the focus here is somewhat different to that of historians like G. Stedman-Jones, *Languages of Class*, (Cambridge, 1983) or P. Hollis, *Pressure from Without*, (London, 1974).

69 See for example A. Redford, *Labour Migration in England*, (Manchester, 1976 ed.) or John K. Walton, *Lancashire: a Social History, 1558-1939*, (Manchester, 1987), chapters 6 and 9.

most of Yorkshire) was a 'gentleman', Feargus O'Connor.[70] O'Connor's leadership of Northern Chartism can be partially attributed to radical Tory and Conservative success in persuading workers to rely upon external leadership instead of developing to the full a political ideology and tactics of their own. As we have seen, political self-development was a feature the working class had tentatively embraced from 1816 up to the reform crisis. O'Connor was benefiting from the work begun for him by the Tory radicals such as Michael Sadler, Richard Oastler, Parson George Stringer Bull and Joseph Raynor Stephens. Several working class Chartists, such as Richard Marsden[71] from Preston, Edward Nightingale[72] from Manchester and the Bradford Chartist, John Jackson,[73] argued that, while O'Connor was a radical, he also shared Tory prejudices and assumptions. They further suggested that he had stepped into the vacuum in the radical Tory leadership left by the arrests of Oastler and Stephens. While O'Connor did pursue the need of political reform, (a measure supported by Stephens but not by Oastler), his ultimate solution to the working man's problems was a return to a simpler life on the land, something which had interested Conservatives as early as 1841.[74] O'Connor's radicalism and rough dress was supplemented by his pose as a landed gentleman of aristocratic birth.[75] One reason why William Lovett and the London Chartists increasingly rejected the tactics of the northern workers was the belief that this group could not be persuaded that they had more in common with the skilled workers than with the gentry.[76] The paternalism of the Tory radicals and the Conservatives of the north-west reinforced the experiences of sections of the working class in the belief that the loss of independence and lack of security was not solely due to the loss of political rights. Arguably, they had never had them at any time before 1832. It was due to the criminal irresponsibility of the 'progressive' Liberal middle class manufacturers and their Whig representatives in Parliament. An element often overlooked was despite its ostensible purpose of political reform Tory Radicalism infused into Lancashire Chartism a viable explanation for their plight. For example, William Smith, a Stockport power loom weaver and trades unionist, told his audience at Blackburn in 1835 that the "Tories were the best masters ... and those who assumed the appellation of 'Liberals' ... [should] reform their own conduct before they talked of reforming others."[77]

Such views had a firm hold on sections of the working class. Paternalism was seen by many of the industrial working classes as not necessarily the patriarchal domination associated with the landed squirearchy, rather it was seen as the need of the elites and the central/local state to fulfil their inherent and customary responsibilities, almost as if it were part of a contractual agreement. Paternalism, to many working people, was equated with its eighteenth century meaning of protection (social, economic, legal and political protection) and was intrinsically linked to deference, status and power in the economic and political matrix of eighteenth century society. Those above had an obligation to those below. And if those above were seen to be lax or wanting in their duty, then those

---

70 For O'Connor's affectations see J. Epstein, *Lion of Freedom, passim,* (London, 1988); for the question of 'gentlemen' leaders see, J. Belchem and J. Epstein, 'The Nineteenth-century Gentleman leader revisited', in *Social History,* Vol. 22, No. 1, May 1997.

71 See *Blackburn Standard,* 9 July 1848.

72 *Manchester Guardian,* 6 December 1841.

73 J. Jackson, *The Demagogue Done Up: An Exposure of the Extreme Inconsistencies of Feargus O'Connor,* (Bradford, 1844).

74 T. Carlyle, 'The Conservative Land Plan', in *The Quarterly Review,* (September 1841).

75 D. Read and R. Glasgow, *Feargus O'Connor,* (London 1959), p. 20, see also James's view in *Lion of Freedom,* (London 1979), who makes a rather different assessment of O'Connor than the one offered here.

76 See Stedman-Jones, *Languages of Class,* pp. 97-9.

77 *Blackburn Standard,* 15 July 1835.

below felt they had right to nudge the elites into fulfilling their responsibilities. Edward Thompson called this relationship akin to a 'field-of-force' which set the limits of political and social power in external, demonstrable displays of crowd actions. Internally this 'field-of-force' acted, "within mens' minds, as taboos, limited expectations, and a disposition towards traditional forms of protest, aimed often at recalling the gentry to their paternalist duties." Thompson suggested that,

> The poor might be willing to award their deference to the gentry, but only for a price. The price was substantial. And the deference was often without the least illusion: it could be seen from below as being one part necessary self-preservation, one part the calculated extraction of whatever could be extracted. Seen this way, the poor imposed upon the rich some of the duties and functions of paternalism. Both parties were constrained within a common field-of-force.[78]

Earlier it was noted that the working class of the north-west became increasingly politicized from the 1790s, a major reason for this was the erosion of traditional responsibilities by the elites, locally and nationally. Sections of the working class maintained that this was compounded by the growth of the factories, unconstrained by custom, given legal backing by statutes and philosophical credence by political economy. The political dimension took the form of attempts to gain adequate working class political representation, but it continued to take the form of nudging the elites into making basic economic and social concessions to the grievances of working people. These people were not revolutionaries; often they did not even demand the vote. What they did want, however, was security, independence and a fair and just system of the redress of their grievances: in short, the basic rights of citizenship. Working people were confronted with difficulties surrounding work practices, wage and piece rates, factory conditions, the price and availability of foodstuffs, welfare provision, housing, public health and sanitation, increased levels of direct and indirect taxation, education and religious reform, essentially the basic necessities for human existence. In the later 1830s and early 1840s, as the Chartists advocated the Six Points as the panacea for these social ills, radical Tories and some local and national Conservatives were addressing these bread and butter issues more directly, they were, after all, in positions of power to effect decisions. It was this that gained them the support of sections of the working class. Liberal leaders tended to dismiss the willingness of the working class to follow Conservative and Radical Tory leadership as a desperate, anachronistic strategy for attacking the Whigs, especially when they were having to make hard decisions in government after 1832. The *Manchester Guardian* was particularly disgusted at the short-sightedness of sections of the working class in allowing their resentment of Whig policy to shape their actions.[79] But to many of the semi- and unskilled workers involved in spinning, weaving and labouring, the Liberal middle classes were men attempting to foist a theory of gross exploitation onto the working class, wantonly destroying the traditional paternalistic relationship between the governed and the governors. If a worker had not come to this conclusion himself, there were several channels through which it was conveyed. As early as 1833 Henry Hetherington, in the *Poor Man's Guardian*, was writing that, "The middle classes, or profit men are the real tyrants of the country. Disguise it as they may, they are the authors of our slavery for without their connivance and secret support no tyranny could exist. Government is but a tool in their hands to execute their nefarious purpose."[80] Or, again, with Bronterre O'Brien noting directly the distinction between the moral economy and political economy:

---

78 E. P. Thompson, 'Patricians and Plebs', in *Customs in Common*, (London, 1991) p. 85.

79 *Manchester Guardian*, 10 November 1837.

80 *Poor Man's Guardian*, 2 November 1833.

> True political economy is like true domestic economy; it does not consist solely in slaving and saving; there is a moral economy as well as political... It is indeed the MORAL ECONOMY that they always keep out of sight. When they talk about the tendency of large masses of capital, and the division of labour, to increase production and cheapen commodities, they do not tell us of the inferior human being which a single and fixed occupation must necessarily produce.[81]

The worker heard the same kind of argument over and over again at the mass meetings called in support of the Ten Hours Movement or protesting against the New Poor Law. But working-class distrust of the Whigs and Liberal manufacturers was nurtured not only by Radical Tory and Conservative rhetoric but also by the bitterness of cumulative disappointment that again served to harden feelings of class consciousness. The Reformed Parliament had turned out to be much the same as its predecessor, indeed, worse in terms of the attacks made on trade unionism, the lacklustre performance over factory reform and the perceived punitive provisions of the New Poor Law. For many workers the indictment that the Whig governments of the 1830s sought only to represent the interests of the middle-class Liberals was proved by their severity in dealing with the Dorset labourers in 1834 or the spinners of Glasgow in 1837. Despite their traditional roots in the land, many Conservatives felt as insecure as the working class. As stated above, the Reform Act, in theory if not immediately in fact, abruptly ended the coalition of conservative Whiggery and Toryism that had held power more or less continuously since 1784. In addition, theories of political economy questioned the economic function of the Tory element of Conservatism, accusing them of being parasitic countrymen or the 'stupid party'. Political economists argued that the nation would benefit if the emphasis were shifted from land to industry, from the traditional paternalism and parochialism of the local gentry to the individualistic and centralized rule of an efficient, rootless, meritocratic bureaucracy clearing the way for systematic progress.

Issues and Political Re-alignments

Old style Tories could not admit that their role as a patriarchal country gentry was superfluous in the changing society, nor could they welcome the direction of that change, begun as it was in the reforming Whig ministries of the 1830s. The Whigs and progressive Liberals appeared to be attacking everything the Tory element deemed inviolable: the established church, the House of Lords, Local government, and the essential social and political relationship which, the Tories (and many Conservatives) argued, had separated Britain from despotic Europe and republican America. In the north-west the Conservatives developed a defensive ideology of social reform, partly as an expedient to attack their political opponents, but also because many felt a genuine sympathy with the isolation and insecurity of working people. It will be seen in the next chapter that this was put over to working people by highlighting the threat posed by Whig/Liberal policies, the pursuance of certain issues whilst at the same time extolling the central tenets of old style Tory paternalism and Conservatism. The salience of issues was reflected in the alliances between Tory radicals and more militant radicals. For example, in November 1837, the radical reformers of Oldham gave a dinner honouring the seventy-fifth birthday of the veteran working class activist John Knight. The two principal speakers at this celebration of fifty years of radical agitation on behalf of the working class were the radical Tories, Richard Oastler and Joseph Raynor Stephens. Oastler said,

---

81 *Bronterre's National Reformer*, 21 January 1837, cited in E. P. Thompson, 'The Moral Economy Reviewed', in *Customs in Common*, (London 1991), p. 337.

> He felt exceedingly proud to be called on to meet the friends of liberty and justice to the poor of Oldham ... Knight was a good man, an honest man and a patriot. They had done him the honour to connect his name with a cause that stood on the topmost pinnacle of honour. So fond had the yearning capitalists become of the labour that produced wealth, that it was now clearly demonstrated that the factory child was of more value than gold or silver... He came because they [the Oldham Radicals] and he agreed on so many sentiments.[82]

Oastler described his first meeting with Knight. He and Michael Sadler were at Oldham in the late 1820s when they were visited by an old man. Oastler asked Sadler who the man was. "Why bless you", said Sadler, "he is one of the oldest Radicals in England, that thinks that we Tories are doing something beneficial, so he came to give me a shake of the hand."[83] Stephens said Knight had taught him,

> much useful knowledge on the subjects of capital and labour, and if there was any one reason more than another that led him to attend these festivals, it was in order to impart to them the knowledge of subjects closely affecting the interests of working men.[84]

Of course, the Conservatives and Tory Radicals were not the only social reformers operating in the industrial districts between 1832 and the 1860s, and the following chapters will examine these regional variations and differentiation of political allegiances among working people. There were many Radicals, Liberals and Whigs who supported working class causes and it is interesting to note the issues these groups supported in the light of their ideological traits, their political aims and objectives. As stated earlier, the Liberals and progressive Whigs lent heavily on the theories of political economy associated with Adam Smith and Ricardo, on the social theories of Malthus, the utilitarianism of Bentham and James and John Stuart Mill. In the north-west, the Liberals and Whig reformers championed the usual issues linked primarily to industry and economics: the repeal of the Corn Laws, taxation reform and the freeing of trade, which they maintained would result in the improvement in society as a whole. But they also supported educational reform, church-rate reform, moral improvement, temperance and public health, which all had a direct or indirect relevance to the working class. However, one historian has suggested that a large part of the radical appeal of Liberalism to a section of the Oldham working class was not related to class issues, but more to do with the popular politics focused by radical Liberals. On "retrenchment, tax reform, democratic accountability and local self-government (which) represented a commitment to a democratic, capitalist environment capable of sustaining material progress and promoting moral and spiritual improvement and individual responsibility."[85] This may have had some relevance to the situation in Oldham but elsewhere was not the case with the Conservative appeal to the working class.

There were a variety of Radicals: moral force Chartists, who adopted the strictly peaceful tactics in pursuit of the Six Points, there were republicans, secularists, primitive socialists and physical force Chartists. These groups also pursued issues that had a direct bearing on working class existence. The best way to gauge the extremity of their respective positions was not the degree to which they advocated the use of physical force to gain their objectives, most were prepared to contemplate it at

---

82 Oldham Reference Library, The Butterworth Manuscripts, 29 November 1837.

83 Ibid.

84 Ibid.

85 Michael Winstanley, 'Oldham Radicalism and the Origins of Popular Liberalism, 1830-1852', in *Historical Journal*, 36, 3, (1993), p. 619.

one stage or another, but rather their willingness to operate within the existing constitution. We must ask, just how revolutionary were they in terms of their complete and total rejection of the existing social and political order? Apart from a very brief period in the early 1830s, or in certain places at the height of the Chartism in 1839, the majority of these groups wished to operate within the existing constitution. They never possessed a sufficient level of mass class consciousness, in a Marxian sense, to carry out their revolutionary objectives at any time up to the 1870s.

There were three distinct approaches by which the three main groups linked the issues they actively supported to basic political principles. The Liberal progressives stressed the necessity of moral improvement through direct action on the baser instincts of the late Georgian, early Victorian working man. Attention was focused on the pursuit of objectives that would both morally and physically transform him and make him less susceptible to the temptations of the 'residuum'.[86] These 'progressive' reformers rejected the Tory and Conservative premise of paternalism, stressing instead individual self-reliance, rather than relying on the good works of others. The Radicals' essential guiding principle was the attainment of equal social and political rights. They affected a high moral tone over issues related to religious, political and social egalitarianism, but it did not have the ideological strength of Liberalism or indeed Conservatism. The basis of early nineteenth-century Radicalism was perceptions of the blatant abuse of natural justice, with many writers focusing on aspects of exploitation. However, although writers such as Thomas Wooler or Bronterre O'Brien pre-date the works of Marx by two or three decades, they did not develop the philosophic rigour that the continental Radicals achieved. Nor, according to Patricia Hollis and Gareth Stedman Jones, did they adequately identify the real enemy of the working class: the capitalist middle classes and the system of production itself.[87] Although at times popular, Radicalism found itself squeezed between the progressive Liberals on the one hand and traditionalistic Conservatives on the other. Stedman-Jones suggests that the decline of Chartism was not due to prosperity or economic stabilization or an immature class consciousness, "but to the changing character and policies of the state — the principal enemy upon whose actions the radicals had always found their credibility depended."[88] The third main ideological strand which operated in the years after 1832 was that of Conservatism, imbued as it was with the strong Tory paternalistic element. Overall, issues, principles and policies arguments were selected and presented within the framework of these developing ideologies.

What then were the main working class issues which the Radical Tories and Conservatives exploited in the north-west region? The relevance and potency of these issues varied over time and from area to area within the region as a whole, but essentially two issues stand out. They were factory reform, and opposition to the 1834 Poor Law Amendment Act. Added to these were a series of issues relevant to working people that local Conservatives promoted from time to time. These included trade union recognition, public health and related issues of sanitation, urban overcrowding, religion and education.

Historically, paternalistically orientated Conservatives and Tories had a long association with factory reform throughout the northern manufacturing districts. The first Sir Robert Peel had placed an Act on the statute book in 1802 that regulated the hours of work of cotton apprentices to twelve hours per day. In 1815, with the development of steam-powered factories employing 'free' children in urban areas, the primitive socialist mill owner Robert Owen began a campaign to limit child labour to

---

86 See the case study of Preston below with reference to Joseph Livesey, and see A. Howe, *The Cotton Masters*, (Oxford, 1982).

87 P. Hollis, *Pressure from Without in early Victorian England*, (London, 1974), Stedman-Jones, *Languages of Class*, p. 107.

88 Stedman-Jones, *Languages of Class*, p. 178.

ten and a half hours per day. Investigations by Committees in Parliament, under the sympathetic chairmanship of the paternalist Tory Lord Kenyon, led to a widening of Peel's Act of 1802, applying it to all children employed in cotton mills. In 1825 three Tory manufacturers from Bradford, John Rand, John Wood and Matthew Thompson, unsuccessfully appealed for a voluntary ten-hour day in the worsted industry. In Lancashire, meanwhile, a group of trades' unionists under the leadership of James Turner and John Doherty maintained a campaign in the cotton areas of Lancashire, eventually with Conservative support.[89] A host of 'experts' from medical men to Anglican priests published information in an effort to influence Parliament. To many Liberals and progressively inclined manufacturers, such interfering with the free operation of labour and wages was, of course, an anathema as long as *laissez-faire* was in the ascendancy. It was in the later 1820s that Richard Oastler and the Radical Tories burst upon the scene and gave dramatic life to the issue which, as will be seen subsequently, was to be for the next three decades one of the most important questions of social reform in north-west politics.[90] Also in the mid-1830s came the implementation of the New Poor Law, administered from London by a centralised commission. Operative Conservatives and Radical Tories as well as many middle-class Conservatives asserted the hypocrisy of the Whig/Liberal position. They pointed to the fact that Liberals would not interfere with the free market with regard to the hours which workers laboured, but were willing to interfere in matters concerning the dispensing of poor relief.

These issues linked working class politics to the paternalistic principles of Conservatism and Toryism. It was the inability of a substantial section of the working class of the north-west to harmoniously adjust to changing industrial and social conditions which played a large part in explaining their receptivity to paternalist theory. But some were also attracted to the security of an ordered, if hierarchical, social order, they were repelled by the *laissez-faire* implications of an industrial society, apparently free but very precarious. Some members of the working class who were attracted to Conservatism may have done so out of a sense of social deference, to rank or those of a superior social station. But the support given, and given freely, becomes more meaningful when seen in the light of issues which the Conservatives of the north-west championed. This was not the politics of influence which Nossiter describes in the north-east but more the politics of conditioned opinion emanating from the social and political environment working people actually existed in during the 1830s, '40s and '50s. What developed in these years was a mutuality of interests between traditionalistic Conservatives and a section of the working class. It was mediated theoretically by a re-working of Tory paternalism and a practical application in the struggle surrounding issues directly affecting working people, and vociferously agitated by the Tory-Radicals such as Oastler and Stephens. The importance, therefore, of the transformation of the support given to Conservatism in the north-west should not be gauged merely by the numerical strength or functions of the local operative associations. These were important, but were probably only the tip of much deeper support among working people. The electoral success which the Conservatives had in the mill towns of the north-west by capturing large sections of the working-class vote in later 1860s and 1870s had a long gestation period, dating back to the political leadership and socialisation which were installed in mid-1830s, both practically and theoretically.

A clear distinction was being made in the battle for working-class political support between

89 See below the case studies of Blackburn and Bolton.

90 Oastler made no secret of his attachment to Toryism, see, for example, *Manchester Guardian*, 24 September 1836, or the Butterworth Mss, Oldham Reference Library, 29 November 1837, or C. Driver, *Richard Oastler, Life of a Radical*, (New York, 1948).

middle-class Liberalism, inspired by *laissez-faire* individualism, and traditionalist Conservatives, influenced by a re-asserting of paternalistic values.[91] North-west Conservatives criticised liberalism because it appeared to assert unlimited progress and simplified human nature contrary to all religious and historical evidence. Tory theorists, (such as Samuel Taylor Coleridge), maintained human nature was not a product of economic self-interest. Man was a complex ethical social being, dependent in his direction on the communal guidance of family, church, society and, in the 1830s, the proselytizing efforts of the political party. Progress was limited by the traditions of the past and by providential design. This position was taken up by traditionalistic Conservatives against the extreme Radicals just as forcefully as it was against the progressive Liberals. In 1839 the Chartists invaded Blackburn parish church, the reply of the vicar serves as an illustration:

> The doctrine of equal right to property … amounts to nothing less than this: You are first to covet, next to demand, and then, if your demands be not conceded, you are directed to take by violence your neighbours goods… You have many excuses my friends, [but] … no equality of property can exist so long as God endows man unequally with gifts mental and personal? And is it not clear, that, if all were made equal in respect of property at some imaginary point in time, they could not … remain equal for a single week?[92]

On the other hand those with wealth had a responsibility for those less fortunate and this was of great significance for the Conservatives of the north-west. As early as 1833, the founder of the South Lancashire Conservative Association, William Hulton, exemplified their position. He said,

> Conservatives had a duty to perform on behalf of the poor which they ought never to forget: and no man deserved the epithet of a true Conservative who did not to the utmost of his power listen to the wants and relieve the sufferings of the poor. I call for a toast to the operatives of England, and may every Conservative show them… they hold them in the same degree of heartfelt esteem as they entertain for the aristocracy.[93]

The importance of the issues such as factory reform, poor relief, or public health for Conservatives in the north-west was that they fitted their theories of paternalism, but, as important, that they also revealed they were not adverse to the reality of change. They argued that change had to be guided by a systematic policy, unless this was so change would not be ameliorative. They realized local action could not meet national problems effectively and insisted that Parliament must intervene to ensure the strong did not prosper at the expense of the weak.[94] The rapidly changing conditions of life in the industrial north-west dismayed many Conservatives almost as much as they did the working class. But for Conservatives they did so because they saw urban life compounding the natural weaknesses of men: their irrationality, helplessness and dependence. To combat these conditions Conservative reformers in the north-west became almost like missionaries to the lower classes, preaching a millennium rooted in social harmony. This mission was all but evangelical, comprising of both

---

91 For example see, T. M. Kemnitz and F. Jacques, 'J. R. Stephens and the Chartist Movement', in *The International Review of Social History*, 19, (1974), or J. Seed, 'Unitarianism, Political Economy and the Antinomies of Liberal Culture in Manchester. 1830-1850', in *Social History*, 7, 1, (1982), J. F. Glaser, 'English Nonconformity and the Decline of Liberalism', in *American Historical Review*, 63, 2, (1958).

92 Rev. T. D. Whittaker, 'A Sermon preached to the Chartists at the Blackburn Parish Church', (London, 1839) pp. 19-20.

93 *Preston Pilot*, 31 August 1833. For more on aspects of Tory paternalism see, D. Roberts, 'Tory Paternalism and Social Reform in Early Victorian England', in *The American Historical Review*, 63, 2, (1958), W. O. Aydolotte, 'Conservative and Radical Interpretations of Early Victorian Social Legislation', in *Victorian Studies*, (December 1967), R. Kirk, *The Conservative Mind*, (London, 1954).

94 See the speech given at Bolton by W. B. Ferrand in *Bolton Chronicle*, 23 December 1843.

Anglicans and Wesleyan Methodists, whose moral and political code came largely from their religious conscience. Unable to accept a morality glorifying individual success instead of social harmony, they emphasized Burke's dictum that social status and social responsibilities were inseparable. In efforts to persuade the working class, these Conservatives and Radical Tories combined Conservatism with social welfare. Richard Oastler echoed the banner of the Leeds Operative Conservative Association, "The Altar, the Throne and the Cottage," with his own heading above the weekly Fleet Papers of "Property has its duties as well as its Rights". He was accepted by many working class people as the 'Factory King', but he denied the need for political change in parliamentary representation. This was similarly unacceptable to many Conservatives in the 1830s and early 1840s, but by the end of the 1840s this position too was changing. In the early 1850s the former Conservative Home Secretary Sir James Graham, said in Parliament that

> The operation and object of the Bill of 1832 was to transfer power to the middle classes. But it is a mistake to hold that the humbler classes also do not take a real and deep interest in elections... Speaking in a strictly Conservative sense, I am convinced that it is infinitely more prudent to make timely concessions to reasonable demands than obstinately to resist them. The demands of the working class for the franchise are reasonable, and can no longer safely be refused.[95]

In the north-west at least the basis of this change of attitude was primarily caused by changes in political culture, of attitudes to political institutions and situations. Here the politics of opinion in relation to a wide range of issues, political parties, and pressure groupings was the important engine of social and political change. This fits Nossiter's definition of 'opinion' based politics and more besides. The 1830s and '40s saw sections of the working class begin to support Conservatism because that party positioned itself, especially locally, in such a way that working class issues could be presented as meaningful without betraying the fundamental tenets of Conservatism. In this chapter we have seen that these were questions which were addressed to working people and made attractive to them in a class sense and were beneficial to them as a class. It was this cultivation of working class opinions coupled with a sense of their insecurity and loss of independence in the industrialized world that began to attract working class support. So far only the role of issues has been discussed, not the issues themselves, in the light of increasing working class support for Conservatism after 1832. These will be addressed in the following chapters, particularly how they related to the changing political culture of the north-west region. The intention now is to examine Operative Conservatism comparatively over several different parts of the region, looking also at the politics of the elites, especially to questions and issues affecting the working class.

---

95   C. S. Parker, *The Life of Sir James Graham*, Vol. II, (London, 1907) p. 370.

5

Operative Conservatism and Local Political Developments: Three case studies

The aim of the next two chapters is to bring operative Conservatism and political change into crisper focus. This will be done by comparing and contrasting their impact not only on the Conservative party and the working class in different parts of the north-west but also in relation to some of the issues we looked at in the last chapter. Parliamentary and municipal politics will be discussed, as will the vital question of local political leadership. The towns of Chester, Clitheroe and Lancaster will be examined briefly, and in more depth the town of Preston with its old Scot and Lot franchise. Chapter six will focus on developments in the newly enfranchised towns of Blackburn and Bolton. We need to discover the amount of working class involvement not only in Operative Conservatism but also their involvement in the respective towns' politics. Naturally, the region had its variations: economic, political and social, and these variations must be examined to serve as a context to the levels of support working people gave to Conservatism.

A core theme is the changing political attitudes within the region, for this highlights a changing political culture, especially with regard to the working class. Political culture is a somewhat contrived term to describe political attitudes held by a society, both to political principles and institutions and also the wider society in which these principles and institutions operate and affect change. This is why the political party is interesting and useful to the historian and political scientist, for it is both an institution and a vehicle which disseminates and mirrors political principles. Earlier it was noted that in the north-west before 1832, the political elites were either uninterested in the working class or on occasions were downright hostile. In their turn, the great majority of the working classes were either hostile to Conservatism or apathetic. We have seen that after 1832 attitudes began to change on both sides. The Conservatives attempted to cultivate a sense of traditionalism and paternalism, extolling the virtues of the prescriptive constitution, highlighting the dangers of unwanted and unrequired progressive reforms. Reforms, which, once enacted, would directly affect the lives of many working people. They called on a section of the working class to support the Conservative Party both as an institution that would represent the interests of working people, and as a set of comfortable and safe traditionalistic principles. In the past the Conservative Whigs and Tories called on the loyalties of working people as a reserve army, to be used to defeat the extreme Jacobins and Radicals and then discarded. However, this does appear to have discouraged thousands of working people after 1832 from joining the party as fully-fledged members and thousands more from giving their support.

The intention now is to compare and contrast the levels of support and the political attitudes of working people in different parts of the region in relation to the local political elites. The main focus of the discussion will centre mainly on the Conservatives, but at times, in the case of Lancaster, the Liberal responses will also be examined. This is because at Lancaster, compared to other parts of the region where the Conservatives took the political lead, it was the Liberals who were the main instigators of political change involving the working class. Essentially the region may be broken down into three categories of political locality. Firstly, the traditional market and county towns; secondly, the old type of borough with an open franchise, both before and after 1832; and thirdly, the post-1832 type of borough, operating with a restrictive franchise. The method used here is both diachronic and synchronic. The former in order to compare and contrast the various political idioms occurring in the north-west across time and the latter to facilitate the examination of divergent socio/political factors operating at the same point in time but in different parts of the region. We begin by looking at the market and county towns of the region, examining developments in Clitheroe and Chester but concentrating most of the detailed description on the town of Lancaster.

The Market and County Towns

A feature of politics that is of concern to this study is that various aggregations of interests became increasingly important after 1832. As noted earlier, this was of major concern to both Whigs and Tories during the reform crisis itself and in the years that followed. Most obvious amongst the various assemblages of interests was that of class. This was by no means as determined a phenomenon as some social scientists maintain. In the politics of the north-west, working class interests did not always find expression in the widespread support of radicalism, although there were of course examples when they did, as during the reform crisis or the early Chartist years when radicalism gained a mass working class following. But it could be argued that even among Chartists there were strongly traditionalistic sentiments to be found.

In the decades following the 1832 Act, the politically salient interests of many people of varying social standing were often linked to their economic activity and that of their locality. Thus we see traditionalistic Conservatives highly suspicious of the effects of industrialism, especially if the industrialists happened to be Liberals. Conversely, the progressives ridiculed the yokel mentality of the agricultural lobby. It is worthwhile to pursue the line of enquiry that in regional politics, the political character of a locality (in terms of leadership, the wielding of power, and the call for, and giving of support) can be examined to a greater or lesser degree by the prevalent economic activity. Therefore, when discussing regional variations of politics the specific social and economic character of a locality needs to be considered, especially if they contribute to the fashioning of local political attitudes.

Nineteenth-century market and county towns were typically non-industrial. But this did not mean that their economies were based solely on servicing agriculture. There were some towns in the nineteenth century whose economic existence was based largely on the weekday markets and the fortnightly auctions and the provision of the attendant facilities needed in an agricultural region. But these tended to be in the smaller type of market town situated largely in predominantly agricultural areas. Those market and county towns with populations of over 2,000 persons tended to have a mixed economy. This was certainly so in Lancaster, Clitheroe and Chester. None could be considered large, even by early nineteenth century standards. Yet Chester, with nearly 28,000 in 1851, was of substantial size. The population of Lancaster in 1821 was 10,144, but by 1851 it had risen to 16,168, a rise of some 58 per cent, which, although large in itself, was not as rapid as elsewhere in a region more dependent on the factories and industrial capitalism. Clitheroe, on the fringe of industrial east Lancashire, grew more rapidly. Its population in 1821 was 3,213 and in 1851, 7,244, a rise of over 125 per cent. A reason for the difference was that Clitheroe began to attract industrial manufacturing much earlier and in greater volume than its larger northern neighbour.

Lancaster had a truly mixed economic base by the mid-nineteenth century. It enjoyed mercantile commerce thanks to Glasson on the Lune estuary and the rapidly growing port of Barrow to its north. Its extensive county prison and hospital coupled with the regular Assizes and quarter sessions made Lancaster a major administrative centre. The town was also the main market centre of the area with all the services noted above and it possessed some manufacturing industry. Lancaster was known for the manufacturing of furniture and upholstery, sail cloths and heavy cotton and worsted yarn, but also had a small silk weaving factory. By the 1830s there were five cotton factories producing finished cloth, all equipped with power looms. However, although the trend throughout Lancashire was of an expanding cotton industry during the early Victorian period, there were pockets of the north-west region where the industry did not flourish. Such was the case with Lancaster, and equally so at Chester. Although the industry did not flourish in Lancaster this does not mean it was of no importance to the town's social and economic foundation. At Lancaster in 1851, out of a total population of 16,168 there were 1,279 engaged in the manufacture of cotton goods, amounting to just over 11 per cent of the population.[1] Lancaster had a mixed economic infrastructure with no single dominant interest, be it manufacture or agriculture which in turn was able to politically dominate the rest by its sheer size and local importance.[2] This mixture of influences greatly assisted the maintenance of traditional forms of political behaviour several decades after 1832 in ways that were not as evident in more industrially developed areas.

Clitheroe was traditionally a market town that developed a domestic textile industry in the seventeenth century. Its political importance was like Lancaster and Chester, it held the pre-1832 franchise and retained one of its seats after the first Reform Act. The census of 1851 indicates that Clitheroe remained essentially a market town despite some limited industrialisation. The figures demonstrate that agricultural employment was a vital element in Clitheroe's economy. Over 35 per cent were classified as agricultural workers, compared to 30 per cent working in textiles.[3] So, again as with Lancaster, in Clitheroe no single economic interest was dominant. This meant that, unlike Preston or Wigan or the new boroughs, in Clitheroe there were no substantial blocks of politically powerful manufacturing elites emerging to press their interests.

Chester in the far south of the region was, by 1851, even more bereft of large-scale industrialization. There was no textile manufacturing, no metal industry and no coal mining. For males the largest employer in a total population of 27,766 was the land, the next largest being the railways.[4] Most women worked in domestic service, with 3,888 described as wives "with no recorded occupation." Chester seems to have been stifled of economic development for opposite reasons to that of Lancaster. In the case of the latter it was its relative remoteness from the great port of Liverpool, in the case of Chester it was its close proximity. As one contemporary put it, Chester was "fed, in great part from the crumbs which fall from Liverpool's table ... being of little importance in comparison with the latter great city."[5] Chester did, however, retain its two-member parliamentary status but again conducted its political affairs in much the same way as in the pre-reform period.

---

1   Parliamentary Papers, Census for 1851.

2   For more on the economic development of Lancaster see P. J. Gooderson, 'The Social and Economic development of Lancaster, 1780-1914', Ph.D. thesis, University of Lancaster, (1975), or D. M. Clark, 'The Economic and Social Geography of Rural Longsdale', M.A. thesis, University of Liverpool, (1968).

3   Census for 1851.

4   Ibid. For a useful contrast with economic and social developments in Chester with York, a town of comparative size at this time, see, J. A. Armstrong, *Stability and Change in an English County Town*, (London, 1974).

5   Sir G. Head, *A Tour Throughout the Manufacturing Districts of England*, (London, 1835, reprint 1968), pp. 59-60.

Until the later 1840s the dominant interest was the land and, after this time, the railways. But this latter interest did not reign long in Chester given the growth of the railway town of Crewe some 12 miles to the south-east in the 1850s.

The first point of contrast with many other parts of the region is that the county and market towns retained their traditional economic framework and were not greatly affected by the consolidation of industrial capitalism taking place nearby. Similarly the towns attempted to maintain the old types of political activity. Before 1831 all three were at various times nomination seats, or boroughs under the influence of a dominant patron. One of Lancaster's seats was, in pre-Reform days, under the influence of those great collectors of boroughs, the Lowthers, both of Chester's seats were firmly under the control of the Earl of Grosvenor and one of Clitheroe's was the property of the Earl of Brownlow, and the other, Viscount Curzon.[6] In the old boroughs (where Nossiter's idioms could be relevant) a multiplicity of politico/economic interests developed alongside an ideology of political reform. However, due to a heightened sense of political respectability after 1832, overt methods of venality and corruption could be safely engaged in or tolerated. There were of course examples of robust confrontations between political rivals as at Preston in 1837 or Wigan in 1832 and 1835, but this type of partisanship indicated the heightened interest in party politics and what the various candidates stood for. Elements of working class support could still be gained through treats, and non-elector and elector intimidation and violence undoubtedly existed, especially in closely contested boroughs, but this does not preclude the possibility of opinion-based politics existing in such places. An alternative to opinion based politics was the politics of influence in places where there was little excitement, or indeed contests. In such places the old system held out the longest. If electors and non-electors had little opportunity to exercise their rights because national leaders and local elites felt the contest useless or deals had been pre-arranged, there was little chance of opinions being formed or political conscience being raised.

At Chester this certainly was the case. Here the grip of the Whig/Liberal Grosvenor family was virtually total. The family owned extensive lands and property in and around Chester and the deference extended to the family by the local population verged on idolatry. Between 1832 and 1859 the Whig/Liberals totally dominated Chester's two seats. It was one of the few places in England where no Operative Conservative Association existed, nor, indeed, a branch of the North Cheshire Conservative Association. Of the twelve parliamentary elections called at Chester between 1832 and 1859, seven were unopposed by the Conservatives and in the rest the Conservative vote was derisory, indeed, up until the 1880s, Chester remained firmly in the grasp of the Liberals.[7] This was also true of local politics, with the Conservatives never gaining more than one-third of the seats on the borough council between 1836 (the year of the town's incorporation under the terms of the Municipal Reform Act) and 1860. If modern politics can be defined as the open vying for power by opposing political groupings, in which policies and opinions are exchanged and discussed with a view to implementation, then Chester remained firmly attached to a traditionalistic and decidedly antiquated form. Members of the working classes involved in political developments between the 1830s and the 1860s followed the two established parties, with the overwhelming majority falling in with the Whig/Liberals. There was very little working-class radical activity. The few radicals that existed

---

6   A. Aspinall and E. Anthony Smith (eds.) *English Historical Documents*, Vol. IX, (London, 1971), pp. 224-36.

7   In 1832, out of an electorate of 2,088, the Conservatives polled 499 compared to the two Whigs, 1,169 and 1,053 respectively. In 1837 the Conservative vote had fallen to 352. With the split in the Conservative party in 1846 and the growth of protectionist reaction under Lord Derby, the Conservative vote began to climb; 645 at a by-election in 1850 and 1,110 in 1859, the only occasion a Conservative won a seat at Chester.

were drawn exclusively from the small artisans made up predominately of tailors and shoemakers. At Chester, therefore, there is little evidence of political development in which political change transformed the functions of political groups after 1832, or of the growing importance of social and economic sectional interest. Indeed, Chester would be an ideal type of case study for those historians supporting the continuity thesis (that little changed immediately after 1832) argued by O'Gorman, Norman Gash or H. J. Hanham.

If the market and county town of Chester continued to be dominated by the Whig/Liberals in the decades after as well as before 1832 then the same was essentially true of Clitheroe. Before 1832 Clitheroe possessed two parliamentary seats, both under nomination. After 1832 nomination ended at Clitheroe and it was stripped of one of its seats. The parliamentary boundary, however, was increased to include the neighbouring town of Whalley and the small villages on its parish borders. This meant that its parliamentary size in square miles increased from 3.6 to 25.3 after 1832, with the result that more electors involved in agriculture, who formerly held the freeholder county franchise, were brought into the borough.[8] This should have been advantageous to the Conservatives as the party of the landed interest. However, in 1830s north-east Lancashire this was not the case. In fact, in these years the local Radical squire, John Fort, dominated the politics of Clitheroe. This anomaly suggests that Fort and the radicals were either guilty of corruption, playing on former loyalties or exerting some kind of influence. The answer probably lies in a combination of all three possibilities. The Conservatives certainly believed that Fort was using dubious tactics. Writing in 1840, a Conservative summed up the position:

> ... since the period when the Reform mania raged and a temporary frenzy took men's judgement by storm, the borough of Clitheroe has been in the hands of the Whig radicals. Various attempts have been made to rescue it from this degradation; but heretofore such attempts have failed. We will not enquire into the causes of those failures — some of them may have been corrupt and wicked, and some of them the result of erroneous political views and delusive hopes.[9]

Much of Fort's support came from the lower middle class shopkeepers and small manufacturers within Clitheroe town. The political character of the majority of this group was radical reformist, a trait that was peculiar to this part of east Lancashire from the 1830s until the later 1850s. Indeed the borough continued to return Liberal members until 1868 when, like the majority of the Lancashire mill towns, it turned Conservative.

Although the parliamentary boundaries were widened after 1832, the constituency remained small: 306 electors before 1832 and 438 in 1865. After the second Reform Act the electorate rose to 1,595, and another member of the local gentry was returned, this time as a Conservative. This suggests that at Clitheroe, like Chester, local influence held sway. The type of radicalism evident at Clitheroe was moderate; Fort and his successor, Wilson were both 'advanced' Liberals, which usually meant they were in favour of a slight extension of the franchise, the secret ballot, but no more. This was true of these two members. At Chester no issues which directly affected working people appeared to play any part in swaying local opinion. Working-class concerns manifested themselves at Clitheroe around the question of the county police, imposition of the New Poor Law and some Chartist agitation up to 1843. After this date little appears with reference to Clitheroe either in the

---

8   Parliamentary Papers, Vol. 23 (1859), p. 121.
9   *Blackburn Standard*, 19 August 1840.

Northern Star, or the National Convention Minutes. Although there was some working-class radical activity, it sheds little light on how many were politically active or apathetic. What is clear is that the majority of working people who expressed any political sentiments during the 1830s supported the Liberals and radicals. Although there was, by 1841, a well-established local Conservative Association dominated, as in other parts of Lancashire, by the local gentry and bourgeoisie, there was no operative branch in the district. By 1837, however, there was an Operative Reform Association, suggesting that the Liberals held the advantage.

By 1841 the controversies aroused by the County Police Act and the New Poor Law saw a shift in local working class political alignments. Many working people saw the County Police Act as a further attempt by the Whig/Liberals to impose centralised control and discipline.[10] It was seen as an intrusion on working-class recreations and pastimes, but further it was viewed as imposing vigorous form of state coercion in issues that impinged directly on working class life. In situations such as strike control and picketing, the use of blackleg labour, public displays of popular grievances, the Poor Law and the Factory Question were all areas which the working class rightly felt the new police would be instrumental in curtailing expressions of discontent.[11] The new police were proof that the Whig/Liberals had no faith in the ability of working people, or indeed the industrial districts, to regulate or govern themselves. In this sense it was seen as an attack on traditional or customary working class liberties, as one speaker said at a meeting called at Blackburn in 1841 to throw out the county police, "... In the matter of the police the people had no say whatsoever: not even a negative voice... At present all self-government was taken out of the hands of the people ... the people ought to choose their own officers."[12] Oastler accused the county police of being a "frenchified gens d'armie in order ... to creep into the cradle of the babes and poison them with gas."[13]

For Radical Tories like Oastler and Stephens the new police was another example of the Whigs pandering to the will of Liberal manufacturers. Local Conservatives in positions of power, however, kept quiet whilst offering tacit support by doing little against working people who demonstrated their anger. They accused the Liberals of using the issue to gain political control of the local Police Commissions and complaining over the increased cost to the county rate.[14] Nationally the Conservatives opposed the new Police Act much on the same lines as in the localities, stressing the measure was used by the Whigs to find jobs and places for their supporters.[15] In the area around Clitheroe the most alarming incidents took place at neighbouring Colne, where the issue rumbled on from April to August 1840. Here the anger of working people was directed at a local Liberal solicitor named Bolton who, as well as being a vociferous anti-Chartist, was chiefly responsible for bringing the new police into the area. The disturbances were extremely violent and resulted in the death of a special constable, but were directed solely at the police. When the army was called in to quell the troubles they found the town at peace, indeed they were cheered as they marched through the streets. As one witness reported, "These fellows know how to behave themselves, but the police do not."[16]

10 For more on the Police Act and its relevance in the north-west see F. C. Mather, *Public Order in the Age of the Chartists*, (Manchester, 1959), E. C. Midwinter, *Social Administration in Lancashire, 1830-1860*, Robert D. Storch, 'The Plague of Blue Locusts: Police Reform and Popular Resistance in Northern England, 1840-1857', in *International Review of Social History*, 20, I, (1975).

11 The First Report, Royal Commission on Constabulary Force, *Parliamentary Papers*, Vol. XIX, (1839), pp. 61-92.

12 *Blackburn Standard*, 6 January 1840.

13 *Northern Star*, 2 March 1839.

14 *Blackburn Standard*, 6 January 1841, *Manchester Guardian*, 3 June 1840, 12 August 1840.

15 British Library, Peel Papers, Ad. Mss. 40427, f 103, Granville Somerset to Peel , undated 1839.

16 *Leeds Times*, 2 May 1840.

The New Poor Law was commonly viewed like the county police, as yet more interference by the central state in the lives of working people, on this occasion in the provision of essential welfare. The actual imposition and the psychological impact it had on the minds of the working class should not be underestimated. Be they urban industrial workers or agricultural labourers, in the opinion of working people the New Poor Law was an attack on their traditional rights to public welfare at periods of most acute need. At Clitheroe the implementation of the New Poor Law in 1837 gave the local Conservatives the opportunity to mount a campaign on an issue which affected the majority of working people. Clitheroe was a large Union geographically, though small in terms of population. In 1841 it numbered only 23,000 people but in area covered some 130,000 acres. The first elected Board at Clitheroe comprised of 35 Guardians, representing 33 townships. The Liberals were confident of success on the basis that the old relief system had been maintained and promised that, regardless of the rumours of harsh measures included in the Act, the poor of Clitheroe would be provided for as in the past.[17] As stated above, Clitheroe was rare in that it was primarily a rural constituency returning to parliament a succession of progressive Liberals, essentially on the basis of the concentration of its industrial population inside the town itself. However, after 1837, even before the actual imposition of the New Poor Law, the situation began to change. In that year the Conservatives won overall control of the Board of Guardians, a position they held until 1848. The township of Clitheroe however, still remained in the hands of the Liberals. This suggests, given the furore that the issue provoked among working people, that the Liberals of Clitheroe town were relatively moderate, but in the outlying parish the Conservatives successfully exploited the issue. As to the Factory Question, that other great working class issue of the 1830s in the north-west, Clitheroe, unlike other parts of the region, was relatively quiet. The earliest sign of any activity came in 1849 and then died away quickly.[18]

In August 1840 the Conservatives of Clitheroe were given an added boost when they gained Edward Cardwell as a prospective candidate. Cardwell was a rising star of the sober-minded bright young men that Sir Robert Peel occasionally bestowed his political blessings. Cardwell was in several ways an ideal candidate. Although his family now resided in Liverpool, they were originally from east Lancashire; they had links with the cotton trade but were now merchants. Cardwell was a young London barrister with a first from Oxford, and came to Clitheroe with the full backing of the Carlton. On 13 August the Clitheroe Conservative Association held a festival to welcome Cardwell. In his speech Cardwell exhibited the classic sentiments of Peelite Conservatism, saying that agriculture and commerce were "inseparably intertwined" and should be made to work in harmony.[19] In the 1841 election Matthew Wilson, a prominent Leeds Liberal, narrowly defeated Cardwell by five votes. In the ensuing petition Wilson was unseated on counts of treating and bribery, and for the first time the Conservatives secured Clitheroe. Cardwell did not stay long however. In 1847 he became the member for Liverpool, and, in the resulting turmoil of the Peelite split, the Conservatives of Clitheroe could find no candidate to bridge the gap between the Peelite and Protectionist wings. Clitheroe was a market town operating very much in the pre-1832 manner. In Clitheroe there were few working class electors, the vast majority of voters coming from the small manufacturers and shopkeepers who were Whig before 1832 and Liberals in the years which followed. Working class pressure was minimal, apart from the implementation of the Whig reforms in the areas of welfare and policing, which, for a brief moment, offered the Conservatives hope. Most of the town's

---

17 *Blackburn Standard*, 4 April 1837.

18 This was a branch of the Fielden Society in 1849, and eventually by 1853 became a branch of the Labour League of Lancashire, Yorkshire and Cheshire.

19 *Blackburn Standard*, 19 August 1840.

manufacturers were Liberal and the absence of the extreme radicals, apart from a flirtation with Chartism in 1839 and 1841, suggests that Clitheroe's working class were either Liberal or politically apathetic. However, a faint trend is appearing. In both Chester and Clitheroe the traditional political practices, methods of selection, corrupt practices, absence of organized pressure groups, and election rituals seem to have been maintained after 1832. This broadly conforms to Nossiter's concepts of influence and market politics in these market and county towns. But before attempting a deeper analysis and appraisal a fuller description of events in Lancaster needs to be considered.

Developments in Lancaster

As was noted above, Lancaster was also a mixed economy with no single dominant interest able to impose its political will. Until the 1820s the town returned a Tory and a Whig, essentially under the influence (but not the direct nomination) of the Earls of Longsdale and Derby respectively. The tendency in the 1820s, however, was for this moderate form of influence to disappear. After the first Reform Act Lancaster returned its MPs free of aristocratic influence. Indeed, after the 1820s none of the three families involved previously in Lancaster politics, the Lowthers, Stanleys and the Dukes of Hamilton, maintained their political links.[20] Even before 1832, therefore, older forms of aristocratic influence were in decline at Lancaster. In fact, the first two contests called under the terms of the 1832 Act returned members unopposed, indeed the Conservative Thomas Greene and the Whig Patrick Stewart were the sitting members from the pre-Reform era.

National issues did not play a great part in Lancaster's politics, and local questions, such as the need for Parliamentary Acts of Improvement, did not impact in parliamentary contests. This indicates some form of political control was operational. There were various reasons why the two aspects of political activity could be so easily separated. These included the maintenance of the older forms of political culture, patterns of recruitment, the roles of the local political leaders in the Corporation, the use of local patronage, control by the elites of the political agenda and the activities of the local opinion formers. Throughout the region many of these features will figure in the analysis below. The point to note, however, is when a comparison is made between the market/county towns and the new boroughs, the most striking feature is how tight controls were in the former with regard to opinions and issues. But in the latter, especially in the 1830s and '40s, how wide and various the crossover of local and national opinions appear and, further, how this ranged across a wide section of social classes. More will be said of this in due course but it is worth stressing here that differing types of political culture were developing in different localities. In the market and county towns older forms of recruitment and attitudes to politics were maintained longer compared to those localities where dynamic and new social, economic and political forces shaped political activities. In Lancaster much of the political focus of its population was centred on the town council and the Improvement Commission, this was because before 1832 parliamentary contests were rare and continued to be so immediately after. The main economic and social interest was that of the small manufacturer and shopkeeper, what might be conveniently termed the tradesman's interest. This centred largely on either local manufactured goods or agricultural produce, with its chief customers being, in addition to the local population, the gentry and professionals attending the local Assize and the magistrates' sessions. Such long-term patterns of patronage made this group extremely rigid in either their Whiggery or their Toryism. It also meant that retention of the Lancaster bi-annual Assizes and the

---

20 Aspinall and Smith, *English Historical Documents*, Vol. IX, pp. 224-37.

Quarter Sessions was of vital economic importance to the traders as well as to the town's status. In the 1830s the retention of the Assize became an important issue between a minority group of radicals and the majority of conservatives. The former advocated the removal of the Assize in order to break the stronghold of the Tory/Whig elites in the Council, and the latter proposing its retention at all costs in order to maintain the town's status and their own political position. It has been noted that in the 1830s and '40s there were few centres of factory industry in Lancaster, which meant that a strong proletarian interest bloc did not exist, either in terms of numbers or in the articulation of an alternative set of political interests. This trend was reinforced both by the dominance of the tradesman's interest, and the proximity of Lancaster Castle, with the prison acting as a visible deterrent to potential disturbers of the political peace.

One indicator which political scientists have focused on in determining political culture is political recruitment. Just who is being recruited into decision-making positions and into the political sphere generally, to a significant extent determines the scope and interest orientation of politics. In Lancaster, both before the Municipal Reform Act of 1835 and after, political recruitment came not through the conduit of the political party, which elsewhere was a vital agency of recruitment, but through the local corporation, and, as was the case in the pre-Reform period, through the local magistracy. Before 1835 the corporation was a typically exclusive body. It consisted of a Mayor, seven aldermen, twelve capital burgesses and twelve common councilmen. The Mayor and capital burgesses were elected from within the council. The common councilmen were chosen again by themselves from a list of the free burgesses. The capital burgesses and the common council were each headed by a bailiff and the two together with the financial officers of the corporation, formed the central core of the town's decision-makers. The council was almost totally dominated by the local elite. In 1831 and 1832, for example, of the fourteen common councilmen who sat at various times, there were four members of the gentry, four manufacturers, four attorneys, one doctor and one tradesman. The exclusive nature of the council was again reflected in the social composition of its entrants. Between 1819 and 1835, of a total of 48 entrants, only 16 were the sons of non-freemen, and the majority of these were members of the professions recently arrived in the town.[21]

The reformers of Lancaster, led by the free-trader John Greg, showed their innate conservatism by their limited demands during the Assize issue. Their chief point was that the corporation (and hence the local government of the town) was essentially rotten and, given the exclusive nature of its composition and patterns of election and recruitment, they were correct. The case attracted the attention of Henry Brougham as early as 1817 who said the council possessed a "dangerous congregating spirit."[22] He called for the election of the council by the body of the town's freemen, and the reformers stuck to this limited end throughout the whole of the campaign that ended with the Municipal Reform Act of 1835. It was limited, in direct contrast to other parts of the region, in the sense that it stopped short of household suffrage or a low property qualification that radicals in most other north-western towns were claiming.[23] The reformers then attempted to organize the freemen voters at large but with little success. The Tory arguments that the town would lose its Assize privileges, parliamentary rights and status swayed the lower middle class service sector. There is little evidence of any working class involvement in the issue. It was one between the two established political groupings; the Tory majority and the Whig/Radical minority. Indeed, there was little radical

21   P. J. Gooderson, 'A Social and Economic History of Lancaster', Ph.D., University of Lancaster, (1975).

22   T. Johns, *An Address to the Freemen of Lancaster on the Subject of their Charter*, (Lancaster, 1817), p. 7.

23   See for example *Blackburn Mail*, 8 September 1826, or *Preston Chronicle*, 24 November 1832.

working class activity throughout the period compared to the rest of the north-west region. Widespread displays of disaffection among the working class occurring elsewhere had little affect among their counterparts in Lancaster.

During the reform crisis the two traditional groupings petitioned parliament and the King, the Tories against parliamentary reform and the Radicals in favour. Neither group thought it necessary to give any political importance to the working class because the working class displayed few signs of interest, and the vast majority were not freemen.[24] This was certainly so in respect of the semi- and unskilled of the working class. Some artisans may have been freemen but this factor again militates against widespread working class political activism in Lancaster. Elsewhere much of the impetus for early working class involvement in politics came from disaffected craft workers like handloom weavers and the skilled artisans.[25] These groups offered the much-needed leadership and the initial articulation of political aims and objectives, whether through early attempts at trade unionism or the simple explanation of political realities. The fact that in Lancaster the artisans may already have been freemen and yet did nothing suggests that they were under the influence of the two main political groupings: the Tory Corporation or the Whig reformers.[26] Indeed, during the reform elections, there was no working-class activity whatsoever.[27] Similarly, there was no trades union organization, only Friendly Societies who were strictly non-political.

After 1832, throughout most of the north-west, the working class became increasingly disillusioned and disaffected with the Reform Act and its results, but the working class of Lancaster were, for the most part, quiescent. Even during the many slumps in business cycles in the 1830s the working class did not demonstrate any grievances. Whatever controls were operating were effective. Little is known of their church attendance but a factor, which could explain their inherent respectability, was the high working-class membership in the Temperance Movement. In 1835 this was put at 1,332 in the Temperance Association,[28] and 2,000 in the draconian Total Abstinence Association.[29] The acquiescence of the working classes to the authorities and elites of Lancaster was rewarded by the retention of Tory paternalism.[30] The Conservatives announced that it was they who were more concerned for "comfort and happiness of the people than the Whigs or Radicals", in Lancaster this meant that the people were expected to confine themselves to their "proper sphere and give confidence to the possessors of property." If they did not, the *Lancaster Gazette* warned, "Disquiet on the part of the people would lead to nothing short of inevitable misery, confusion and destruction affecting the lower classes first of all."[31] However, both public and private charity was relatively adequate for the needs of the poor during times of industrial recession; the poor were given free access to the large Lancaster Dispensary and Lying-in Hospital, two charity schools were

---

24 Gooderson, *op. cit.*, or Armstrong, *op. cit.*, for the similar situation existing at York at this time.

25 I. Protheroe, *Artisans and Politics in Early Nineteenth-century London*, (Folkstone, 1979), D. Bythall, *The Hand Loom Weavers*, (Cambridge, 1969), E. P. Thompson, *The Making of the English Working Class*, (Harmondsworth, 1978 ed.).

26 Gooderson, *op. cit.*, p. 123.

27 *Lancaster Herald*, 1 April 1831.

28 *Lancaster Gazette*, 31 January 1835. Nor can these relatively high abstinence figures be attributed to the work of any particular nonconformist group. There were a mere 240 Methodists in the town in 1839, (Returns of the Lancashire Wesleyan Methodists, 1839, Lancaster Reference Library), nor again were the numbers particularly high in 1850, see *Parliamentary Papers*, Census Returns.

29 *Lancaster Gazette*, 5 September 1835.

30 Gooderson, *op. cit.*, p. 158.

31 *Lancaster Gazette*, 1 August 1835.

initiated, as well as Sunday Schools and several alms houses built.[32] The New Poor Law was introduced into Lancaster without much protest, the situation remaining effectively unchanged. In the winter of 1840, for example, outdoor relief was given without constraint to 720 families.[33] Displays of paternalism continued, as at Christmas, 1841, when some 8,000 people were entertained at a "Special Poor Dinner" at which 100 sheep were consumed at a cost of £162. Middle-class Conservatives voiced their disapproval of the New Poor Law on the grounds that it was yet another example of Liberal rationalism.[34] But that is all they did. The only attempt at any mobilisation came in 1841, when thirty people petitioned over the 'unconstitutional' centralising powers of the Commissioners.[35]

The arrival of the county police aroused a brief display of aggression among working people. At Lancaster races in July 1840, as the county police dispersed those enjoying the festivities the crowd turned on the officers referring to them as 'bloody rurals', 'blue bottles', 'rural rascals', 'soldiers in disguise', and threatening violence if they returned. The police assembled in greater force the following day and were pelted with sticks and stones, they rallied, however, and managed to capture three prisoners. The crowd followed the officers and on the outskirts of Lancaster the police were ambushed. They were forced to flee the road and made their escape across the open fields.[36] The widespread popular disgust shown toward the county police even ran as high as the magistracy bench where, in actions redolent of eighteenth century social protest, some Tory justices refused to pay the increased county rate.[37] Indeed, the county magistrates of Lancaster (Longsdale south) attempted to expel the county police by appointing a committee to look into the possibility of withdrawing from the terms of the Act of Parliament.[38] In the main, however, the lower orders of Lancaster knew their place. On the issue of public welfare provision population pressure was not as critical in determining the relief of poverty as in other centres of urban expansion, this explains why the working class of Lancaster did not feel threatened by the New Poor Law. The demographic trend at Lancaster was that growth was static or in actual decline. This suggests that working people were moving out of the town, especially so with the continued decline in the West India trade after 1815 and the failure of the corporation to maintain the town's port facilities in the later 1830s and 1840s.[39]

The Liberals had some success in municipal politics but this was not reflected in parliamentary politics. In 1837 and 1841 the Conservatives took both seats, mainly because of their superior organization of the registration contests. In September 1837 the Conservatives won acceptance for 66 out of 89 voters names submitted, while the Liberals successfully defended only 30 out of the 115 names submitted.[40] Similarly, a year later, the Conservatives won 37 of their claims while the Liberals won only 4.[41] Much of this Conservative success was due to the national unpopularity of the Whig government, but improved organization of the Conservatives was also a factor.

The Lancaster branch of the Conservative Association was known as the Heart of Oak Club. It

---

32 Gooderson, *op. cit.*, pp. 136-7.

33 *Lancaster Gazette*, 20 February 1840.

34 Ibid., 11 April 1840.

35 Ibid., 3 April 1841.

36 Ibid., 1 August 1840, *Preston Chronicle*, 15 August.

37 *Lancaster Gazette*, 25 July 1840.

38 Ibid.

39 Gooderson, *op. cit.*, p. 29 and *passim*.

40 *Lancaster Gazette*, 30 September 1837.

41 Ibid., 29 September 1838.

was formed in November 1835 and set out its aims in a manner typical of the narrow nature of Lancaster politics. There was no mention of the need to involve the working class or anyone else other than the Conservative middle classes. The only stipulation they made in the 1830s was that they expected their Conservative MPs to protect Lancaster in Parliament whilst at the same time respecting their traditional independence of giving 'pledges', but this again came last in their list of principles, which were,

> to secure the return of members for the borough of Lancaster, who without giving any of those pledges which are so highly to be depreciated, will, nevertheless, be steadfast supporters in Parliament of those who diffuse principles of loyalty and attachment to the throne ... to watch over, protect and foster the town and trade of Lancaster and its local and foreign interests.[42]

This reflects the retention of traditional 'no issue' and 'no pledges' politics so prevalent in eighteenth century British politics. But it also reflects the fact that Conservative party organization in Lancaster was of individual representation; of the middle class dominated Conservative Associations as opposed to the more social integrationary operative or tradesman's associations. This also says something about the nature of Lancaster politics, especially in relation to the political recruitment of the local elites. Obviously the closed clique of the freeman-dominated corporation was a channel of selection and recruitment in the municipal arena. But, as noted earlier, this group had traditionally little involvement in the recruitment and selection of parliamentary candidates and this remained the case after 1832. Power was still in the hands of the county gentry located in the immediate vicinity of Lancaster.[43] The introduction of the clubs, the 'Heart of Oak' and the 'Reform Association', reveals the formalization of this feature at Lancaster. In other areas these developments opened up the political process to a limited extent, but in Lancaster, the initiation of the clubs had the effect of closing or formalizing the existing political system and method of recruitment.

The Lancaster Heart of Oak Club contained the names of all those Tory families who had been the chief members of the town's elites for decades before 1832: the Martons, the Greens, the Garnetts, the Braddylls, the Wilsons, and others of agricultural areas of Longdale. Partly because the Heart of Oak Club was made up chiefly of members from the rural districts, making regular attendance difficult, and partly because it functioned mainly as a middle class and lesser gentry party of individual representation, it had not the desire or need to constantly proselytize its membership. Nor did it provide the kind of amenities found in the working class based associations elsewhere. Finally, on the existing evidence, the working class were so devoid of radical sentiment that there was little need to politically direct them away from anything. If working class issues did not feature significantly in any of Lancaster's parliamentary contests, nor did they in the politics of the town until the later 1840s and early '50s and then only to express fears of Lancaster's industrial decline and the question of public health. Increasingly, Lancaster's parliamentary politics became a struggle between two sets of elites: the Conservatives of the traditional families, and the Liberals of the new manufacturers: the Gregs, the Armstrongs and the Gregsons. The Conservatives held on successfully throughout the 1830s and early 1840s. It was not until 1847, and the Peelite/Protectionist split, that the first Liberal member was returned for Lancaster, and even then Samuel Gregson the Liberal

---

42 *Preston Pilot*, 5 December 1835.

43 This point was made clear by George Marton, the Tory MP for Lancaster, in a letter to Sir Robert Peel in 1841, requesting that the new Prime Minister place his name on the list of newly created baronets. Marton had been advised to contact Peel by Lord Stanley (the Conservative member for north Lancashire), and stated that in the elections of 1837 and 1841 he "spent a great deal of money on behalf of the cause." British Library, Peel Papers, Ad. Mss. 40494, ff. 327-9, Marton to Peel (undated, 1841).

manufacturer was unseated for bribery. After 1847 and the Conservative split, the independent Tories were in the majority at the expense of the Peelites, but the split in voting terms was enough to let in the Liberals and dashed any hopes of the continuation of the Tory gentry monopoly of Lancaster's two seats. From 1847 the Liberals, in the shape of Gregson and Armstrong, assiduously pandered to the electorate by making the decline of local industry a major issue. This was a tactic which the Conservatives, no matter how paternalistic and anti-industrial their private sentiments may have been, could not afford to ignore. However, throughout much of the 1850s the parliamentary politics of Lancaster followed the national trend in blurring party political differences. In the ensuing contests after 1847 the Tory Longsdale gentry and the Lancaster Liberal manufacturers took one seat each. After the retirement of Thomas Green in 1857, a Conservative, W. J. Garnett, took his place. In 1859 a Palmerstonian Liberal, E. M. Fenwick, ousted Garnett and kept the seat until the disenfranchisement of the borough in 1866.

Significantly, and in contrast with the situation at Clitheroe and Chester, from the mid-1830s both of Lancaster's main political parties attempted to integrate target social groups into their respective orbits. The Conservatives, in 1836, for example, formed a branch of the Heart of Oak Club especially for tradesmen, who, in turn, were expected to bestow a message of paternalism as well as a political one, as the President, the Vicar, Rev T Mackreth said, "The societies aim was to retrace our steps and take back the labourer into the social chain."[44] However, only in the mid-1840s did the local Conservatives come to terms with an issue which had a direct bearing to the working class and it came in the form of the Conservative *Lancaster Gazette*'s lukewarm support for factory reform in the winter of 1843-4.[45] The Conservatives tended to confine their activities to the Anglican tradesmen and the freemen. They attempted to obtain, for those favourable to the party, the status of freemen through their control of the Court of Admission. This was the main device of political recruitment of the local Conservatives rather than the Heart of Oak Club, which remained primarily a county clique for parliamentary politics.

Only on one occasion did the Liberals attempt to politically integrate sections of the working class. This was in February 1839, when a local manufacturer, John Greg, tried to form an Operative Anti-Corn Law Association.[46] But, as the *Gazette* derisively asserted, it was made up of "principally the servants and dependants of the manufacturers."[47] Indeed, this attempt ended in failure, for the body met only once. The Chartists fared little better. In June 1839 the Radicals held a camp meeting at Green Acre near Skerton, but only 50 turned up.[48]

The Liberals in the council gave their support to the Anti-Corn Law League under the leadership of Gregson and Greg, but opposed the Chartists, alleging that they were not representative of Lancaster's working class and were led by outsiders from Preston. However, despite the lack of support from the middle-class radicals, the 'outsiders' (who came mainly from Ashton-under-Lyne) were successful in producing strikes at all three of Lancaster's mills in 1842. The local working class radicals, led by the weaver Jonathan Earl, directed their anger not at the Liberal manufacturers, but towards the local working class for "cowering to the local Conservatives."[49] Chartism had little success in Lancaster due in equal parts to the paternalism of the local Conservatives, the antagonism

---

44 *Preston Pilot*, 10 July 1836.

45 *Lancaster Gazette*, 13 January 1844.

46 Ibid., 4 February 1839.

47 Ibid.

48 Ibid., 8 June 1839, see also Lancaster City Library, 'Political File'.

49 Gooderson, thesis, p. 287.

of the Liberal radicals and the numerical weakness of the towns' working class. This meant that the politically and numerically important shopkeeper and tradesmen sections of the local population were less reliant on profits derived from the working class, thus less likely to succumb to exclusive dealing, should it be attempted, which, incidentally, it was not. The tradesmen class had a wider variety of customers allowing them greater independence than in most Lancashire towns. At Lancaster the party battle was fought between the town's elites to gain the support of the tradesmen class. By the late 1830s and 40s the conflict was between the elites representing old money, commerce and the land, (the Conservatives) and the Liberals representing the interests of new money in the professions and industry.[50] It was only the advent of the Small Tenements Act and the relatively rapid expansion of the working class electorate that forced the elites to shift their attention away from the tradesman class and consider the working class, and make firm commitments on policy. The only major issue that galvanised the parties into action at Lancaster in which the working class were a point of focus was the public health question. The basis of the public health question was that the local Conservatives were in favour of raising expenditure from the rates and the Liberals were not. The Conservatives argued that it was imperative that all classes in the town are safeguarded, especially the working class, who were most at risk and from whose districts disease would spread to the rest of the town.

Table I
Average Age of Death of Different Groups in Lancaster Union 1838-1844[51]

	Average age of all			Average age of all over 21		
	Town	Rural	Total	Town	Rural	Total
Gentry, Professionals and families	50.26	49.59	49.94	61.30	65.25	63.07
Tradesmen and families	30.22	33.63	31.38	52.01	56.06	53.49
Farmers and families	50.66	46.39	46.71	70.36	65.25	65.57
Artisans and families	26.04	30.84	27.28	53.24	54.55	53.62
Agricultural Labourers and families	33.05	32.61	32.77	52.81	55.74	55.58
General Labourers and families	23.02	24.87	23.37	55.64	54.92	55.49
Factory Hands and families	15.34	13.77	14.80	39.67	43.12	40.65
Workhouse Paupers	40.18	49.28	43.38	60.29	68.95	63.51

The figures in the 'average age of all' category show the importance of the infant mortality rate and may be accounted for by the state of working class living conditions. The figures shown in the 21 plus category are probably more a reflection of general conditions of work, but taken together they display the stark gap in the town's health between the various social groups. The Conservatives argued that the slur of being unhygienic was tainting the towns' stature and that this was discouraging moves by the new rich of South Lancashire to Lancaster. The presentation of Lancaster as a villa town for the South Lancashire bourgeoisie was the Conservatives answer to the town's dwindling population and probably underlay their attempts to exploit this issue as much as any attempts to care for working class health. However, they did make such claims and whilst they were not directly aimed at the working class, the Conservatives were engaged in courting local public opinion and thus the issue is of significance, as well as being an interesting example of local politics in a county town. Meanwhile the Liberals countered by saying that the death rate in Lancaster was no worse, indeed

50   For a more detailed description of the importance of this see D. Fraser, *Power and Authority in the Victorian City*, (Oxford, 1979).

51   Dr. Robert Owen, *Report on the State of Lancaster, Health of Towns Commission*, (1846).

probably much better, than in many of the newer industrial towns of south and east Lancashire. They relied for their evidence on the town's density of population in relation to other towns in the region.

Table II
Density of Population in Six North-West Towns, 1831[52]

	Persons per acre
PRESTON	16.08
MANCHESTER	67.71
LIVERPOOL	47.79
CHESTER	7.09
CARLISLE	2.67
LANCASTER	10.17
LANCASHIRE	1.20

The table shows that population density in Lancaster had, for several years, run substantially below Manchester and Liverpool, and significantly below Preston which underlay the Liberal claims that the situation did not warrant municipal attention. The Liberals also asserted that Lancaster should not have been included on the list of boroughs whose death rates exceeded 23 per 1,000, which, under the terms of Morpeth's 1848 Public Health Act meant they required statutory action.

Another bone of contention was which of the two municipal bodies was responsible for what was the main cause of the public health question, the so-called 'Mill Race'. This was the main sewerage outlet for the town as well as its main water supply, and, as well as being in urgent need of repair, was tidal and prone to 'back-up', bringing the effluvia with it. The Liberal Police Commission charged the Council with ownership of the Mill Race and responsibility for the purity of the town's water supply. The Conservative controlled council denied responsibility, and, as well as charging the Commission with ultimate responsibility, also campaigned against the Liberal owners of worker dwellings, most notably the solicitor, Thomas Lodge.[53] They also used the findings of Dr Robert Owen (Table I above) to show that the poor classes housed in the worst dwellings were most at risk. As noted above, the Liberals claimed that from the evidence of population density (Table II above) Lancaster was not as bad as other north-west towns, save Chester and Carlisle, who, they pointed out, had not even the limited industrial basis which Lancaster possessed. What was not in doubt was that in certain parts of the town, close to the Mill Race, the housing was poor. For example, in Hargreaves Court, 54 people lived in five cottages, and there were similar patterns in the Irish dominated Lucy Court. The Liberals again countered by saying that Lancaster's ratio of doctors' per-head-of population was better than other towns in north Lancashire. They cited the following figures to support of their case: Lancaster, one doctor per 400 of the population, Blackburn, one doctor per 915 and Preston, one doctor per 761.[54] The two sides became locked in political conflict both producing evidence for their case, and each claiming the other was responsible for the one cause which both agreed required local statutory action. The leader of the public health movement in Lancaster in the initial stages was the Peelite Conservative, Dr. Edward De Vitre. He had been elected to the council in 1841, but in 1844 joined the Health of Towns Association, along with Dr Arnott of Lancaster Infirmary, Richard Owen and Edwin Chadwick. The dispute as to precisely whose responsibility the Mill Race was ran through 1846, whilst at the same time the Council set up a special committee to

---

52 *Parliamentary Papers*, Vol. XXXVI, Population, (1833), pp. 286-305.

53 Gooderson, thesis, p. 287.

54 *Parliamentary Papers*, Vol. 53, 2, 'Population', (1863).

investigate the ownership and responsibility of the Mill Race. On 5 May 1847 the Town Council Committee on the Mill Race reported its findings and it was confirmed that it was indeed owned by the Corporation and thus its responsibility. It proposed that the Council should undertake the cleansing and refurbishing of the Mill Race and that this would require a rate increase of 6*d* to 9*d* in the pound. The Council vote was split on the motion, with the Conservatives unanimously in favour and the Liberals against. The motion was lost by the casting vote of the Liberal Mayor. The cabinet maker John Richardson, and Thomas Wise, a manufacturer of railway carriages and a substantial owner and developer of property, led the opposition to sanitary reform. Both were political economists of the Manchester school and representatives of the small ratepayers of St Ann's Ward. Throughout the early years of the 1840s the Public Health question was an increasingly important political issue. But the loss of the crucial vote, and the mounting opposition of Richardson and Wise, spurred the Conservatives into action, when, as a united party, they fully backed direct municipal intervention. It was from this time, the middle of 1847, that the party political battle really began. The *Lancaster Guardian* defended the actions of the Liberals in their defence of the small ratepayers. The Conservative *Lancaster Gazette*, meanwhile, stressed the need to cleanse the town to preserve law and order, demonstrating the classic Tory device of couching a question in terms of it being crucial to the peace and stability of society.

In the autumn of 1847 Lancaster was hit by cholera and the rapid increase of outpatients of the Dispensary again pushed the question of sanitary reform to the fore. At a special meeting of the Council, called in late October 1847, the Conservatives demanded that a memorial be sent to Parliament to sanction a special rate signed by the entire population.[55] These were Chartist-style tactics used on a question of local social reform and it ensured that the Conservatives gained a majority of seats in the Council elections of November 1847.[56] The Conservative majority meant that resolutions in favour of sanitary reform were now carried in Council and resulted in the formation, in 1848, of a voluntary local Board of Health. This Board proposed an entirely new sewerage system and a new waterworks and was empowered by the Council to prepare a report to outline cost and feasibility. An engineer, Robert Rawlinson, sent by the Health of Commission, prepared it and in December 1848 he reported his findings.[57] The total cost was estimated at a minimum of £45,000, a phenomenal sum that appeared to place the cost of sanitary reform prohibitively high. But the report was also political in that in the interests of efficiency it proposed to transfer the powers of the Police Commission to the Town Council, enabling the town to borrow and levy special rates. These proposals were defeated by 22 votes to 20, with the Peelites voting with the Liberals. The line was now drawn between the Conservative sanitary reformers (the so called 'Whites') and the Liberal retrenchers (the 'Blacks'). The largest single group in the Council were the Conservatives, next largest were the Liberals but the power lay in the casting votes of the three Peelites. Although both sides maintained that they championed working-class interests neither group attempted to engage their active participation. For the first time at Lancaster, opinion politics were tentatively emerging but, importantly, although the issue directly affected the working class, no party made a serious attempt to involve them in the campaign, a trend typical of Lancaster politics.

The Liberals objected to the cost, arguing it would fall heaviest on cottage property owners who had to pay the combined rates of all property valued at £5 or less. This, the Liberals maintained,

---

55 *Lancaster Gazette*, 30 October 1847.

56 Ibid., 7 November 1847.

57 E. Sharp, *A History of the Progress of Sanitary Reform in Lancaster*, (Lancaster, 1876).

would mean raising the rents of the poorest working class. Not surprisingly, the two largest investors in cottage property were leading 'Blacks', the building contractor, Wise, who owned property to the rateable value of £450 per year, and the solicitor, Lodge, with £305 worth of property. But there were also some 'White' property owners, for example, Edward Sharp, who owned over £100 worth of property. The Conservative case was strengthened by the authoritative views of two local men. The first was Superintendent Registrar, James Grant, who maintained that mortality rates were increasing, and the second, John Smith, who, after a preliminary survey, announced that the local water supplies were heavily polluted. De Vitre attacked the building standards of the Liberal cottage owners. He mocked their reluctance to sanction the measure on the basis of the increased costs of their £5 per year rented cottages even though the returns on these investments could be as large as 10 to 12 per cent annually. Wise rejected such claims, revealing his economic motives with unusual frankness by suggesting that if the Conservatives owned as much property as he did, they too would oppose the reforms.[58] However, the Liberal case was finally scotched in May 1850 when it was discovered that a petition of 1,954 signatures, raised by them, contained the names of only 992 ratepayers. An Act of Parliament was finally applied for in 1851, it was passed in 1853 and work began in April. The project was finally completed and opened amid all the usual nineteenth century municipal grandeur in June 1855.[59]

The public health question is interesting because it was a test of local leadership and power relations between the two political parties. Both geared their arguments towards working class welfare without actually politically mobilizing them as a social group to defend their party's position. Increasingly the question hinged on whether the town would take its instructions from a small group of professional men, some of whom were relatively new to the town and whose position on the town council and in the local Conservative party seems to have influenced the party on the issue. Or alternatively, was the town to be led by a large number of small tradesmen who, the Liberals argued, were being asked to shoulder the majority of the increased rates burden, and whose voice were heard loudest on the Police Commission. The leadership of Edward De Vitre and Edward Sharp locally, and Edwin Chadwick nationally provided much of the catalyst for political action. But also crucial was the decision of the Conservatives to back a local issue as a party for the first time. The issue was won when the cotton manufacturers, on whom the town was increasingly economically dependent, stepped into the debate and backed the sanitary reformers. This indicated that working-class opinion, in so far as it existed, was led by the important industrialists, a situation, as will be seen below, similar to other parts of the region at this time.

The public health question revealed the contrasts in the nature of party politics up to 1847. It is interesting in the sense of the relative lack of party spirit in municipal politics before the emergence of the question, the absence of any direct working class involvement in politics and, overall, the relative shortage of imaginative local political leaders, especially on the Conservative side. For the urban historian, the public health question in Lancaster offers a classic example of the weaknesses of mid-nineteenth century political institutions in a traditional county town: the paralysis caused by the Police Commission and the Town Council, each negating the actions of the other. The issue was also interesting in the way the Conservatives, particularly, mobilized support through the local press, utilizing the *Lancaster Gazette* as an extension of the local party apparatus. The fact that it was the Conservatives who were cast in the role of reformers and the Liberals in that of resisters should not

---

58   Gooderson, thesis, p. 302.

59   *Lancaster Guardian*, 20 June 1855.

provoke undue surprise, for, as will be seen when we look at other areas of the north-west, this was the norm, particularly in social-related questions. What is of interest in the case of Lancaster is that the Conservatives began to operate so tentatively and so late in the period. In other parts of the region this was occurring from the mid-1830s. Overall the study of developments in the market and county towns bear witness to the longevity and the resilience of the traditional political order. There were virtually no contrasting party lines over national issues or in any significant area of local government policy up until the mid-1840s. Thus the scope for unlimited local party political opportunism was very narrow in these places.

Particularly in Lancaster, but also in Clitheroe and Chester, the old ways of conducting political business, both local and parliamentary, remained virtually unchanged both before and after the Reform Act. The evidence for the market and county towns seems to reinforce the position of the gradualists like O'Gorman, Gash and others. It also suggests that Nossiter's idioms of influence and the politics of the market held precedence over opinion/interest politics, especially with regard to working class orientated political developments and issues. However, opinion/interest politics did appear to be strengthening at Lancaster from the later 1840s, especially with regard to the economic prospects of the town in parliamentary politics and public health in its municipal affairs. Working class involvement in politics was minimal, there were few working class leaders and issues like constitutional reform, opposition to the New Poor Law or the Factory Question received scant attention by either of the two main political groupings. This further reinforces the point that the elites dominated the affairs in the these towns in terms of their own political interests, only rarely considering the wider local community. Attempts at politically integrating the working class were rare up to the 1860s, and, in the case of the Conservatives did not involve the working class at all in the organization of the party. The situation of the market and county towns now needs to be contrasted and compared with another type of locality within the north-west; that of the old Scot and Lot borough of Preston.

The Old Industrial Boroughs, Preston: Economic and Social Background

One of the chief reasons why the north-west is interesting to the historian is its diversity. By 1830 the capitalist factory system dominated the region. But this was not universally the case. The region contained a mixed and fluid population: religious, economic, demographic and political, and it contained several types of political constituency.

If the market and county town constituencies appeared to be the least susceptible to changing influences of post-Reform political culture it will be interesting to see how they compare with the new towns which emerged as constituencies as a result of the 1832 Reform Act. What is needed at this stage is the examination of a locality that lay politically and historically somewhere between the two, and here lies the importance of Preston. Both before and after 1832 Preston enjoyed a rate-payer franchise very similar in type to the 1867 Reform Act; it was a borough which possessed a householder franchise, which meant that the majority of its electors (although the numbers declined in the 1840s) were made up of the working class. This gives us an ideal opportunity to compare the findings of the foregoing with that of a largely industrial town which, although having all the old political traditions, also had the added advantage (for us at least) of possessing a largely working class electorate. Preston, like Lancaster, had for most of the eighteenth century an economic make-up which, although mixed, relied strongly on its status as a major centre for the marketing of agricultural produce. It possessed a similar corporate structure to Lancaster, and, although it did not have the latter's status as a centre of the full quarter sessions, a Court of Common Pleas was sited at Preston. On the face of it, therefore, as the eighteenth century gave way to the nineteenth, there were important points of similarity between the two towns. The chief differences in the case of Preston were, firstly, the maintenance of dramatic industrial growth, and, secondly, its remarkably open franchise.

As elsewhere, factory development began in the spinning section of the textile industry. The first spinning mill was established in Preston in 1777. Developments on the weaving side began in 1791 with the arrival of John Horrocks. Between that date and 1802 John, and his brother Samuel, built six factories, mostly in the south east of the town in Fishwick Ward. Thus Preston's social and economic development at the end of the eighteenth century can realistically be compared to both Lancaster and Chester but, crucially for the town's immediate development, the Horrocks family began to significantly expand their textile enterprise.

Preston differed from the market and county towns in the sheer size and speed of its population growth. In 1801 the population of Lancaster was 9,030 and in 1871 17,245. In contrast, the population of Preston in the corresponding period was 11,887 persons in 1801 and 83,515 in 1871, or, put in percentage terms, Lancaster increased by 89 per cent in seventy years but Preston by 700 per cent in the same period. The years between 1831 and 1861 imposed great strain on the physical resources of the town in terms of poor relief, housing, water supply, waste removal and burial grounds, on education, and, of course, on public order and social control. This period was the key one in the development of the commercial and industrial enterprises that fed, clothed, housed, warmed, shod, transported and instructed the town's population. It was a good time to set up in business at the peaks of the trade cycle, but alarming in the troughs. It was also the period of dramatic change in the structure of parliamentary and local administration. The census of 1851 reveals that Preston was bigger than Salford and Oldham, and much bigger than Blackburn, and therefore provides useful material for analysing a town in the middle of a transition from an old style mixed economy to that of a fully developed industrial society. This is underscored when the varied nature of Preston's occupational structure is considered, the continuation of spinning and weaving, the disparate factory size, the patterns of mobility, and the sex and age distribution of the town's population.

The demographic analysis reveals that it was predominantly a young population, 46.6 per cent (32,372) were under 20 years of age. According to the census of 1851 more than half (52.5 per cent) of the population were born outside the borough, and amongst the adults (those over 20) 70% were migrants. This suggests that the traditional practices of the town in, say, political activity, and the bestowing of familial or community political allegiances, would probably not have affected these migrant groups as they did in Lancaster's more stable and less migrant population. Preston's incomers would have brought their traditions and social mores with them, but they would have been drawn to others in the town in a similar situation who could offer psychological, spiritual or material support. In the case of such a substantial influx, this factor may prove to be significant when the political changes in Preston are analysed over time. Population density could also have been a factor in political change, as it is an important dimension of the local experience of life. K. M. Spencer has done some work on this for Preston, but there is little comment on how the pattern as a whole affected local society.[60] Briefly, the town was geographically small and becoming very crowded. The built-up area hardly changed whilst the population had roughly doubled and the development of mill-owner housing was relatively late at Preston compared to Bolton and, especially, Blackburn. Unlike

---

60   K. M. Spencer, 'A Social and Economic Geography of Preston, 1800-1865', M.A. thesis, University of Liverpool, (1968).

other mill towns in the region, the fact that Preston's population was housed without the early intervention of the manufacturers should be borne in mind when considering the relationship between the working class and the manufacturing elites. At Preston the sheer size of its growth marks it out from Lancaster and Chester, and gives it a pattern of development like that of the larger conurbation's of Salford and Manchester up to 1850. This placed enormous social and political pressures on the community and the local elites respectively. A large number of people were living in a relatively small town, and their density was increasing. As any schoolteacher or supporter of popular sport is aware, overcrowding usually raises levels of excitement, tension and dramatises events. The working class of Preston became literally huddled masses. The objective reality of their position coupled with a heightened subjective awareness or consciousness of their experiences as a class created severe potential problems for the authorities. Moreover, what makes Preston so uniquely interesting to this study is that a significant proportion of the town's post-1832 electorate was made up of the male members of this huddled mass. Certainly, contemporary commentators were concerned about working-class living conditions. In the late 1860s a contemporary writer offered a retrospective impression of Preston's poorer districts:

> Smokey workshops, old buildings, with windows awfully smashed in, houses given up to 'lodgings for travellers here', densely packed, dirty cottages, and the tower of a windmill... Pigeon flyers, dog fanciers, gossiping vagrants, crying children, old iron, stray hens, women with a passion for sitting on doorsteps, men looking at nothing with their hands in their pockets... And the mirage of perhaps one policeman on duty constitute the signals of the neighbourhood [Trinity Ward]. Townwards you soon get into a region of murky houses, ragged children, running beerjugs, poverty ... the plot thickens until you get into the very jaws of ignorance, depravity and misery.[61]

In terms of occupations, the textile industry accounted for 48 per cent of the total recorded labour force in 1841, and 50 per cent in 1851, and more than a quarter of the entire population of the town between 1847 and 1862.[62] Figures for earlier dates are harder to come by, due in part to the occupational instability of handloom weavers, but the poll book of 1830 reveals the political importance of the textile workers. Out of a total electorate of 7,122 there were 2,032 spinners and weavers eligible to vote, some 28.5 per cent of the electorate. Trade recession and the terms of the Reform Act meant that holders of the old franchise tended to disappear from the register due to removal, failure to pay rates or the receipt of poor relief. Thus the number of spinners and weavers qualified to vote in parliamentary elections declined. Nevertheless, this group still counted for 20 per cent of the total electorate in 1838 and 18 per cent in 1841, but gradually fell away throughout the later 1840s and 1850s. However, it is safe to assume that from the 1820s roughly a quarter of Preston's population were involved in the textile industry and that they were a salient feature of electoral politics. Analysis of the development of Preston's textile industry is complicated by a number of factors. Firstly, some mill-owners owned several mills and others held partnerships in branches of the trade, for example, in cotton finishing, which makes it difficult to say categorically and precisely which cotton master controlled which set of employees. Secondly, during the 1830s particularly, not all of Preston's cotton factories were fully mechanized, and several still put work out to handloom weavers.[63] A third complicating factor was that the industry itself was in a state of

---

61 Attilus, *Our Churches and Chapels*, (Preston, 1869), p. 12.

62 Spencer, thesis, pp. 75-7.

63 For a more detailed description of this see, J. Bythall, *The Sweated Trades*, (London, 1980), and J. A. Schmiechen, *Seated Industry and*

constant change, with firms adjusting to the state of the market by combining spinning and weaving or, at other times, concentrating on a specific branch of the industry. Patrick Joyce has suggested that levels and trends of worker deference and employer-inspired paternalism may be detected from the size of the factory units, especially from the period after 1850.[64] Larger employers tended to be able to exact deferential attitudes from their employees in a way that was impossible for smaller employers. This analysis may have a bearing in our study of the slightly earlier period for the industrialized parts of the region, especially in relation to the political allegiances of the working class. It is therefore important to establish the pattern of economic and industrial development in Preston from the 1830s in order to appreciate the relationship between the cotton manufacturers and their employees. Also relevant is the speed of change, noting what proportions of masters and men retained the older work practices. If in Preston it can be demonstrated that capital was concentrated amongst a few large-scale manufacturers, as was the case in Blackburn (the chief source of Joyce's research) then Preston may provide a useful source of comparison.

At Preston the textile industry was mixed, containing both small and large manufacturers putting work out to handloom weavers.[65] One reason for the dramatic growth of Preston could be the maintenance of industrial diversity, a feature that was not to be found at Lancaster for example. Even though by the 1830s handloom weavers had become extremely impoverished, there were still estimated to be 3,000 in the town itself and another 10,000 in the district, although one witness, Robert Crawford, said this was "less than 15 or 16 years ago."[66] Individual businessmen could display a diverse set of economic interests, as the auction of the effects of William Dixon, a bankrupt tea dealer and grocer, reveals. Included in the sale was a "counting house, warehouses behind the same, also two large buildings containing 159 self-acting looms."[67] A serious setback came not only from the boom/slump cycle but also from the spinners' strike of 1836-37 when the major mill-owners advised handloom weavers to seek other employment. However, as late September 1847 the *Preston Guardian* reported that, "Amidst the depression connected with mill work in the cotton business... handloom weaving is unusually brisk."[68] Indeed, handloom weavers were still plentiful and politically significant enough to warrant particular mention by one of the candidates at the 1852 election.[69] Handloom weaving survived partly because of the growth of power loom factories, providing a conveniently elastic outlet to be expanded or contracted as the market dictated, without unduly disturbing the regular mill hands. However, it must be noted that these handloom weavers were still essentially waged factory workers operating in 'dandy sheds' attached to, or close by, the powered plant. Their status, earning capacity and numbers declined but they fiercely retained a level of independence not found in the powered workshops. This substantial group are relevant to the independent nature of working-class political affiliation, especially in the early 1830s. The growth of cotton mills in Preston followed the trade cycle almost exactly in the first half of the nineteenth century. There was an initial spurt between 1815 and 1826, then a slump from 1827 to 1836. After 1836 there was a gradual recovery and a tremendous boom in the mid-1840s.[70] S. D. Chapman

---

Sweated Labour, (London, 1981).

64   P. Joyce, *Work, Society and Politics*, (Brighton, 1980).

65   Harris Library, Preston, 'Assessment of Cotton Mills', (1844).

66   *Parliamentary Papers*, 'Report on the Select Committee on Handloom Weaver's Petitions', Questions 5862-5865, (1834).

67   *Preston Pilot*, 15 February 1832.

68   *Preston Guardian*, 18 September 1847.

69   *Preston Pilot*, 26 June 1852.

70   V. A. C. Gatrell, 'Labour, Power and the Size of Firms in the Lancashire Cotton Industry in the Second Quarter of the Nineteenth Century', in

explained this was due to the extra abundance of credit facilities.[71] At Preston the period of moderate growth between 1826 and 1845 corresponds almost exactly with the continuing presence of the small non-mechanised concerns and the handloom weavers.

Firstly Horrocks's and then Horrocks, Miller and Co. dominated the cotton industry of Preston, in size, number of mills, capital invested, and number of hands employed. The scale of the Horrocks enterprise compared with others in the industry was vast. Balance sheets for 1836, for example, show a total of both capital and profits of £432,485, and a net profit of £30,432 to be distributed pro-rata amongst the five partners.[72] Their exports rose from 99,457 pieces in 1840 to 132,827 in 1853, with the largest quantities going to the Indian sub-continent. But Horrocks, Miller and Co. were not at all typical of Preston's mill owners.[73] Out of 30 mills valued for rating purposes in 1844, Horrocks's were rated at £61,376, Catterall's at £18,000 and a further 21 at under £8,000.[74] Horrocks employed over 2,000 workers, two other factories over 1,000, 9 others more than 500, and 19 employed fewer than 150. The average size of the cotton mills in Preston was 300.[75] Preston's main and quickest period of growth took place in the 1840s. The factory inspector, Leonard Horner, reported in 1845 that there were "many new factories now building or being completed."[76] In fact there were eight, and his statistics reveal that capital had been invested in ten new factories between July 1844 and March 1845. This again separates Preston from Lancaster where no such growth occurred and, indeed, from Blackburn and Bolton, where the growth of the 1840s was a consolidation on existing plant and buildings. Preston's social and economic growth was remarkable even by the standards of the time. The chief reason was possibly the town's proximity to the two great mercantile and commercial centres of Liverpool and Manchester. Similarly, Preston was favourably placed with regard to the key industrial raw materials, labour and power. The town may also have been attractive for migrants, not only because of work opportunities but also because of its reputation for religious toleration (it had, relative to its size, the largest Catholic population in the north-west), and political reform.

It is important to outline the social and economic background to Preston's growth because it also enables us to examine working class political development. It offers an insight into the wider political organization in a burgeoning industrial area where, in the initial years after 1832, the majority of working men were allowed to vote. It provides an opportunity to examine a largely working-class electorate subject to a wide and changing mixture of influences. Forces of community and employer paternalism may have pushed it towards deference politics; market influences may have pressed towards 'corruption'; whilst new impersonal capitalism, allied to the survival of handloom weaving, may have bred independence and thus opinion politics. These questions are important but at this stage a brief look at Preston's religious make-up is needed, and its general political trends between the 1820s and the 1860s.

Assessing religious composition is difficult for any locality in the nineteenth century but what is clear in the development of Preston, was the relatively large number of Catholics in the town. However, the Anglicans seem to have possessed the allegiance of the overwhelming majority of the town's leading citizens. In 1827, the Clerks of the Peace, Gorst and Birchall, obtained figures for the

Economic History Review, 30, (1977).

71 S. D. Chapman, 'Financial Restraints on the Growth of Firms in the Cotton Industry, 1790-1850', in *Economic History Review,* 32, (1979).

72 Lancashire County Records Office, Horrocks Papers, DDHS, 76, (1836).

73 See T. Banks, *A Short Sketch of the Cotton Trade of Preston for the last 67 years*, (Preston, 1888), p. 15.

74 Harris Library, Preston, 'Assessment of Cotton Mills', (1844).

75 *Preston Guardian*, 15 June 1836, and 8 May 1847.

76 Factory Inspector's Report, (1845), quoted in Spencer, thesis.

nonconformist sects of the town. They found ten places of worship occupied by Independents, Primitive Methodists, Wesleyan Methodists, Huntington's Connection, Independents, Presbyterians, Baptists, Quakers, and Independents, which added up to a total of 3,160 souls. The Catholics at this time numbered 10,900 at Fishergate and Friargate chapels in the town centre. This was approximately one third of the 1831 population. By 1851 the census recorded that Catholics had declined to 10,200 persons, or 15 per cent of the population, in spite of large-scale Irish immigration. The Catholic presence was an important and well-represented feature of the town's political life. There were, in due course, outbreaks of sectarian trouble, especially in the 1850s, but generally the Catholic population were relatively well integrated in Preston if one compares the situation with Wigan or Liverpool. Indeed some of the most respected families in the town were Catholic.

Municipal Politics

In terms of political change, prior to the 1855 Municipal Reform Act there were three separate governmental bodies. Preston's corporation was the most constitutionally visible, but this self-electing body had only marginal powers that barely affected the lives of the ordinary citizens, its chief roles being control of the markets and the borough magistrates. Responsibility for the condition of the streets, policing and lighting lay with the Improvement Commission, a body that was only open to ratepayers, and owners of property worth £100 per year. Responsibility for the poor lay with the Vestry which was open to all ratepayers. Both the Improvement Commission, made up of the elites, and the Vestry, composed chiefly of the masses, had the power to levy rates. Older forms of commercial wealth were predominant on the Council from the 1800s, a situation that was similar to Lancaster. Aside from four cotton spinners, the majority of the Council from 1825 was made up of 6 attorneys, Horrocks and Thomas Miller, 3 bankers, a doctor, a surveyor, a furrier, a draper, and several other tradesmen. There was little influence of the older county or agricultural money, such as corn or flour dealers, whose relative numerical strength in the trade directories is so apparent. This again bears out the findings of Derek Fraser, especially his work on Leeds.[77] Even before the Municipal Corporations Act of 1835 the situation locally was perceived as being in urgent need of reform. One petition sent to the House of Commons read:

> ... praying the House to pass such a Bill as will relieve the present Mayor's and Aldermen of the Municipal Corporations of their magisterial duties... will prevent the Corporation property from being wasted and misapplied, and will vest the election of all the members of Corporations in persons entitled to vote at elections of [MPs], so that Corporations may be placed under vigilant popular control, and because, what they were in fact intended to be, for the benefits of the inhabitants at large.[78]

This signified a more direct involvement in the arena of local government by the ordinary citizens than took place at Lancaster. For, although the Preston Corporation did not associate itself with the freemen and burgesses in this petition, it willingly cooperated with the Municipal Corporation Commission when it took evidence in Preston in September 1833, which was not the case at

---

77 D. Fraser, *Urban Politics in Victorian England*, (Leicester, 1976), pp. 129-32. E. Baines, *History of Lancashire*, (Manchester, 1825), P. A. Whittle, *A History of Preston*, (Preston, 1886).

78 *Commons Journal*, 15 June 1835, p. 339.

Lancaster.[79] Indeed, the remarks of Preston's Mayor, John Addison, were those of a man welcoming the prospect of relief from old-fashioned and restricting traditions. The Council, he maintained, "might be considered a self-elected body. This was not satisfactory."[80] Seemingly many members of the Corporation were not adverse to a measure of reform, but, although the Tory Addison wished for reform, he did not want the open franchise operating as in the parliamentary elections. He stated in 1833 that he considered it "desirable that harmony should exist in the institutions of the country, and should therefore prefer giving the power of election to the same class of voters ... as the Reform Act ... namely the £10 householders."[81]

The case of Preston confirms the conclusions reached by Derek Fraser, that moves for municipal reform and parliamentary reform "were but two horses in the same harness."[82] Public meetings on Corporation reform were like those on parliamentary reform but on a reduced scale in terms of numbers and passion. The leading radicals and reformers present at these meetings held throughout 1835 included Robert Segar, Joseph Livesey, Robert Ashcroft and Joseph Mitchell. There was in fact little difference coming from the spokesmen of the working class over the question, between popular radicals like Mitchell and the middle class Liberal reformers like Segar. It was the Conservatives who, whilst agreeing to a measure of reform, still wished for a £10 franchise and attempted to block the use of public buildings for debate, which provoked an attack from both the middle class reformers and working class radicals. It prompted Richard Arrowsmith, a Roman Catholic banker, to remark that the Conservatives were intent on retaining office by fair means or foul, he said they "did not want anyone of those present to become a mayor, or an alderman, or a councillor."[83] The reformers had two main objectives. Firstly to gain political recognition for the rising power of the new rich and the upwardly mobile 'professionals'. As Arrowsmith put it,

> He saw many at the meeting who had raised themselves to stations of eminence from their industry, integrity, and uprightness... These were the sort of men ... who were the most proper persons for them to choose to manage their local affairs.[84]

A second objective was a more efficient administration and a wholly new type of relationship between the Corporation and the rapidly growing urban community. The Liberal, Robert Segar, said that if the Corporation was in debt, as indeed it was,

> they should sell off the Corporation's farms and pay off their debts... If their local affairs were well-regulated, many improvements might be effected out of the Corporate fund, without perhaps the heavy taxation imposed by the Police Commissioners. They might then, perhaps, be able to ... keep the streets clean ... and put some other streets in repair besides Fishergate Lane and some other fashionable thoroughfares which were attended to while others, equally important to a large class of the community, were left even without sewers and neglected. He should welcome a general improvement in the conduct from the new Corporation whom they could elect, and if not, could turn them out.[85]

---

79 See pp. 137-40 above.
80 *Preston Chronicle*, 15 August 1833.
81 Ibid.
82 Fraser, *Power and Authority in the Victorian City*, (Oxford, 1979).
83 *Preston Chronicle*, 15 August 1835.
84 Ibid.
85 Ibid.

These were clear statements by the radicals and reformers in favour of representative local government based on effective political administration and on the opinions of a broadly based electorate. But in fact the 1835 Act made little immediate difference to the responsibilities of the Corporation, with the important exception of the transference of the powers away from the Improvement Commission, thus allowing the Corporate bodies to levy a watch rate. The magistrates' bench also ceased to be the exclusive preserve of council members, but the council continued to send forward council candidates for the magistracy to the Home Office. Locally, the impetus for reform had come from the popular radicals and the reformist wing of the emerging Liberal Party, personified by the leadership of Mitchell for the radicals, and Segar and Livesey for the Liberals and, importantly, these people did have a working-class following. As to the franchise, the new Act made the distinction between the 'burgesses' and the rest of the inhabitants. "The burgess role ... was limited to occupiers of rateable property in the borough residing within seven miles of it, who had paid rates for the previous two and a half years." [86]

This meant that recent immigrants to Preston were unenfranchised, as were those whose rates were compounded and paid by their landlords, which applied to most rates under £7, until the operation of the Small Tenements Act after 1853. It is at once clear from Table III that the working class of Preston suffered an absolute decline in their involvement in local politics from the introduction of the Municipal Corporations Act until 1853.

Table III
Relative Size of Preston's Municipal Franchise, 1835-1860[87]

Year	Total Burgesses	% of Population	% of Adult Males	%of Parliamentary Franchise	% of Ratepayers
1836	2,369	5.8	3.3	6.3	31
1852	1,892	2.7	1.4	6.57	not known
1853*	4,484	6.1	3.1	15.8	—
1857	4,385	5.6	2.8	16.0	—
1859	5,728	7.3	3.7	20.9	—

* Introduction of the Small Tenements Act.

These figures also show that the municipal electorate in Preston was small in relation to the whole population, similar in fact to what Hennock found in Leeds and Birmingham. They indicate as many as a third of adult males were able to participate in 1836 but only 14 per cent in 1852. This was due to the restrictions placed on compounders written into Preston's new municipal charter of 1836/7. It was further due to the fluidity of Preston's population with people moving in and out of the town, and as many moving about within it, especially after the building of new housing in the mid-1840s.

The most striking contrast is with the parliamentary franchise. Preston's householder franchise up to 1832 meant every male householder could vote as long as he was 21 years of age and upwards, had resided in the town for six consecutive months immediately preceding an election, and who was free from pauperism and crime.[88] The imposition of the £10 property qualification after 1832 gradually

86   Quoted in E. P. Hennock, *Fit and Proper Persons*, (London, 1973), p. 16.

87   Harris Library, Preston, Burgess Lists, Census for 1841, 1851, 1861, Poll Books, 1837, 1852, 1857, *Preston Chronicle, Preston Pilot, Preston Guardian, passim.*

88   A. Hewison, *History of Preston*, (Preston, 1883), p. 129.

reduced the parliamentary electors of Preston "as they fell into their graves."[89] Thus, the municipal franchise between 1836 and 1853 was less representative of the working class, comprising less than two thirds of the parliamentary electorate for most of the intervening years. After 1853 the situation was reversed, for every 10 working men who could vote for MPs, 16 could vote for councillors. This situation was, of course, redressed after the 1867 Reform Act when once again Preston gained a householder franchise.

There were six wards created under the terms of the 1835 Municipal Reform Act: St John's, Trinity, Christ Church, St George's, Fishwick and St Peter's. The Burgess Roll reveals that the most concentrated working class wards, whose average rateable value per house was £5 or less between 1835 and 1838, were St Peter's, Fishwick, St George's and Trinity. These were the main focus of factory development. The wards with the highest number of 'respectable' working class members, whose rateable value was put between £5 and £10 were in St John's, Trinity and Christ Church. And the highest percentage of middle class ratepayers, valued at £10 or over, was in Christ Church and St George's. The deference thesis gains some limited credence when one considers that according to the Poll books for 1832 and 1835 Christ Church ward polled over 80 per cent Conservative in those years. This embraced most of the new factory district, and three out of the four mill owners, Messrs. Rodgett, Clayton, and Hincksman plumped Conservative, with only George Corry splitting for the Liberals, at all elections up to 1847.[90] A further implication was that the ruling Conservative Corporation attempted to confine the electorate most traditionally hostile to them, containing both the Liberal shopkeepers and the radical or Catholic working class in St Peter's and Fishwick wards. Even if the electors of these wards filled the full 16 seats available with radical councillors and aldermen, they could do little against the Conservative superiority in the four other wards. These factors, coupled with the high property qualification for candidates (real or personal property of £1,000 or occupation of premises of £30 rateable value), meant that the structure of Preston's local politics were heavily biased against direct working class involvement and in favour of respectable, 'safe' government by the elites.

The level of electioneering over the twenty-five years of 1835-1860 reveals a clear three-phase pattern. The initial excitement of 1835-36 was followed by three years of intense activity. There was then a long, quiet period with few council contests. The only significant change was the admission of a few of the politically active Liberal cotton manufacturers: George Smith, John Goodair and John Hawkins, and the Liberal attorney James German, to a council dominated by the established manufacturing and professional elite. The Conservatives held power for most of the period, the main Liberal challenge coming in 1847-48. Finally, with the increase in the voters in 1853 there was a marked revival in political activity, with an upsurge in treating and popular electioneering.

Parliamentary Politics

Turning to the development of Preston's parliamentary politics it is worth noting three general points of contrast with the county town of Lancaster. First, at Lancaster local questions were confined to municipal politics and national issues to the constituency, whereas at Preston they often overlapped. Secondly, the Corporation of Preston was closely involved in parliamentary politics, unlike

---

89   An incidental fact regarding the first Reform Act was that one of Sir Robert Peel's objections to the Reform Bill was that it would deny these customary elective rights, and he cited Preston as an example. *Hansard*, 14 October 1831.

90   Harris Library, Preston, Poll Books, 1832, 1835, 1847. See also Appendix 3 below.

Lancaster. Thirdly, at Preston there was considerable working class involvement, especially in parliamentary politics, which was not the case at Lancaster.

In the election immediately following the Act, every male person of full age could vote; by 1859 only one in five could do so. Under Clause 31, existing voters retained their franchise. However, the terms of the retention under the old franchise in Preston was six months residence in the borough prior to 7 June 1832. By 1857 only 8 per cent of those qualified in 1832 remained on the register. However, by far the biggest loss, and the one most serious for a study of working class political behaviour, occurred within ten months of the Reform Act. Following the Court of Revision in October 1833, the number of voters under the old franchise had been almost halved; of the 6,291 able to vote in 1832 only 3,412 (54%) were left.[91] The *Preston Chronicle* ascribed this partly to apathy but also to the cost of the actual registration, "… to the poor man who reckons his earnings by pence … a shilling is a very serious and important amount."[92] One of the practical functions of the Operative Conservative Associations was to pay the annual registration fee on behalf of their members, importantly this was one of the inducements which attracted working-class supporters possessing the right to vote. However, many working class electors were forced off the register at Preston for reasons other than cost. One was that in the 1830s the middle-class and new overseers were zealous in striking out radical working class electors, a crucial factor in controlling a potentially troublesome, numerically large working class electorate. Table IV illustrates the development of Preston's electorate over a thirty-year period.

Table IV
Size of the Electorate of Preston, 1832-1868 in Relation to the Old and New Franchise.[93]

Election year	Total voters	Old Franchise	New Franchise	% of Old Franchise Remaining	% of Old Franchise Total
1832	6,325	6,291	37	100	99
1835	3,744	3,354	828	53	90
1837	3,738	2,785	973	44	75
1847	3,054	1,570	1,463	27	51
1857	2,742	806	1,936	13	29
1862	2,834	504	2,330	8	18

Unquestionably it was the working class who were most affected by this change but enough of the working class electorate remained to make an analysis of their voting behaviour meaningful.

Traditionally in parliamentary elections the corporation nominated one seat, usually in the interest of Lord Derby, the largest landowner in the town, with the other open to contest. The bye-election of 1830 saw a victory for Henry Hunt and radical organization in the town against Derby's son, Edward Stanley. So angered was Stanley that he severed all ties with Preston, never visiting the town again and ending almost two hundred years of influence. Although the Corporation still nominated one seat, the other was open and, as elsewhere during the reform crisis, the Preston Radicals strengthened their hold on local popular politics. At Manchester and Bolton the working class threw off the lower middle class leadership, but at Preston this did not happen. The two main Radical leaders at this time were Joseph Mitchell and Joseph Livesey, but even at this early date differences in popular radicalism can be detected. Mitchell was a thoroughgoing Paineite, Livesey more a 'philosophical'

---

91   Lancashire County Records Office, Register of Electors, 1833, 1834, 1835.

92   *Preston Chronicle*, 19 October 1833.

93   Lancashire County Records Office, Register of Electors, figures for election of 1841 not available.

radical, prone to the tactic of pressure group politics, his greatest crusade being the cause of temperance. Both claimed a large working class following. The poll book for the 1830 election reveals a strong working-class feeling towards radicalism. The table below shows the voting pattern of the 2,032 textile workers on the register at the 1830 by-election.

Table V
Voting Patterns of Spinners and Weavers at the 1830 Preston By-Election[94]

| | Stanley (Whig) | | Hunt (Radical) | | Total |
	Total Votes	%	Total Votes	%	Total
Spinners	184	32.7	378	63.3	562
Weavers	239	16.3	1,231	83.7	1,470

Clearly Preston's mill hands were Radical in this early, pre-Reform period and the weavers were marginally more prone towards radicalism overall than the 33 percent of spinners who voted for Stanley. An important variable was the Tory-induced support for Hunt, explained by the fact that there was no Tory candidate and Stanley, as a leading Whig reformer, was hated by local Tories. The first elections held under the terms of the Reform Act show that the opponents of popular radicalism had become more organized. The Conservative dominated corporation brought forward Peter Hesketh-Fleetwood, a member of the lesser aristocracy and large landowner on the Fylde coast. The reforming Whigs chose as their candidate H. T. Stanley, the future earl of Alderney, and the Liberals, Charles Crompton. Hunt stood again for the popular Radicals, and a fifth candidate was Joseph Fortes, who shared many of Hunt's radical principles. Back in 1830 the Conservatives realised that working-class radicalism in Preston was a considerable threat to the maintenance of their power, constitutional stability and local harmony. The Conservative paper, the *Preston Pilot*, put the onus of blame on those manufacturers who shirked their responsibility to lead their employees.

> ... the fact is, that men in this town are actually forced into the ranks of radicalism by the want of due consideration in those with whom rests the power of preventing such desertion. For example, we will suppose the employer of two or three hundred men to express ... just previous to an election, an intention of holding himself neutral during such election. What follows? The people, finding their master feels no interest in directing them one way or the other, consider themselves at liberty to parade what they are pleased to call their independence. This we may be sure is done in all taproom coteries, and, as in such assemblies, there are never wanting discontented spirits to take advantage of moments favourable to their wishes ... by which the radical faction become embolden to look out for the most notorious demagogue they can find...[95]

From an early stage Preston Conservatives were aware of the need to politically direct and contain the working classes. The working class tendency towards extreme radicalism in the first four years of the 1830s only served to reinforce these predispositions, but Preston was not unusual in this respect amongst the industrial towns of the north-west. Throughout the region the politics of Reform, coupled with a high level of infra-class awareness and consciousness, raised the fortunes of the popular or extreme radicals. But Preston was noteworthy for the tight grip the lower middle class radicals held on local politics in the first years of the 1830s, although cracks were beginning to appear.

---

94 Lancashire County Records Office, Poll Book, (December 1830).

95 *Preston Pilot*, 14 August 1830.

From the basis of their parliamentary success, the popular radicals of Preston moved in on local politics, particularly the Vestry. This assault was led by Joseph Mitchell, but at a time when his own popularity had suffered following a dispute with Hunt. This was not, however, a local split, it assumed national proportions. It was begun in 1831 when the extreme radicals, such as Mitchell and John Irvin locally and, for a time, Hunt himself nationally, pressed for economic and physical force to gain a radical constitutional reform. The more moderate lower middle class radicals, known as the 'ten pounders' or the 'Russell Rads' because of their adherence to Lord John Russell's proposals, were led by Livesey and Robert Segar who were genuinely frightened by the turn of political events. Mitchell continued his violent oratory, attempting to stir passions through issues directly affecting working people. In December 1831 he spoke of fires burning in six counties, "and how did they know they might come nearer to home? Particularly as he had heard that … six and twenty factories were about to be stopt [*sic*] for the purpose of destroying the trades union."[96] The implication being that if their opponents were using economic weapons, (though there is no evidence of this), then so should the radicals. In such a climate the moderates began to distance themselves from extremism (as, indeed, did Hunt). Earlier in 1831 the *Pilot* had reported that:

> Fellows of the most notorious stamp struggling to divest themselves of the taint of radicalism … our Russell Rads — the ten pounder people — recoil from contact with their old play fellows.[97]

In September, Hunt's supporters in Preston placed Mitchell on 'trial' at four open air meetings for "having gone off from Hunt", and attempting to bring in William Cobbett in his place; it would seem that Mitchell had gone over to moderation.[98]

It is often overlooked by historians of the period, especially those of the Marxist school, that although class consciousness was high among working people, political sectionalisation still existed. The Tories and Conservatives were held to be responsible for blocking the Whig measure and received the wrath of the masses for their pains; but so too did many moderate reformers and Liberals. The radical leadership was in disarray for much of late 1831 and 1832 and this gave their opponents the opportunity to regroup. Extreme radicalism dismayed many of the middle classes and those professing 'respectable' opinions. At this time there were three main political groupings in Preston. There were the rapidly reorganising Conservatives backed as they were by the Corporation. There were the moderate reformers and radicals led by Livesey and Segar who backed Russell and called for step-by-step reform over several years. Finally, there were the extreme radicals, led now by John Taylor and John Irvine, who called for total and complete reform, including universal suffrage and the secret ballot. At this time, this latter group held the majority of working-class support with the moderates holding the lower middle-classes, and the Conservatives gaining support from various social groups who were rapidly becoming disillusioned and frightened by the discord and acrimony. It was in this climate that the Conservatives began their long campaign to regain the political initiative and were assisted unwittingly by the radical leadership. Although the radical leadership was split they maintained their hold on the popular support, and their ability to mobilise their supporters is indicative of some power, both in terms of action and organization. They had their own newsheet, the wordily titled *Address from one of the 3,730 Electors* that ran from January 1832 until the end of the

---

96   Ibid., 11 December 1831.

97   Ibid., 18 June 1831.

98   *Preston Chronicle*, 3 September 1831, 10 September 1831, 17 September 1831.

Reform elections in January 1833. Its tone of class antagonism was in marked contrast to the Liberal *Preston Chronicle* or Joseph Livesey's occasional sheet, *The Moral Reformer*. The popular radicals set the precedent for efficient mass political organization with the formation of the Political Union in June 1832 in readiness for the first Reform elections. According to the resolutions passed, the body favoured universal suffrage, vote by ballot, annual parliaments and no property qualifications for MPs. They then began a system of organization. "Each district," ran the report in the *Address*, "was to be divided into classes and each class was to have his own leader, the classes to pay equal proportions to a small fund to be placed in the hands of 'The Council'."[99] They refined the organization by resolving that there should be a general meeting of the Union once a month, only admitting those producing their 'red card', the membership certificate of the Union.[100] This form of localised organization was not new; the Methodists and Friendly Societies in England had used it, as had O'Connell's Catholic Association in Ireland, but two points are worth noting. Firstly, it was the first time such tactics had been used in mainland Britain for party political and electoral purposes. Secondly, the use of the term 'class' suggests an awareness of social divisions and the possibility that they could be turned to popular radical advantage.

The Political Union was an immediate success, meetings were "crowded to excess" with applications flooding in to form new classes giving credence to the boast of the *Address* that "hundreds, nay thousands [were] binding themselves together in one common bond having in view one common object."[101] To accommodate this increase in interest and membership it was necessary to take a larger room for general meetings, and, more interestingly, for "each representative to be provided with a list of the names and residence of each individual in his class". This was a precaution that reflected not only the size of the membership but also the infiltration by spies or opponents.[102] This use of the list is interesting, revealing that in Preston, at this early date, face-to-face community contact was disappearing, the traits of anonymity associated with modern urban social life evident. It also enhanced the degree to which new forms of political organization based on class or interest aggregation was needed and a subsequent decline in the older, more traditional forms of political organization. Divisions among the Radicals intensified in the run-up to the elections of December 1832. The Political Union, unashamedly Huntite in character, condemned the Cobbettites, a report in the *Address* ran,

> ... in consequence of the prevalent report of Cobbett being put in nomination at the approaching general election, we wish it to be generally known that we would feel ourselves disgraced as radical reformers and as men for having anything to do with him or his self-interested partisans.[103]

For their part, the Cobbettite radicals were equally vitriolic in condemning the Huntite Political Union. The *Preston Chronicle* reported that the Political Union was an anathema, and its methods, if truthfully reported, were abhorrent. "The Political Unions are now organizing plans of intimidation, which are disgraceful to the parties concerned in them."[104] By now local Tories and Conservatives had reached their nadir of support, and, as the old system began to crumble, they became united as a

99 *Address from one of the 3,730 Electors*, 9 June 1832.
100 Ibid., 16 June 1832.
101 Ibid., 23 June 1832.
102 Ibid.
103 Ibid., 16 June 1832.
104 *Preston Chronicle*, 11 August 1832.

party in their opposition to reform, adopting the political tactics of their opponents, and the deepening divisions among the Radicals would eventually assist the Conservatives. Those radicals who were uncompromising in their demands were doomed to oblivion as the 'respectable' political parties reasserted themselves and as local methods of political containment and control were fashioned. Others, backward looking, like Cobbett, Sadler, Oastler, who desired the return of former customs, privileges and rights were informed by natural conservative instincts. They attacked those reformers who embraced economic progress, the group who merged into Liberal Party. What was occurring at this stage was the formation of parties and ideologies, with radicalism momentarily in the ascendant but about to be torn apart into moderate Liberal progressives, radical Tories, and an extreme radical rump. This last group was to grow again during the Chartist years, but by the end of the 1830s and the beginning of the 1840s, the party political system had taken root and the radical extremists posed nothing like the threat they had in the early 1830s.

The voting in the first Reform election reflected a clear divide between the working classes and the rest, according to the *Preston Pilot*,

> The lower orders are notoriously for Hunt and Forbes ... as to the higher, the whole [are] pledged to either Mr Hesketh-Fleetwood or Mr Stanley.[105]

This was confirmed by the *Preston Chronicle* in its inquest on the failure of the Liberal, Crompton. It reported that any feeling for Crompton "was completely overpowered by the strong determination entertained by one class of voters to throw out, and by another to bring in Mr Hunt."[106] Among the working class trades it was the weavers who were most solidly radical at this election.

Table VI
Voting Patterns of the Spinners and Weavers of Preston, 1832[107]

	Weavers	Spinners
Voted for Whig, Tory, or both	197 (22.75%)	159 (53.36%)
Votes for Radicals, Hunt and Forbes	699 (72.25%)	139 (46.64%)
Total	866 (100%)	298 (100%)

Arguably the spinners were more directly subjected to influence by their employers, supported by the fact that 53 (75%) of the 71 spinning overlookers voted for the Conservative and Whig, and only 10 (14%) for both radicals. The overlookers were more obviously dependent upon the mill-owners for their higher status, as well as their jobs. However, there were a few independent spirits, as witnessed by the 10 who voted for the Radicals and the 14 (20%) who split between the Radicals and another party. This suggests that influence or coercion was not an insurmountable obstacle to free voting or to 'opinion' politics even among the elite of working class operatives.

If the main strength of middle class politics was in the trading district of Trinity ward in the centre of town and the genteel housing area of St George's ward, in terms of geographical spread, the main area of working class radicalism was in St Peter's ward on the northern fringes of the town. Here 55 per cent of spinners and 82 per cent of weavers voted radical, and where the employers were evenly split between Whig and Conservative. If this gives little support to the notion of employer influence, there was even less in Fishwick ward to the south-east. Here the influence of the Conservative

---

105 *Preston Pilot*, 1 December 1832.

106 *Preston Chronicle*, 15 December 1832.

107 Lancashire County Records Office, Preston Poll Book, 1832. The main spinning firms were Napier and Goodain, (Liberal/Whig), Catterall's (Liberal/Whig), Birley Bros, (Conservative), H. and A. Dawson, (Conservative).

Horrocks might be expected to be greatest. Yet 75 per cent of weavers and 40 per cent of spinners voted radical. Again employer influence or coercion played little part in the way that the working class polled at this election. The key factors, even at this early stage, were organization and leadership and, in relation to the working class, the radicals, even though they were split, possessed these two important elements in 1832-33 in both local and national politics. The strength of radical feelings among the working class was worrying for both Whigs and Conservatives for, if it could not be contained, both could be affected by an organized working class voting in unison against them despite the effects of the Reform Act. This form of 'political' working-class activity profoundly disturbed moderate middle-class opinion who, previously to 1832, believed that the 'lower orders' were only capable of spasmodic and spontaneous violence or being led by zealous, self-interested demagogues. The examples of 1830 and 1832 alerted the middle classes to the dangers of extreme radicalism amongst the working class. They were, of course, assisted by the terms of the Act itself. Here D. C. Moore's point that the Act was more of a 'cure' than a concession, and that it served to stabilise the system by imposing tighter controls on precisely who was allowed into the political contract, is reasonable.[108] In Preston this was to be a long-term effect. In the short term the working class were still the largest single social group on the electoral register and strategies were formulated to steer them away from extreme radicalism.

In other industrial towns various methods were utilised, either wittingly or unwittingly, to contain the working class, through tighter middle-class leadership, control of welfare provision, education, or heightened levels of dependency on the middle class manufacturers. However, at Preston the levels of dependency remained fairly low until the mid-1840s. Therefore other methods were attempted and it is here that party political organisation, political integration and the perseverance of working class-based issues became important. What is noticeable about Preston, marking it off both from its own previous political history and from the market and county towns examined earlier, is the extent of working class political involvement in the later 1820s and early 1830s, and the uncompromising nature of that group's radicalism. Similarly, the national picture appeared to bode ill for the established political groups. The reforming Whigs held a majority but little was known about the loyalties of the independent radicals in Parliament or the nationalistic radicals. The Conservatives and Tories had been decimated in the reformed House of Commons, though their control of the Lords was apparently safe. Overt coercion on the part of the authorities had worked in the past, and, indeed, was continued in the agricultural counties of the south, but the growth of industrialisation and the densely packed urban centres were seen as impossible to control by the force of arms. It was in this atmosphere that new methods of party political control were attempted in the decade after 1832.

If Preston's radicals failed in 1832, then the progressive Liberals suffered an even more disastrous result, their candidate, Crompton, polling a derisory 118 votes. This is, however, a false picture because, in both national and local politics, advanced Liberalism and reforming Whiggery were becoming identified as being but two wings of the same party. A party that by 1836-7 was to be formally organized with local branches much in the way that the Conservatives began to do in 1833-4.

At Preston the formation of the local Conservative clubs and associations took place rather later than in other industrial boroughs in the north-west. Part of the reason was the solid middle-class support given to Conservatism at Preston in 1832 plus the confidence of the Conservative Corporation and their ability to maintain their influence in parliamentary politics. This involvement

---

108 D. C. Moore, 'Concession or Cure. The Sociological Premises of the First Reform Act', in *Historical Journal*, (1966).

of the Corporation in constituency politics, absent in Lancaster, had at Preston been a permanent feature since the eighteenth century. Crucially between 1833 and 1836 there were regional developments in party organisation, beginning early in 1833 with the formation of the South Lancashire Conservative Association, but in Preston itself there was little activity on this front. As the election of 1835 approached there is evidence that older and more traditional political rituals were being fused into more overtly opinion-based tendencies, as this letter from the Conservative MP for Preston, Peter Hesketh-Fleetwood shows:

> On my way to Preston today ... I beheld a procession of persons coming towards me. I observed that they had a banner, it was not what one would call a splendid one, to me, however, nothing could be more so — it was a shawl of true blue colour, they had also some instruments of music. On approaching my carriage they insisted on taking the horses from it, and thus having the opportunity of escorting me themselves ... Respect like this could not be given I think from any other motive than a respect for my public principles ... I said that I would vote for a repeal of the Poor Law Amendment Act and toasted England's greatness: Capital and Labour.[109]

This was a popular display of traditional eighteenth-century political ritual, but now directly linked to popular issues.

As the 1830s progressed, working-class issues fell loosely into two broad categories. Firstly there were those questions which the middle classes deemed relevant to working class existence: education, religion, improved standards of moral behaviour, health and the dispensation of both public and private charity. Arguably some areas like health and charitable aid might be seen as something which any sane person would desire. These were policies that in the 1830s and 1840s were deemed good for the working class but which the latter did not perceive as central to their direct interests. The second category of issues were those which the working class themselves believed to be important, often quite independently of the middle classes. These questions included rights of citizenship, the New Poor Law and a range of issues, which centred on the place of work and the community. In a sense, it is a test of relative working class and middle class power to see which sort of issue became part of the political agenda at any given point. It is also important to see who caused it to be so. On occasions local politicians, and some national figures, pursued working class questions to further their own and their party's fortunes. This is not a cynical judgement but one which suggests that informed, opinion-based politics were emerging as the salient factor in political life in the post-Reform era.

The Preston election of 1835 was a particularly vicious affair, religious bigotry and party animosity ran high spilling over into riot.[110] The Radicals did badly; although the electorate was still predominantly working class they suffered because of the improved organisation of other movements in the town. As early as 1835 the popular radicals were being squeezed between the two established parties. These parties began to establish a commanding influence over the voters even during the Chartist years. They diverted attention away from the Radicals' sweeping political aims that seemed beyond hope of realization in the post-1832 political world, towards the more mundane, but realizable issues connected with the material interests of the working class, and, in the case of Preston, religious sectarianism. In the broad political spectrum the popular radicals can be viewed as

---

109 Reprinted in the *Preston Pilot*, 24 January 1835.

110 *Preston Pilot,* 28 March 1835. The result was a victory for Hesketh-Fleetwood, (2,165 votes), and Stanley (2,092), the Radical T. P. Thompson, polled 1,385, and the Liberal T. Smith, 789 votes.

operating on the left of Preston's politics with the moderate reformers, made up of an alliance of the Anti-Corn Law League and prominent Roman Catholic leaders, occupying the area slightly to the left of centre. The right wing became identified with the zealous Protestant squire of Cuerden Hall, Robert Townley Parker, who managed from an early date to exploit the sectarian and anti-Irish feelings of a section of the town's working class. In the 1830s the chief Conservative issues were the defence of protestantism and the opposition to the New Poor Law. The Liberals possessed an able leadership and their use of the Factory Question and the issue of cheap food enhanced their fortunes. It was not until the 1840s with the decline of Chartism and the growth of working-class suspicions of the Anti-Corn Law League, that Preston Conservatives took up the Factory Question. As will be seen shortly, this was not the case in other industrial towns in the region. Livesey was unquestionably a powerful leader of working-class opinion for the Liberals in Preston, and the Conservative chief tactic was to ridicule his moral self-righteousness, seen in the mockery heaped upon his followers by the *Pilot* in chapter four. However, they also utilised a more practical avenue of political control, and this was the annual registration of electors. They did this in two ways. The first was through the control of the overseers, deriving from their domination of the Corporation and its appointees. The second was through the Conservative Associations. By 1837 there were three Conservative Party clubs in operation at Preston. The first was the North Lancashire Conservative Association, the second the Preston Operative Conservative Association and, finally, the Conservative Registration Society. Before discussing the issues in more detail, the organization of the local Conservatives needs examination.

Operative Conservatism in Preston

The North Lancashire Association was formed as an affiliate to the South Lancashire Conservative Association but was based in Preston and catered for the organisational needs of the party outside the Parliamentary boundaries of the boroughs. This body was also the controlling Conservative organization in the northern half of the region to which all other party bodies, including those in the boroughs, was subservient. Formed in Preston in June 1835, the Association met only intermittently but held a General Meeting in September, its committee of 115 was made up of the most powerful members of the party, drawn from both the boroughs and county.[111] The President was Lord Skelmersdale, the chairman, Sir Thomas Darlymple Hesketh, the treasurer was the Preston banker, James Pedder, and Charles Buck and Edward Gorst were joint secretaries. As a body the Association was essentially Peelite in character rather than Tory, as Hesketh made clear at the outset:

> ...the protection of property is the principle upon which all Conservative Associations are founded... We not only own that we must go along with the spirit and temper of the age, but declare our willingness to countenance and cooperate on every useful reform of abuses.[112]

The assembly was told in no uncertain terms what the precise purposes of the Association were. According to Hesketh it was, "to give the whole weight of your influence to furthering the spread of Conservative principles, and thus arrest the spirit of innovation and destruction which all interests are being threatened or disregarded."[113] The General Committee was split into regions and linked to the

---

111 *Preston Pilot*, 6 June 1835.

112 Ibid.

113 Ibid.

various local associations whilst the management committee retained an office in Preston which received information about new members and information concerning the various registers throughout the region. This was forwarded to Bonham, the Conservative's national agent in London.

For their part, the Liberals acted swiftly to counter the increased level of organization of their political opponents. On 27 June they formed the Preston Constitutional Reform Association which, in terms of the locality, completed the symmetry of the political organization of the established parties and further squeezed the popular radicals of the working class between the two main party groupings. The Preston Constitutional Reform Association called for the secret ballot, biennial parliaments and the formation of a committee "whose especial responsibility it would be to take care of the registration."[114] Shortly afterwards the Conservatives formed the second and third local associations. In February 1836 they created the Preston Operative Conservative Association and, later, the Preston Conservative Registration Committee.[115] For our purposes the Operative branch was the most important. But the existence of a separate Registration Committee meant that although the operative branch was expected to forward registration information, it was not its main function, rather it was intended from the start as a distinctly working-class based branch with separate objectives. The Registration Committee acted as an overall coordinator of registration information for the whole borough in both Parliamentary and municipal politics, but in organizational terms was a separate body.

The Operative branch had an initial membership of around 200 and, from the composition of its 15-man committee, was genuinely representative of the working class. Of the committee whose occupations can be traced there was one grocer (George Addison), one clerk (Edward Vardy, Vice-President), four spinners (Robert Hart, Thomas Baxter, John Barrow and Richard Chadwick), and four weavers (William Ambler, John Walmesley, John Fletcher and William Alanson). The Association's President, Philip Addison, was a shopkeeper. Membership was free but the wealthier members were encouraged to pay subscription in 'shares' (2s) and 'half shares'. Out of these funds the annual voters' registration fees of one shilling were paid by the society for its members and they were enrolled into the party's building society.[116] It was openly acknowledged at the time that this superior organization had been a major factor in the party gaining both of the seats for the town in 1837, with Hesketh-Fleetwood being partnered by Robert Townley Parker. At this election Parker said he would vote for a repeal of the New Poor Law and oppose the principles of political economy.[117] The party's success was analysed in a subsequent article in the *Pilot*:

> Who can doubt for a moment that the triumphs obtained in the late borough elections viz, those of Liverpool, Preston, Lancaster, are attributable in a very great degree to the Conservative feeling infused into those towns through the operations of the respective Conservative Associations in them... We trust therefore that the advantages which have resulted from these associations will be kept carefully in mind, not however to be merely remembered as things past and no longer of further use, but rather as an encouragement and stimuli for future unremitting exertion in increasing and employing those means, ... which have been so productive of such important advantages.[118]

---

114 Ibid., 27 June 1835.

115 Ibid., 6 February 1836, and 7 October 1837.

116 *Preston Pilot*, 26 March 1836.

117 Ibid.

118 Ibid., 5 July 1837.

Parker himself acknowledged the work done by the operative Association when he said "… the services rendered to the late elections by these bodies of men have been felt to be of the highest importance."[119] He was quick to point out that employers had not influenced those working class electors who voted Conservative. According to Parker:

> It had been imputed that their support had been under the slavish feeling of subservience to the dictation of their masters, but I will repel such slanderous imputations with the most unqualified denial. The operatives had given their consent first, and then consulted with their masters afterwards, regardless of any attempts, which might have been made to prevent them from proving their determination.[120]

What is noteworthy on this evidence is not that they should consult at all, but, further, that they should do so when they had made up their minds.

By 1837-38 the Preston Operative Conservative Association numbered over 500 and in the summer of 1839 this has risen to 650 members.[121] To gauge the significance of these figures we can compare them with the working class membership of the Preston Radical Association, the governing body of the local Chartists. On the eve of the Sacred Month in July 1839 the Chartists claimed a membership of 400.[122] Thus working class membership of the Conservatives were more than the equal of the popular radicals, and this also tells us that working-class support in Preston for the Charter and the Sacred Month was not great. This last point was illustrated in a letter from the president of the Radical Association, Robert Walton, and its Secretary, George Halton, in late July to the Chartist National Convention in London:

> I am directed by the Committee of the Preston Radical Association to inform you that they have communicated with eight of the principal trades of the town and with the exception of two or three they are decidedly against the Sacred Month. Our Association numbers about 400 members, many of the members possess influence over their brethren and are very determined but the Committee conceives that there has not been the organisation for a successful struggle.[123]

The Conservatives claimed that the proposed general strike had been a complete failure in Preston. They claimed that working class support for constitutional principles had grown as a direct consequence of the efforts of the Operative Conservatives, suggesting that if the 400 members of the Radical Association possessed influence over the opinions of their peers, then so too did the members of the Operative Conservatives.[124] Thus the resurgence of popular radicalism at the end of the 1830s "which was rife in places of no great distance" had, in Preston, been contained by the setting up of operative branches by the Conservatives.[125] The operative branch of Preston's Conservative Association functioned in a way typical of these early political clubs. It was divided into ward

---

119 Ibid., 12 August 1837.

120 Ibid., 5 July 1837.

121 British Library, Ad. Ms. 34245B, Vol. II, 'General Convention of the Industrial Classes', (1839), ff. 119, Walton and Halton to Lovett.

122 Ibid.

123 Ibid. Nor, indeed, was support within Preston itself particularly strong in the next phase of Chartism, the General Strike of 1842. At that time, according to the *Preston Pilot*, most of the disturbances were created by outside activists, with Prestonians having little or no involvement. A fact borne out by the subsequent arrests of the 'outsiders'. *Preston Pilot*, 13 August 1842.

124 *Preston Pilot*, 17 August 1839.

125 Ibid.

organizations which met twice a month to receive new members, but more frequently during local or national elections. In the town centre there was a central clubroom with discussion classes, reading rooms and social facilities.[126] There were tea-parties, fêtes, outings, a brass band, a sick club (from 1838) and a building society.[127] All these benefits served to bind the member closer to his party, and, in turn, benefited the party by showing to the world that it catered to the needs of all social groups and not merely the elites. This meant that by 1838 Preston's Conservatives had organizationally outpaced the radicals and Liberals. In terms of local power, this effectively took four related forms. Firstly, the Conservatives had increased their grip on the apparatus of power by effecting a breakthrough in the development of the formal party structure by integrating a section of the working class. Secondly, they began to outstrip their opponents in the various contests for local power. From 1837 to 1841 the Conservatives returned both of the town's MPs and had a council majority. Thirdly, the Conservatives expanded the sources of their support and thus the sources of their power. Fourthly, the structure of power in terms of the issues the party allowed to be discussed, particularly those affecting their members' direct interest. This brings us directly to the role which issues played in the restructuring of Preston's politics after 1832 and the integration of sections of its working class effectively on equal terms.[128]

It will be seen shortly that in the north and east of the region radical Toryism played a significant part in determining working class political orientation. But in Preston it does not appear to have been a major feature. This is linked to leadership. In Preston the Conservatives began to take the lead in the Poor Law question from 1836-37, but they were not especially radical. They adhered to the law and focused their efforts on gaining a majority on the local Board of Guardians and administering the Act with the least possible pain. The view of the Operative Association in March 1838 was that:

> ... there cannot be any question that some provisions are of a character not only repugnant, but, more properly speaking, revolting to the best feelings of human nature... the most reasonable conduct would seem to be, preserve a course of opposition, but still in a temperate and legal manner.[129]

This course of action was generally followed, but the Conservatives also displayed their resolve, keeping popular issues within their political orbit when, in April 1838, they managed to gain the chairmanship of the Board of Guardians from Livesey, who had mounted a strong campaign that year.[130] The chief theme of the Conservative campaign was the moderate operation of the New Poor Law in the town, but also that Operative Conservatism and hostility to the New Poor Law were synonymous. They further suggested that Townley Parker's election to Parliament in 1837 was greatly assisted by his appeasement of the working class and his opposition to the New Poor Law. On reflection, the editor of the *Pilot* saw this as a major turning point in the town's political history:

> The present appeared to be a remarkable anal in electioneering matters, for on all former occasions the higher orders were always in advance, but at Mr Parker's election the operatives took the lead. There was no forcing the votes of the operatives... The first man to put his name

---

126 The meeting rooms were in Cannon St. *Preston Pilot*, 20 January 1838.

127 *Preston Pilot*, 10 February 1838.

128 *Preston Pilot*, 30 June 1838. This equanimity is evidenced by the *Pilot* when it reported that it was pleased to observe such gentlemen as Joseph Bray, John Latteral and John Armstrong, "sitting familiarly side by side with the respectable operative members."

129 Ibid.

130 Ibid., 14 April 1838.

to the requisition inviting Mr Parker to stand was an operative.[131]

This is an example of opinion politics, but one of the problems with opinion politics for the politician is that if he offers pledges and fails to deliver, the electorate can subsequently turn nasty. This indeed happened to Parker in 1841 when, in the election of that year the popular radical, Sir George Strickland, defeated him. The erosion of Parker's working class base was probably less to do with his own record on the question of poverty as with the fact that the Liberals had now set up their own Operative Reform Association in 1841. The issue was seen as less important than factory reform which at this time in Preston was under the control of Livesey and the radicals. The Conservative split of 1847 had a dramatic impact at Preston. It will be seen shortly that this was not the case in other parts of the north-west, but in Preston the small Peelite fringe effectively wrecked Parker's attempt at a political comeback in the election of 1847. Nevertheless, Operative Association continued to function even if its membership was being eroded, and working-class support for Conservatism seems to have been steady throughout the period 1841-1851. For example, in the ward in which most of the mills were concentrated (Christ Church) in 1841, Parker polled 211 votes to Fleetwood's 180, and Strickland's 174 votes.[132] The situation is difficult to assess precisely because of the serious decline of the old franchise holders who tended to be working class. Furthermore, the defection of Hesketh-Fleetwood, the eventual winner, to the Liberals just prior to the election of 1841 was especially hurtful to the Conservatives. By 1852 Parker had returned to be top of the poll. His links with the working class were stressed, but his incitement of religious bigotry coupled with rising tensions in this area was also contributory reasons for his success.[133] There was a Conservative Club in operation in 1852 that boasted "considerable working class support amongst its ranks".[134] Between 1847 and 1850 Operative Conservatism in Preston waned but by 1852 it was active again, complete with ward branches.[135] In Fishwick ward a meeting was held to offer a vote of thanks to Samuel Oddie, a weaver, for his work on behalf of Townley Parker. Elsewhere, at nearby Wigan for example, throughout the 1850s Operative Conservatism continued to be a significant force but, as at Preston, the Conservatives used religious intolerance in an attempt to secure the support of the working class.[136] From the later 1840s the Conservatives of Preston began increasingly to become involved in the Factory Question. In other parts of the region they had done so from the 1830s but in Preston Livesey controlled the issue with his leadership. In 1841 Livesey joined the Anti-Corn Law League, announcing that capital and labour "mutually and reciprocally acted for each others advantage" and that "the repeal of the wicked bread tax was emphatically a WORKING MAN'S QUESTION".[137] Many working people, however, remained highly suspicious of political economy and the free trade Liberals, and Livesey began to loose his following within the local Ten Hours Movement.

This left the way open for the Conservatives to begin to involve themselves in the issue. In July 1849 they invited the elderly Richard Oastler to speak in Preston in defence of the 1847 Act and against the machinations of the 'Manchester League' who were in the process of attempting to get the

---

131 Ibid., 28 April 1838.

132 Harris Library, Preston, Poll Book for 1841.

133 *Preston Pilot*, 3 July 1852.

134 Ibid., 20 March 1852. Townley Parker's election committee was made up of Revd. Parr, E. Pedder, H. Pedder (manufacturers), J. Paley (banker), R. Threllfall (manufacturer), J. Heywood (seedsman), and T. Walmey (weaver).

135 Ibid., 9 October 1852

136 Ibid., 5 June 1852.

137 J. Livesey, *The Struggle*, (December 1841), pp. 1-8.

Act repealed. In his speech, Oastler issued a scarcely veiled attack on the former friends of factory reform, like Livesey and Mitchell, who had now deserted it. He said,

> Now we have some of our leaders, as they call themselves, those whom we formally trusted ... advising us to take the law and unsettle it; and they advise to put on again those chains which have just been taken off ... I do not like snakes in the grass. I would rather face League.[138]

The mouthpiece of the Protectionists, the *Preston Pilot*, put the issue in a more basic way. What the working class required of the law was a measure of protection against unscrupulous (Liberal) mill-owners to protect them

> against avarice and tyranny, and oppression — protection against their own wants and their own weakness — and this through the unbridled lust and love of gain, that seeks its own end and pursues its own object, unchecked and unrestrained by any case at what cost to those below them.[139]

Even before the 1847 Act, Robert Gardner, a Conservative mill-owner, adopted an eleven-hour day without cutting wages, maintaining there was no fall in production, "his 700 workers' happiness and productivity had both increased and he would adopt a ten-and-a-half hour day without the slightest fear of suffering a loss". When John Bright challenged Gardner's figures and assertions, Gardner's workers defended him.[140] Later, in 1850, an address appeared in the Conservative press from the "factory operatives of Preston" to the mill owners. It began,

> Gentlemen. We the factory workers of Preston beg leave to tender you our sincere and grateful thanks for the fair and honourable manner in which, as a body, you have acquiesced in the recent law for the regulations of factory labour.[141]

At approximately the same time, in the national context, Disraeli was making his "state of the Nation" speech in the House of Commons. Here he attacked the Liberal's record, *vis-a-vis* the working class, and further attacked the New Poor Law, demanding to know why the number of paupers had increased by 74 per cent since 1846 while expenses on the poor were up by only 25 per cent.[142] However, overall (the New Poor Law apart) the Conservatives of Preston were slow to pursue working class issues. In the 1830s, and later in the 1850s, the Conservative manufacturers attacked strikes called by the working class in as vehement terms as the Liberals, and such strikes were, at times, particularly bitter.[143]

The Conservatives of Preston attracted the support of sections of the working class by a combination of means. As befits an old borough, deference and paternalism were still in evidence, as were the older rituals of political activity, some merely for show and others for direct gain. They also utilized the deep religious differences between the majority Protestants and the minority Catholics, continuing in the 1850s and 1860s with especial hostility to the Irish. They attracted some support by

---

138 Anon, *Report of the Public Meeting held at the Assembly Rooms, Preston, On the Ten Hours Movement*, (Preston, 1849), p. 19.

139 *Preston Pilot*, 9 March 1850.

140 Quoted in J. T. Ward, 'The Factory Movement in Lancashire, 1830-1855', in *Transactions of the Lancashire and Cheshire Antiquarian Society*, (1965-66), p. 196.

141 *Preston Pilot*, 27 April 1850.

142 Ibid., 14 September 1849.

143 In 1837, for example, there was a bitter strike of spinners that lasted over three months and in the mid-1850s the famous '10 percent' dispute.

their down-to-earth approach to working-class pursuits like gambling and drinking, whilst at the same time debunking the pretensions of the moral crusaders like Livesey. But they also organized effectively, and, from an early date, utilized issues and working class opinions, particularly with regard to poverty, stressing the old responsibilities of wealth and paternalism. They organized acts of private charity, they built Sunday and day schools in poor parishes, but they stuck to their principles by maintaining the Church Rate and objecting to voluntarism. However, it was the substantial working class vote that marked Preston out and their continuing involvement in politics, particularly up to 1847. Preston was a mixture of the politics of opinion and of influence. The size of the electorate worked against the widespread use of market politics, yet on occasions there were electoral riots and intimidation. But the overall trend was more towards the appeasing of electors and non-electors through the force of argument and opinion, and this was much more apparent than in Lancaster or the traditional market towns. After 1832, moreover, the Corporation attempted to put an end to the old disruptive political rituals and traditions. They banned the use of traditional party colours, the use of musical bands, and the chairing of candidates. The Bribery Acts of 1854 that heralded the age of the working-class electorate carried this process further. Preston was developing a 'respectable' political character. In 1857 the Mayor, Lawrence Spencer, told the electors at the end of the poll,

> whatever pains have been taken in your education, whatever advantages you derive from society, on occasions like this, when you would be expected to be excited to a great degree ... without drink ... without bribery, corruption or violence ... you have elected the members.[144]

By the end of the 1850s the electors and the working class of Preston could be contained and directed by the established political parties. The Conservative Party in Preston managed to counter the growth of Liberalism for most of the period under discussion. Only in the early and mid-1840s did they fail when the Anti-Corn Law League was at its height, especially with its appeal to the lower middle classes, led as they were by the redoubtable Joseph Livesey. But Livesey, by moving closer to Manchester School Liberalism, alienated much of his working-class support by abandoning the Factory Question, and here the Conservatives took advantage, especially after 1847. This trend of the Conservatives, alternating or for the most part sharing power with the Liberals, did not occur in municipal politics. Throughout the 1820s and the early 1830s the Tories and Conservatives controlled the Corporation. In the years following the imposition of the Municipal Reform Act they dominated local politics. The main reason for Conservative domination was their level of organization and the fairly extensive powers given over to the Liberal dominated Improvement Commission leaving the Conservatives to control the Council. However, such was the Conservatives level of organization that even after the full operation of the Small Tenements Act after 1853, which gave the municipal franchise to the working class, they maintained their advantage. This point is underscored by the success of the Conservatives during the mid-1850s in those wards (Trinity,

---

144 Harris Library, Preston, Poll Book for 1857. Further evidence of this climate of respectability came from one of the candidates of the 1857 parliamentary election. In March of that year the prospective candidate for Preston, the future Home Secretary, R. A. Cross, wrote to the Liberal solicitor, Henry Hall, regarding the Bribery Acts. He asked four questions relating to, a) the hiring of printers, writers, canvassers, messengers and attendants, (this was legal); b) living rooms (which was regarded as hazardous as it may sway the owners vote); c) hiring transport to convey voters (answer as in b and d) whether he could pay shopkeepers whose assistants wished to give their time in his cause. Answer. "This is too hazardous to be allowable and should not be adopted." Such was the fear of the Acts that the Radical Strickland had dismissed all his paid canvassers. British Library, Ad. Ms. 51269, Cross Papers, Cross to Hall, March 1857.

Fishwick, St George's and St Peter's) with the greatest concentration of working class voters.[145] In terms of local politics, the progressive Liberals were not popular with the working class before 1870. This was largely due to their poor record in industrial relations. In both major disputes of the period, the spinners strike of 1837-38 and the "10 percent" dispute of 1853-54, it was the Liberal employers who resisted the demands of the working class and came in for the most criticism from working-class leaders.[146] Indeed, during that especially bitter struggle the strike leaders asked Robert Townley Parker to act as their 'umpire' in the dispute.[147] The Conservative *Preston Pilot* openly supported the working class. The operatives had no other choice left to them at present but [to] strike to resist the tyranny of the manufacturing class, and to force, to some extent, a modification of their demands upon their employers.[148]

Over the period covered here the Conservatives were more united in the local political arena than the Liberals and, importantly, had superior organization. At Preston this was due to the Conservatives history in the town, of being the standard bearers of Anglicanism and, importantly, the experience of dealing with a large working-class electorate over many decades. The Liberals, for their part, were relative newcomers to the political game at Preston, being in the 1830s, '40s and '50s an amalgam of not necessarily compatible components. Included in their ranks were radicals, old Whigs, Manchester School economic hard-liners and various reformers drawn to the party through religion or special interest group zeal. These benefits and drawbacks were reflected and to a significant extent informed the direction of municipal politics at Preston. It was common for local politicians in the first half of the nineteenth century to play down party conflicts in the council chamber whilst maximising them at elections. The Preston Conservatives were masters of this tactic. In 1837 for example they utilized the power of the Operative branch of the party to full effect. According to the editor of the *Pilot* the municipal contests in 1837 were "set up from political motives" which he stated as "an object altogether foreign to the purpose of securing the most efficient guardians and managers of the corporation's funds". In Fishwick ward the leading member of the Operative Conservative Association, Philip Addison, defeated Barton, a Liberal cotton spinner with two years experience on the council. The *Pilot* positively gloated:

> But he [Barton] is a cotton spinner, and has his mill in the ward, and that is an accidental circumstance of no mean advantage on the occasion of an election where local influence and interest are much needed.[149]

Addison was "the President of the Operative Conservative Association, without the local influence of Mr Barton or his experience in municipal affairs."[150] After the 1835 Municipal Reform Act some may have desired that municipal politics be free of party political battles, but not so the Conservatives. Resolution seven of the Operative Conservative Constitution ran:

> that this Association holds itself pledged in all elections, borough or municipal, to use all its energy in returning Conservative members, and each member individually to delineate as much

---

145 *Preston Pilot*, 5 November 1853, 4 November 1854, 10 November 1855, 22 November 1856, 7 November 1857.

146 See H. I. Dutton and J. E. King, *Ten per cent and No Surrender: The Preston Strike of 1853-54*, (Cambridge, 1971), *passim*.

147 *Preston Pilot*, 1 October 1853.

148 Ibid., 8 October 1853.

149 Ibid., 4 November 1837.

150 Ibid.

as possible the principles of this society.[151]

Finally, there are three points of note here which encapsulate how far and how quickly the party political system had developed by 1837. Firstly, the working class were officially being allowed into the party structure; secondly, that these operatives were aiming at winning elections for the party and, thirdly, that they were extolling the policies and principles of Conservatism to a wider audience.

Looking at Preston, we have seen that the old traditional ways of political activity did continue in the post 1832 world. But we have also seen how the opinions of this largely working-class electorate were courted and how the Conservatives came to terms with the post-1832 situation much more successfully than the Liberals. Extreme working-class radicalism was nullified and the two established parties sought to gain working class support and attempted to integrate sections of the working class in order to steer them away from extreme radicalism. The political history can be seen as a mixture of the old form of political activity and of the new.

By 1860 opinions and the influence of interest groups were the mode of political contests. The Conservatives had come to terms with the experience that in return for support and votes something had to be given back. The interests of the working class had to be considered. This may appear to be a tautological statement but in the analysis of power and the politics it represented, it was a significant departure from the pre-1832 situation. Throughout the eighteenth and early nineteenth centuries the plebeian and working classes were viewed as a mob, fickle, often intemperate, open to corruption, backward looking and politically ignorant of worthwhile opinions. The fact that they possessed the vote in Preston was seen as an anomaly. By the 1860s this was not the case. Preston's interest to the historians is that the elites attempted to control and direct a large working class electorate at this crucial intervening period of the two political cultures. What of the boroughs created by the Act of 1832? Here the working classes were mainly non-electors, but this did not mean that they had no political muscle or were not involved in the political affairs of their towns.

---

151 Ibid., 7 October 1837, 'Rules and Constitution of the Preston Operative Conservative Association.'

6

The New Boroughs

So far we have looked at working class politics and Conservative Party development in the old boroughs of various types. The intention now is by way of comparison to examine similar developments in some of the north-west boroughs created by the Reform Act of 1832. The main focus will be on the Blackburn area but also the general trends occurring in Bolton and we shall finally be looking briefly at developments in Manchester, Salford and radical Oldham. But let us begin by moving in geographical terms some twelve miles south east of Preston to the town of Blackburn.

The Economic and Social Structure of Blackburn

It was noted earlier that radicalism and working class political consciousness grew in Preston from the mid 1820s to 1832, but became less effective after this date because of leadership splits which, in turn, sectionalized the working class radicals. Working class developments in Blackburn followed a similar pattern, with some important qualifications. The first is that in Blackburn working class consciousness reached a very high level before 1826 and during the trade disputes of that year and, secondly, that by 1837-8 working class radicalism in Blackburn was not simply split, but scarcely existed. Another important difference is of course, whereas in Preston the great majority of working class males enjoyed the franchise before and after 1832, Blackburn was not enfranchised prior to the Reform Act, and afterwards only those holding property of £10 rateable value were given the vote. Thus the working class were effectively left out of the political contract. In local politics at Blackburn the town did not become an incorporated borough until 1851. But this did not mean a lack of working class participation. The occupational and economic structure of Blackburn is interesting. It differed from both Lancaster and Preston in that its populations was far larger than the former and smaller than the latter in the 1820s. Neither was it at the geographical centre of a major road network in the way both the others were. It was predominantly a weaving town with a few manufacturers, the Feildens, Hornbys, Eccles, and Hopwoods, expanding their concerns to include spinning and the finishing of cotton goods. There was some coal mining in the area but in the main Blackburn was a weaving centre with women becoming increasingly involved in the spinning of yarn, and handloom weaving the preserve of males. But there were several types of weavers in Blackburn in the 1820s. In Preston by the middle of the 1820s the weavers had switched over to power very peacefully and quickly, and there were other large scale industrial enterprises in that town, such as machine making, not to be found in Blackburn. Conversely, what was found in Blackburn in the mid 1820s was a large proportion of handloom weavers still operating in the town centre or within a couple of miles of the town itself.

Early Working Class Militancy

Throughout the period from 1815 to the onset of the Reform agitation, the handloom weavers of Blackburn appear to have been extremely militant and politically radical. In 1818, for example, the women of Blackburn had formed the Female Reform Society.[1] But by far the most serious display of militant radicalism and violent behaviour by the weavers came in 1826 with the resumption of widespread machine breaking. What is noteworthy was all of Blackburn's textile workers, power loom weavers, spinners and handloom weavers acted in complete harmony with high levels of class and political consciousness being displayed and little sign of occupational intra-class status differences. We know this comes from the existence of a trades committee which coordinated the dispute and was made up of all three sets of textile workers and was, in effect, a general association of textile workers (led by the working class themselves) which remained united throughout the dispute.[2] The dispute itself lasted from April to the end of July, spreading from East Lancashire to south of the region and into Yorkshire and coinciding with a sharp depression in trade.

The disputes in East Lancashire have been detailed elsewhere but with regard to the discussion of working class development and consciousness there are two important points of note.[3] The first is that at this point in their development the working class of East Lancashire were operating with a will to act around questions organized and formulated within the class itself and not from any outside agencies, such as middle class inspired pressure groups or, indeed, political parties. This latter agency, at this stage in its evolution, did not get involved in working class-based issues. Secondly, the harmony of the Blackburn weavers suggests strong leadership from within the working class themselves. Evidence for this comes from a memorial sent by the mechanics of Blackburn to the first Sir Robert Peel. It reveals that the two chief causes of working class action were, firstly, the loss of independence brought by the factory system and also the frequent breakdown in that system which created such widespread privation and insecurity. The language is important for it suggests a heightened sense of awareness that a body of workers had for the plight of their fellows in another. It ran,

> No adequate idea can be formed of the sufferings of those who are unemployed, of whom there are upwards of 7,000 in this town and neighbourhood. Were a humane man, Sir to visit the dwellings of four-fifths of the weavers and see the miserable pittance which sixteen hours of labour can procure divided between the parents and the little ones, he would sicken at the sight and blush for the patience of humanity.[4]

Powerful forces were at work on the consciousness of the working class of Blackburn. Those engaged in factory work shared the insecurity and loss of independence, especially prevalent in the handloom sector. To the working class entering the factory meant the loss of independence, coupled with the fact that there was still no guarantee of job and wage stability as the severe trade slumps bore witness. In crude terms, where was the value of entering the factory, becoming utterly dependent on that manufacturer when those workers inside the factories appeared just as prone to the trade cycles as those weavers outside it. Yet the manufacturers who pleaded the inviolate vagaries of the market and were laying workers off or reducing their rates of pay, could still embark on the building of new factories or fitting out existing ones with the expensive power looms. This leads to a related factor, namely the appalling poverty prevailing in Blackburn in the mid-1820s. Indeed, as noted earlier, the situation of the Blackburn weavers prior to the outbreak of the disturbances became so bad that it gained national notoriety. Support came from parts near and distant; Liverpool, Bristol,

---

1   Thompson, *The Making of the English Working Class*, pp. 454-6.

2   *Blackburn Mail*, 15 February 1826, *Annual Register*, (1826).

3   D. Walsh, 'The Lancashire Rising of 1826', in *Albion*, vol. 26 No. 4, (Winter, 1994).

4   PRO (Kew) HO 44/16, The Mechanics of Blackburn to Sir Robert Peel, 9 April 1826.

and London. Indeed, the weavers of Yeovil in Somerset organized meetings and collected money specifically for the weavers of East Lancashire.[5] Given this situation and the level of local working class unity, organization and leadership an explosive social atmosphere prevailed.

The spark was produced locally by the attitude of the employers of East Lancashire. The manufacturers remained adamant in their refusal to discuss the joint weaver/spinner demands. This was unlike the situation at Bolton, Preston or Stockport, where discussions and meetings were held between the various antagonists, and serious disturbances averted.[6] A further worry for the local and national authorities of the worsening situation in East Lancashire was that some of the military sent to quell the disturbances appeared as a source of solace for the weavers as Thomas Duckworth, an apprentice weaver from Haslingden, recalled,

> That morning we set off to the loom breaking. When we had got on the road we saw the soldiers. There was a stop then, the horse soldiers came forward, their drawn swords glittering in the air... Some threw their pikes over the dyke and some didn't. When the soldiers had come into the midst of the people, the officers called out, 'halt!' All expected that the soldiers were going to charge, but the officer made a speech to the mob and told them what the consequences would be if they persisted in what they were going to do... 'What are we going to do? We're starving. Are we to starve to death?' The soldiers were fully equipped with haversacks and they emptied their sandwiches among the crowd. Then the soldiers left and there was another meeting. 'Were the looms to be broken or not? yes, it was decided, they must be broken at all costs.'[7]

A letter from a cavalry officer to Home Secretary Peel is indicative of the lack of awareness on the part of the elites when confronted by a determined, organized and violently disaffected civil population, on this occasion at Chadderton near Oldham:

> Several of the mob were killed and it is to be feared from the incessant firing, which was kept up for more than a quarter of an hour, that a considerable number must have been wounded. Between 500 and 600 shots were fired. The populous then dispersed gradually, but with the avowed intention of returning with overwhelming force. The obstinacy and determination of the rioters was most extraordinary, and such as I could not have credited had I not witnessed it myself.[8]

So the forces of the state acted and the disturbances were quelled. The county magistrates swore in large numbers of special constables who, under the cover of darkness, began to round up suspected leaders and were sent immediately to Lancaster gaol. David Whitehead, a manufacturer from Rawtenstall, described developments in his locality in a letter to Peel:

> The inhabitants were all in amazement, one telling another that such and such had been fetched out of bed... This method of arresting them and taking them away completely put a stop to the breaking of power looms... The rioters were so frightened that a-many durst not go to bed in their own houses. Some left for the country, others hid themselves for weeks, some in one

5   *Bristol Gazette*, 4 May 1826, see also L. Mumby, *The Luddites*, (London, 1971), pp 46-7.

6   Bolton Reference Library, Local History Archive, Meeting Sheets, Addresses and Advertisements, Spencer thesis, pp. 50-8, *Manchester Mercury*, 6 May 1826.

7   Quoted in C. Aspin, *A Local History of Helmshore*, (Helmshore, 1969), p. 48.

8   PRO (Kew), HO 44/74, unsigned officer to Peel, 26 April 1826.

place, some in another, some in local pits, some who few, if any, would have thought would have been guilty of such a crime.[9]

Report after report makes the same point that the disruption caused by mechanization was turning moderate sober-minded individuals into insurgents and 'radical demagogues', and was indicative of the homogenous nature of working class consciousness at this time. However, a further question is whether the working class of the north-west were displaying any political manifestations and aspirations prior to the 1830s?

It has already been noted that there was a widespread perception of the denial of industrial and political rights to working people held by the majority of the working class themselves and by the lower-middle class popular radicals. This can be detected in both the actions of the working class and what they said throughout the north-west industrial region, especially from 1818. The popular radicals utilized this disaffection amongst the working class as evidence of their own popular support 'out of doors'. The important point is that increasingly the moderate, respectable middle classes and the authorities believed them. However, the violent disputes of the mid-1820s were not overtly political in the sense that the struggle was mounted directly for the purpose of recovering lost rights of citizenship. But the political element lay just under the surface, as the *Blackburn Mail* bore witness when it referred to those involved in the 1826 dispute as "the disciples of Paine and the blasphemies of Carlile."[10] The logic of the situation also evinces a strong political element. Here was a large section of people suffering appalling privations due to trade recession and industrial rationalisation and the state appeared not to be acting in their interests. The state appeared to back the interests of that group who the working class believed were the cause of their problems: the industrial manufacturers of nascent capitalism. Not only this, but the government seemed unwilling, hostile to combating the high food prices by the allowing into the country cheaper foreign grain and sticking rigidly to the 1815 Corn Laws. Indeed, the *Gentleman's Magazine* ascribed the onset of the disturbances to Whitmore's failed motion to the repeal the Corn Laws.[11] Significantly the Enabling Bill, to open the ports and allow grain stored in bonded warehouses, like those at Liverpool, was made by Canning in parliament when the House of Commons was debating the situation in the industrial north.[12] The realization on the part of the working class was that the government was protecting one group in society at the expense of another. It is thus only a short step, as was the case at Blackburn in the 1820s, from being able to objectively recognise one's class position in economic terms, to forming a political consciousness. A consciousness that identifies the problem as the states' inability or unwillingness to act or to legislate on behalf of those who feel they are being repressed. It is also reiterating the point made earlier that no efforts were made by the agencies of governmental or manufacturing opinion, for example political parties, which could have acted as a countervailing corpus of understanding against the views held by the working class. In effect the popular radicals had the field to themselves. The obvious solution that developed by the late 1820s was that the working class had to organize collectively into trades unions. But also to attempt to gain working class representations within the institutions of local and national political control. In the local context this was focused on the Open Vestry and Select Vestry, and in the national sense on the growing realization of the necessity of reforming parliament to include more representatives of the working

---

9   PRO (Kew), HO 44/19, Whitehead to Peel, undated.

10 The press at the time certainly believed a strong political element was motivating the crowd, see *Blackburn Mail*, 14 June 1826.

11 *Gentleman's Magazine*, (May 1826), p. 458.

12 *The Times*, 2 May 1826.

class interest. These feelings were strongest in those boroughs denied representation before 1832. It is worth stressing that the disputes of the 1820s did not end with the 1826 disturbances. The developing theory of general unionism and the way the various trades were able to cooperate with each other assisted in the homogeneous nature of the class response. At Accrington, for example, the dispute of 1826 was signalled by a demonstration of weavers. But it was led by a shoemaker and a chair-maker, whilst elsewhere those arrested included farmers, mechanics, confectioners and other assorted trades.[13] We have already observed that in East Lancashire the handloom weavers, power loom weavers and spinners were able to work together on equal terms. Throughout the region as a whole many other artisans and labourers were involved in pre-Reform Act working class politics. There were shoemakers, hatters, tailors, mechanics, builders, joiners, etc., etc., all of high status in occupational terms and mixing quite freely and equitably with those (such as power loom weavers) of a lesser occupational grade in terms of status. Moreover, this was true of the period of Parliamentary Reform.

Reform and Parliamentary Politics in Blackburn

In Blackburn particularly the Reform agitation galvanized local working class radicals into a concerted call for remedying a range of working class grievances. The public meeting was one way in which information was disseminated and supporters recruited, but the popular radicals of Blackburn also utilized the Vestry as a focus for their political agitation. Here George Dewhurst (reed maker) Robert Witherington (weaver) and George Meikle (bookseller and distributor of the unstamped press) led them.[14] At this time the Whigs/Liberals came in for less vitriol than the Tories, unsurprising considering that in the national context it was the Tories who were perceived as being the group most resistant to constitutional change. The Blackburn Political Union passed a resolution during the 'days of May' crisis calling for the names of local Tories be read at a public shaming "in order to show that they may be exposed to the detestation of their fellow townsmen."[15] But as soon as the Bill was passed and notification came through of the two seats Blackburn had been given by the Act, the views of the Radicals were diverted by the conciliatory attitude adopted by the Conservatives to the new electorate. One proposed candidate, John Fowden Hindle (one of the local county gentry), issued a public address at end of May in which he said, "...I shall always be found among the advocates of every constitutional reform, having for its object the happiness of the community."[16] At Blackburn the Conservatives acted swiftly after the passing of the Act. They endeavoured to present a face of moderate conciliation, and this seems to have had an immediate effect. One member of the Political Union, as early as October 1832, stated publicly that he was intending to cast his vote for Hindle, an early indication of opinion politics in the new parliamentary borough.[17] Other evidence testified that at Blackburn the local elites were attempting to place politics at a more advanced level. John Bowring for example, one of the reforming candidates, pledged that no treats would be given to electors or non-electors, hence he and his supporters were known as the 'Dry Party'.[18] A second came from a ban on 'chairing' and the wearing of party ribbons, evidence that

13 *Blackburn Mail*, 10 May 1826, 24 May 1826.

14 *Blackburn Alfred*,17 September 1832.

15 *Blackburn Gazette*, 22 May 1832.

16 Blackburn Reference Library, Local Studies Collection, PO 1832, 'The Election Address of John Fowden Hindle.'

17 *Blackburn Alfred*, 29 October 1832.

18 W. A. Durham, *A History of Parliamentary Elections for the Borough of Blackburn*, (Blackburn, 1868), p. 8, also *Blackburn Alfred*, 23 January

the magistrates were attempting to keep party feelings as low as possible whilst not allowing the town to be encumbered by the political traditions and rituals of an earlier age. It is interesting to compare this situation with Preston, where tradition was enthusiastically maintained. At Blackburn however, there were some important political shifts in the 1830s and '40s.

A major development in the first years of the 1830s was the growth of radical Toryism in north east Lancashire. Among the still numerically significant handloom weavers of Blackburn there were strong links with that brand of radical Toryism associated firstly with Michael Thomas Sadler and later with Richard Oastler and the Rev Rayner Stephens. Even middle class Conservatives seem to have been sympathetic to this group. After Sadler's defeat in the elections of 1832, referring to his work on the Factory Question and the resistance of the Whig/Liberal manufacturers in Yorkshire, the *Blackburn Alfred* commented, "His Toryism and impatience of Reform would have been freely forgiven, but for his unpardonable offence against the mill tyrants of that pious and slave-whipping neighbourhood."[19]

The condition of handloom weavers and the issue of factory reform were central to working class politics in Blackburn from the early 1830s through to the 1850s. Initially it was the popular radicals who took up these issues. From 1830 to 1834, and briefly in 1837, the popular radicals under the leadership of George Dewhurst and the two weavers, Witherington and Gifford, dominated the Vestry. The Radicals and Liberals also seem to have been powerful in the Police Commission that replaced the Vestry in 1841. Up to the incorporation of the borough in 1851, the local Conservatives took little interest in the town's local government. They were, however, active in parliamentary politics, and returned a member for the town in every election from 1832 to 1852, and regained the seat after a successful petition against defeat in 1853. In 1865 and 1868, the Conservatives took both seats, the 1868 election was particularly important as the electorate was greatly swelled by working class votes under the householder suffrage.

The Political Culture of Blackburn

The town's leading Conservatives were Robert Hopwood, James Forrest, James Pemberton, William Eccles, William Feilden MP, John Hornby and his brother William Henry, and all the substantial mill-owners. The lawyer Richard Backhouse, the shopkeeper Christopher Parkinson and the surgeon Richard Martland ably assisted them. Although the leading Conservatives were willing to leave some aspects of local government to the Liberals, they continued to control key areas such as the local county magistracy. However, in the early 1830s the Conservatives became concerned with the way the working class popular radicals were attempting to control local government. William Henry Hornby realised early in 1833 that the attack on the Conservatives and on the future of local government came from the seemingly irresistible progress of Liberalism and the radical inclinations of the working class. Through the Conservative newspaper the *Blackburn Alfred* he said,

> There is a party in this town, who are working night and day to bring all our municipal affairs under their immediate control ... and endeavouring to set the lower and higher class at variance. Let the radical and revolutionary characters once get ahead in the country, and there is an end to the constitution.[20]

1833.

19   *Blackburn Alfred*, 7 January 1833.

20   Ibid., 21 January 1833.

Although the leading local Conservatives were willing to leave the Liberals those areas of local government where they felt their damage could be contained, the union of a 'revolutionary' class and the 'radical' Liberal party was a threat to not only local stability but also to local Conservatism. [21] As noted earlier, in some parts of the region during the reform crisis, the alliance of the lower middle-class radicals and the working class had been broken. At Bolton, Oldham and Manchester, after the King's proclamation banning political meetings in November 1832, the working class radicals took over their respective political unions. [22] At Blackburn, however, the alliance of the lower middle class radicals and the working class was maintained, which made it vital that the Conservatives reorganise quickly.

Religion was also a motivating factor of many local Conservatives in this early stage of re-organization, both in terms of attempting to convince the working class of the moral worth of religious instruction, and also to gain support to defeat Liberal attempts of reforming the Anglican Church. From 1829 and the acceptance of Catholic Emancipation through to 1835 and the Litchfield House compact, where the Whigs were partially successful in binding Joseph O'Connell to moderation and to the party line, the reform of the Anglican Church was fiercely resisted by the Conservatives. This threat served to rally Anglicans of all classes to the party's colours. In Blackburn feelings ran high, according to one source the reformers were unleashing "a power anti-social and revolutionary in its principles, and constituted for the avowed purpose of plundering our church of her revenues... Let them succeed in dismantling one single barrier of our now tottering constitution, and the revolutionary flood rushes in."[23] Although Conservative opinion in Blackburn was at times vehemently anti-Catholic and anti-Irish, they were willing to compromise in some areas. On the church rate question in 1837, for example, the *Standard* reported, "If the Church rate were abolished, a bone of contention would be taken away — Dissenters and Churchmen would meet and be more happy and friendly, the effect in local situations would be the preventing of that unpleasantness which had existed in Blackburn for so many years."[24]

Let us consider the political preferences of Blackburn's electorate in 1835 in relation to their religion. The figures below show the numerical strength of the Anglicans and the Conservatives, and clearly the Anglicans were not averse to voting tactically for the Whig reformer Turner in order to keep out Bowring, the Liberal high-flyer from London. However, they only reveal the religious denominations of Blackburn's middle and lower middle class electorate; little is known of the religious persuasions of town's working classes. It is known that until the 1850s working-class religious attendance was at best spasmodic. Even after 1850, when participation is believed to have increased, Horace Mann, the author of the 1851 census report, stated that in the large towns and cities of England "fewer than one person in ten attended either Church of England or Nonconformist worship on census day."[25] This denotes Church attendance on one day in one year and may not of course be reflective of overall working-class religious feelings. But given that the middle classes

---

21 The powers of the Vestry were extremely limited after the introduction of the Sturges Bourne's Select Vestries Act of 1819 and were reduced even more in the mid-1830s by the effects of the 1834 Poor Law Amendment Act. However, the point regarding the Vestries was not their power to effect meaningful change or to levy local taxes, but that they were becoming rallying points of the disaffected and as such were a platform for the wider dissemination of dangerous political doctrines.

22 See W. Brimelow, *Parliamentary History of Bolton*, (Bolton, 1880), pp. 109-110, *Manchester Guardian*, 5 December 1832, *Bolton Chronicle*, 5 December 1831.

23 *Blackburn Alfred*, 28 January 1833.

24 *Blackburn Standard*, 18 January 1837.

25 *Parliamentary Papers*, Census, Vol. 89, (1852-53), p. 158.

spent enormous amounts of time, money and energy in attempting to make the working class learn the moral teaching of religion, this suggests that irreligion was perceived as a problem before 1850. It cannot be proven with any degree of certainty that because the majority of Blackburn's elites were Anglican the working class would be similarly inclined. Religion was important, especially in relation to social control. But at Blackburn, at least, at this critical stage greater organizational efficiency was at least of equal importance.[26]

Table VII
Analysis of Voters by Religious Denomination: Blackburn, 1835
Fielden (Conservative), Turner (Whig Reformer), Bowring (Lib. Reformer)[27]

Name of Candidate and Type of Vote Given

Religious Denomination	Plumped Fielden	Plumped Turner	Plumped Bowring	Split F&T	Split F&B	Split T&B	Total
Anglican	4	15	34	263	9	58	383
Independent	0	2	66	15	3	25	111
Catholic	2	1	15	4	2	15	39
Methodist	0	0	21	10	3	16	50
Baptist	0	0	2	0	0	3	5
Quaker	0	0	5	0	1	2	8
Unitarian	0	0	20	0	0	3	23
Total	6	18	163	292	18	122	619

Total votes including splits	Anglican	Independent	Catholic	Methodist	Baptist	Quaker	Unitarian
Fielden	276	18	8	13	-	1	-
Turner	336	42	20	26	3	2	3
Bowring	101	94	32	40	5	8	2

Political Organization in Blackburn

It was the local Conservatives who began the process of party organization in Blackburn. The Conservative Association was formed in late 1834 at the time when Peel formed a minority ministry and the prospect of an early election seemed likely. In February 1835 the Committee of the Association met for the purpose of admitting "members, appointing officers and adopting resolutions in furtherance of the objects of the Association."[28] Its first President was John Fowden Hindle, and his deputy was W. H. Hornby. William Feilden, MP for the town, was a member, and the first committee was composed of the leading members of the local Conservative elites, especially the

---

26 Orangeism was factor in some areas during the 1830s (Wigan and Liverpool) especially after 1835 and the Orange Lodges were banned by parliament and many Orangemen felt they were being persecuted. At Blackburn extreme protestantism was not a salient feature, nor was it in the 1850s and 60s when the anti-Irish and anti-Catholic battles were being fought in and around Manchester.

27 Ibid., 4 August 1835.

28 *Blackburn Standard*, 4 February 1835.

manufacturers, gentry, wholesalers and retailers.[29] These included William Alston, J. Hargreaves, Joseph Makinson, James Cross, R. S. Dodgson, James Dodgson, W. B. Maymon, Dixon Robinson, John Lister, Benjamin Brierley, Henry Hargreaves, Christopher Parkinson, James Forrest, and the secretary was Peter Ellingthorpe. Many of these men were to play important roles in the political life of the town in the next four decades. However, even at this early stage the local Conservatives were anxious to widen the net of the party. In February 1835 they announced that the annual subscriptions had been, "placed as low as 5 shillings, to afford an opportunity for such as the working classes as are disposed to stem the progress of revolutionary doctrines to become members of the association."[30] By November 1835 the Conservatives realized that 5 shillings was far too high a figure to be paid by the working classes and with the formation of the Operative Association the entry fee was 6 pence, with 6 pence annual subscription.[31]

The middle class Conservatives of Blackburn, who made the first move toward greater political integration in their local party, made it clear why they had done so. This concerned three areas of the party's ideology: the defence of Anglicanism, the Constitution, and the need to further the Conservative message in order "to stem the progress of revolutionary doctrines."[32] The Liberals followed quickly in forming their main association on 4 March 1835, headed by the prominent local manufacturer James Pilkington, suggesting that the need to take care of the annual registration of electors was also an inducement to organize. These three themes of religious and constitutional preservation, political proselytization, and local politico/electoral organization lie at the foundation of the associations in the new boroughs, but in due course they were joined by a fourth, that of the dissemination of Conservative policy, and issues directed at working class opinion. The Conservative Association launched the Operative Conservative Association late in November 1835. The *Blackburn Standard* made some optimistic but still significant statements as to the reactions of the political opponents of Conservatism. It stressed party political rather than religious distinctiveness in an article entitled 'The Whig Radicals and the Operative Conservatives',

> The Whig Radicals and the Revolutionists are suffering the most excruciating tortures, from the contemplation of the result of the revision of the elective register, and the prospect of an extensive establishment of Operative Conservative Associations. In the former they see the certainty of an early and complete defeat ... and in the latter they behold an efficient instrument for such a wide dissemination of sound political information as shall render it absolutely impossible for interested and unprincipled agitators any longer to retain their hold upon the prejudices of the people.[33]

The prime movers in the forming of the Operative Association in Blackburn were James Martin, the editor of the *Blackburn Standard* and Dixon Robinson, the clerk to the magistrates. However, both the Liberal *Blackburn Gazette* and the *Manchester Guardian* reported that two 'strangers' were at the meeting, suggesting that the impetus for the setting up the association came from outside, but neither the *Gazette* nor the *Guardian* claimed the Operative Association was linked to Orangeism.[34] Elsewhere in other parts of the region the situation was very different. In 1835 Parliament had

---

29 Blackburn Reference Library, Trade Directory, (1834).

30 *Blackburn Standard*, 18 February 1835.

31 Ibid., 18 November 1835.

32 Ibid.

33 *Blackburn Standard*, 25 November 1835.

34 *Blackburn Gazette*, 2 December 1835 and 9 December 1835, *Manchester Guardian*, 5 December 1835.

outlawed the Orange Lodges, but the Lodges continued to exist, and the *Manchester Guardian* mounted a campaign accusing the Salford Conservatives of setting up Operative Branches as vehicles for Orangeism. The Operative Conservatives of Manchester and Salford were quick to repudiate the assertions of the *Guardian* and placed an advertisement in the *Guardian* and other newspapers stating that "persons from all persuasions being members of the society; and are admitted providing they acknowledge themselves to be Conservatives." They asserted not only Orangemen were members "but also Protestant Dissenters and Roman Catholics, who though differed on many points, are still agreed in their attachments to the existing institutions of the country, and are prepared to support them by every constitutional means in their power."[35] At Liverpool and Wigan there were links between Orangeism and the Conservative party,[36] but elsewhere caution is needed, especially considering that prominent Catholics like Trafford and Sir John Gerrard were members of both the Manchester Conservative Association and the South Lancashire Association.[37] In Blackburn the Liberals suspected that the Operative Association was not so much the hotbed of Orangeism but rather the tool of the national party attempting to interfere in local political organization. In an article written in the *Gazette* in late November 1835 it came to light that the Conservative *Blackburn Standard* was being run from London,

> ...it is said under the auspices of the Carlton Club... the *United Services Gazette*, the *Alfred*, and *Old England* newspapers; and from these are manufactured, by simply *changing the name*, [*Gazette's* emphasis] of country journals [including] the *Blackburn Standard*, the *Surrey Standard*, the *Dover Telegraph*, the *Oxford Conservative*, the *West Devon Standard*, the *Worcester Guardian*, the *Greenwich Guardian* and the *Leicester Herald* — such are the attempts of the Tory Faction to spread their noxious principles in the country.[38]

It seems therefore that Conservatives at the centre were indeed making an effort to influence opinion in the localities. However, such outside influence in the setting up of the clubs is difficult to prove, although it is known that Robert Scarr Sowler, one of the leaders of the Manchester Conservatives, employed a barrister, one Charles Wilkins, to tour the north-west.[39] A key moment at Blackburn came when William Henry Hornby became President of the Conservative Association in 1836, and he immediately began to cultivate a body of support among the Blackburn working class. In his inauguration speech he defined Conservatism as loyalty to the monarch, "attachment to the constitution, obedience to the laws and kindness to the poor."[40] At the annual dinner of BCA in April he suggested that the existence of an Operative branch of the Conservative Party in Blackburn:

> give[s] a proof to Conservatives of wealth and station, so far from regarding the working classes with feelings the least approaching to contempt or indifference, that it is their great pride to acknowledge that they themselves can only stand or fall with them.[41]

---

35 *Manchester Guardian*, 5 September 1835, 12 September 1835.

36 *The Times*, 21 October 1836.

37 It is also worth making the point that at Salford, for example, as far as the Association being a cover for extreme Protestants, the Operative Association was formed months before the Orange Lodges were banned.

38 *Blackburn Standard*, 28 November 1835, *Manchester Guardian*, 19 December 1835. This information validated the evidence of Alfred Mallalieu given in his memorandum to Lord Aberdeen some four years earlier, see British Library, Ad. Mss 57420, Herries Papers, for how Mallalieu suggested the Conservatives could control the provincial press.

39 *Manchester Guardian*, 26 November 1836.

40 *Preston Pilot*, 27 February 1836.

41 Ibid., 23 April 1836.

Hornby began to foster the image of a good and fair master, a device not peculiar to the Conservative manufacturers, but especially relevant in the era of doctrinaire Liberalism and Manchester school reformism. Furthermore, this tendency reached working-class audiences further afield than Blackburn. In Stockport, for example, during a power loom weavers dispute, one weaver, William Smith, said that in Stockport "those persons whom it was sought to stigmatize by calling them 'Tories' were the best masters and paid higher wages than those who assumed the appellation of Liberals."[42]

1836 was a key year in the development of Operative Conservatism, it saw the consolidation of the branch societies and their legitimization by Conservative Party leaders in London, through the National Conservative Institution, based in Pall Mall.[43] There was also considerable activity within the region with delegates from one town visiting those from another. The Blackburn branch was represented at the Preston Operative Conservative meeting held in October 1836, as were delegates from Lancaster, Ormskirk, Manchester, Liverpool, Bolton, Wigan and Chorley. The 'professional' organizer of the region, Charles Wilkins, came up with an interesting ploy when he urged the working class "make the women your allies", adding that "... my knowledge of electioneering matters enables me to declare that women are the best possible agents."[44] Charles Tiplady, a bookbinder representing Blackburn, claimed his was the first town in the region in which the Conservatives had actively organized the working people. He said that members of the working class felt that it was "right that we should meet and endeavour to arrive at a unity of opinion, and arrange plans for a coincidence of practice." As to reform, Tiplady's speech makes it clear that a section to the working class clearly believed that the Conservatives could represent their interests and repay their loyalty. He asserted that if such bodies were maintained throughout the nation at large they would bring "every benefit that the greatest reformer could desire." The principal object and operation of operative associations, he said, were, "... the dissemination of knowledge amongst the people and especially amongst the poor and uneducated."[45] This dissemination and widening of the basis of support was, as noted previously, one of the key objectives of parties of social integration.

From an initial membership of 300 in its first year, the Blackburn branch steadily increased its support annually.[46] In 1839, Wilkins visited the town urging greater organization and recruitment in the face of the mounting challenge of the Chartists.[47] By the 1840s the membership topped over 600.[48] The branch had several of the other features of a party of social integration as well as those of proselytization, political socialization and what Tiplady termed 'arriving at a unity of opinion.' It provided educational facilities at the central clubrooms; there was a Sick and Burial Club, discussion classes, fêtes, lectures and outings. Also a mark of this sort of party was the development of a strong middle class leadership within the Conservative party in Blackburn, and an increasingly close relationship between the local leaders and issues which directly affected the working class interest. In spite of the split of 1847, the Operative branch was maintained with Hornby being the prime mover

---

42 *Blackburn Standard*, 15 July 1835.

43 For a full transcription of the aims, objectives and key players in this body see Appendix 2.

44 *Preston Pilot*, 16 July 1836.

45 Ibid., similarly the opposition began to realize the situation as the Liberal MP for Bury, Richard Walker, made clear when he called that "new breed of Operative supporting the Conservatives, 'Conservative Reformers'", *Manchester Guardian*, 11 January 1837.

46 *Preston Pilot*, 29 October 1836.

47 Ibid., 30 November 1836, for a list of the leading members of the Blackburn Operative Association, see also Appendix 3 below.

48 The Eight Annual Report of the Blackburn Operative Conservative Association. *Blackburn Standard*, 3 January 1844.

until the mid-1850s, it being revived in February 1864.[49] But it was issues that gave working class support for Conservatism a wider dimension than was reflected in the overall membership. Wider working class support for Conservatism in Blackburn to a large degree resulted from the radical Tory agitation over, once again, the Factory Question and the New Poor Law. In the 1840s the respectable middle class Conservatives, led by Hornby, began to champion these issues, particularly when physical force Chartism rapidly declined after 1842 in the Blackburn area. From the mid-1830s there existed a body of working class opinion in the town that began to associate issues they were concerned about with, firstly, the radical Tory critique of Liberalism and political economy and, secondly, in the early 1840s when constitutional reform appeared to have been defeated, concern with the bread and butter questions of industrial relations and social reform. Both sets of local Conservatives utilized these issues at the expense of the Liberals. From the mid-1840s grandiose libertarian sentiments and sweeping constitutional and economic reform were replaced with the more practical working-class questions. Issues of industrial relations, welfare provisions, education, public health, rate increases, and social recreation held sway. But at Blackburn the foundation of this pragmatic approach to opinion based politics had been laid in the 1830s.

The Role of Issues and Working Class Politics

We have seen already that there was a tradition of violent opposition by working people in Blackburn to the imposition of the new work practices of industrial capitalism as it consolidated, and the subsequent loss of independence was felt especially strongly by weavers. In terms of political sentiment, this placed the workers of East Lancashire closest to the working class of the West Riding of Yorkshire than, say, the libertarian values which motivated the radicals of Oldham, or Unitarian Manchester.

In parts of Lancashire the working-class Radical Tory faction was as vocal as that in West Yorkshire and leaders like Oastler and Stephens had great influence in parts of industrial Lancashire. Undoubtedly Oastler was a popular character in Blackburn; indeed he produced one of his most violent speeches against those manufacturers opposing the Factory Acts. At a large meeting held at Blackburn in September 1839, Oastler addressed the question of factory reform, the power of his oratory can be gauged from the following extract:

> Oh, we must have men that will fight up to their knees in blood for the Ten Hours Bill. For perhaps we may have to fight for it yet; but mind you don't begin until you see me lead the way. I will tell you, however, how we can beat them. If they resist, I will teach every factory child in the Kingdom how to use a knitting needle among the machinery. Oh yes, I'll do it for them. I'm taking lessons now to learn little children how to do more harm than good... I am resolved that the laws of England shall triumph over the factory masters, or that the factory masters — shall breathe their last![50]

This was powerful stuff and it was little wonder that the middle-class elites of Blackburn were nervous. This was particularly so among the conventional Conservative manufacturers who, as yet, had not warmed to the issue as they were to do in the 1840s, and also because it allowed the Liberals to level the charge of extremism at Oastler and his supporters. However, the town's working class

49   Blackburn Reference Library, Local Studies Collection, B329, The Report of the Blackburn Conservative Club, 1864-5.

50   *Manchester Guardian*, 24 September 1839.

was won over by Oastler and his speech certainly had the effect of placing the issue at the forefront of local working class politics. Oastler's radicalism stemmed from deeply held Tory sentiments regarding human responsibility. On the one hand he believed the Reforming Whigs and 'progressive' Liberal manufacturers were shirking their responsibilities in allowing the appalling conditions in the factories to continue. Similarly Oastler believed that the New Poor Law was an inhuman piece of legislation which effectively worsened the precarious existence of the factory worker. Thus Oastler, with his radical rhetoric combined with sound constitutional ideology, was providing an alternative to Liberalism and extreme radicalism, whilst at the same time extolling the virtues of traditional Toryism. In such a situation some members of the working class would be swayed to the Conservative side on the back of issues like factory reform and the New Poor Law. Especially so after the decline of the mass appeal of Chartism in the early 1840s and the less abrasive posture adopted by the government of Sir Robert Peel toward the working class. This served to forge a lasting link in some parts of the north-west between the working class and old Tory principles. However, in Blackburn, as elsewhere, working class Conservatives were unsurprisingly not encouraged to support any form of electoral or constitutional reform. In 1839, for example, the Conservative agitator Charles Wilkins, correctly detected that the relationship between the physical force Chartists and the radical Liberals was deteriorating, "…let them hang today their companions in treason of yesterday."[51]

What was happening in these new boroughs was that, firstly, working people saw a political party enjoin its traditional and constitutional principles with issues which directly affected working class existence, and (a point which requires reiterating) something which the Conservatives and Tories had shown little desire to do before 1832. Secondly, this led to a sectionalising of the political opinions within the politically conscious working class, which in turn reduced the level of their overall class consciousness and thus its potential effectiveness. Finally, the Conservatives were helped by the weak and disunited leadership at the highest level of the Chartist movement and the calling into question by local radicals of the supposed libertarianism of the Whig reformers and their Liberal fellow travellers.[52] This last point was being painfully underscored to the working class of the mill-towns by the introduction of the New Poor Law. Also the Whig ministry's backing of those Liberal manufacturers who resisted factory reform and trades union recognition whilst attacking the acceptance of limited working-class industrial independence within the factory system.

In Blackburn the radical Tories led the way in attacking both the New Poor Law and the anti-Factory Act manufacturers. Local Conservatives began to build on this fairly quickly. In the case of the New Poor Law, they stressed the need to obey the law. But they built their campaign around the idea that the Act would be best administered by friends of the working class who basically opposed the legislation and would find every means of making it less draconian than Liberals who, in essence, accepted the theory and practice of the Act wholeheartedly. That the Conservatives managed to do this from the introduction of the Act into Blackburn in late December 1837 through their control of the Board of Guardians, came from a statement made by the Board's chairman some five years later. From May 1841 the Commissioners in London attempted to impose restrictions on what they saw as the lax manner in which the Blackburn Union was run. In a series of letters to the Commissioners, the Conservative chairman of the Guardians, Peter Ellingthorpe, offered little short of an ultimatum:

---

51 *Blackburn Standard*, 27 November 1839.

52 See *Bolton Chronicle*, 8 August 1835, speeches by Halliwell and Rothwell, or the same newspaper, 24 February 1838, or *McDouall's Chartist and Republic Journal*, 24 April 1841.

I need not inform you, of the difficulty and impolicy, I must say utter impossibility in disturbed times like the present, of suddenly urging any severe regulations, with the hope of benefit or advantage… The result of any attempt to do so would be a popular revulsion against the law, one of the effects of which would be the resignation of most of the present Board.[53]

Ellingthorpe advocated the extension of outdoor relief, the payment of rates and rent for those in most distress and to support wage increases.[54] The local Conservatives whilst obeying the law, but not the letter of the law, similarly maintained their opposition to the Commissioners between 1844 and 1846 over the question of the Labour Test and the treatment of the unemployed and workers experiencing short time. The *Standard* left its Conservative supporters in no doubt as to what they should do when, in July 1846, Commissioners appeared to be vacillating:

We hope that the unexpected chance which has given a national opportunity of inflicting deserved vengeance upon the Poor Law Commissioners will not be suffered to pass. A series of experiments made with the view of finding out if it were not possible to render the destitute more contented without making the wealthy less satisfied might be set on foot.[55]

Frequently the question of the welfare provisions for the working class was linked by the Conservatives of Blackburn with factory reform and the strict adherence of the laws already in existence which regulated the hours of labour and factory conditions generally. The Blackburn Short Time Committee was formed in January 1842, and its initiation was, according to the *Blackburn Standard*, brought about by the Operative Conservatives. They further claimed that by taking up these practical working-class questions the Conservatives had convinced the working class to abandon "the extravagant notions of revolution."[56] The Short Time Committee had three basic aims that the Conservatives of Blackburn went along with. These were, firstly, a complete abolition of the New Poor Law; secondly, the adoption of some extensive scheme of internal colonization; thirdly, they wanted changes in the Factory Bill that would include four amendments: i) That no person from the ages of 13 to 21 should be employed more than 10 hours per day in any mill, ii) That no young person be employed between the hours of 6 at night and 6 in the morning. iii) That all females should be gradually withdrawn from the factories. iv) That dangerous machinery should be boxed off and compensation for individual injuries provided by law.[57] In that same year of 1842, William Kenworthy, Hornby's business partner, published his famous appeal for shorter hours, *Inventions and Hours of Labour*. Here he made the claim that increased productivity made reductions in the hours of work possible, and refused to accept the Liberal argument of the threat of foreign competition, concluding with the point, "Are the poor, toiling factory hands our only security from foreign competition? If so, they are a vastly more important class of people than they have ever yet been generally considered."[58]

At Blackburn it was the radical Tory element who took the initiative on the Factory Question and, to a lesser extent, opposition to the New Poor Law, but by the later 1840s these issues of work practices and working class welfare had become issues of mainstream local Conservatism. This

---

53   PRO, Poor Law, MH 125529, Ellingthorpe to PLC, 6 September 1842.
54   Ibid., 12 August 1842.
55   PRO, Poor Law, MH 125529, Ellingthorpe to PLC, 5 July 1846.
56   Ibid., 19 January 1842.
57   Ibid.
58   W. Kenworthy, *Inventions and the Hours of Labour*, (Blackburn, 1842).

alliance of Conservatism with the remnants of local radicalism was unusual but not unknown in the mill towns of the north-west, which were particularly suspicious of Manchester School Liberalism.[59] This, combined with a powerful and charismatic leader in Hornby, makes working class support for Conservatism understandable in the 1830s, '40s, '50s and '60s. By the later 1840s and early 1850s the Conservatives of Blackburn could count on considerable working-class support. In 1847 for example the Chairman and Vice-Chairman of John Hornby's non-elector Committee were both former radicals. William Watson, a former handloom weaver, was one and the other gloried in the pseudonym of the 'Gas Pipe Fusilier'. This was Christopher Gifford, who gained his notoriety during a particularly bitter dispute at Fielden, Throp and Townley Parker in 1833. The spinners had asked for a wage rise in the light of working longer hours. The employers brought the strike instigators before the county bench where Addison, the Chairman of the magistrates, after jailing and fining the men informed them that in his view that in trying to raise their wages the strikers were effectively "robbing the masters."[60] In an assault on the factory in May, Gifford converted a gas-pipe into a crude bazooka and destroyed half the mill.[61] Gifford served 9 months in Lancaster gaol but 14 years later he had been completely rehabilitated and was a leading working class Conservative.

Further evidence of working class support for Conservatism came in 1853 when William Henry Hornby made the clearest statement of his attachment to working class issues and causes. Before addressing an audience of 20,000 on the balcony of the Railway Station, Hornby was presented with sliver candelabrum by the Operative Conservative Association. The inscription read, "In a token of sincere esteem of his zealous promotion of the best interests of the town, HIS GENEROUS SUPPORT OF USEFUL AND CHARITABLE INSTITUTIONS. And particularly as the well-tried, FAITHFUL AND CONSTANT FRIEND OF THE WORKING CLASSES."[62] On the question of short hours and factory reform, Hornby said that on the Liberal side of the town the argument was that the measure would ruin the capitalist. But the argument on the Conservative side was, "We don't see why a man's constitution should be racked through before he is five and forty, merely to save the capital of the country."[63] He advocated that the working class should stick to the Conservative Party "like leeches, both at the hustings, at the shops and at all other places." Hornby accused the Liberals of building £10 rated worker housing and of abusing the Small Tenements Act. He was asked what, in his view, was Conservatism. "This is Conservatism", he replied, "to obtain for the working classes the benefits of short-time ... each in their particular sphere and in their particular district has a power and an influence, which, when you unite together, like a bundle of sticks, is somewhat powerful."[64] On the question of trades unions he said, "Have you not as much right to have an association to protect yourselves as the masters have. Is there anything illegal in working men associating together to prevent a chopping of their wages... You have your own interests to look after both in the House of Commons, and out of it, and I for one should support any Act which you might request to be passed to protect you from the attacks of tyrannical masters."[65]

Earlier in 1853 Hornby had gone even further in taking up popular issues. He had stated, for

---

59 See for example R. N. Soffer, 'Attitudes and Allegiances in the Unskilled North', in *International Review of Social History*, X, 3, (1965), pp. 429-54.

60 *Blackburn Alfred*, 17 April 1833.

61 Ibid., 15 May 1833, 22 May 1833, *Northern Star*, 23 February 1839, *Blackburn Standard*, 28 July 1847.

62 *Preston Pilot*, 10 September 1853, (*Pilot*'s emphasis).

63 Ibid.

64 Ibid.

65 Ibid.

example, that he had no objection to a gradual extension of the parliamentary franchise and that he was inclined to be in favour of the Secret Ballot.[66] This was Hornby extolling working class based issues in the course of attempting to win (and winning) a parliamentary seat. But he still used the local party as an opinion-generating agency aimed at the working-class electors and non-electors. At the same time as Hornby was attempting to win the representation of Blackburn, elsewhere in East Lancashire meetings of the 'Lancashire, Yorkshire and Cheshire Conservative Labour League' began to be held.

The radical Tory, W. B. Ferrand, and the former London Chartist, Samuel Kydd, attended one such meeting held at Padiham, near Burnley. It was stated that the aim "was to clarify the position between masters and men by law, and that disputes should be settled by arbitration or the Board of Trade, whereby the mutual interests of masters and operatives would be discussed calmly and deliberately."[67] The opening address noted that the working class had no other course "at present, but strikes to resist the tyranny of the manufacturing classes... [The] Labour League was designed to find the middle ground: to induce both the employers and the employed to concede something."[68] Later in 1853 Kydd spoke at Blackburn and at Preston.[69] Thus throughout Lancashire the Conservatives were active in attempting to influence working class political opinion and action.

At Blackburn throughout the rest of the 1850s and the 1860s, the Conservatives and Hornby commanded the loyalty of a section of the towns' working class, primarily by the propounding 'safe' working-class issues noted above. It is a testimony to their success in integrating significant working-class support over the previous three decades that in 1868, with the enlargement of the franchise to include the majority of working-class men, the Conservatives won both parliamentary seats.

We have stressed two possible reasons for the success of the Conservatives amongst the working class of Blackburn. Firstly, there was a tradition of Radical Toryism among a section of the town's working class. Secondly, the middle class Conservatives utilised the local operative clubs as opinion generating agencies and as bodies of political integration between the mid 1830s and 1870. However, there were other factors that have to be briefly mentioned before we look at developments in other new boroughs. Firstly, Blackburn had a number of very large factories and factory communities which were developed much earlier than in other north-west towns.[70] This may have led to a higher level of working class dependency than elsewhere. Secondly, this feature is compounded by the fact that at Blackburn the manufacturers began to build worker housing on a far greater scale and much earlier than in other parts of the region. For example, the three largest employers in the town, the Conservative Hornby's and Hopwood's and the Liberal Pilkington's housed up to 90 per cent of their workers by 1845, and, by 1851, 41 per cent of Blackburn's total housing was under the control of the large mill owners.[71] These large factories encouraged the type of 'flamboyant' political leadership indulged in by Hornby for the Conservatives and men like Feilden, Jackson and Pilkington for the Liberals.[72] What we have seen in Blackburn is the development of a powerful party structure. The Conservatives operated to politically integrate a section of the working class but also acting as an opinion-generating agency for the wider working class. That they could do this was due on the one

---

66   Ibid., 23 March 1853.

67   Ibid., 8 October 1853.

68   Ibid.

69   Ibid., 22 October, 1853.

70   *Parliamentary Papers*, 'Factory Inspectors Report for 1841', Appendix No. 1, pp. 45-51.

71   Blackburn Reference Library, Rate Books, 1830-1860, *passim*.

72   For a detailed discussion of this aspect in relation to Blackburn after 1860 see, P. Joyce, *Work, Society and Politics*, (Brighton, 1980), *passim*.

hand to the traditional sympathy many radical weavers felt towards what was widely perceived as the pursuance of 'fairness' and justice by the radical Tories combined with the acceptance of the older types of work practices and worker independence. However such sympathies were bolstered by high levels of worker dependency, control, and containment exacted by manufacturers and a growing hostility felt by many working people for the progressive Liberals and the 'reforms' of the Whigs after 1832.[73] Further factors at Blackburn, as indeed at Preston, were the divisions within popular Radicalism and its loss of purchase on working class opinion. Even during the height of the Chartist period, between 1838 and 1842, the only major disturbance that occurred in Blackburn was the Plug Strikes of 1842, and this to a large extent came from workers outside the Blackburn area. The Sacred Month of the summer of 1839 passed off in Blackburn without any disruption, save a slight disturbance at the Parish Church, where the invaders, received a salutary lecture from the Vicar on the need to keep public order to gain their reforms.[74] Local Conservatives were willing to take up working-class issues and even brought former Chartists into their ranks. The former President of the Operative Conservative Association, the bookbinder, Charles Tiplady, for a time presided over a Chartist Sick and Burial Fund, up to the time it began devoting its funds to O'Connor's Land Labour Scheme, which he regarded as foolhardy.[75] At the 1847 Parliamentary election one of the candidates, the radical Chartist lawyer, W. P. Roberts, went on record saying that, "So far as practical freedom was concerned the Conservatives had done more than the Whigs ever did."[76]

From 1833 through to 1870 therefore, the political attitudes of the Blackburn working class had been pulled in various directions. As we move into the 1840s, increasingly, this was achieved by powerful middle-class leaders using the working class political clubs both as agencies of wider political opinion dissemination, and in practical terms as a means of social and political integration. Opinion politics were far more important at Blackburn than at Preston, Wigan or the county and market towns of Chester, Lancaster and Clitheroe. But Blackburn was particular, both in the size of the Tory radical support of its weavers and its geographic proximity to the Radical Tory heartland of the northern and eastern parts of Lancashire and, of course, the West Riding of Yorkshire. But what impact did the Conservatives make on the political opinions of working people in other new boroughs in the north-west?

Developments in Bolton and the South of the Region

As stated above, in two key structural areas of its socio/economic development, Blackburn was unusual when compared to other parts of the north-west region. The first was the predominance of male weavers, many of whom were imbued politically with radical Toryism from the mid-1830s, working alongside semi-skilled 'throstle' type spinners, the majority of whom were females.[77] The

---

73   For example, in 1838 the Benthamite John Bowring stood as a Liberal at Blackburn in the parliamentary elections of 1832 and 1835, he told an audience of the Blackburn Reform Association in 1838 that, "I felt grieved when I heard that the flame of freedom was burning less bright here, [and] that Toryism was in the ascendant." *Blackburn Standard*, 26 September 1838.

74   J. W. Whittaker, *Sermon Preached to the Chartists at Blackburn Parish Church on Sunday August 4*, (Blackburn, 1839).

75   Blackburn Reference Library, 'The Diary of Charles Tiplady', entry dated 21 March 1848.

76   *Blackburn Standard*, 29 July 1847.

77   In 1851 the population of Blackburn was 46,536, of whom 8,355 (18.1% of total population) were females involved in cotton manufacture, compared to 9,464 (20.5%) male weavers. In Bolton in the same year the population was 61,172, of whom 6,450 females (10.5%) of the population worked in cotton manufacture, compared to 8,237 (13.5%) males involved in weaving. No other part of the region ,save the Ashton township of Manchester, had a higher population of working females in its total population of working females. *Parliamentary Papers*,

second was the size of Blackburn's industrial factory units, the large and clearly demarcated community boundaries that grew up around these large factories created by employer housing, shopping, educational and recreational provisions. The significance of the size of firm in the various towns and also the question of occupational differentiation are subjects worth considering as we look in the final part of this chapter at developments in other towns created parliamentary boroughs by the Act of 1832. Let us begin by tracing developments at Bolton, one of Blackburn's closest neighbours to the south.

In recent years two historians have made the suggestion that factory size may be related to working class political activity and patterns of middle class leadership. Joyce has suggested that in those towns where the factory size was smaller and more compact it was probable that employer influence was less pronounced throughout a community.[78] Garrard's analysis is based on the formula that a) small factories meant a more independent working class in terms of the policies they pursued and b) larger factories seem to indicate less evidence of independent working class policies.[79] Joyce compares Blackburn, with its large-scale factory units and the widespread involvement of the middle-class manufacturers in local political leadership, with Bury and the West Riding of Yorkshire where this process was slower to develop. Garrard compares Bolton and Salford, where there were larger factories and relatively low working class political involvement after 1850, with Rochdale, where the factories were mainly small and where working class involvement in Parliamentary and local politics was more visible and continuous from the 1830s through to 1870. To a significant extent after 1832 the giving of a political lead to the working class became increasingly important, which further attests to the importance of policies and to the politics of opinion.

At Preston the working class became gradually less involved in politics partly due to their gradual numerical erosion on the electoral role. But also because the existing working class leadership in Preston in the 1840s and 1850s became more concerned with the more mundane questions of industrial relations. However, there was a retention of working class and lower middle class leadership, even though after 1833 this appeared hopelessly split. Preston was susceptible to traditional political practices of both influence and the market, although opinion politics did become more important in the 1840s with the rapid industrial development. Moreover, the experience of the Blackburn workers was of a dramatic reduction in the scale of working-class led radical politics from the mid-1830s around issues they were concerned with, and the assumption of this leadership role by the middle class manufacturers of both political parties.

Certainly Bolton's industrial development was different from both Blackburn and Preston. As noted, Preston was a mixed economy providing agricultural and legal services, and a limited textile base that mushroomed in the 1840s. At Blackburn, textiles dominated the town and had done so increasingly from the end of the Napoleonic wars. Indeed, by the mid-1830s the basic consolidation of the towns staple industry was in place, with the manufacturers merely adding to their stock of factory buildings and worker housing from 1836 through to 1850. Bolton differed in several respects. Firstly, although it was neither a legal or agricultural centre, its industrial and service sector was diverse. For example, in 1851, in occupational sectors other than textiles there were 2,784 colliers as against 896 at Blackburn, in the engineering trades there were 2,114 working in Bolton compared to

---

Census, Occupations of the People, (1851).

78 Joyce, *Work, Society and Politics*, especially chapter 5, also worth considering by the same author is, 'The Factory Politics of Lancashire in the Later Nineteenth Century', in *Historical Journal*, 18, 3, (1975).

79 J. Garrard, *Leadership and Power in Victorian Industrial Towns*, (Manchester, 1983).

624 in Blackburn.[80] In both examples there were three times as many working men involved in these industries in Bolton as in Blackburn. These differentiations may be indicative of distinctions in the type of relationship between the working class and their employers. This is not to say that the working class of Bolton would be less susceptible to the regimentation of the factory with its attendant loss of worker independence at the point of production. It would mean there were alternative form of employment open to the Bolton workers, and, if it can be established that the factory size was noticeably less than at Blackburn, the workers of Bolton may not have experienced the same level of all-embracing dependency on their employers as at Blackburn. In such a situation the workers of Bolton experienced more political autonomy and, in effect, had been more likely to develop their own politics around issues which they believed to be important for the whole of their class and to be led by men drawn from their own class.

Let us pursue this by looking comparatively at the size of firms in nine north-west locations.

TABLE VIII
Comparative Factory Size of Nine North-West Areas
Spinning and power loom weaving by the same firm, 1841.[81]

	Total number of Firms	Total number of Workers	Average Workers per Firm
Blackburn	18	10,885	605
Manchester	35	14,833	424
Ashton-under-Lyne	13	6,783	521
Bolton	12	3,660	305
Bury	37	11,386	307
Whalley	49	10,758	219
Rochdale	17	3,073	181
Oldham	32	7,137	223
Preston	15	7,801	520

The figures reveal that Bolton was one of those middling towns where ratio of workers-per-factory was not as high as Blackburn, nor was it particularly low as in the case of Rochdale. However, the Factory Inspectors reports show that in those factories which combined spinning and weaving, employing both males and females, can be reasonably expected to be the largest employers of factory labour at the time. The largest figure employed in a single factory unit at Bolton was 712, whereas at Blackburn it was 1,400, followed closely by another three manufacturers employing over 1,000 hands.[82] Thus overall the factory size was low at Bolton when compared to Blackburn, and, as we noted above, it was more industrially diverse with more small-scale engineers and other lower-middle-class employers. At Bolton there was a lower level of capital concentration. Thus, in the event of worker militancy, the employer had less chance to overcome or negotiate out of existence working-class resistance by the sheer size of the economic power of the manufacturing elite. Such could have been the case at Horrocks's of Preston, or the Hornby's, Hopwood's and Pilkington's of Blackburn. These considerations should be borne in mind when the political developments in Bolton are examined.

---

80 *Parliamentary Papers*, (1852), Occupations of the People, Census (1851), pp. 634-46.

81 *Parliamentary Papers*, 'Factory Inspectors Report for the Half-Year ending 31 December 1841', pp. 45-51. See also V. A. C. Gatrell, 'Labour, Power and the Size of Firms in the Lancashire Cotton Industry in the Second Quarter of the Nineteenth-Century', in *Economic History Review*, 2nd Series, 30, (1977). R. Lloyd-Jones and A. A. LaRoux, 'The Size of Firms in the Cotton Industry', in *Economic History Review*, 2nd Series, 33, (1980).

82 Factory Inspectors Reports, (1841).

What then of the political development of the working class of Bolton, the incidence of Conservatism among this social group and the pattern of political leadership in local and, especially, parliamentary politics? In the pre-1832 period at Preston and Blackburn, (particularly the latter), the working class became increasingly radical, ostensibly in the area of industrial relations but importantly this developed politically out of their industrial experiences. At Bolton the pattern is similar in the later eighteenth century and the first decade of the nineteenth, but in the 1820s there was not the same scale of working class militancy found at Blackburn. Nor did the workers of Bolton possess the level of political sophistication of those at Preston, the great majority of whom, it will be recalled, possessed the householder franchise. But residing near to Bolton during this crucial early stage of consciousness formation were Ralph Fletcher and William Hulton, two of the foremost and formidable opponents of radical working class politics in the region. The 1820s do appear to have been a fairly quiet period in Bolton. In 1826 for example when disturbances over the imposition of power looms and the general down turn in trade raged across the north-west, Bolton was peaceful. Even though power looms were deployed and the trade slump severely hit the handloom weavers there were few disputes. In Bolton, unlike Blackburn, the weavers did not attack machinery and during the worst of the distress allowed acts of private charity to be organized by the Manufacturers Committee on their behalf.[83] At Blackburn the weavers rejected such moves by the local manufacturers and magistrates, but at Bolton they seem to have been accepted. The pattern was that the development of the larger factories at Blackburn was sudden from the mid-1820s, and this was a likely factor in the rise of worker militancy at this time, whilst at Bolton it was much more gradual and not on the same scale. By the later 1830s and the rise of Chartism, the factory size of Blackburn was far larger than that of Bolton but, as we have noted, Blackburn was relatively quiet, whilst at Bolton, with its smaller units and greater occupational mix, the situation, conforming to the general model, was very serious.

During the 1820s, the main lead of the workers of Bolton in the sphere of industrial relations came from the spinners, and not, as in the case of Blackburn, from the weavers.[84] It was the spinners who formed a committee in 1825 to look into conditions of the Bolton factories, a move that initiated the wider interest of the working class in the factory movement. It was the spinners who had been introduced to the factory system first and it was they who began to politicize the male weavers after 1826 through factory reform and the need to unite by the forming of a general union of Bolton textile workers on the model of John Doherty. Moreover, it was the spinners who remained the single largest body of employed workers in Bolton throughout the period under discussion. There were two types of spinning in the town: course, which employed mainly women and children, with men acting as overlookers, and fine, which was the preserve of the men. However, the weavers, both power and handloom, did not follow the lead given by the spinners, at least in any mass sense. The apparent quiescence of the Bolton weavers before 1832 is given credence by a fellow weaver, John Miller, who, when looking back from 1836, said,

> In 1809 we petitioned Parliament for a minimum wage, in 1811 we petitioned Parliament for a tightening up of the apprentice rules of entry, both refused. In 1826 when throughout the county rioters smashed the power looms, Bolton was at peace. We now need a strong union, we have

---

83   Bolton Reference Library, Local History Archive, handbill calling for a meeting of leypayers and the Manufacturers Committee to consider the distressed state of the handloom weavers. Dated 29 April 1826.

84   J. Clegg, *Annals of Bolton*, (Bolton, 1888), see also J. T. Ward, 'The Factory Movement in Lancashire', in the *Transactions of the Lancashire and Cheshire Antiquarian Society*, (1965-66), pp. 186-210.

relied too much on outside help.[85]

The spinners were quite different. During the great spinners' strike of 1829-30, the Bolton spinners were actively supportive of their Manchester colleagues. This resulted in a long and violent dispute in 1830, initiated by a wage reduction, and later by the fierce hostility to the spinners union displayed by the manufactures. When the weavers were faced with similar reductions the spinners again attempted to bring them into the General Textile Union.[86] They had already persuaded the dyers and bleachers to join their ranks, but again the weavers refused, placing their hopes on memorials to masters and attempting to form committees of employers and men. At one firm the tactics of the weavers appear to have been successful for at Green's, after a meeting addressed by one of the weavers' leaders, William Pilling, the weavers gained their list of prices.[87] Thus in the period before the onset of the agitation surrounding the Reform Act, the workers of Bolton did not exhibit the high levels of class consciousness of those at either Blackburn or Preston. The reluctance on the part of the weavers to join the more active spinners is suggestive of a heightened sense of status differentiation among the Bolton work force.

Throughout 1830 and 1831 the spinners became more agitated on both the industrial and political front. The main targets of their attacks were two of the largest employers in the town, Bolling's factories and the Ashworth brothers. The former was Conservative and the latter advanced Liberals. In April 1830 there was a serious riot at Ashworth's factory,[88] and in May a bomb was thrown at the window of Bolling's factory, followed by a battle between the spinners and Bolling's knobsticks.[89] By the end of July 1831 the spinners dispute was over with an agreed list accepted by both sides and any outstanding prosecutions dropped by the employers.[90] In mid October 1830 the Bolton Political Union was formed. Its rank and file was made up of spinners and craft workers, whilst its leadership was in the main composed of the lower-middle-class shopkeepers and small manufacturers. The chief leaders were William Naisby, a draper, John Mitchell, a small-scale counterpane manufacturer, Joseph Skelton and his brother Peter, linen drapers, who were all drawn from the Huntite wing of popular radicalism.[91] However, the weavers became involved in the Political Union shortly after its formation. At a meeting of the Union in late October the leading spokesmen were three weavers, John O'Brien, Charles Wood, John Aston, and two spinners, Edwin Barker and John Trevor, indicating that, as the Reform agitation got under way, the previously moderate weavers began to become politically involved.[92] It took a great constitutional issue of reform to raise their class consciousness and work alongside the spinners.

What is not so easy to ascertain is the nature of the popular politics these working class leaders of the Political Union espoused. They did not oppose capitalism in the manner of Hetherington, O'Brien and the *Poor Man's Guardian*, for these same leaders were willing to work alongside the employers in a body formed in 1834 called the Weavers' Committee.[93] Furthermore, some members of the

85 *Bolton Chronicle*, 6 February 1836.

86 Ibid., 20 February 1830, 17 April 1830.

87 Ibid., 24 April 1830.

88 Ibid., 17 April 1830.

89 Ibid., 8 May 1830, 15 August 1830.

90 Ibid., 24 July 1830.

91 Ibid., 14 August 1830, for reports of when all attended a dinner called to honour Hunt and the recent revolt in France.

92 Ibid., 23 October 1830.

93 Ibid., 1 February 1834.

Political Union went on to become supporters and members of the Bolton Operative Conservative Association. Some, indeed, were already displaying signs of overt racial bigotry, attitudes played upon by some middle class Conservatives in later decades when attempting to rouse working-class feelings. In 1830 for example, at a meeting of weavers, John O'Brien blamed the Jews of Manchester for the decline in trade. "Our ancestors would have died to a man before they would have submitted to these Jews with their baboon faces", and Richard Starkie expressed similar feelings of intolerance towards the Russians.[94] Even at this early stage in Bolton's politics fissures of political sectionalism can be detected within popular radicalism. As at Preston, a split took place between the lower-middle classes who supported the radicalism expressed by Burdett and Cartwright, and members of the working class radicals who supported Hunt. At Bolton the radical working class spinners also drew on the proto-socialism of O'Brien and the *Poor Man's Guardian*, and the weavers whose leadership was drawn towards Radical Tory elements. Within the wider Tory leadership of the Bolton area there had been a long history of rabid anti-Jacobinism and, more recently, Orangeism. Here two men stood out. One was a local squire, William Hulton, and the other was the local agent for the Duke of Bradford, Ralph Fletcher. Hulton was the magistrate who ordered the Yeomanry to charge at Peterloo and it was he who was the driving force in the formation of the South Lancashire Conservative Association. He prided himself on his skills at political organization but lamented what his endeavours had cost him in personal and financial terms without reward. As he told Sir Robert Peel in 1842, "No one could have devoted more energy, and few made greater pecuniary sacrifices in proportion to their means, than I have done especially for the establishment of Conservative Associations... I abandoned personal ambition in order more successfully to accomplish what I believed proved of national importance. In truth I have devoted too much to public and too little to private care."[95]

Hulton began to organise local Tories as early as 1813, mainly around the sedentary auspices of the local Pitt Club, along with the notorious Colonel Ralph Fletcher.[96] Fletcher acted as Hulton's partner during the anti-Jacobin campaign when Fletcher and his vigilantes visited those suspected.[97] Fletcher supplied the Home Office with reports of scores of secret meetings of trades unionists and reformers from the 1790s until his death in 1832. Fletcher combined his anti-Jacobin pro-Tory activities with an ardent advocacy of Orangeism. The *Bolton Chronicle* noted in his obituary, anti-radicalism and religious intolerance for Fletcher equated to a defence of the British Constitution.

> The whole policy of the spy system, of which, in this part of Lancashire he was the prime mover, is too well known ... suffice to say, that the scenes which occurred under that system ... can never be forgotten ... in the instance of Colonel Fletcher, this particular policy resulted from the circumstance of his being an inveterate Orange man ... and from a belief that the absolute ascendency of the Orange or Protestant interest, was necessary to the safety of what he called the British Constitution.[98]

Although both men were hated by radicals, and mistrusted and despised by many moderate men, the activities of Hulton and Fletcher go some way to explaining the lack of cohesiveness in working class activities in Bolton before 1830. It was the sheer exuberance, and feelings of realization and hope

94 Ibid., 24 April 1830.

95 British Library, Peel Papers, Ad. Mss. 40508, ff 305-9, Hulton to Peel, 14 May 1842.

96 Lancashire Records Office, Preston, DDU 53/82/11, List of Members of Bolton Pitt Club, 1813.

97 Anon., *The Blackfaces of Bolton*, (Bolton, 1831), Bolton Reference Library.

98 *Bolton Chronicle*, 25 February 1832.

that drew many working people to the reform agitation in 1830, and this included the weavers who had suffered under Fletcher and, previously, were rightfully wary of incurring his wrath. However, it should also be remembered that at Bolton, Fletcher found some support amongst a small section of working weavers and colliers. This serves not only to underline and highlight the complexity of the politics of Bolton's working class, but also shows there existed a core of working-class support for Orangeism, closely identified with Toryism in the area before 1832, as was the case at Liverpool and Wigan. Part of the reason for this was the substantial proportion of Anglicans within the population. Also important were the tactics employed by the extreme Tories against the radical weavers.

A major point of distinction has to be noted here. Working class acquiescence and support for Loyalism and Toryism before 1832 was built on the twin foundations of intimidation and fear, especially among the weavers, who up to 1811-12 had been militantly radical. After 1832 however, through the integration of sections of the working class into the party structure, working class Toryism was based on mutual consent, freely offered and accepted, and the inculcation of political opinions through local Conservatives taking up working-class based issues. Of course there were elements of intimidation, and corruption, but these became less important than the role and function of the party. What needs also to be borne in mind at Bolton was the industrial and religious differentiations that facilitated the development of opinion-orientated politics after 1830 and the onset of the reform crisis. The weavers now felt safe to involve themselves in politics, but the complicating factor is that they did not advocate similar strains of politics and policies as a single trade as, say, the spinners did. They were politically disparate and the lines of demarcation do not coincide with the crude distinction between handloom and power loom weavers. As at Blackburn, from 1831-2 the leadership of the Political Union began to involve itself in local politics, initially through the Vestry but also on the Boards of Trustees, particularly those of Little Bolton with their less self-perpetuating membership and lower property qualification.[99] This latter area engaged the attention of the lower middle class leadership; the rank and file (which by November 1831 was put at 4,000) contented themselves with Vestry packing and assembling public meetings to air their increasingly radical views.[100] How the Bolton Political Union was organized in 1831-2 indicates a marked heightening of class consciousness and political awareness among key sections of Bolton's working class, particularly the formally moderate weavers. By 1831 a committee had been formed comprising of 25 persons who Brimelow describes as being "chiefly working men."[101] In October 1831, after the House of Lords had rejected the Reform Bill, a public meeting was called. A letter from Edward Curren, the leader of Manchester Political Union, called upon the "brave men of Bolton" to attend a "great demonstration" in Manchester, "but do not go as before [unarmed] to Peterloo."[102] The radical nature of the leadership is revealed in the type of reform they desired. Effectively, they would not support any measure of reform which was not founded on universal suffrage, vote by ballot and annual parliaments. The lower middle class leadership attempted to moderate the actions of the rank and file by attempting to operate within the law by asking for all their public meetings to be sanctioned by the magistrates with responsibility for Great and Little Bolton. When this was refused, the leadership vacillated and the working class effectively took over the Political Union. They organized a procession and meeting on October 15, a workday at which 6,000 gathered in Bradford Square in the centre of the town. Prominent at this meeting was a

---

99   Ibid., 16 April 1831.

100 Ibid., 10 January 1831.

101 W. Brimelow, *The Political and Parliamentary History of Bolton*, (Bolton, 1880), p. 109.

102 *Bolton Chronicle*, 12 October 1832.

handloom weaver, Walter O'Carroll, and a spinner, Findley Frazer, reinforcing the point that by now the spinners and weavers presented a united front. Throughout the meeting the King and his ministry received support, the wrath reserved for the Bishops and Lords.

The forces of authority, increasingly alarmed after the Bristol riots and the actions of the various Political Unions, issued a Royal Proclamation on 2 November declaring meetings of political societies illegal. This had the effect of splitting the moderates from the extremists. A meeting of the Bolton Political Union was held on November 28, whereupon, after a series of angry exchanges, the Union split and its former lower-middle class leadership consisting of Naisby, Staton, Robinson, Waring, Greenalgh, Black, Starkie, Brown and Hayhurst, left the governing council. The remaining working-class spinners and weavers held a (strictly illegal) meeting in Bradford Square. The militant tone of class politics at this time can be gleaned from the savage attacks the speakers made upon the holders of property. For example, Walter O'Carroll suggested somewhat arbitrarily that anyone who owned or rented property above £5 rateable value was a coward. Other weavers, John O'Brien and John McQuirk, called for a Declaration of Rights. John Aston advised the audience to read the entire works of Paine, which would have kept them out of mischief for some considerable time. But he also moderated the tone of the meeting by suggesting that while the Council insisted on all their demands being delivered, eventually they would not oppose gradual reform as a precursor to further reforms.[103]

There are some important points here regarding the levels of working class consciousness among the working people of Bolton between 1831-3 which constitute striking similarities with their counterparts at Blackburn and other new boroughs. The first is that the working class of Bolton formulated and organized their political demands as a means of benefiting the whole of the working class, not merely sections of it. Secondly, they acted independently of political groupings existing at the time, the Whig reformers, the lower-middle class progressives or indeed the Ultra Tories. These were class-based issues being organized by the working class themselves, and this leads to a third important point in that the leaders of popular working class radicalism in Bolton between 1831 and 1833 were drawn exclusively from the working class regardless of occupational or status differentiation. This was a heightening of class consciousness, associated as it was with a mass sense of political awareness. This state of anticipation and high levels of working class consciousness continued throughout the 'days of May' crisis, up until the elections themselves in December 1832. The Bolton Political Union was also agitating around other issues than the reform of Parliament. They supported the Ten Hours Bill and the opening up of local government.[104] However, after the passing of Reform in June 1832, divisions began appearing, particularly over the limitations of the Act itself and the retention of the Corn Laws, orchestrated in the main by Naisby and the lower middle class radicals. As for this group, once the Reform Act had been passed they increasingly regained the initiative. They mounted assaults on the Board of Trustees in both Great and Little Bolton, and won control of the Overseers of the Poor in both townships.[105] In short, they became increasingly important as the first parliamentary elections drew near. The Conservatives for their part took cover. As at Blackburn they did not oppose parliamentary reform and this may have been an important factor in their future success. But they wished above all to curb the extreme radical tendencies of the working class and to put a brake on the reforming zeal of the various sets of

---

103 Ibid., 5 December 1831.

104 Ibid., 3 March 1832. They also had contacts with other parts of the north-west and sent delegates to the National Convention of the Working Classes held in early 1832 in London. Ibid., 25 February 1832.

105 Ibid., 1 September 1832.

reformers.[106]

The four candidates at this first election were William Bolling, a local-large scale manufacturer and the Conservative candidate, J. A. Yates, an 'advanced' Liberal from Liverpool, Robert Torrens, a Whig reformer and a leading Philosophic Radical, and William Eagle, a Manchester lawyer. Torrens and Yates were favoured candidates of the lower-middle class popular radicals, whilst Eagle was the man favoured by the bulk of the non-electors and the now depleted Political Union. The close association between radical Toryism and the opposition to reforming Whiggery was again in evidence at Bolton, as witnessed by the presence of Charles Rothwell and Staten on Eagles's non-elector committee, both of whom were to play important parts in the future Bolton Operative Conservative Association.[107]

Although some working class leaders remained active, especially among the weavers, the spinners appear to have lost interest in politics after what they may have seen as the failure of 1831-2. In fact, in the first few years after the passing of Reform the spinners of Bolton did not even engage in trade union activities. Now the weavers were the focus of activity, and, as at Blackburn, it was issues that dominated the agitation. Moreover, it would seem that many of these leaders, as at Blackburn, became attracted by Conservative attempts to address working class problems. Early in 1834 the Bolton Committee of Manufacturers and Weavers was initiated.[108] This effectively split the formerly united Weavers Union between the extreme radicals, led by McQuirk and Edward Hamilton, and those moderates who joined the Committee, several of whom (Halliwell, Staten, Needham, Rothwell, Makin and Monks) went on to become Operative Conservatives. Bolling took the chair of the Committee, a large mill-owner as well as the Conservative MP. The body was an attempt to alleviate the plight of the handloom weavers, particularly in the light of a serious down turn in trade. But its added significance was that it was an attempt to address a working-class issue. Moreover, it was an acknowledgement by the Conservative manufacturers that the working class themselves could be part of the consultation and decision making process. In this sense it was the beginning of an attempt in political toleration.

Meanwhile, as noted above, the lower-middle-class radicals were gaining access to the decision making process in local government. This culminated in the Liberals gaining control of the first municipal council after the towns' incorporation in 1838, and keeping their majority until 1844 when the Conservatives won control. However, as the moderate working class were beginning to be integrated into the middle class dominated politics of the factory, some working-class radicals were becoming more extreme. Like extreme radicals across the north-west, the Bolton radicals were disillusioned by the effects of the Reform Act and the attitudes of the Whigs and Liberals. This group was the remnant of the old Political Union, its name now changed to the Bolton Political Union of the Working Classes. It became the organizational basis of Chartism later in the 1830s. In June 1833, however, the Union made its feelings clear in a letter to the *Poor Man's Guardian*. Commenting on the bad effects of the unjust and tyrannical Reform Bill, McQuirk and Hamilton gave their assessment of the Whig/Liberal government:

---

106 Ibid., 3 March 1832.

107 Ibid., 1 August 1832.

108 Ibid., 1 February 1834. The full Committee was, Manufacturers: Messrs Brodie, Crook, Dean, Tong, Bailey, Heaton, Blinkhorn, Hitchen, Green, Haslam, Arrowsmith, Horrocks, Mallet and Wood. Weavers: Phillip Halliwell, Richard Needham, John Aston. Ibid., 1 August 1832. John Young, William Pilling, James Whiteford, John Welsby, Walter O'Carroll, William Hatch, Thomas Makin, George Thompson, Charles Rothwell, Richard Wood and Thomas Wolf.

The government of this country are not friends but enemies of the people and that we are now subject to complete military despotism. And further, we, the unionists of Bolton do honestly declare that the circumstances that lead us to pass these resolutions further convince us that there can be no effectual relief for our sufferings without an efficient change in the representation of the people, which has determined us that we shall never cease seeking in a constitutional way that reform which has its basis in universal suffrage, vote by secret ballot, short Parliaments and no property qualification.[109]

The political picture presented by 1834 was multi-faceted, with opinion being stretched in various directions. Whether this can be attributed to a lack of deference among the working class due to the smaller size of the factory units, imbuing them with greater freedom of political expression, is impossible to prove with certainty. But the situation continued throughout the 1830s and into the early 1840s. The support given by the working class of Bolton to the extreme radicals should not be underestimated, as the events of 1839 reveal. The existence of a significant element of support for the radicals and the need to contain it was probably an inducement to the Conservatives to throw their support early behind the Weavers' Committee, and in 1835, to establish an Operative branch of the Bolton Conservative Association.

The Bolton Operative Conservative Association was formed in September 1835[110] and by 1838 possessed a membership of over 800.[111] With the coming of municipal incorporation it had branches in every ward in Bolton with 30 officers operating throughout the town.[112] Its relationship with the Weavers Committee was close, as the extreme working class radicals lost no opportunity in pointing out.[113] However, it included in its supporters some former ardent radicals of the militant stamp. Among these were Walter O'Carroll, the secularist radical, and Charles Rothwell, the trades' unionist.[114] Rothwell's commitment to trades unionism was apparent when he defended the rights of the striking spinners of Preston in a speech at a meeting called in their support in Manchester early in 1837. "The spinners of Preston", he said, "had been unjustly dealt with by the proceedings of their employers, in attempting to hinder them from taking such steps as the law of the land allow."[115] The tone of this meeting was radical Tory, a fact underlined by the speech of the Rev Joseph Raynor Stephens, who described the manufacturers as, "those bloody, murdering, swindling, smuggling, plundering, tyrannical murderers of Preston."[116] At Blackburn, throughout the 1830s, the radical Tories and later Operative Conservatives grasped the issue of factory reform as a rallying cry. In Bolton however, the chief issue during the 1830s and early '40s was opposition to the New Poor Law. It was over this question that the various leaders of popular opinion attempted to capture working-class support. Initially the Liberal-inclined lower middle class radicals, led by William Naisby, were ambiguous on the question, preferring instead to concentrate on moral-force Chartism and repeal of the Corn Laws. The Operative Conservatives argued for adjustments to the New Poor Law by petitioning Parliament, ultimately with the aim of repeal. The extreme radicals advocated

109 *Poor Man's Guardian*, 22 June 1833.
110 *Blackburn Standard*, 9 September 1835.
111 *Preston Pilot*, 22 September 1838.
112 Ibid., 15 June 1839.
113 *Bolton Chronicle*, 15 August 1835, 9 July 1836.
114 J. Belchem, 'English Working Class Radicalism and the Irish, 1815-1850', in *North-West Labour History Society Bulletin*, No. 8, (1982-3), p. 9.
115 *Manchester Guardian*, 7 January 1837.
116 Ibid.

ignoring the law and incorporated the tactic of refusing to elect Guardians into the general agitation of constitutional reform and the Charter.[117] The Operative Conservatives, whilst obeying the law and electing Guardians, attempted to soften the effects of New Poor Law. But they also exploited working-class traditions and sentiments, especially in the decent treatment of those caught in the trap of poverty, and, ultimately the relatives of those who died. At a public meeting Giles Marsh said that Warburton's Anatomy Bill proved, like the Factory system and the New Poor Law, that the Whig ministry cared little for working people. The Anatomy Bill "robs the grave of its victims and the New Poor Law provides the schools of anatomy with subjects, the former wets the knife which is to be plunged into my body, and the latter prepares me for the dissection table."[118] This aspect of playing on the traditional feelings of working people should not be underestimated. There is a growing body of research that suggests that the treatment of the dead was of great religious and physiological concern to the working class, indeed, spurring them on to riot over the perceived mistreatment of the dead.[119] This may have been a tactic on the part of the Conservatives but if so was one that had powerful symbolic, historical and practical connotations for working people.

When the elections for the Guardians of the Bolton Union eventually went ahead in April 1839, the three groups were represented but the Conservatives held a slender majority that they maintained well into the 1840s. During this period of Conservative control the Guardians administered relief as if the New Poor Law did not exist, much to the chagrin of Chadwick and the Commissioners in London.[120] However, whatever support the Operative Conservatives, and Conservatives generally, found among the working class of Bolton in 1839 as a result of their liberal treatment of the poor, was offset in this particular year by the high level of support by working people to the physical force Chartists.[121] The local manufacturer-turned-gentleman, Robert Heywood, tells us in his diaries (confirmed in the Home Office papers) that the popular support given to the Chartists was out of control by the summer of 1839.[122] The Mayor of Bolton, the Liberal Charles Darbyshire, told Home Secretary Russell that the membership of the Bolton Working Men's Association had increased from 700 at the beginning of the year to 2,100 by July 1839. In comparison the membership of the Operative Conservatives remained slightly over 800 throughout 1839.[123] The explosion of working-class anger came during the strikes surrounding the Sacred Month of August. By August 12 the *Chronicle* reported that, "The town was in the greatest state of alarm, most shops and businesses closed. People believed a terrible attack to be at hand."[124] The riots duly came and lasted four days, culminating in the Chartists successfully storming Little Bolton Town Hall. In the end the Military assumed control and the leaders were arrested, but Bolton remained in a state of uneasy calm. The only other mill town to be affected in anything like the scale of Bolton was Bury.[125] Elsewhere, at

---

117 *Bolton Chronicle*, 28 January 1837.

118 Ibid.

119 See, for example, P. Linebaugh, *The London Hanged; Crime and Civil Society in the Eighteenth-Century*, (London, 1991), see also, by the same author, 'The Tyburn Riot against the Surgeons', in Douglas Hay, Peter Linebaugh, Edward Thompson, *Albion's Fatal Tree: Crime and Society in Eighteenth-Century England*, (London, 1975).

120 PRO, MH 12, 5593-4 Correspondence, 4 April 1839, and April 1840, *passim*.

121 See R. Sykes, 'Popular Politics and Trade Unionism in South-East Lancashire, 1829-1842', Ph.D thesis, University of Manchester (1982). See also PRO, HO 40-42, Correspondence between Darbyshire and Russell, *passim*.

122 Bolton Reference Library, Heywood Papers, ZHE/35 L55, (1839).

123 PRO, HO 40/44, Darbyshire to Russell, 21 July 1839.

124 *Bolton Chronicle*, 12 August 1839.

125 PRO, HO 40/37, Grundy to Russell, 5 August 1839.

Oldham and Rochdale, the situation was calm, with no strikes taking place. In the larger mill towns the strike was at best lacklustre. In Ashton the leadership was badly divided, and at Blackburn the Sacred Month passed off with scarcely a murmur.

Robert Sykes asserts that while the various conspiratorial schemes were being hatched in other parts of the country, most notably South Wales and Yorkshire, only Bolton, of all the towns in the north-west, organized a response. This tells us something of their commitment even though ultimately these plans came to nought.[126] The eventual defeat of 1839 reduced the strength of support for the extreme radical faction in Bolton and, in the years which followed the Sacred Month, the working class of the town became less militant and more interested in issues not connected with far reaching constitutional reform.[127] The radical Tory MP for Knaresborough, W. B. Ferrand, re-kindled the interest in the Factory Question in 1843 when he visited the town for a 'Oastler Liberation' rally in December. Speaking as a "Tory of the old school" in favour of "ten hours," repeal of the New Poor Law and of the need for industrial arbitration, he gained the backing of the Bolton Operative Conservative Association.[128] But the Liberals, under the leadership of a major employer, Robert Knowles, also took up the issue, much to the displeasure of the leading Manchester School Liberals, Henry and Edmund Ashworth, and the Liberal MP Dr John Bowring.[129]

Increasingly the picture of working class politics in Bolton in the 1840s, 1850s and 1860s was one in which both of great parties vied for the support of the working class over issues that they, the middle classes, felt were important. This was irrespective of whether the working class believed them to be so, these included issues such as religion, public health, education, temperance, self-help and moral reform. However, the parties also became involved in issues which the working class themselves viewed as important, such as factory reform, trades unions, industrial negotiation and poor relief. The Conservatives remained a force in the town throughout the period and although the operative branch did not survive the great split of 1846-7, it was revived in the later 1850s. At the election of 1868, called under the householder suffrage, Bolton, like Blackburn, Preston and Salford, returned two Conservative members. Until its decline in the mid-1840s, the Bolton Operative Conservative Association fulfilled the same functions in education, proselytization, provision of sick benefits and entertainment as in other north-west towns. It also served to integrate sections of the working class into party political activity, and it legitimized that activity. The operative branch acted as an agency for generating opinion and for its wider dissemination, galvanizing a measure of working-class support behind the party. For example, taking a year when the Conservatives of Bolton did badly in a parliamentary election, 1841.[130] This was a year when the Operative Association was at its height. We find that of the total electorate of Bolton, the working class made up 22.5 per cent. Of this 14 per cent voted for the losing Conservative candidates, Bolling and Rothwell, whilst 8.5 per cent for the Liberal pair of Bowring and Ainsworth.[131] As a statistic it reveals the overwhelming

---

126 R. Sykes, 'Physical Force Chartism: the Cotton District and the Chartist Crisis of 1839', in the *International Review of Social History*, 30, 2, (1985), p. 234.

127 For example the great strike of 1842 passed off in Bolton without any serious disturbance, see Sykes, thesis.

128 *Bolton Chronicle*, 23 December 1843.

129 *Bolton Free Press*, 20 April 1844.

130 From 1832 the Conservatives of Bolton only lost both of the parliamentary seats twice out nine elections fought, these were in 1841 and 1852, in all others, apart from 1868 when they took both seats, they shared the representation with the Liberals.

131 *Bolton Chronicle*, 7 July 1841, Bolton Reference Library, Poll Book for 1841. Out of the 553 split votes for Ainsworth and Bowring there were 48 working class votes; out of the 406 votes for the Conservatives, Bolling and Rothwell, there were 56 working class votes. Other splits were so small as to be barely meaningful.

strength of the lower-middle-class electorate, but it does show that among the working class electors, particularly the weavers, the Conservatives held majority support.

In Bolton then, even in the years of high levels of working class consciousness, particularly the later 1830s, there was a section of the working class integrated into the Conservative Party. And it is also noteworthy that from the mid-1830s, the Operative Conservatives involved themselves in working class based issues. This tells us that some working people were seeking other solutions to their problems than that of directly challenging the forces of authority, whilst at the same time displaying a will to act on behalf of what they perceived as their class interest as a whole. This suggests that working class consciousness may have been operating at different levels. However, it also signifies that even when class consciousness was high and working class leadership was prominent, political parties and key individuals still had the power to influence sections within the working class. In Bolton, as at Blackburn, the Conservatives utilised this, but at Bolton it was not the prominent manufacturers like Hornby, but largely the lower-middle class and the working class themselves. However, the local Conservative leadership carefully cultivated support among the moderate working class, giving publicity to their problems and at the same time denigrating the Liberals as the chief cause of their miseries. To some working class members this may have been seen as an attack on the systematic progressiveness of Manchester School Liberalism. This was the basis of the success of men like Ferrand in gaining widespread support among the working class in the 1840s, Booth Mason in the '50s and W. R. Callender in the '60s. However, in the case of these last two leaders it should be remembered they used religious bigotry, sectarian and racial conflict as weapons in their political campaigns. The point is that working class sectionalism and support for Conservatism had a fairly long history.

We saw in Bolton that in the 1820s it was the spinners who were active; by the 1830s it was the weavers. Unquestionably the weavers' economic situation was an important factor, but so too was the effect of the transformation of their political awareness. Even in the 1830s, working-class politics were sectionalized with opinions as to the solutions, varying from the largest section, the extreme radicals, through to the moderates, and the Conservatives. However, all maintained they had genuine solutions to the plight of the working class. Thus, even in the radical '30s a plurality of opinion existing around working class based issues. After the débâcle of the Sacred Month mass radicalism in Bolton grew weaker until, by the later 1840s, political activity amongst the working class was minimal. Support was now split between the two main party groupings over issues like industrial relations, factory reform, the New Poor Law, the rating question, education, temperance, public health and so on.

The point that greater working class political autonomy and the motivating of a wide set of political attitudes among the working class of Bolton was due to the relative smallness of its factories is interesting but contradictory. There is evidence on both sides of the argument. Certainly there were not the charismatic leaders in Bolton of the type found in Blackburn or even Preston. But there is the anomaly of the spinners, a group who worked in some of the largest factories in the town, who were active on the industrial front but passive on the political. The engineers, as a group, tended to work in the small workshop environment and throughout the 1830s became increasingly radical, and, in 1841, those who possessed the franchise voted overwhelmingly for the reformers and against the local iron-founder, Rothwell. However, when one looks at the 27 electors who plumped for Rothwell one finds that 9 were working class, either mechanics, millwrights or moulders, thus even within this trade, where radicalism was in the ascendancy, there was political sectionalism.[132]

The split among the workers of Bolton between Conservative and radical Liberal took place in the early to mid 1840s. In Blackburn we saw this came in the 1830s. In Radical Oldham it was in the 1850s, but even here Operative Conservatism established a foothold in the 1830s.[133] The Oldham Operative Society was formed in September 1835, and by January 1836 they were attracting 200 to their branch meetings.[134] Apart from 1835, the town returned radical Liberal members. However, the radicals of Oldham believed that in the 1830s they could influence the county elections with their weight of numbers. At the election of 1837, for example, they concentrated their attack on the Conservative member for South Lancashire Lord Francis Egerton. They failed but left this genteel member of the nobility with an enduring memory of the contest, as Egerton told Peel. "We have given the Radicals another stunning blow in this country… The two candidates were more active and efficient than my former opponents … then they insulted all precedents by perambulating many minor districts through which I was compelled to follow them, for which I hope God may forgive them but I never will."[135] From the period of the French Wars through to the 1850s the political leadership of Oldham was dominated by radicals of various persuasions and coming from different occupational and status backgrounds.[136] Throughout the 1820s, '30s and '40s popular radicalism in Oldham gained enormously from the working class leadership of John Knight, Alexander Taylor, John Earnshaw, Richard Cooper and William Fitton and from the national prominence of the middle class MPs Cobbett, Fielden and Johnson. After becoming members immediately after 1832 the radical MPs of Oldham pledged their loyalty to the radical cause. They considered themselves representatives of their constituents, (not merely electors), and regularly discussed the salient issues of the day affecting working people, as well as submitting their voting record and parliamentary performance with the popular radical organization in the town, the Oldham Political Association.[137] But even here in the 1830s the Operative Conservatives gained a foothold through the leadership of John and George Nield and by the later 1840s and the decline of radicalism had grown into a considerable force. Indeed as at Blackburn even veteran radicals like Alexander Taylor and John Earnshaw attended their meetings.[138] With householder suffrage in 1868, a Conservative was returned for Oldham and in 1874 the town had two Tory MPs. Also in 1868, in Manchester, a Conservative finished top of the poll and at Salford two Conservatives were returned. In these two cities the Operative Conservatives appear to have had thriving branches. Mr Richie of the Salford branch expressed, in 1836, an early form of Tory democracy when he said, "The almighty has not made different codes of law, one for the rich and one for the poor, in his eyes all are equal."[139] This branch vehemently denied the charge levelled at them by the *Manchester Guardian* that they were the political manifestation of an Orange Lodge. In March 1836 they opened up their membership books

132 Bolton Reference Library, Pollbook for 1841.

133 J. Foster, *Class Struggle and the Industrial Revolution*, (London, 1974), see also The Butterworth Manuscripts, Oldham Reference Library.

134 *Manchester Courier*, 7 January 1836.

135 British Library, Peel Papers, Ad. Ms. 40424, ff 17, Egerton to Peel, undated August 1837.

136 See Foster, *Class Struggle*, pp. 100-118, 200. Also D. Gadian, 'Radicalism and Liberalism in Oldham: a study of conflict, continuity and change in popular politics, 1830-1852', in *Social History*, Vol. 21, No. 3 (October 1996).

137 See Butterworth Diaries, Oldham Reference Library, 20 October 1833 and *passim*, also Foster, *Class Struggle*, p. 69.

138 See Butterworth Diaries, Oldham Reference Library, 1835-37, *passim, Manchester Guardian*, 7 October 1848, 11 October 1848, 13 October 1849.

139 *Manchester Guardian*, 7 January 1836.

to the *Guardian* in order to prove that out of 380 members only 14 were Orangemen.[140] According to *The Times*, in 1838 Salford Conservatives held a tea party and ball, 3,000 persons attended.[141] In the same year, when the Manchester Operative branch invited Sir Francis Burdett to address them, he sat down to a subsidized dinner along with 2,000 others.[142] Speaking at Warrington in December 1836, the editor of the *Manchester Courier* said that in south Lancashire alone the Operative membership amounted to 7,000, and Charles Wilkins, at the same meeting, put the total membership for the whole of Lancashire at 12,000.[143] Also in 1836, Wilkins defended the right of working people to agitate over industrial relations and to form trades unions.[144]

As noted above, many of these operative associations faded with the split in the party after 1847. Part of the reason for this was the deep divisions that Corn Law Repeal created among the propertied middle classes, who, as we have seen, provided much of the financial backing for the operative branches. Without such financial help the branches folded. This reinforces the point that these operative associations were heavily reliant on the middle classes. By the 1850s many had been re-formed. This was partly due to the need to re-organize because of the effects of the Small Tenements Act in local government, but also a feature was the heightened ethnic and religious tensions of that period.[145] In terms of mass membership, the political clubs came into their own in the 1870s, with the need of both Liberals and Conservatives to organize a mass working class electorate, this, however, has been covered elsewhere.[146]

The concern of this chapter was to compare developments in three different types of north-west towns, but the most decisive indications of political change among the working class came in the new boroughs. Here the Conservatives, whilst maintaining the need to preserve the constitution in Church and State, also began to integrate sections of the working class into their ranks. They were integrated not merely as bigoted political pawns, but on the basis of issues that the working class were directly concerned with, and thus sought to influence opinion and gain support around these issues. In Blackburn the local Conservatives, while attempting to politically socialize sections of the working class and control them, and indeed to use them as organizational tools of the party, concerned themselves with practical, bread and butter issues which the working class themselves felt were important. Thus the Conservatives began to become involved in opinion politics. Also noted was the growth of radical Toryism throughout the Blackburn area and a form of popular Conservatism in the 1840s, '50s and '60s centring on key charismatic leaders, usually large scale middle class manufacturers. At Bolton during the 1820s the trades were split and there had been a history of loyalist Tory sentiment among key sections of the working class some four decades before 1832. In the first two decades of the nineteenth century this centred on the reactionary magistrate, Ralph Fletcher. The reform crisis brought a level of unity to the trades and a general heightening of class consciousness. The extreme radicals claimed a large section of working class support up until the end of the 1830s, whilst the lower middle class Liberal reformers predominated among their social peers. Both sides looked to their class interests in politics, with the Liberal reformers concerning themselves successfully with local politics and the working class looking increasingly towards major, and

---

140 Ibid., 12 March 1836.

141 *The Times*, 20 April 1838.

142 Ibid.

143 *Manchester Courier*, 3 December 1836.

144 Ibid.

145 See N. Kirk, 'Ethnicity, Class and Popular Toryism, 1850-1870', in K. Lunn, (ed.) *Hosts, Immigrants and Minorities*, (Folkstone, 1980).

146 See for example, J. Garrard, 'Parties, Members and Voters after 1867: A Local Study', in *Historical Journal* 20, 1, (1977).

possibly violent, constitutional reform. But even in this seemingly barren political environment the Conservatives could claim some working class support. They began to influence working class opinion, especially among the weavers and their specific problems and the working class as a whole over the imposition and operation of the New Poor Law.

After the events of 1830, more and more working people began to become involved in industrial relations and again the Conservatives in parts of the north-west lead opinions on the Factory Question. Working class politics, however, became increasingly quiescent, and what interest the working class had in politics, even when the Small Tenements Act was operating in the 1850s, became polarized between the two main party alignments. We noted that after the majority of working men received the vote, Bolton returned two Conservatives in both 1868 and 1874. This may have been due to the prevailing political situation of the time, but, as we have seen, sections of the working class at Bolton and Blackburn had been harbouring Conservative sympathies for possibly three decades.

In both Blackburn and Bolton, and in the majority of the new boroughs, religious distinctions do not appear to have played a major role in the political choices of the working class in the 1830s and 1840s. At this time they were more concerned with material and practical questions. Some sections of the working class turned to major constitutional reform as the answer, but others looked to practical solutions within the existing system. The Conservatives aimed their dart at this second group, and it seems that on occasions they were successful. Religion, in fact, was of minimal importance to the majority of the working class Conservatives in the 1830s and '40s, although the middle classes may have believed it was important to the working class. The working class themselves apparently used religion as an institution for gaining the basic educational needs of their children rather than a means of spiritual solace. However, in terms of generational influence, Sunday Schools of the 1830s and '40s may have played an important role in the rise of working class religious observance in the 1850s and '60s. In these two decades religion became an important political question in the mill towns and the large cities of the region. With the influx of the Irish immigrants, the Conservatives, locally and nationally, played the 'Orange card', but even this, in a sense, illustrates the power of parties to generate and influence opinion, even despicable opinion, among sections of the working class.

7

Working Class Political Integration and the Conservative Party

It was suggested at the outset that, at national and local levels, the form and structure of politics in Britain began to change after 1832. The interest lay in two key areas of political change: firstly, the development of political parties (specifically the Conservatives), especially in the light of the social and structural changes of the 1830s and 1840s, and, secondly, the political development of the industrial working class in the north-west, the most economically and industrially advanced region in the country. The 1850s and '60s had effectively absorbed the impact of change. The immediate aftermath of the first Reform Act became the cornerstone of the discussion surrounding the nature of political change, along with the consolidation of industrial capitalism in the 1830s and '40s, stressing the links between political change, economic change, and, more pertinently, social change. In order to account for these developments the investigation required research and discussion on a broad, as well as on a narrow, canvass, to look at the situation before 1832 as well as concentrating on the key changes occurring after the passing of Reform.

The historiographic debate surrounding the emergence of the modern political party before 1867 is important in two senses. Firstly the contrast between the way political factions operated in the eighteenth and early nineteenth centuries and the evolving party system after 1832, taking the effects of the Reform Act itself as points of assessment of changes both at the centre and in the localities. Secondly, it provided a series of explanatory concepts, more normally associated with political science and political sociology, in order to bring the points of departure between the pre- and post-Reform period into sharp relief. Before 1832 political parties did not in any qualitative sense reveal the features nor perform many of the functions that both the major parties after 1832 quickly developed. These included a more co-ordinated and systematic method of selection and recruitment of the local political elites in both national and local politics and, in the case of the latter, a broader stage on which these elites could operate politically. This was especially so in the new boroughs, and, after the 1835 Municipal Reform Act, in the sphere of local government. Political selection and recruitment of the elites did of course take place before 1832 but the trend was for the county gentry or large-scale landowners in or around the constituencies, or the closed corporations to select and recruit potential political leaders. To a certain extent, in parts of the north-west this process was continued after 1832, especially in the county towns of Lancaster and Chester, and, to a lesser extent, in the old borough of Preston. However, in the new boroughs the local party seems increasingly to have taken over this function. The political elites realised the new post-1832 political situation required new approaches. The memorandum of Alfred Mallalieu to the national leaders of the Conservatives made explicit the need for such localized party activity.

If the debate surrounding the development of political parties is well established, that concerning the emergence of working class conservatives is not. Historians have assumed that because the working class were excluded from the formal political contract there was little point investigating the localised political clubs. To be sure, there is research devoted to the post-1867 period but little or nothing for the preceding period. The only study, which touched on working-class conservatism before 1850, was R. L. Hill's *Toryism and the People*, published in 1929. Hill notes the existence of the operative associations but says nothing of their organization, role or function. For Hill they were merely a tactical ploy to be used during elections and later as a means of offering deferential displays of popular adoration.[1] More recently, for Joyce, the operative associations of the 1830s were little more than vehicles allowing the mill-owning elites opportunities for ostentatious patronage and the receipt of working class deference.[2] Garrard, on the other hand, while primarily concerned with developments after 1867, acknowledges the vital role such working class based associations played before that time.[3] For the historians of party the incidence of Operative Associations in the localities in the 1830s merits little more than a footnote. They are more concerned with developments at the centre and the actions of the political elites. Norman Gash, for example, whilst acknowledging the need for the study of Conservative Associations pays them scant attention and totally ignored the involvement of the working class.[4] What has been demonstrated here may go some small way to rectify this imbalance. After 1832 local political parties played an increasingly important role in the coordinating and organizing electoral activity. The discussion of the old boroughs revealed the traditional methods of electoral organization were maintained longer after Reform than in the new boroughs where local Conservatives were noticeably quick off the mark. The need after 1832 to control the registration process, and local politics after the 1835 Municipal Reform Act, even in the market and county towns and old industrial boroughs, saw local parties increasingly and permanently involved in the coordination of electoral activity. The crucial point was that sections of the working class, the great majority of whom were non-electors, became permanently involved in local party political organization to a greater extent than had ever been the case before 1832. Political parties after 1832 began to act as the main agencies of disseminating both governmental and opposition principles and policies. Indeed, in the localities parties began to champion those issues which were of direct concern and consequence to the working class. There were local factional cliques who took up particular grievances in specific places before 1832, but, as with the radical Tories, and later with mainstream Conservatives in the 1840s, '50s and '60s, this become a region-wide phenomenon. Modern parties play a vital role in politically coordinating both governmental and opposition actions in the localities and not long after 1832 political parties began the same process. For example, in the north-west over the perceived harshness of the New Poor Law, but it must be noted that at this early stage local party political activity was essentially opportunistic and was rarely informed by 'hard' ideological imperatives. Thus the taking up of issues varied from place to place and over time in any given place. In many parts of the north-west it is highly debatable whether ideological distinctions of national politics had any relation with the essence of the local political battle, although they may at times have had a peripheral bearing.

Other functions and features included political integration, political socialization and education. Political integration meant parties began to allow groups, individuals and sections of classes who previously had been excluded from mainstream politics, a legitimate role in localized political

1   R. L. Hill, *Toryism and the People*, (London, 1929), p. 51, and *passim*.

2   P. Joyce, *Work, Society and Politics*, (Brighton, 1980), p. 269.

3   J. Garrard, 'Urban Elites, 1850-1914: The Rule and Decline of a New Squirearchy', in *Albion*, Vol. 27, No. 4, (Winter, 1995), p. 593. Also 'Parties, Members and Voters after 1867', in T. R. Gourvish, and A. O'Day (eds.) *Later Victorian Britain*, p. 145.

4   N. Gash *Politics in the Age of Peel*, (London, 1953), p. xvii.

society. At no time before 1832 did continuous activity occur as it did between 1832 and 1852. From 1834-5 the Conservative Party particularly was acting as party of social integration in the industrial areas of the north-west. It is important to establish how parties began to perform a range of ongoing activities after 1832, enabling political society to operate more effectively. Political parties, for example, need not necessarily undertake political socialisation. It may be, and indeed was, also carried out by the education system, or the family or the press, but increasingly after 1832 parties took up this role. So too with other functions which may easily have been carried out by other means. These included the determining of the political agenda, which could be done by the press or interest groups. The dissemination of basic ideological principles (which could have been effectively performed by educational institutions, the press, Church or Chapel) or indeed the provision of sick and burial facilities which could be, and were, provided by Friendly Societies. However, in all these spheres the Conservatives were active after 1832. There was another set of functions that only the parties themselves could perform. These included the disciplining of the members and the articulating of the aggregated interests and demands of members and supporters. Parties began to perform these functions in the 1830s. However, some of these functions may be detected among the various factions operating before the Reform Act, especially in the 1820s. It was the range and the extent of the roles performed by the Conservative Party that is noticeable after 1832. Although the focus of activity was the localities, Peel's Conservative Party at the centre gave an important lead. Peelite Conservatism built on the central traits of old Toryism; the conservative Whigs, liberal Tories (in economics and religion) and those leaders closely associated with Peel himself. Between 1833 and 1856 (indeed for some time after) Peelite Conservatives represented a synthesis which made up the Conservative Party. Peel attempted to maintain what he believed to be the essential constitutional and institutional prescriptive rights of the monarch, the aristocracy, the Established Church and the landed interest. At the same time he wished to cater to the needs of the rising economic interest, of manufacturers and employees, the Catholics (especially in Ireland) and the Nonconformists on mainland Britain. He wished for government and a party, which truly represented the interests of society's material, religious and social needs. Peel was a believer in *laissez-faire* in economic matters but he was not averse to executive intervention to achieve economic and social cohesion. By reducing prices, lowering tariffs and relieving the burden of taxation on the less well off by shifting fiscal policy away from indirect to direct taxation, he was introducing measures that would increase the purchasing power of those at the bottom of the social and economic order. This would eventually diffuse class tensions between labour and capital. John Foster correctly pointed out that it was Peel's belief in liberal values and putting these into effect during his 1841-46 administration, that helped shift the political attitude of the majority of working people away from extreme radicalism and towards a more moderate, indeed apathetic, stance on great political questions. Foster writes,

> In Peel's eyes government was a trust to be exercised on behalf of the entire people, and to this extent he sought to remove the main material basis of popular discontent: cutting the length of the working day, repealing the Corn Laws, passing the first systematic health legislation. The equation of political power with the roots of economic misery no longer held... At this point ... the language of radicalism was no longer able to hold together the diffuse alliance that had previously given it mass influence.[5]

For Peel, even the repeal of the Corn Laws, albeit done to assuage famine in Ireland, was a

---

5   John Foster, 'The De-classing of Language', in *New Left Review*, 150, (1985), p. 33.

measure vital to the material well-being of working people, as well as in the interests of the Conservative Party. He wanted to go to the polls on a cry of cheap bread, as well as the other more traditional Conservative principles, because, in his words:

> I have thought it consistent with true Conservative policy to promote so much happiness and contentment among the people that the voice of disaffection should no longer be heard, and the thought of the dissolution of our institutions should be forgotten in the midst of physical enjoyment.[6]

He was asking his party to back him in his policy of true political representativeness, at the same time killing extreme radicalism (or Chartism) and class tensions with kindness. Peel's chief problem was not that he neglected party organization, either at the centre or in the country at large, but his psychological inability to adequately communicate and convey his feelings to his backbenchers. He remained aloof and unapproachable to his Tory wing, the majority of whom represented the agricultural interest, whilst others were remnants of the Ultra faction who were mistrustful of Peel after his *volte-face* on the Catholic Question in 1829. The party at the centre was split by the repeal of the Corn laws in 1846, but this had little impact on overall party development in the north-west, especially in the sphere of local government.

If party development was mutable, what of the other element of concern to this study: the political development of the working class? More specifically, the historical relationship between the Tory/Conservative party and the working class up to and beyond the Reform Act of 1832. Levels of working class consciousness rose between 1790 and 1832, as workers in the north-west saw their traditional work and customary practices undermined by the factory system. On the one hand this reduced their independence, and on the other produced an apparently hostile and uncaring attitude on the part of the Tory political elites. From the end of the 1810s, class consciousness took the form of an enhanced sense of awareness on the part of working people of their social and economic position, and the need to seek redress through increased political representation. The conclusion reached by many working people was the need for a wholesale reform of the constitution.

Traditional eighteenth-century forms of social control based on mutual respect, the mediatory role of the magistrate and subtle forms of 'moral economy' were increasingly replaced by a Tory inspired system of overt coercion. This system included the widespread use of spies, suspension of habeas corpus, the Gag Acts and, in short, crude intimidation. This served only to harden the will-to-action of many working people in the newly industrialised parts of the region. Their outrage was vented on the objects perceived as the chief cause of their problems, namely the factories and owners of the new machinery. The need was to replace the rotten political system with one where working people would gain a form of representation and restore their sense of citizenship as a class. In effect they began to think politically in a class-conscious way. To an extent the working class accepted the prevailing political theory of virtual representation. But they demanded that proper weight be given to their increasingly important economic and social status as a productive class within the nation as a whole and to their perceived lost rights as free citizens. In the later 1820s and the revival of the agitation for Parliamentary reform, many working people believed their best hope of success lay in placing their support behind the middle and lower middle-class radicals. Tory/Conservative attitudes continued to be hostile, a posture maintained throughout the reform crisis. Indeed, this was transformed into genuine fear when a united working class, not divided by craft of status differentiations, were allied

---

6   *Hansard*, 3rd Series, Vol. 83, p. 95.

to a radical urban middle class. Older forms of social and political controls had broken down, alarming not only the political elites, but also the middle class radicals of the north-west and, indeed, middle class leaders of reform in London, like Francis Place.

In the Bolton district working class consciousness reached its height when many working class radicals, realizing the bill was expressly designed to exclude them, took over the middle and lower middle class Political Unions, flying in the face of a Royal Proclamation banning such associations. It has been argued that the working-class radical movement lacked a comprehensive theory of social and political change. Rather working class radicalism harked back to recapturing previous lost rights.[7] What was in place in the early 1830s was a working class unity devoid of status differentiation and a mass will to act around the economic, social and political problems. The mass march on London by the workers of Manchester early in May 1832, and the disturbances at Derby, Bristol and Nottingham reveal some of them were quite prepared to violently confront the state authorities.

High levels of mass working class consciousness during 1830 to 1834 across the region have to be set in contrast with the sectionalization of subjective class unity and the gradual, but eventually widespread preponderance of status differentiation among the working class. Several factors caused this. These included the discipline of the factory system, the high levels of working class dependency on the manufacturers, particularly welfare relief, education, religion, housing provision and recreation. Working-class political allegiances were being pulled in various directions by the two main political parties, various pressure and special interest groups, trades unions, the press and the radical rump. It was not only the Conservatives: the great bulk of moderate middle-class opinion was alarmed at the radical shift in working class attitudes between the late 1820s and the early 1830s. Local and national Conservatives were moved to defend the institutions of the secular and spiritual state against what seemed their imminent destruction by the reforming Whigs and the progressive Liberals, but they were further motivated by the desire to deflect working class opinion away from the dangers of extreme radicalism. The Reform Act rendered it necessary that the Conservative Party be radically and urgently reorganized. This was not only concerned with changes in party structure at the centre but also in the localities. An important change wrought by the Reform Act was the introduction of the annual registration contests in the boroughs that meant the party in the locality was organized on a permanent basis. Conservatives at the centre recognised that a new situation existed. One solution was to have a flow of reliable information from the various localities into a permanent standing committee at the Carlton. Mallalieu's memorandum supported the argument that the party was aware of the changing nature of politics. A standing committee was initiated, performing a variety of functions. These included advice on organizational tactics to the constituencies, especially in the new, larger boroughs providing prospective members with constituencies and *vice-versa*. They collated relevant information from the constituencies, marshalling the semi-professional organizers and helpers for the constituencies who required such assistance, catching the political mood of the various constituencies, organizing the press, logging registration and electoral returns and keeping the party's leadership informed as to developments and reactions in the localities. It was the sheer scope of these activities that marked the period off from the pre-reform political system; the scale of the change, the originality and the dynamism the Conservatives evince, particularly, immediately after 1832 evince that is so notable. As an opposition they were in a far better position to effect the re-organization of the party than when in government,

---

7   See G. Stedman Jones, *Languages of Class*, (Cambridge, 1983).

and may partly explain why the Whig/Liberals were so slow off the mark. The manner in which the leading politicians, including the initially sceptical Peel, accepted the need for the party to be permanently organized at the centre, coupled as it was with the autonomous but closely monitored local branch associations throughout the country. This is a striking feature of the immediate post-1832 situation. Moreover, and importantly, the local parties began to canvass support from groups previously denied access to the political system: namely the non-electors and sections of the working class in the industrial areas, a group the Tories and Conservatives had previously shown no great interest in. However, before expanding this key theme, it has to be established whether any political integration of this kind had taken place among the lower orders before the 1830s.

The tendency of the majority of the working class between the 1790s and the 1820s was of increased class solidarity, based loosely around the principles of Paineite radicalism. Developing alongside this was the articulation of a collective consciousness based on the defence of traditional working class independence that led to the transformation of Friendly Societies into trade union organizations. In contrast to the Loyalist Associations and Reeves Societies of the 1790s, the main objective of political parties after 1832 was the eliciting of party political support at the expense of the rival political party. Neither did the middle-class Pitt Clubs of the early 1800s realistically correspond to the Conservative Associations of the 1830s. They performed limited functions in political recruitment or occasionally raised subscriptions but were not interested in integrating other social groups, and were at pains to maintain and support the traditional system of political influence, be it corporate or aristocratic. They did set a precedent of sorts, but if any organization was a genuine antecedent of the political associations of the 1830s then it was O'Connell's Catholic Association of the later 1820s and the Political Unions of the early 1830s. The overall tightening of national party structures, coupled with a range of permanently organized functional features, marks the Conservative Associations off from the Pitt Clubs of the first three decades of the nineteenth century. Also, the localized political associations after the 1830s engaged in another feature of the modern party system as they began to allow members of the working class into their party, endeavouring to enlist the support of groups representative of the various social and economic interests of the north-west region.

Initially the middle class Conservative Associations were essentially autonomous bodies and were viewed with suspicion by some leaders of the national party. However, when their utility became manifest in terms of the detailed information that the party could use, these fears were allayed. The main aims of the local Conservative Associations were to regain the political initiative from what they saw as the threat posed to the constitution by the Whig reformers and the progressive Liberals, and also to place the party on a firm organizational footing within the region as a whole. This was seen as especially important given the success of the Whig/Liberals at the first elections held under the first Reform Act. A further aim was to convince the moderate working class (including non-electors) of the dangers of extreme radicalism but also to point out that Liberalism and political economy was no friend of the inherent needs, culture and traditional practices of working people. In this early stage of development, local Conservatives played on feelings of working-class loyalty to the protestant religion and the state, but also on their deference to long-standing institutions and local men of distinction and worth. They emphasized eighteenth century paternalistic values, customary rights and the sense of natural justice. Such values struck a chord with those workers who saw their independence rapidly disappearing, and others witnessing the regimentation of the factory. Although the factory system itself was not condemned, difficult given that many of the leaders of the Associations in the boroughs were local factory owners, what was stressed was that the best employers tended to be Conservatives, with Liberals portrayed as cold, hard-headed, uncaring people concerned more with the relentless pursuit of profit and the radical re-organization of society according to the tenets of political economy, rather than with the real needs and wants of working people. The core of the Conservative ideological message at this time was the need to preserve the chief institutions of Church and State and especially to work within the existing law. There emerged, however, a group of radical Tories, especially strong in the north and east of the region and particularly antagonistic to the Liberal factory owners, men like Oastler and Stephens, prone to wild and violent speeches to get over their message regarding the abuses of the factory system. They too made a strong impression on sections of the working class.

Working class support for Conservatism was seen as beneficial to both the party and the members. Peel, particularly, wished the party to be truly representative of all sections of society, and the incidence of working-class support for Conservatism was visible proof of that representative aspect. The working classes were useful as foot soldiers both in the process of electoral organization and the annual registration contests. Acting as agents of communication, from the party's leadership to wider working class society, the party's local and national leaders became aware of what questions and issues particularly concerned working people at any given time. The party had also the ability to control and politically direct influential leaders of working class opinion. This ability to direct opinion, to determine what is allowable or legitimate and what was excluded was, after 1850, according to Alastair Reid, important in gaining the rights of participatory citizenship for the working class their consent for the political and social system.[8] But again the study of the political integration of the working class of the north-west shows that this was begun some two decades before the 1850s. For those working class who became members of the operative branches the chief benefits were that they were now incorporated into a legitimate political party, and, in a sense, had become integrated into the wider political system. In the long term this meant that sections of the industrial working class had begun the process of what Peter Hennock, echoing the contemporary usage, termed 'fit and proper persons' to be allowed into the political contract. These Conservative (and Liberal) working men were, by their acceptance to the existing political norms, demonstrating their suitability for admittance to the responsibilities associated with holding the franchise. But by so doing they were also being socialised into the conventions of pluralistic party politics. Moreover, so was the party. As such, these moves were the first stages towards a wider, capitalist-based, incorporational pluralist democracy at the local level, built around the party structure. There were, however, benefits of a more material nature such as the Sick and Burial Clubs, a vital facility in periods of economic recession and personal hardship. There were trips and outings, literary and social facilities such as free libraries and newspaper reading rooms, some had bowling greens or brass bands. There were educational opportunities, evening classes available for both adults and children, dinners, tea-parties, dances and guest speakers, all of which served to underscore both the worth of working people themselves and the worth they were held in by their social superiors.

The setting up of the operative clubs took place very quickly from 1834 to 1836. But although middle class Conservatives aimed their message and recruitment at a certain type of working man, at this stage there was not the overt sense of sectarian bigotry or Orangeism which became prevalent in some working class Conservative clubs after the 1850s. In the mid-1830s Orangeism was on the defensive and, indeed, was outlawed in 1837, which was a major reason why some national leaders were suspicious of these local societies. The concern was that the party should not be tainted by

---

8   A. J. Reid, *Social Classes and Social Relations in Britain, 1850-1914*, (Basingstoke, 1992), pp. 49-59.

charges of crudely absorbing the fanatics of Orangeism; this is why branches like the Salford Conservative Association opened their membership lists to the scrutiny of the *Manchester Guardian* in order to prove that they had no links with Orangeism.[9] Certainly some elements of the local and national Conservative press were hostile to Irish Catholics in particular, and the Anglican Church was lauded to the heavens, but it is worth recalling these working-class associations were set up and financed by local middle class Conservatives who tended to be Anglicans. But religious or racial bigotry was not what these clubs embodied in this early phase, (not even in traditional areas of Orange activity such as Liverpool and Wigan).[10] Rather the imperatives were to maintain the prescriptive constitution in Church and State; the urgent need to direct working people away from extreme radicalism, and, from the later 1830s, to show concern with some of the social and economic issues which the working class themselves felt were important.

The Conservative Party in the localities began promoting working class based issues which the local Conservatives felt were safe and in tune with the basic philosophy of the party. By 'safe' is meant issues which would not rock the constitutional boat, electoral reform was out of the question as was sweeping church reform and the full repeal of the Corn Laws. The championing of working class issues, such as lessening the effects of the New Poor Law, factory reform, non-political trades unions and public health was innovative, but equally remarkable were the changes in political attitudes of Conservatives in positions of power. Such moves corresponded to changes in the overall political culture, the on-going traditions, attitudes, style and behaviour in which politics was conducted. The dominant trend in the politics of the north-west after 1832 (among a wide set of social and economic groupings) was towards the politics of opinion, rather than influence or corruption. The significance was twofold. Firstly, competing political elites saw far more advantage in winning public opinion and electoral support by argument over issues and policies than by influence or crude corruption. This is not to say that the politics of the market or influence disappeared immediately, but the growth of social and political respectability from the 1830s meant they increasingly came to be seen as devices of considerable risk.[11] As the pressure and interest group system became increasingly accepted, party political leaders in the localities began to be associated with the various blocs of potential support; similarly, they related to questions which concerned key interest groups and social classes. Hence the desire of local Conservatives to ally themselves to working class based issues, a feature particularly objectionable to many Liberals, as it ran in direct opposition to the central tenets of *laissez-faire* political economy.

Sections of the working class began to support Conservatism not merely because they were Anglicans or were deferential but because they saw in that party and its elites distinct signs that the Conservatives supported the core issues they themselves were concerned with. This was especially so across the north-west as a whole with the decline of Chartism after 1842, but also previously in those parts of the region (the north and east) where Chartism did not possess a mass following. Given the recent radical history and the contentious nature of those questions, coupled with the uncompromising nature of some of the leaders of radical Toryism, like Oastler and Stephens, it becomes clear why some working people supported the party. They did so because it addressed their concern directly, as opposed to the unfeeling abstractions of progressive Liberalism. Of equal importance was that by the 1840s the Conservatives had their local organizational and structural

---

9   *Manchester Courier*, 12 March 1836.

10   See F. Neal, *Sectarian Violence: The Liverpool Experience 1819-1914*, (Manchester, 1988).

11   T. Nossiter, *Influence*, D. Fraser, *Urban Politics*, N. Gash *Politics in the Age of Peel*.

apparatus in position to influence such opinions through their working-class based clubs, and through the press and the personal message of their own working class party members. The mutable nature of working class consciousness became evident not long after the passing of Reform. In certain parts of the region (in Stockport, in Blackburn, Preston, Wigan and Warrington) it had begun to decline from the mid-1830s, and in most other parts of the north-west after 1842. Sections of the working class gave their support to Conservatism because they were less enthusiastic to the harsh capitalism that Liberalism was seen to represent and promoted issues related to the working class which Liberals fundamentally opposed on points of principle. From the 1830s sections of the working class came to realize that of the two established political parties, they could support the Conservatives because it was in their wider interests to do so. By following an established political party, especially in the absence of a radical alternative after the decline of Chartism, which pursued policies of working class interest, it can be seen why sections of the working class believed supporting Conservatism served their immediate class interests. This is especially understandable if the local party began to put their words into action, as the Conservatives of Lancaster, Blackburn, Bolton, Preston, Wigan and Salford did from the later 1840s. Indeed, in the 1850s and '60s prominent Conservatives were supporting issues of constitutional reform, such as the extension of the franchise and the secret ballot in the constituencies.[12] It could be that, therefore, we need to re-think the notion that the mid-Victorian period was one of class lacunae. In terms of practical day-to-day questions, as we move through the period, the Conservatives were increasingly able to claim sectionalized working-class support. However, this is not a blanket statement; it was not true that the party claimed majority working class support in all parts of the region. Popular Liberalism flourished in Rochdale, Bury, Stockport and Oldham, but by 1874, even in the last example, the householder franchise ensured the return of one Conservative in this former bastion of radicalism. Earlier, in 1868, the householder franchise ensured that Conservatives won both the seats at Blackburn, Bolton, Preston and Salford, and won the single seat constituencies of Ashton and Clitheroe, and they even won a seat at Manchester, the capital of Liberal political economy.

Although deference could have motivated some who joined the party in its early stages of development, there were other reasons, like religious belief, the use of issues, and the range of sick and benefit, educational and recreational inducements, which were contributory factors. Furthermore, by the mid-to-late 1830s, Conservative employers engaged in overt displays of paternalism to their employees. These covered a range of areas including housing provision and schools and, by the 1840s, offering trips, fêtes and dinners to their workers. Whilst this increased the dependency of the working class to the employer in ways other than that of the wage nexus, allowing the employer tighter control over his workforce, it also gave the Conservative employer an opportunity to display publicly his paternalistic attributes. Many Liberals were doing the same sort of thing in the period of increased profits after 1847-8, they too expected a form of deferential respect from their factory communities, but the effect served to polarize working class support between the two established parties. Often however, this was not blind deference; it was based, particularly for the Conservatives, on a form of reciprocal and negotiated mutual respect. The status and local standing of the employer demanded that he be treated with deferential attitudes, but Conservative employers were quick to point out that the overall success of the business depended on the harmonious operation of mutual esteem of capital and labour. Thus deferential attitudes can be seen as part of the negotiated politics

---

12   See the speech of W. H. Hornby at Blackburn, *Preston Pilot*, 23 March 1853, speech at Padiham by W. B. Ferrand, *Ibid.*, 8 October 1853, speech by Sir James Graham in the House of Commons, reprinted in C. S. Parker, *The Life of Sir James Graham*, Vol. II, (London, 1907), p. 370.

of industrial relations, which by the later 1840s were based on conciliation and compromise rather than confrontation. There were still disputes, but prominent Conservative mill-owners in particular appear to have been more willing to accept working class representation through trades unionism than their Liberal counterparts. Social and political deference and respect was a widespread cultural norm of the early and mid-Victorian period. It was part of the wider contemporary social culture that the Conservatives utilized.

However, working-class support for Conservatism varied within the region. Given the advanced state of industrial capitalism of a great part, but not all, of the region, the wider political developments need to be understood in terms of both local and national politics. In order to gauge the relative success of working class development and the Conservative Party in the light of different economic and social structures of various areas within the north-west it was necessary to outline and correlate the economic, social and political developments of different localities. This was needed in order to compare them with other parts of the north-west and the region as a whole.

Chester was a market centre for the surrounding area, it also possessed a sizeable group of lawyers, bookkeepers, managers, teachers, clerks and others who were located at Chester because of its position as the administrative centre for the county. However, by the 1850s light industry and the advent of the railways made Chester a key network point prior to the development of neighbouring Crewe. By mid-century a modestly sized wage-earning working class had become established. However, in terms of its general political development, Chester was relatively untouched by the great events of the period, both before and after the first Reform Act, or, indeed, the Act of 1867. Given the lack of a wage-earning working class until relatively late in the period (and even then it was extremely small) and, further, the absence of a viable radical leadership and the tight control of the reforming Whigs, it is not surprising that Chester had no Operative Conservative Association. The politics of influence, the maintenance of long established political traditions, not to mention the paternalism of the Grosvenors and other leading Whig families, and the deferential respect in which they were held, ensured their dominance in both local and national politics at Chester. This supports Norman Gash's argument for the continuation of the traditional practices of the pre-reform period.[13] However, Chester, like all of Gash's boroughs, were market and county towns who held the parliamentary franchise for hundreds of years before 1832. But, in spite of this Whig domination and the influence of the Grosvenor family, towards the end of our period, when the franchise was extended, the Conservatives gained a seat and, in 1874, they finished top of the poll. Therefore although in socio-economic terms a working class presence was marginal, even by the 1870s, there was an element of Conservative support among them.

Clitheroe, in contrast, by the 1830s had a limited industrial sector with its small textile industry, but again the political impact of the working class was minimal, even though the influence of John Fort ensured considerable radical presence from the 1830s to the early 1850s. Between 1832 and 1866 the Conservatives only won the seat once, in 1853. In the 1830s and '40s, although a middle class Conservative Association existed, the local elites showed no inclination to proselytize or rally the support of the town's working class. But again after 1867, in the two elections of 1868 and 1874, the Conservatives won the seat outright. As with Chester, at Clitheroe there was the feature of new electors tending toward Conservatism. Earlier, in the 1830s and 1840s, what working class political activity existed was directed toward radicalism of Fort. Tory Radicalism had a foothold in the neighbouring Pendle towns of Colne and Burnley but largely passed by Clitheroe. Through the 1830s

---

13   N. Gash, *Politics in the Age of Peel*, chapters, 7 to 9 and Appendix D.

and '40s, few local issues (let alone working class questions) found any purchase on the decisions of the town's elites or in the consciousness of its industrial working class. Again, as with Chester, the traditional form of political culture was carried over into the post-1832 period. Activity in local government was minimized by the fact that Clitheroe was controlled, and largely financed, by rates levied by county magistrates, but even at the level of the Vestry there was little involvement by the working class. Chartism only held a brief term of influence in 1842, never reaching the levels seen in the electorally unrepresented neighbouring towns of Burnley and Colne. Thus, neither Chester nor Clitheroe were shining examples of working class political integration or Conservative Party development after 1832.

In comparison the situation looked more favourable at Lancaster, with its potentially useful set of economic and social variables. Although possessing an industrial base and a proportionate working class, Lancaster was a county town and an administrative centre, serving also as a market for the agricultural district of north Lancashire. The town had a relatively equal social mix of waged labourers, skilled artisans, lower middle-class service sector, middle class professionals and manufacturers and small but significant gentry. The balance in political terms at Lancaster was that the local gentry and aristocracy controlled the town's parliamentary politics but did not interfere in its local government, and the corporation did not involve itself with the recruitment and selection of candidates, nor with the organising and running of parliamentary elections. Two sets of informal, elite political caucuses existed, one confined to parliamentary contests and the other to corporate affairs.

Before 1832 and the Municipal Reform Act of 1835 both sets of political elites were exclusive and ran their affairs independent of each other. Overall control remained in the hands of a small and tightly organized group up until the 1850s, after which new blood was infused into the organising body as, for the first time, the Conservatives lost both of the town's seats to the Liberals in 1852. The new recruits were drawn from the ranks of the professionals and the larger manufacturers, and it is noticeable that issues, which had not figured in Lancaster politics, surfaced in parliamentary contests.

At Lancaster it was the Liberals who began to utilise opinion politics and attempted to integrate sections of the working class into their political orbit through the Anti-Corn Law Association, but with little success. For their part, the Conservatives, up until the early 1850s, retained their exclusive nature using the Court of Admissions to attract votes. The working class of Lancaster did not agitate over issues prevalent in other parts of the region. There was little support for Chartism or opposition to the New Poor Law or factory reform. Nor did they figure in the actions of the two main political parties until the later 1840s, save the aborted Liberal attempt to establish the Operative Anti-Corn Law Association, which failed through lack of support. At Lancaster the old system of corruption and the influence of those elites drawn from the immediate vicinity of Lancaster were the dominant trends in the area, that is, as long as the Conservatives remained in control. After 1847 however, when the Liberal merchants and manufacturers began to take the initiative, the system began to change, especially when the Conservatives took up the issue of public health. In both local and parliamentary affairs, changes in the pattern of Lancaster's politics can be detected in both structure and behaviour in the years following Peel's fall and throughout the 1850s and '60s. For the Conservatives the split of 1847 explained this change. This was because the parliamentary boundary of Lancaster included areas where the agricultural interest dominated, either directly (as with the farmlands to the north, south and east) or indirectly, affecting those electors in the town itself whose living was dependent on providing services based on agriculture. The town's two Conservative members voted on opposite sides over the repeal question. At this point the Liberal elite, led by the three big manufacturers of Greg, Armstrong and Gregson, began to apply pressure in both parliamentary and municipal politics, culminating, in the early 1850s, in the struggle between Schneider and the Conservatives over the representation of the town.

The two main issues in local politics were the Conservative pursuance of public health reform and the Liberal's policy of low rates and *laissez-faire* in local government. In local government the Conservatives fared better through the widening of the municipal franchise in the 1850s, brought about by the Small Tenements Act, than did the Liberals. Thus, at Lancaster, by the later 1850s, the Conservative party was developing features and functions similar to local parties in other parts of the region, albeit over twenty years later. Up until the end of the 1850s political integration into the Conservative Party by groups other than the propertied elites was minimal. Moreover, in the intervening period from 1830 to 1860, working class political development in the town was virtually non-existent. Of primary importance was the relative smallness of the working class and their marginal importance as an economic, social and political force when compared with other groups within Lancaster itself, (for example, the tradesmen), and with other parts of the region. Although traces of opinion politics could be detected on the Liberal side at various times in the municipal arena, these tended to be directed at the electors and not those below the level of the lower middle class. This supports the view that working class political integration and Conservatives displaying opinion/interest politics were the only phenomena where industrial capitalist development was advanced and, importantly, where there existed a numerically large and class-conscious working class to make such exercises worthwhile. This was significantly not the case at Lancaster.

In terms of party organization the Reform Act of 1832 made little impact, even the annual registration contests, which were occasions of deep party rivalries elsewhere in the region, appear in Lancaster to have been decided by agreements between the parties. Also, at least until the early 1850s, the Conservatives kept their recruitment of both leaders and members firmly in the hands of the traditional elites. For much of the period the political culture of Lancaster was changing only very slowly, and if any group forced the pace of change it was the Liberals. They appear to have been the more dynamic of the two major parties. There was virtually no radical presence and very little working class activity either in the politics of constitutional reform or in matters of direct concern to themselves as a class.

Conservatism in Lancaster was traditionalist county Toryism with a smattering of conservative Whiggery. Liberalism at Lancaster was not that of popular reformism or libertarianism, but strongly influenced by Greg's link to the Unitarian and Manchester School political economy.[14] Traditional Tory attitudes to paternalism were maintained in the outlying agricultural areas of the town, but there were few instances of Conservative urban paternalism. Some help was given to the working class of Lancaster, but this was not paternalism as understood by the Conservative or Tory. For most Tories this meant a prescriptive customary obligation and responsibility. For the Liberals of the political economy school the aim was to make assistance as unacceptable to the respectable poor as possible and as painful to the residuum and those deemed undeserving. The ideological key here was thrift, sobriety, self-help and the education of the rational intellect that would redeem the individual from immorality and superstition. Intellectual self-improvement with an emphasis on hard scientific rigour was the Liberal remedy to halt the effects of irrationality that sustained dependence, pauperism, superstition and, eventually, the corrupt political system itself. Such features figured prominently at

---

14 For a more detailed analysis of the importance of this in a general context see John Seed, 'Unitarianism, Political Economy and the antinomies of Liberal culture in Manchester, 1830-1850', in *Social History*, 7, 1, (January 1982).

Preston, but overall the market and county towns were resistant to political change, at least in the first two decades after 1832.

Preston was an open borough, possessing a householder franchise before 1832 for all adult males who had not received parochial relief twelve months prior to an election. It was an administrative centre with its own Assize, a market centre for the fertile Fylde district to its west, and, importantly, it was the location for a large industrial sector based primarily on textiles. Corresponding to its mixed social and economic base, Preston was also multi-denominational, with Roman Catholics a significant and influential part of the town's population, but only on relatively few occasions were there any overt displays of anti-Catholic feeling. Preston, then, was a tolerant society and, coupled with its wide parliamentary franchise, one in which open political participation of most social groups was part of the political culture of the town. Although the working-class were the largest single group on the parliamentary register, even after 1832, the majority of them were excluded from participation in the local government of the town until the advent of the Small Tenements Act in 1853. Hence the only forum open to the working class was the Vestry, but with the imposition of the Poor Law Amendment Act in 1834, this institution too was rendered useless in political terms. This meant that parliamentary contests with the large working class voting strength became the focus points where working class grievances could be aired. Local government power was shared equally between the Liberal and Conservative elites, the latter holding a majority on the Council and the former on the Improvement Commission, a situation similar to Lancaster. The leaders of these parties were drawn mainly from the industrial and merchant sectors of the town's economy. However, there was some involvement of the professional sectors comprising of bankers, lawyers, doctors and the like, and also a sizeable proportion of tradesmen and shopkeepers. Those in positions of genuine power came from the propertied and manufacturing classes and throughout the period from 1830 to 1870 key wards in the town retained their political colour. Traditional political practices and allegiances were therefore maintained, especially in the sphere of local government. Before and after the introduction of the Small Tenements Act the Conservatives held their majority in the largely working-class wards of Trinity and St. George's. Clearly working class political support, whether arising out of religious, deferential, or opinion/interest causes, once located was resistant to change in Preston.

Meanwhile in parliamentary politics, the size of the town's electorate, over 3,700 in 1835 and almost 2,800 in 1857, made attempts at large scale bribery financially impractical but not impossible. Corruption was a facet of electoral practice before 1832 and seems to have continued throughout the 1830s and early 1840s. There were rowdy scenes at elections in 1835, 1847 and 1852, and allegations of treating were levelled by both sides in 1837 and 1841.[15] But Preston, with its relatively large electorate, was not an especially corrupt or riotous constituency.

Aristocratic influence was not prevalent as the defeat of Edward Stanley by the radical Hunt at the by-election of 1830 showed. Neither was employer influence a notable feature of the town's parliamentary development. In order for this to be effective a manufacturer would have to be a fairly large-scale employer of voters, or of workers who could act as rabble-rousers on his behalf. Up to the mid to late 1840s the size of Preston's leading factories was small; only the Conservative Horrocks's possessed a workforce of over 1,000. In the mid-1840s large factories began to be built, but here again there is little evidence that Liberal or Conservative employers were attempting to influence their workers. The working class Conservatives of St. George's ward and Liberal Fishergate ward maintained political allegiances for many years. But this was attributable to a range of factors,

---

15   See Dobson's *Parliamentary History of Preston*, (Preston, 1868), pp. 68-71.

including both social and political deference and respect, or employers looking to working class/community interests, or the existence of cohort tendencies in the political consciousness of the working class. In 1838 the Preston Conservative Association triumphantly declared that their parliamentary candidate, Robert Townley Parker, gained his victory as a result of the operatives "taking the lead".[16] A point which the Liberals made no effort to deny. So although influence may have been attempted, it was not conspicuously successful. Intimidation was spasmodic and if treats were given it was a manifestation of traditional political culture integral to the ritual of an old open borough. From the later 1820s and increasing through the 1830s and '40s, it was opinion politics and the open recognition of the interest orientations of key social groups, including those of the working class, which were the dominant trend of Preston's parliamentary politics. The Preston Operative Conservative Association operated in a manner consistent with trends throughout the north-west during this early phase. The Association was expressly designed to fulfil the functions and features outlined earlier, but an important addition at Preston was the existence of a separately named branch devoted solely to the gathering of annual registration information. The size of the working-class vote rendered it necessary to form the Conservative Registration Committee that acted as an organisational co-ordinator for both the Preston Conservative Association and the operative branch. Its existence is evidence against the suggestion that the operative branches were purely set up for organizing the registration process. The existence of a separate society purely for that purpose at Preston makes apparent, as do the smaller committees in the new boroughs, that clearly demarcated functions were being performed by these local political associations. The Conservatives, by 1839, began to exploit working class issues in order to secure broader support, especially over questions like factory reform and access to welfare provisions. Their stance on the factory and short hours issue challenged Joseph Livesey's and the popular Liberals near monopoly of purely working-class questions, whilst acting as a rallying point of opposition to the harsher elements within the New Poor Law. In these areas the working class Conservatives gained the support of their parliamentary representative, Robert Townley Parker. By the end 1830s this combination of factors meant the working class had gained access to the party structure and all that that entailed.

By empirically and analytically examining the hitherto limited picture of both Conservatism and party organization, and also that relating to working class allegiances, a clearer picture of intra-class political and social relationships emerges. Political culture and patterns of political organization were mutable, impinging directly on both middle and working class attitudes to politics and to wider society. In Preston, as in other towns, the middle classes began to control local education, local justice and the relief of poverty after the decline of the Vestry, replacing, in effect, the old eighteenth-century rule of the gentry through the greater powers of the borough council and the Improvement Commission. However, at Preston there was not the same level of overall working class dependency on the manufacturing class in, for example, the sphere of housing provision, as there was at Blackburn, hence there was less chance of direct influence, suggesting a more open political atmosphere.

Sections of the working class of Preston maintained their interest in politics throughout the 1830s, which was not the case at Blackburn, even though throughout much of the central years of the decade extreme radicalism was in decline. Towards the end of the decade Chartism, for example, was not of the physical force variety, unsupportive of the general strike and, as a movement in the town, was slow to develop. Their organizational base was the Preston Radical Association which, in July 1839,

---

16   *Preston Pilot*, 28 April 1838.

claimed a membership of 400, compared to the Preston Operative Conservative's 650 members. Part of the reason why the workers of Preston did not wish to engage in a general strike was due to the recent failure of the great spinners' strike of 1836-7 and its demoralizing effect on the class consciousness of the workers of Preston. However, another reason was the concerted action of each of the two main party groupings that flourished at the expense of the flagging appeal and weak organization of the extreme radicals. Once the established parties began to recognise pressure group politics and took on board the aggregated demands of groups within their respective orbits, working class mass agitation around platforms of extreme radicalism increasingly began to be less of a problem for the forces of authority. There were of course trade disputes involving both Conservative and Liberal mill-owners, but these tended to be devoid of political aims and objectives. From an early stage in their development the Conservatives of Preston embraced the traditional practices and customs of the working class as a means of punching holes in Liberal theories of moral regeneration directed toward the working class. The Conservatives saw nothing inherently wrong with working class bawdy culture, drinking, gambling and traditional past-times, but the Liberals either found such distractions meaningless and thus irrational, or dangerous to the moral fibre of society as a whole. The Conservatives, whilst not condoning excess, made light of Liberal pretensions of righting the wrongs of society by some strict formulae and denying the working class their slight excesses. This attitude was attractive to some sections of the working class and made the Conservatives appear more tolerant than the Liberals. Those who accepted Conservatism did so in the belief that, by the later 1840s, industrial capitalism was a permanent feature. Chartism had effectively failed, and the hope of major constitutional reform looked remote. The Conservatives pursued basic working class bread and butter issues, expressing not only a willingness to look at these questions, but also to integrate sections of the working class themselves into the party structure. In the later 1840s and early 1850s, as economic conditions were gradually improving, the Conservative approach, though still elitist, hierarchical and exclusive in terms of office holding within the party, was based on mitigation and extenuation rather than reproach and harsh remediation. By the 1850s these tendencies were joined by the more unsavoury aspects of popular Conservatism, religious and racial bigotry and jingoism, which again served to influence a section of the working class.

The local party was badly affected by the split of 1846-7, but interestingly the Operatives continued to support Sir Robert Peel, indicating the esteem that the statesman was held in by some working people.[17] As one working man said at the election of 1847, if the Operative Association "did their best at the next election we would have Sir Robert Peel back in office again."[18] Working class deference and the re-working of paternalistic attitudes by many Conservative employers was a factor in attracting the support of working people, as was the heightening of the tensions between religious groups due to the influx of Irish Catholics after the famine of 1846-8.[19] But the rejection of Liberalism by a substantial section of the working class and the opinion-orientated support for Conservatism throughout the 1850s and '60s greatly assisted the party in both municipal and parliamentary politics. It may be worthwhile to make a slight but important distinction between what political scientists regard as the politics of opinion and the actions of the Conservatives of Preston in the 1840s and '50s. During these decades the town still possessed a significant working-class electorate. The politics of opinion that the Conservatives (and Liberals) utilised was not always the

---

17 *Preston Pilot*, 20 July 1850.

18 Ibid., 5 June 1847.

19 See M. Anderson, *Family Structure*, Spencer, thesis

call to the individual conscience of the open minded, non-partisan elector acting on the basis of his own interest and the best policies or arguments put forward. Rather it was an appeal to sectional, group or class interests. What the parties were attempting was to appeal to the interest orientation and aggregated demands of as many people as possible of a given group or class without sacrificing the central tenets and basic ideological principles of the party as a whole. The key to success was to cast a wide net.

This explanation fits reasonably well with the development of pressure or single interest groups from the 1840s, and these pressure groups proliferated across a wide range of issues and interests, from church reform to education, public health to trades unionism, the brewing interest to temperance, (often within the same party). The aim was to cast wide and to gear party policy to the salient and preferably numerically prevalent interest in a given locality. After a slow start, the Conservatives of Preston managed this balancing act well from the 1840s, at Blackburn, for example, it was begun in the early 1830s. The party at Preston however, seems to have played the political percentages, gaining the maximum amount of support, not from small-scale single interest groups, such as the Anti-Gambling League, but from numerically strong pressure groupings like trades unions or the Protestant Association and the like. Increasingly, and with a degree of calculation, they conceded more as pressure from their client groupings became more intense. Examples of this could be seen in the way the Preston Conservatives carefully began to take questions like franchise extension seriously in both municipal and parliamentary politics from 1849. The leaders of the various interest groups could assess the commitment of the party to their cause, and also the results. They would advise their followers accordingly, their peers clearly seeing for themselves which party deserved their support. A more definitive term than the politics of opinion in cases like this may be the politics of interest. The Conservatives of Preston did not command the majority of workers' support until late in the period, due largely to the strong leadership qualities and libertarian values of the local Liberals, particularly Joseph Livesey. However, at the end of the period the Conservatives were successful because they controlled the allegiances of the key majority groups. They derived regular support from the Anglican middle and lower middle classes, also from substantial section of the industrial working classes, and, for a time, they even captured the support of some Catholics.[20] The Conservative elites of Preston adapted to a changing political culture, based on a form of proto-pluralism and recognition of the power of the masses, particularly the working class, in a locality increasingly dominated by industrial capitalism. Compared to the other large towns and localities, Preston reveals some of the traits of market and county centres, especially the retention of traditional political values. But even before 1832 the large working-class based popular franchise meant that in Preston limited concession to the popular will had to be made. This was seen especially during the disturbances across the region in 1826 with the generous piecework prices given to textile workers at Preston (where there was no trouble) and the easy access to the old Poor Law.[21] Conversely, old-style aristocratic and gentry influence declined after the reform crisis and never returned in the same form. The gentry (such as Townley Parker) attempted to influence the political opinions of the electorate by way of an appeal that combined social deference with the principles of Conservatism and recognition of the needs of key social groups. A pattern of continuity can be detected up to the later 1830s, after which the pace of changing political culture quickened appreciably.

The clearest evidence of the changing political culture after 1832 came from the new industrial

---

20 *Preston Pilot*, 30 April 1859.

21 See Ibid., 8 April 1826, 29 April 1826, *Blackburn Mail*, 19 April 1826; *Preston Chronicle*, 22 April 1826, 29 April 1826, 7 January 1832.

boroughs by virtue of the fact that they were not encumbered with the baggage of rituals, customs, and political idioms of the pre-Reform period. Furthermore, they were relatively advanced examples of industrial capitalism, with the social and economic characteristics, such as large-scale factory development and a population made up in the majority of a wage earning proletariat, features not found elsewhere in Britain. However, important questions remained. The most vexing was, for example, why did the working class switch away from the agitation around long held principles of extreme radicalism, manifesting as it did in high levels of class consciousness? And further, why did the north east of the region for the most part support Conservatism from the mid-1830s until the end of our period, while the south veered towards mainstream Liberalism? Related questions include, why did allegiances change in Bolton from radicalism to reforming Liberalism and, over time, switch to Conservatism, and why elsewhere did support for popular Liberalism remain consistent throughout the period?

In a sense these questions of fixed and changing political allegiances encapsulate the two dominant themes of this book, firstly working-class political development and eventual integration, and secondly, Conservative Party development and organization. However, despite the sub-themes of political idioms, national policies, the incidence of paternalism and deference, working class issues are important in trying to provide an overall evaluation. Some conclusions can, however, be made. Firstly, from the later 1830s through to the decline of Chartism as a movement in the north-west after 1842, the political leadership of the middle class became increasingly important in directing and controlling working class political orientation. This can be envisaged as a clash between, in the 1830s, middle class radicalisms and working class radicalisms being replaced in the 1840s and after by party political battles dominated, in the north-west at least, by the middle classes. Secondly, this was coupled with the considered but pragmatic use of basic issues that the working class in a given locality felt was of direct relevance to them. It was from this crucial period of the decline of popular radicalism in an area or town that the dominant political party and its leaders began to emerge initially. If strong and attractive leadership based around opinion/interest questions was maintained, then the party seemed to be able to retain power, control and a wide basis of support. The working class are important in this explanation but so too were the attitudes of other social groups, for example key religious minorities, like the Roman Catholics at Preston, or Unitarians in Manchester, or Nonconformists in Rochdale. Similarly, middle class professionals as well as the manufacturers began to play an important organisational role in the urban centres, as did the lower-middle-class electorate. In the new boroughs this latter group were the majority of the ten pound qualifiers under the 1832 franchise. Although the working class might seek to influence them through exclusive dealing or some other form of collective influence, as a group the lower middle class tradesmen were the key to power for many party political leaders after 1832 in these new boroughs. The successful placation of the working class might afford security but the successful appeasement of the lower-middle class brought power.

Manchester, Rochdale, Bury and Stockport, towns with proportionally high numbers of Unitarians, Methodists and other Nonconformists, remained firmly under Liberal control throughout the entire period under discussion. Here the lead came from these middle and lower middle classes, even before the decline of Chartism. In Ashton, for example, physical force Chartism was pre-dated by the working class being influenced by the Primitive Methodists and the extremely violent rhetoric of the Tory Radical, Joseph Raynor Stephens. This was lower-middle-class leadership attempting to influence working people around issues and sentiments that were tailored to the needs of working people. In Rochdale the high level of flexibility displayed by the Liberal textile owning elite in responding to working class demands and protests over the New Poor Law may have been a factor in ensuring substantial working class support. Also at Rochdale these middle-class elites were willing to integrate working class issues into local governmental programmes as, for example, by their provision of a gas supply to working class homes. At Bolton, during the reform crisis the working class threw off the middle class leadership primarily because it failed to address itself to the needs and aspirations of working people. By the later 1830s into the '40s, this middle-class and lower middle-class leadership had become once again the primary focus of working, and middle-class political authority. It must not be forgotten that this party domination and leadership, although it may have had a fairly long history with a given party in a given location, still had to take into account the interests and aggregated demands of its client groups. The party may have been able to persuade and argue its case under favourable conditions predicated on the fact that its client groups were intrinsically sympathetic, but the party and its leaders had to at least listen to what concerned their supporters.

Firmly linked to this last point was that political tradition of a given locality and community were still important, even in this period of rapid political change. In the market and county towns traditional forms of politics, both in terms of customs and rituals, and in the maintenance of institutions and practices, continued well into the 1840s, and, at Chester into the 1850s. In these types of localities changes in political allegiance and the idioms of politics took place very slowly. Conversely, in Preston and Bolton allegiances shifted from Radicalism to Liberalism and then to Conservatism. In these places, as in Oldham and Rochdale, there was openness in political discourse, and this had a long history, dating back to well before the reform crisis. Thus the switching of allegiances may have in part been due to the willingness of the local leadership to play to a wide variety of social and economic influences. Recognising the various forces of opinion and interest, they were not afraid to make their disenchantment with the previous party's policies widely felt. The importance of this is that it marked the beginning of a pluralistic form of politics. Increasingly in the industrial boroughs local leadership skills were an important factor. Unquestionably in Preston, for example, the retirement of Joseph Livesey from politics in the later 1850s was a profound loss to local Liberals, opening up the previously staunch Liberal areas of control to attack from the Conservatives. Meanwhile at Bolton improved organization by the Conservatives, coupled with their use of practical working class issues after the decline of Chartism in 1839, dramatically improved their fortunes among the working class and the lower middle class tradesmen. The popular Liberals held on to Rochdale, Bury, Stockport (and to a lesser extent Oldham and Salford) for the whole of the period. While at Manchester the power of Unitarian Liberalism, strongly influenced by political economy and a talented press, remained in control for most of the period under discussion. Yet, even at Manchester, the Conservatives eventually broke through, though it must be said they pandered to the darker, more bigoted sentiments of Hugh Stowell and W. R. Callender from the mid-1850s.[22] At Salford the allegiance to Joseph Brotherton and his version of popular Liberalism was a consistent force among the middle classes from 1832 until the advent of the Second Reform Act, after which the Conservatives broke through, taking the most densely populated ward of Crescent with a 512 majority.[23] So while in some parts of the region traditions were eventually eroded with strong leadership and the use of issues, in others they were maintained. Control of popular politics in Bury, Stockport and Rochdale ensured the Liberals retained the initiative for virtually the whole of the

---

22   For further discussion of this see N. Kirk, 'Ethnicity, Class and Popular Toryism, 1850-1870', in K. Nunn, (ed.) *Hosts, Immigrants and Minorities*, (Folkstone, 1980), or by the same author, *The Growth of Working Class Reformism in Mid-Victorian England*, (Beckenham, 1985).

23   *Salford Chronicle*, 21 November 1868, see also R. L. Greenall, 'Popular Conservatism in Salford', in *Northern History*, (1974).

period. Here the Conservatives failed to offer up viable policies or, importantly, popular leaders. Meanwhile in the north and east of the region the Conservatives dominated Blackburn in a converse fashion, with the Liberals unable to offer a serious challenge to Hornby's popular Conservatism.

At Blackburn a combination of factors can be put forward to explain this situation. Firstly, the control of the propertied and manufacturing Conservative elites over the industrial working class was begun the earliest, in the mid-1830s, and was the most comprehensive of any of the towns in the north-west region. The area in which this control was manifested was in the housing of workers by the textile-owning elites of Blackburn. These communities were, by the 1840s, completely self-contained units, with their own public houses, chapels or churches, schools shops and the like, all under the supervision of the mill-master or his appointees. Thus in Blackburn the majority of the town's working class were highly reliant on their employers from a very early date in spheres such as work, education, welfare relief, recreation and religious instruction.

The political organization of the Conservatives in Blackburn was particularly strong, as it was to become in Bolton and Preston, ostensibly through the use of the political clubs. Also, the Conservatives of Blackburn possessed in W. H. Hornby a man of quite exceptional leadership skills, a feature which the Liberals could not match. Thirdly, by the mid-1840s Blackburn's Conservatives had become the party of popular politics, as the Liberals were in some of the towns of the south-east of the region. This was primarily because they captured the opinions/interests of several key sections within the working class and, of course, the middle classes. By the 1850s there were a range of issues which key interest groups regarded as important, and parties vied with each other in an effort to gain support through the use of these issues. Fourthly, change in the political culture of Britain occurred initially in the localities and in the north-west particularly, not at the centre of politics, and the momentum of change was begun in the 1830s. Fifthly, a form of cohort action can be detected in the political developments of the region in this period.[24] This meant individuals, families, community groups, factory workers, trades unions, religious associations and local political clubs began, over time, to be so thoroughly socialized into the party that they accepted their political allegiance as a matter of course. A situation different to the fluidity of political expression found at Preston. This cohort allegiance was backed up at Blackburn by party political propaganda which filtered through a variety of sources and agencies, trades unions, the public house, the place of work, political clubs, newspapers, chapel or church, or even over the back-yard wall. It was a process of both formal and informal ideological reinforcement as a function of party political change which became a much more salient feature from the 1830s. This goes some way to explain, along with the politics of opinion/interest and aspects or deference, why certain parts of a locality, even entire towns, consistently supported a particular political party. Increasingly political allegiance took the form of an almost inherited collective consciousness akin to the way football supporters give allegiance to their team. It was passed on from father to son like the proverbial gold watch.

Working class sectionalisation and the decline of class consciousness, coupled with an increase of intra-class status differentiation, meant that by the 1850s a set of working class policy alternatives did not exist within the ambit of a single political grouping as they did, say, during the height of Chartism. Some individuals and groups began to support political parties because their appeal lay not only in their policies or how they handled power, but also due to a range of factors, which varied from community to community, and from town to town. At times this came through the charisma of the individual leader. This was the case with Hornby at Blackburn, Livesey at Preston, Callender at

---

24 For an exploration of this concept see P. Norton and A. Aughey, *Conservatives and Conservatism*, (London, 1981), pp. 178-9.

Manchester, Brotherton, and later Stowell, at Salford, or Tommy Mellor at Ashton, but also because in political terms in the mid-Victorian period political parties were becoming a more powerful force than class.

Far from being the organ of resentment toward the working class, as was the case between the 1790s and 1832, the ongoing discussion has shown that Conservative Party development in the north-west began to accommodate their interests and aggregated demands. Also, importantly, it was the Conservatives who were the first major political party to integrate sections of the working class into their organization in a modern sense. Several motives for this have been suggested which stretch from the features pointed out by political scientists to the possibility of elites playing on the prejudices and deference of working people. In the north-west, as in many other parts of the country, the Conservatives were, in 1833, fighting for their very existence. Many middle-class Conservatives felt passionately for the maintenance of their central principles and the party's ideology. What developed after 1832 was a process of reorganization and reformulation, both at the centre and in the localities, that modernized the party. In some small way this study of the north-west has attempted to validate this assertion.

When looked at in relation to the features and functions of modern political parties these local Conservative clubs and associations were a remarkable historical departure from the pre-1832 political norm. For their working class members and supporters the Conservatives embarked on original methods not witnessed in eighteenth century political culture. What was novel was their methods of integration and recruitment, their facilities and proselytization, their techniques of socialization and local organization, their use of issues and by their utilization of the opinions/interest. However, not all of the features and functions of modernity were evident in this period. At no time was policy formulated at a grass roots level, nor were the 'ordinary' members in positions of real power within the party. The party legitimised working class political activity; it did offer status to the member, and, although it controlled the agenda of politics, it could not ignore the interests of its client groups. Importantly, post-1832 political parties began to control and politically direct sections of the working class, through opinion, ideology and party discipline. Up until 1832-33, and in parts of the north-west beyond that date, the industrial working class began to pose a serious threat to social and political stability. The development of political parties after 1832, although not the sole agency of the reduction of this threat, was an important part of the process.

With the theme of working class development and their social and political integration, the foregoing has gone some way to pointing out how this took place. By 1870 the working class of the north-west were politically sectionalised between the two main party groupings. In 1800 or in 1832 the working class presented a very different picture, one in which class consciousness was high and intra-class status differentiation was low. In certain parts of the north-west the process of reducing working class consciousness had begun by the mid-1830s, in some areas it came later, and in others (like Lancaster) it scarcely existed. This highlighted the usefulness of the comparative method. However, even at the height of Chartism the authorities did not appear as threatened as they had during the 'days of May' crisis of 1832. A change in attitudes had taken place and this involved the nature of social and economic variables as well as those of a political nature. It was at this point that the two central themes came together, and it was here that the key sub-themes of the idioms of politics, of issues, paternalism, deference, religion, bigotry and ethnicity became relevant.

What has been shown above was that the Conservative Party was a dynamic force in the 1830s and '40s. The split of 1846-47 may have interrupted this process, but this was chiefly at the centre of politics. In the localities some political clubs in the north-west became dormant. However, in Liverpool, Wigan and Blackburn they remained in existence throughout the 1850s (years of political quiescence at the centre) and local Conservatives remained active. By the 1870s working class political integration was complete, and this study may have gone some way in explaining how this process occurred.

Appendices

APPENDIX ONE

Full text of the inaugural meeting of the National Conservative Institution

Meeting held at the British hotel, Cockspur Street, London on 25 April, 1836, Lord Sandon (MP Liverpool) in the chair.

It was unanimously resolved:

1) That an institution be established in the Metropolis under the name of the National Conservative Institute and it's objects shall be as follows. First- To promote by all lawful means the advancement of the Conservative cause in general. Second- To collect and afford information on every subject connected with that cause. Third- To diffuse the principles of loyalty, good order, and obedience especially amongst the middle and lower classes of society. Fourth- to support the constitution of the United Kingdom, as established in Church and State.

2) That a reading and newsroom shall be opened, to be furnished with papers, periodical works, and other such publications as shall be deemed of a suitable charder.

3) That every paper offered shall be made by the Institution, to extend the circulation of Conservative publications and other works tending to improve the religious, moral and political condition of the people — and that it should afford facilities to private individuals for the distribution of pamphlets and other works of a desirable nature.

4) That the formation of Conservative Associations shall be encouraged wherever it is practicable, especially amongst the trading and labouring classes — and that the establishment of reading rooms for the above named portions of the community, shall be aided promoted by the Institution.

5) That the Conservative Associations shall be furnished by the Institution with such publications as the Committee may think proper (when arrangements are made and funds permit), either gratuitously, or on the payment of a certain sum, to be hereafter determined.

6) That proper arrangements shall be immediately made for procuring subscriptions, donations and contributions.

7) That members be balloted for; and that an Annual Subscriptions of Two Guineas, or a donation of twenty guineas, be paid by every member resident in London, or within a circle of 7 miles; beyond that limit members of Conservative Associations to be eligible as members of the Institution, on the payment of one guinea annually, or a donation of ten guineas. Gentlemen from the country to be admitted to the reading room, on the recommendation of two subscribers, for a period not exceeding one week.

8) That the following noblemen and gentlemen constitute a committee of management — three to form a quoram, with power to add to their number — and from this body Sub-Committees of finance and for other purposes be chosen:- Committee. Lord Sandon, MP, Henry Ashley, MP, Lord Ashley, MP, Col. Baille, MP, John Barneby, MP, John Barwise, Sir J. P. Beresford, MP, F. R. Bonham, MP, J. Clutton, Sir W.R.S. Cockburn, J. Crisp, E. Dalton, Col. Daubeney, C. Dodd, Lord Francis Egerton, MP, C. Francis, Sir Roger Gresley, MP, Mr. Hartley, T. Hawks, MP, S. W. Henslow, H. Hoare, William Holmes, J. B. Hoy, MP, A. L. Irvine, Andrew Lawson, G. B. Lafroy, Earl of Lincoln, MP, John Nichol, MP, Foster Owen, J. Pluckett, W. M. Praed, MP, S. G. Price, MP, A. Quinn, Rossiter, Col. Rushbrook, MP, Marquis of Salisbury, Wingfield Stratford, D. T. Shears, J. Wilkins.

9) That any contributions of any amount be received in aid of the Institution friendly to the Conservative cause be deposited at Messrs Coutts and Co., The Strand, Messrs Drummond and Co., Charring Cross Road, Herries and Farquar, St. James Street and the offices of the Institution. Publishers, Messrs Rivington.

10) That cordial thanks be given to Lord Sandon.

OBJECTS AND VIEWS OF THE NATIONAL CONSERVATIVE INSTITUTION

One great and leading object of this Institution is that it should become the focus of Conservative intelligence, and afford a place of meeting for individuals holding constitutional principles from all parts of the Empire where members of the House of Commons may see their constituents — and where an intercourse may be established between Conservatives of the several grades of society.

It is well known that sedition and disloyalty, irreligion and immorality, have been infused like poison into the minds of the lower and middle ranks of society, by means of cheap and illegal publications; that every art that hatred and malignity could devise against all that is pure and good, has been most industriously and perseveringly exercised, to sap and overthrow the principles of the people. Unhappily, good and loyal publications have not been so accessible nor so freely offered to the mass of the community. To supply this defect, the Institution will use all its energies to diffuse sound and constitutional principles; by which all means it seeks to strengthen and support all that is valuable in the institutions of the Empire; and to improve the moral and religious condition of the people.

The British Constitution has hitherto presented to all other nations a model of mixed government. It's excellence is best tested by its permanence, and by the unexampled growth and prosperity of Great Britain — a permanence and prosperity which have been owing in no small degree, to a proper admixture of aristocracy, and to the power which this has been has exercised through the House of Peers, acting as an independent branch of the legislature, without this the force of popular movement would at times have become omnipotent, and swept away in its momentary violence the most venerated of our institutions. It is against this aristocratic power that Liberalism is now waging war, and aiming a fatal blow at the main root of the British Constitution.

Amongst the lower orders Conservative principles are rapidly beginning to develop themselves, and it requires only that these principles be encouraged to produce the best results. Already, the nucleus of an Operative Conservative Association has been fostered by the Institution in the Metropolis, whilst in Lancashire and other places, lately the stronghold of radicalism, the most striking political changes have been affected among the people, who are beginning to feel, that they have been most grossly deceived by a democratic faction, and that they, above all other classes, are interested in upholding that Constitution, which secures to the poor as to the rich, and fullest enjoyment of civil and religious liberty.

With these views, and offering a place of resort for the commercial man of the city, for the landed proprietor, the noble lord of the West End, and for a gentleman of Conservative principles resorting occasionally to the Metropolis, this Institution has been established has taken vigorous root, and now appeal confidently to the support of Conservatives in town and country.

Reprinted in the *Preston Pilot*, 26th June, 1836.

APPENDIX TWO

Parliamentary Election Results of Boroughs discussed in this book.

1) Ashton-under-Lyne (One Seat)

Election	Electors	Candidate	Party	Votes
1832	433	G. Williams	Lib.	176
		C. Hindley	Lib.	163
		T. W. Helps	Con.	33
1835	515	C. Hindley	Lib.	212
		T. W. Helps	Con.	105
		G. WIlliams	Lib.	63
1837	603	C. Hindley	Lib.	237
		J. Wood	Con.	201
		J. R. Stephens	Tory/Rad.	19

1) Ashton-under-Lyne (One Seat)

1841	713	C. Hindley	Lib.	303
		J. Harrop	Con.	254
1847	871	C. Hindley	Lib.	Unopp.
1852	937	C. Hindley	Lib.	Unopp.
1857	1085	C. Hindley	Lib.	Unopp.
(Death of Hindley)				
1857	1085	T. M Gibson	Lib.	522
		B. Mason	Con.	390
1859	1081	T. M. Gibson	Lib.	Unopp.
1865	967	T. M. Gibson	Lib.	Unopp.
1868	4822	T. W. Mellor	Con.	2318
		T. M. Gibson	Lib.	2109
1874	5471	T. W. Mellor	Con.	2612
		A. Buckley	Lib.	2432

2) Blackburn, (Two Seats)

Election	Electors	Candidate	Party	Votes
1832	626	W. Feilden	Con.	376
		W. Turner	Lib.	346
		J. Bowring	Lib.	334
1835	761	W. Turner	Lib.	432
		W. Feilden	Con.	316
		J. Bowring	Lib.	303
1841	906	W. Feilden	Con.	441
		J. Hornby	Con.	427
		W. Turner	Lib.	426
1847	1121	J. Hornby	Con.	641
		J. Pilkington	Lib.	602
		W. Hargreaves	Lib.	392
		W. P. Roberts	Chartist	68
1852	1258	J. Pilkington	Lib.	846
		W. Eccles	Lib.	580
		J. Hornby	Con.	509
(Election of Eccles declared void on petition)				
1853	1325	M. J. Feilden	Lib.	631
		W. H. Hornby	Con.	574
1857	1518	W. H. Hornby	Con.	Unopp.
		J. Pilkington	Lib.	Unopp.
1859	1617	W. H. Hornby	Con.	832
		J. Pilkington	Lib.	750
		J. P. Murrough	Lib.	567
1865	1894	W. H. Hornby	Con.	1053
		J. Feilden	Con.	938
		J. Pilkington	Lib.	744
		J. G. Potter	Lib.	577
1868	9183	W. H. Hornby	Con.	4907
		J. Feilden	Con.	4826
		J. G. Potter	Lib.	4399
		M. J. Feilden	Lib.	4164

2) Blackburn, (Two Seats)

1874	11195	H. M. Feilden	Con.	5532
		W. E. Briggs	Lib.	5538
		D. Thwaltes	Con.	5323
		R. Shackleton	Lib.	4851

3) Bolton (Two Seats)

Election	Electors	Candidate	Party	Votes
1832	1040	R. Torrens	Lib.	627
		W. Bolling	Con.	492
		J. A. Yates	Lib.	482
		W. Eagle	Radical	107
1835	1001	W. Bolling	Con.	633
		P. Ainsworth	Con.	590
		R. Torrens	Lib.	343
1837	1340	P. Ainsworth	Lib.	615
		W. Bolling	Con.	607
		A. Knowles	Lib.	538
1841	1471	P. Ainsworth	Lib.	669
		J. Bowring	Lib.	614
		P. Rothwell	Con.	536
		W. Bolling	Con.	441
1847	1479	W. Bolling	Con.	652
		J. Bowring	Lib.	645
		J. Brooks	Lib.	
(Death of Bolling)				
1848	1479	S. Blair	Con.	Unopp.
1849	1437	Sir J. Walmsley	Lib.	621
		T. R. Bridson	Con.	568
(Resignation of Bowring)				
1852	1671	T. Barnes	Lib.	745
		J. Cook	Lib.	727
		S. Blair	Con.	717
		P. Ainsworth	Lib.	346
1857	1933	W. Gray	Con.	930
		J. Crook	Lib.	895
		T. Barnes	Lib.	832
1859	2050	J. Crook	Lib.	Unopp.
		W. Gray	Con.	Unopp.
1868	12650	J. Hick	Con.	6062
		W. Gray	Lib.	5848
		T. Barnes	Lib.	5451
		S. Pope	Lib.	5436
1874	12595	J. Hick	Con.	5987
		J. K. Goss	Lib.	5782
		W. Gray	Con.	5650
		J. Knowles	Lib.	5440

4) Bury (One Seat)

Election	Electors	Candidate	Party	Votes
1832	535	R. Walker	Lib.	306
		E. Grundy	Lib.	153
1835	526	R. Walker	Lib.	Unopp.
1837	637	R. Walker	Lib.	251
		J. P. Cobbett	Lib.	96
		R. Spankie	Con.	87
1841	768	R. Walker	Lib.	325
		H. Harriman	Con.	288
1847	868	R. Walker	Lib.	Unopp.
1852	959	F. Peel	Lib.	472
		Viscount Duncan	Lib.	410
1857	1218	R. N. Phillips	Lib.	565
		F. Peel	Lib.	530
1859	1289	F. Peel	Lib.	641
		T. Barnes	Lib.	478
1865	1352	R. N. Phillips	Lib.	595
		F. Peel	Lib.	572
1868	5587	R. N . Phillips	Lib.	2830
		Viscount Chelsea	Con.	2264
1874	6236	R. N. Phillips	Lib.	3016
		O. O. Walker	Con.	2500

5) Chester (Two Seats)

Election	Electors	Candidate	Party	Votes
1832	2028	Lord R. Grosvenor	Lib.	1116
		J. Jervis	Lib.	1053
		J. F. Maddock	Lib.	499
1835	2053	Lord R. Grosvenor	Lib.	Unopp.
		J. Jervis	Lib.	Unopp.
1837	2298	Lord R. Grosvenor	Lib.	1282
		J. Jervis	Lib.	1109
		Hon. F. D. Ryder	Con.	352
1841	2445	Lord R. Grosvenor	Lib.	Unopp.
		J. Jervis	Lib.	Unopp.
1847	2450	Earl Grosvenor	Lib.	Unopp.
		Sir J. Jervis	Lib.	Unopp.

(Resignation of Jervis)

Election	Electors	Candidate	Party	Votes
1850	2529	Hon. W. O. Stanley	Lib.	986
		E. C. Egerton	Con.	645
1852	2524	Earl Grosvenor	Lib.	Unopp.
		Hon. W. O. Stanley	Lib.	Unopp.
1857	2428	Earl Grosvenor	Lib.	1244
		P. S. Humberstone	Lib.	924
		E. G. Salisbury	Lib.	729
1859	2502	Earl Grosvenor	Lib.	1464
		P. S. Humberstone	Con.	1110
		E. G. Salisbury	Lib.	708

5) Chester (Two Seats)

1868	6062	Earl Grosvenor	Lib.	2270
		H. C. Ralkes	Con.	2198
		E. G. Salisbury	Lib.	1283
		R. Hoak	Lib.	1071
1874	6268	H. C. Ralkes	Con.	2356
		J. G. Dodson	Lib.	2134
		Sir T. G. Frost	Lib.	2126

6) Clitheroe (One Seat)

Election	Electors	Candidate	Party	Votes
1832	306	J. Fort	Lib.	157
		J. Irving	Con.	124
1835	351	J. Fort	Lib.	Unopp.
1837	368	J. Fort	Lib.	164
		W. Whalley	Con.	155
1841	387	M. Wilson	Lib.	175
		E. Cardwell	Con.	170
1847	504	M. Wilson	Lib.	Unopp.
1852	448	M. Wilson	Lib.	221
		J. T. W. Aspinall	Con.	187

(Election of declared void on petition)

Election	Electors	Candidate	Party	Votes
1853	456	J. T. W. Aspinall	Con.	215
		R. Fort	Lib.	208

(Election of declared void on petition)

Election	Electors	Candidate	Party	Votes
1853	456	G. N. Starkie	Lib.	216
		J. Peel	Con.	205
1857	457	J. T. Hopwood	Lib.	Unopp.
1859	469	J. T. Hopwood	Lib.	Unopp.
1865	438	R. Fort	Lib.	Unopp.
1868	1595	R. Assheton	Con.	760
		C. S. Roudell	Lib.	693
1874	1790	R. Assheton	Con.	892
		E. E. Kay	Lib.	804

7) Lancaster (Two seats)

Election	Electors	Candidate	Party	Votes
1832	1109	T. Green	Con.	Unopp.
		P. M. Stewart	Lib.	Unopp.
1835	1207	T. Green	Con.	Unopp.
		P. M. Stewart	Lib.	Unopp.
1837	1161	T. Green	Con.	614
		G. Marton	Con.	527
		P. M. Stewart	Lib.	453
		W. R. Greg	Lib.	347
1841	1296	T. Green	Con.	699
		G. Marton	Con.	594
		J. Armstrong	Lib.	572

7) Lancaster (Two seats)

1847	1377	S. Gregson	Lib.	724
		T. Green	Con.	721
		E. D. Salisbury	Con.	621

(Election of Gregson declared void on petition)

1848	1377	R. B. Armstrong	Lib.	636
		Hon. E. H. Stanley	Con.	620
1852	1398	S. Gregson	Lib.	699
		R. B. Armstrong	Lib.	690
		T. Green	Con.	509
		J. Ellis	Con.	432

(Election of Armstrong declared void on petition)

1853	1420	T. Green	Con.	686
		J. Armstrong	Lib.	554
1857	1328	S. Gregson	Lib.	827
		W. J. Garnett	Con.	773
		R. Gladstone	Con.	537
1859	1288	W. J. Garnett	Con.	660
		S. Gregson	Lib.	641
		W. A. F. Saunders	Con.	509
		E. M. Fenwick	Lib.	459

(Resignation of Garnett)

1864	1394	E. M. Fenwick	Lib.	682
		W. A. F. Saunders	Con.	525
1865	1465	E. M. Fenwick	Lib.	713
		H. W. Schneider	Lib.	685
		E. Lawrence	Con.	665

WRIT SUSPENDED

8) Liverpool (Two seats from 1832, three seats from 1868)

Election	Electors	Candidate	Party	Votes
1832	11283	W. Ewart	Lib.	4931
		Lord Sandon (Snr.)	Con.	4260
		T. Thornley	Lib.	4096
		Sir H. Douglas	Con.	3249
1835	12492	Lord Sandon (Snr.)	Con.	4407
		W. Ewart	Lib.	4075
		Sir H. Douglas	Con.	3869
		J. Morris	Lib.	3227
1837	11179	Lord Sandon (Snr.)	Con.	4876
		C. Cresswell	Con.	4652
		W. Ewart	Lib.	4381
		H. Elphinstone	Lib.	4206
1841	15539	Lord Sandon (Snr.)	Con.	5979
		C. Cresswell	Con.	5772
		Sir J. Walmesley	Lib.	4647
		Lord Palmerston	Lib.	4431

8) Liverpool (Two seats from 1832, three seats from 1868)

1847	17004	E. Cardwell	Con.	5581
		Sir T. D. Birch	Lib.	4882
		Sir D. Mackworth	Con.	4089
		Lord John Manners	Con.	2413
1852	17433	C. Turner	Con.	6693
		W. F. Mackenzie	Con.	6367
		E. Cardwell	Con.	5247
		J. C. Ewart	Lib.	4910

(Election declared void on petition)

1853	16182	T. B. Horsfall	Lib.	6034
		Sir S. G. Bonham	Con.	5543

(Succession of Lidlell to the Peerage 'Lord Ravensworth')

1855	16182	J. C. Ewart	Lib.	5718
		Sir S. G. Bonham	Con.	4262
1857	18314	T. B. Horsfall	Con.	7566
		J. C. Ewart	Lib.	7121
		C. Turner	Con.	6316
1865	20618	T. B. Horsfall	Con.	7866
		S. R. Graves	Con.	7500
		J. C. Ewart	Lib.	7160
1868	39645	S. R. Graves	Con.	16766
		Lord Sandon (Jnr.)	Con.	16222
		W. Rathbone	Lib.	15337
		W. N. Massey	Lib.	15017
1874	54952	Lord Sandon (Jnr.)	Con.	20206
		J. Torr	Con.	19763
		W. Rathbone	Lib.	16706
		W. S. Caine	Lib.	15801
		W. S. Simpson	Rad.	2435

9) Manchester (Two seats from 1832, three seats from 1868)

Election	Electors	Candidate	Party	Votes
1832	6726	M. Phillips	Lib.	2923
		C. P. Thompson	Lib.	2068
		S. T. Lloyd	Lib.	1832
		J. T. Hope	Con.	1560
		W. Cobbett	Rad.	1305
1835	8432	C. P. Thompson	Lib.	3355
		M. Phillips	Lib.	3163
		B. Braidley	Con.	2535
		Sir C. Wolseley	Lib.	583
1837	11185	C. P. Thompson	Lib.	4158
		M. Phillips	Lib.	3759
		W. E. Gladstone	Con.	2224

(Resignation of Thompson)

1839	11185	R. H. Greg	Lib.	3421
		Sir G. Murray	Con.	3156

9) Manchester (Two seats from 1832, three seats from 1868)

1841	10818	M. Phillips	Lib.	3695
		T. M. Gibson	Lib.	3575
		Sir G. Murray	Con.	3115
		W. Entwistle	Con.	2696
1847	12841	J. Bright	Lib.	Unopp.
		T. M. Gibson	Lib.	Unopp.
1852	13921	T. M. Gibson	Lib.	5762
		J. Bright	Lib.	5475
		Hon J. Denman	Lib.	3969
1857	18044	Sir J. Potter	Lib.	8368
		J. A. Turner	Lib.	7854
		T. M. Gibson	Lib.	5588
		J. Bright	Lib.	5458
1859	18334	T. Bazley	Lib.	7545
		J. A. Turner	Lib.	7300
		A. Heywood	Lib.	5448
		Hon. J. Denman	Lib.	5201
1865	21542	T. Bazley	Lib.	7909
		E. James	Lib.	6698
		J. Bright	Lib.	5562
		A. Heywood	Lib.	4242
1868	48256	H. Birley	Con.	15486
		T. Bazley	Lib.	14192
		J. Bright	Lib.	13514
		J. Hoar	Con.	12684
		E. C. Jones	Lib.	10662
		M. Henry	Lib.	5236
1874	60222	H. Birley	Con.	19984
		W. R. Callender	Con.	19649
		Sir T. Bazley	Lib.	19325
		J. Bright	Lib.	18727

10) Oldham (Two seats)

Election	Electors	Candidate	Party	Votes
1832	1131	J. Fielden	Rad.	677
		W. Cobbett	Rad.	645
		B. H. Bright	Lib.	150
		W. Burge	Con.	101
		G. Stephen	Lib.	3
1835	1029	J. Fielden	Rad.	Unopp.
		W. M. Cobbett	Lib.	Unopp.
1837	1372	W. A. Johnson	Lib.	545
		J. Fielden	Rad.	541
		J. Jones	Con.	315
		J. F. Lees	Con.	279
1841	1467	J. Fielden	Rad.	Unopp.
		W. A. Johnson	Lib.	Unopp.

10) Oldham (Two seats)

1847	1691	W. J. Fox	Lib.	726
		J. Duncraft	Con.	696
		J. M. Cobbet	Lib.	624
		J. Fielden	Rad.	612
1852	1890	J. M. Cobbett	Lib.	957
		J. Duncraft	Con.	868
		W. J. Fox	Lib.	777
(Death of Duncraft)				
1852	1978	W. J. Fox	Lib.	895
		J. Heald	Con.	783
1857	2098	J. M. Cobbett	Lib.	949
		J. Platt	Lib.	934
		W. J. Fox	Lib.	898
1859	2151	W. J. Fox	Lib.	1039
		J. M. Cobbett	Lib.	966
		J. T. Hibbert	Lib.	955
1865	2285	J. T. Hibbert	Lib.	1104
		J. Platt	Lib.	1075
		J. M. Cobbett	Lib.	899
		F. L. Spinks	Con.	846
1868	13454	J. T. Hibbert	Lib.	6140
		J. Platt	Lib.	6122
		J. M. Cobbett	Con.	6116
		F. L. Spinks	Con.	6084
(Death of Platt)				
1872	16063	J. M. Cobbett	Con.	
		Hon. E. L. Stanley	Lib.	
1874	18560	F. L. Spinks	Con.	
		J. M. Cobbett	Con.	
		J. T. Hibbert	Lib.	
		Hon. E. L. Stanley	Lib.	

11) Preston (Two seats)

Election	Electors	Candidate	Party	Votes
1832	6352	P. H. Fleetwood	Con.	3372
		Hon. H. T. Stanley	Lib.	2273
		H. Hunt	Rad.	2054
		J. Forbes	Lib.	1926
		C. Crompton	Lib.	118
1835	3734	P. H. Fleetwood	Con.	2165
		Hon. H. T. Stanley	Lib.	2092
		T. P. Thompson	Lib.	1385
		T. Smith	Lib.	789
1837	3656	P. H. Fleetwood	Con.	2726
		R. T. Parker	Con.	1821
		J. Crawford	Lib.	1562

11) Preston (Two seats)

1841	3371	Sir. P. H. Fleetwood	Lib.	1655
		Sir. G. Strickland	Lib.	1629
		R. T. Parker	Con.	1270
		C. Swanson	Con.	1255
1847	3044	Sir G. Strickalnd	Lib.	1404
		C. P. Grenfell	Lib.	1378
		R. T. Parker	Con.	1361
1852	2854	R. T. Parker	Con.	1335
		Sir G. Strickland	Lib.	1253
		C. P. Grenfell	Lib.	1127
		J. German	Lib.	692
1857	2793	C. P. Grenfell	Lib.	1503
		R. A. Cross	Con.	1433
		Sir G. Strickland	Lib.	1094
1859	2657	R. A. Cross	Con.	1564
		C. P. Grenfell	Lib.	1208
		J. T. Clifton	Con.	1168
(Resignation of Cross)				
1862	2773	Sir T. G. Hesketh	Con.	1527
		G. Melly	Lib.	1014
1865	2562	Sir T. G. Hesketh	Con.	Unopp.
		Hon. F. A. Stanley	Con.	Unopp.
1868	10763	E. Hermon	Con.	5803
		Sir T. G. Hesketh	Con.	5700
		Lord E. G. F. Howard	Lib.	4846
		J. F. Leese	Lib.	4782
1874	12073	E. Hermon	Con.	6512
		J. Holker	Con.	5211
		T. Motterhead	Rad.	3756

12) Rochdale (One Seat)

Election	Electors	Candidate	Party	Votes
1832	687	J. Fenton	Lib.	277
		J. Emtwistle	Con.	246
		J. Taylor	Lib.	109
1835	746	J. Entwistle	Con.	369
		J. Fenton	Lib.	326
(Death of Entwistle)				
1837	857	J. Fenton	Lib.	383
		C. Royds	Con.	339
1837	857	J. Fenton	Lib.	374
		A. Ramsay	Con.	349
1841	1016	W. S. Crawford	Lib.	399
		J. Fenton	Lib.	335
1847	1026	W. S. Crawford	Lib.	Unopp.
1852	1160	E. Miall	Lib.	529
		Sir A. Ramsay	Con.	375
1857	1255	Sir A. Ramsay	Lib.	532
1859	1340	R. Cobden	Lib.	Unopp.

12) Rochdale (One Seat)

(Death of Cobden)

1865	1358	R. B. Potter	Lib.	646
		W. B. Brett	Con.	496
1865	1358	T. B. Potter	Lib.	Unopp.
1868	9280	T. B. Potter	Lib.	4455
		W. W. Schofield	Con.	3270
1874	10352	T. B. Potter	Lib.	5614
		R. W. Gamble	Con.	3716

13) Salford (One Two seats from 1868)

Election	Electors	Candidate	Party	Votes
1832	1497	J. Brotherton	Lib.	712
		W. Garnett	Con.	518
1835	2336	J. Brotherton	Lib.	795
		J. Dugdale	Con.	572
1837	2628	J. Brotherton	Lib.	890
		W. Garnett	Con.	888
1841	2443	J. Brotherton	Con.	991
		W. Garnett	Lib.	873
1847	2605	J. Brotherton	Lib.	Unopp.
1852	2950	J. Brotherton	Lib.	Unopp.
(Death of Brotherton)				
1857	2950	E. R. Langworthy	Lib.	Unopp.
1859	4222	W. N. Massey	Lib.	1880
		Sir E. Armitage	Lib.	1264
1865	5397	J. Cheetham	Lib.	Unopp.
1868	15862	C. E. Crawley	Con.	6312
		W. T. Charley	Con.	6181
		J. Cheetham	Lib.	6141
		H. Rawson	Lib.	6018
1874	19177	C. E. Crawley	Con.	7003
		W. T. Charley	Con.	6987
		J. Kay	Lib.	6827
		H. Lee	Lib.	6709

14) Stockport (Two seats)

Election	Electors	Candidate	Party	Votes
1832	1012	T. Marsland	Con.	551
		T. H. Lloyd	Lib.	444
		H. Marsland	Lib.	431
		E. D. Davenport	Lib.	237
1835	922	H. Marsland	Lib.	582
		T. Marsland	Con.	482
		E. D. Davenport	Lib.	361
1837	1192	H. Marsland	Lib.	467
		T. Marsland	Con.	467
		R. Cobden	Lib.	412

14) Stockport (Two seats)

1841	1238	H. Marsland	Lib.	571
		R. Cobden	Lib.	541
		T. Marsland	Con.	346
1847	1108	R. Cobden	Lib.	643
		J. Heald	Con.	570
		J. Kershaw	Lib.	537
		J. West	Chartist	14

(Cobden elects to sit for the West Riding of Yorkshire)

1847	1205	J. Kershaw	Lib.	
		T. Marsland	Con.	
1852	1341	J. Kershaw	Lib.	
		J. B. Smith	Lib.	
		J. Heald	Con.	
1857	1417	J. Heald	Lib.	
		J. B. Smith	Lib.	
		W. Gibb	Con.	
1865	1348	W. W. Watkin	Lib.	
		J. B. Smith	Lib.	
		W. Tipping	Con.	
1874	7814	C. N. Hopwood	Lib.	
		F. Pennington	Lib.	
		W. Tipping	Con.	
		P. Mitford	Con.	

15) Wigan (Two seats)

Election	Electors	Candidate	Party	Votes
1832	438	R. Thicknesse	Lib.	302
		R. Potter	Lib.	296
		J. Whittle	Lib.	212
		J. H. Kearsley	Con.	174
1835	495	J. H. Kearsley	Con.	296
		R. Potter	Lib.	181
		C. S. Standish	Lib.	166
1837	539	C. S. Standish	Lib.	249
		R. Potter	Lib.	245
		J. H. Kearsley	Con.	229
		P. Greenall	Con.	211

(Resignation of Potter)

1839	551	W. Ewart	Lib.	261
		J. H. Kearsley	Con.	259
1841	586	P. Greenall	Con.	273
		T. B. Crosse	Con.	268
		C. S. Standish	Lib.	264
		C. P. Grenfell	Lib.	263

(Death of Greenall)

1845	517	Hon. J. Lindsay	Con.	274
		R. A. Thicknesse	Lib.	211
1847	637	Hon. J. Lindsay	Con.	Unopp.
		R. A. Thicknesse	Lib.	Unopp.

15) Wigan (Two seats)

1852	718	R. A. Thicknesse	Lib.	366
		Hon. J. Lindsay	Con.	356
		F. S. Powell	Con.	324
(Death of Thicknesse)				
1854	788	J. Acton	Lib.	339
		F. S. Powell	Con.	334
1857	797	F. S. Powell	Con.	492
		H. Woods	Lib.	476
		Hon. J. Lindsay	Con.	309
1859	835	Hon. J. Lindsay	Con.	500
		H. Woods	Lib.	476
		F. S. Powell	Con.	273
(Resignation of Lindsay)				
1866	863	N. Eckersley	Con.	411
		J. Lancaster	Lib.	349
1868	3939	H. Woods	Lib.	2166
		J. Lancaster	Lib.	1920
		N. Eckersely	Con.	1875
		J. Pearson	Con.	2493
1874	5062	Lord Lindsay	Con.	2493
		T. Knowles	Con.	2401
		J. Lancaster	Lib.	1883
		W. Packard	Rad.	1134
		H. Woods	Lib.	1029

APPENDIX THREE

Blackburn Operative Conservative Association Membership Lists 1835 -1846

Name	Office held	Occupation	Address	Able to vote	
				1835	1847
Thomas Ainsworth	Committee 1844	Hatter	Blakey Moor	No	Yes
James Appleton	President 1837 Committee 1844	unknown	unknown	No	No
Henry Ashcroft	Committee 1834/6	Shoemaker	Church St	No	Yes
John Barber	Committee 1840	unknown	unknown	No	No
Thomas Banister	Committee 1837/42	unknown	unknown	No	No
James Bell	Committee 1840	unknown	unknown	No	No
John Bennett	Vice-President 1839 President 1840/1 Committee 1842/3	Headmaster	St Peters Place	Yes	Yes
Thomas Bennett	Treasurer 1837/46	Cloth Finisher	21 Montague St	No	Yes
James Brogden	Committee 1837	Attorney	Ainsworth St	Yes	Yes
William Brooks	Vice-President 1844 President 1845 Committee 1842	Draper	King William St	No	Yes
Thomas Bury	Committee 1842	Pawnbroker	Whalley Banks	No	Yes
Robert Cliffe	Committee 1840	unknown	unknown	No	No
John Clough	Vice-President 1842 President 1843	Operative	Montague St	No	Yes
Richard Cardwell	Vice-President 1837	Operative Spinner	unknown	No	No

Joseph Cowell	Committee 1839	unknown	unknown	No	No
Thomas Dewhurst	Committee 1835/7	Operative Joiner	Brown St	Yes	Yes
William Dobson	Committee 1838	unknown	unknown	No	No
Henry Elgin	Vice-President 1840 President 1841 Committee 1839	unknown	unknown	No	No
William Ellison	Librarian 1846	unknown	unknown	No	No
Edward Fisher	Committee 1837/9	unknown	unknown	No	No
Thomas Fisher	Committee 1839	Operative	King St	No	Yes
Thomas Forrest	Committee 1842	Draper	King William St	No	Yes
Jonathan Gate	Committee 1841	Clothier	Richmond Terr	No	Yes
Thomas Gillibrand	Committee 1839	Cotton Mfr.	Old Bank St	No	Yes
Richard Greenwood	Committee 1840	Operative Weaver	Strawberry Bank	No	Yes
Richard Hall	Committee 1841	Grocer	Fleming Square	No	Yes
George Heyes	Committee 1837	unknown	unknown	No	No
William Holden	Committee 1841/2	Shopkeeper	Whalley Old Rd	No	Yes
Charles Holland	Committee 1836/8	unknown	unknown	No	No
James Holland	Committee 1840	unknown	unknown	No	No
Henry Ibbotson	Vice-President 1838	Quarry Owner	Grimshaw Pk Rd	Yes	Yes
James Isherwood	Committee 1838	unknown	unknown	No	No
William Jones	Committee 1838	unknown	unknown	No	No
George Jackson	Committee 1841	Operative Spinner	Ainsworth St	Yes	Yes
Henry Kenyon (Jnr.)	Secretary 1835/46	Solicitors Cleark	Richmond Terr	Yes	Yes
William Kenyon	Committee 1837/8	unknown	unknown	No	No
Roger Kellett	Committee 1843	unknown	unknown	No	No
Issac Lloyd	Vice-President 1841 President 1842/3/4	Operative	unknown	No	No
John Littlefare	Committee 1837	unknown	unknown	No	No
J. S. Livesey	Committee 1837	Shopkeeper	Northgate	No	Yes
James Mullington	Committee 1837/8	unknown	unknown	No	No

[END OF LIST]

Bibliography

A. Primary and Contemporary Sources

1) Private Papers

Aberdeen Papers, The British Library, London
Ainsworth Archive, Bolton Reference Library
The Ashworth Papers, Lancashire County Records Office, Preston
Bowring Papers, John Rylands University of Manchester Library, Manchester
Butterworth Mss, Oldham Local Studies Library
Chadwick Archive, University College, London
Croker Papers, William L. Clemens Library, University of Michigan, Ann Arbor, Michigan, USA
Cross Papers, Lancashire County Records Office, Preston
Cuerden Hall Archive, (The Townley Parker Estate), Lancashire County Records Office, Preston
Correspondence of Lord Francis Egerton, The British Library, London
Feilden Papers, Blackburn Reference Library
The Grosvenor Archive, Cheshire County Records Office, Chester
Goulbourn Papers, Surrey County Records Office, Guildford
Graham Papers, Bodleian Library, Oxford
Hardinge Papers, McGill University Library, Montreal, Canada
Herries Papers, The British Library, London
The Hesketh Archive, Lancashire County Records Office, Preston
The Diary of Robert Heywood, Bolton Reference Library
Home Office Papers, Public Records Office, Kew
Hulton Documents, Lancashire County Records Office, Preston
Lovett Papers, (The General Convention of the Working Classes), British Library, London
Palatinate of Lancashire, Public Records Office, Kew
Peel Papers, The British Library, London
Plaice Collection, The British Library, London
Privy Council Papers, Public Records Office, Kew
Russell Papers, William L. Clemens Library, University of Michigan, Ann Arbor, Michigan, USA
Stanley of Alderney Papers, Cheshire County Records Office, Chester
The Letters of Lord Granville Somerset, The Archive of His Grace the Duke of Beafort, Badminton, Gloucestershire. (I would like to thank His Grace for permission to view his private collection of these letters.)
The Diary of Charles Tiplady, Blackburn Reference Library
The Windmarlegh Archive, (John Wilson Patten MP) Lancashire County Records Office, Preston and in the collection of Lord Scarborough, Sandbeck Park, Maltby, Yorkshire
The Returns of the Loyalist Associations and Reeves Societies, British Library, London
Treasury Solicitors Papers, Public Records Office, Kew

2) Government and Official Publications

Census Returns (for the years) 1821, 1831, 1841, 1851, 1861
Commissioners Files on Poor Law Returns, Public Records Office, Kew
Commissions of Enquiry: Corruption at Elections, Parliamentary Papers; **Blackburn**, 1837 (withdrawn); 1841, (Dismissed); 1852, (Election of Eccles declared void); **Bolton**, 1835, (withdrawn); 1837, (withdrawn); 1847, (dismissed); 1848, (withdrawn); 1852, (dismissed); **Bury**, 1857, (dismissed); 1859, (dismissed); **Clitheroe**

241

1853, (election declared void on petition); **Lancaster**, 1847, (election of Gregson declared void); 1848, (dismissed); 1852, (elections of Armstrong declared void); 1853, (withdrawn); 1865, (void election, writ suspended); **Liverpool**, 1852, (void election); 1853, (withdrawn); **Manchester**, 1868, (dismissed); **Oldham**, 1868, (dismissed); **Preston**, 1859, (dismissed); 1868, (withdrawn); **Salford**, 1837, (dismissed); 1868, (dismissed); **Stockport**, 1847, (withdrawn); 1868, (withdrawn); **Warrington**, 1868. (dismissed); **Wigan**, 1839, (dismissed); 1841, (election of Crosse declared void); 1845, (dismissed); 1868, (dismissed).

Commissions of Enquiry: Handloom Weavers; 1835, 1838
Commissions of Enquiry: Health of Towns; 1838, 1847
Commissions of Enquiry: Conditions in Factories; 1845
Commissions of Enquiry: Inspector of Factories; 1845
Hansard; 1830-1868

3) POLL BOOKS AND BURGESS ROLLS

Blackburn, 1832-1868, Blackburn Reference Library
Bolton, 1832-1868, Bolton Reference Library
Chester, 1820-1868, Cheshire County Records Office, Chester
Clitheroe, 1820-1868, Lancashire County Records Office, Preston
Lancaster, 1820-1865, Lancaster Reference Library and Lancashire County Records Office, Preston
Manchester, 1832-1868, Central Reference Library, Manchester
Oldham, 1832-1868, Oldham Local Studies Library
Preston, 1820-1868, The Harris Reference Library, Preston and Lancashire County Records Office, Preston
Rochdale, 1832-1868, Rochdale Reference Library, and The Local History Library, Institute of Historical Research, Senate House, University of London, London

4) NEWSPAPERS AND PERIODICALS

A) THE LOCAL PRESS

The Ashton Reporter
The Blackburn Alfred
The Blackburn Gazette
The Blackburn Mail
The Blackburn Standard
The Blackburn Times
The Bolton Chronicle
The Bolton Free Press
The Bolton Weekly Journal
The Bury Times
The Chester Courant
The Lancaster Gazette

The Manchester Courier
The Manchester Guardian
The Manchester Mercury
The Manchester and Salford Advertiser
The Manchester Times
The Oldham Chronicle
The Preston Chronicle
The Preston Guardian
The Preston Pilot
The Rochdale Observer
The Wigan Gazette
The Wigan Times

B) THE NATIONAL PRESS

Blackwood's Edinburgh Magazine
Cobbett's Weekly Political Register
The Conservative
Fraser's Magazine
McDouall's Chartist and Republican Journal
The Annual Register

The Gentleman's Magazine
The Northern Star
The Poor Man's Guardian
The Times
The Westminster Review

5) CONTEMPORARY ACCOUNTS

ABRAM, W. A., *History of Blackburn*, (Blackburn, 1877)

ANON., 'Liberals and Conservatives and their policies toward the working class', The Chadwisk Mss, University College Library, (London, undated)

ASHWORTH, H., 'An Enquiry into the Origin, Progress and Results of the Strike of the Operative Cotton Spinners of Preston from October 1836 to February 1837', Harris Reference Library, Preston

_____ *The Preston Strike: Its Causes and Consequences*, (Preston, 1854)

BAINES, E., *A History of Lancashire*, (Manchester, 1827)

BROMLOW, W., *A Parliamentary History of Bolton* (Bolton, 1880)

Dobson's Parliamentary History of Preston, (Preston, 1868)

The Trade Directories of Lancashire and Cheshire Towns

STRACHEY, L., (ed.), *The Memoirs of Charles Cavendish Fulke Greville Esq*, (London, 1938)

LIVESEY, J., *An Autobiography*, (Preston, 1868)

OASTLER, R., 'Infant Slavery in Preston, 1835', Harris Reference Library, Preston

PAUL, W. M., 'A History of the Operative Conservative Societies, 1838', Leeds Reference Library

SOWLER, R. S., 'Thoughts on the State and Prospects of Conservatives with special reference to the Association of Gentry, Tradesmen and Operatives', Manchester Central Reference Library, 1837

B. SECONDARY SOURCES

1) THESES

BOOTH, A., 'Reform, repression and revolution: Radicalism and loyalism in the North-West of England, 1789-1861', Ph.D., University of Lancaster, 1979

KIRK, N., 'Some aspects of working life in South-East Lancashire and North Eastern Cheshire, 1850-1870', Ph.D., University of Pittsburgh, USA, 1978

DOYLE, M. B. S., 'Social control in Over-Darwen, 1839-1871', MA., University of Lancaster, 1979

FOSTER, D., 'The social composition of the Lancashire magistracy, 1820-1850', Ph.D., University of Lancaster

GADIAN, D. S., 'A comparative study of popular movements in North-West industrial towns, 1830-1850', Ph.D., University of Lancaster, 1976

GASKELL, S. M., 'Housing estate development, 1840-1918; with special reference to the Penine towns', PhD, University of Sheffield, 1974

GOODERSON, P. J., 'The Social and Economic History of Lancaster', Ph.D., University of Lancaster, 1975

JOYCE, P., 'Popular Toryism in Lancashire', D.Phil., Oxford, 1975

MORGAN, N. B. B., 'Social and political leadership in Preston, 1820-1860', M.Litt., University of Lancaster, 1980

SPENCER, K. M. R., 'A social and economic geography of Preston, 1800-1865', Ph.D., University of Liverpool, 1976

SYKES, R., 'Popular politics and trade unionism in South-East Lancashire, 1829-1842', Ph.D., University of Manchester, 1982

WALSH, D., 'Working class development, control and New Conservatism, Blackburn, 1820-1850', M.Sc, University of Salford, 1986

2) ARTICLES AND REVIEWS

ALLEN, J., 'Voices of the People: Democracy and Chartist Political Identity, 1830-1870', (review),*Victorian Studies*, Vol. 51, No. 1, Autumn 2008

ASPINALL, A., 'English party organization in the early nineteenth century', *Historical Review*, Vol. XLI, 1926

AYDELOTTE, W. O., 'The House of Commons in the 1840s', *History*, 39, 1954

_____ 'Conservatism and radical interpretations of early Victorian social legislation', *Victorian Studies*, No. 11, 1967

_____ 'Parties and issues in early Victorian England', *Journal of British Studies*, No. 5, 1966

243

Beales, D., 'Peel, Russell and reform', *Historical Journal*, Vol. 17, No. 2, 1974

Booth, A., 'The United Englishmen and radical politics in the industrial north-west of England, 1795-1803', *International Review of Social History*, Vol. 31, Part 3, 1986

Clark, J. C. D., 'A general theory of party, opposition and government, 1688-1832', *Historical Journal*, Vol. 23, No. 23, 1980

Christie, I. R., 'The emergence of the British two-party system, 1760-1832', *History*, Vol. 68, No. 223, 1983

Cragoe, M., 'The Great Reform Act and the Modernization of British Politics: The Impact of Conservative Association, 1835-1841', *Journal of British Studies*, Vol. 37, No. 3, July 2008

Cruickshank, M. A., 'The Anglican revival and education: A study of school expansion in the cotton manufacturing areas of the north-west of England, 1840-1850', *Northern History*, Vol. 15, 1979

Dunkerly, P., 'Paternalism, the magistracy and poor relief in England, 1795-1834', *International Review of Social History*, Vol. 24, Part 3, 1979

Dutton, H. I. and King, J. E., 'The limits of paternalism: The cotton tyrants of north Lancashire, 1836-1845', *Social History*, Vol. 7, No. 1, 1982

Eccleshall, R., 'English Conservatism as ideology', *Political Studies*, Vol. 25, Issue 1, 1977

Foster, D., 'The politics of uncontested elections: North Lancashire, 1832-1865', *Northern History*, Vol. 13, 1977

Foster, J., 'Conflict at work', *Social History*, Vol. 14, No. 2, 1987

———— 'The de-classing of language', *New Left Review*, 1985

Garrard, J. A., 'Social history, political history and political science', *Journal of Social History*, Vol. 16, No. 3, 1980

———— 'Parties, members and voters after 1867: A local study', *Historical Journal*, Vol. 20, No. 1, 1977

Gash, N., 'F. R. Bonham: Conservative 'Political Secretary', 1832-1847', *English Historical Review*, Vol. 63, Issue 249, October, 1948

———— 'The organization of the Conservative Party, 1832-1846, Part one, The Parliamentary Organisation', *Parliamentary History*, Vol. 1, 1982

———— 'The organization of the Conservative Party, 1832-1846, Part two, The Electoral Organization', *Parliamentary History*, Vol. 2, 1983

Gray, R. Q., 'The de-construction of the English working class', *Social History*, Vol. 11, No. 3, 1986

Gregory, D., 'Rates and representation, Lancashire County in the nineteenth century', *Northern History*, Vol. 12, 1976

Greenall, R. L., 'Popular Conservatism in Salford, 1868-1886', *Northern History*, 1974

Gunn, J. A. W., 'Influence, parties and the constitution: Changing attitudes, 1783-1832', *Historical Journal*, Vol. 17, Issue 2, 1974

Gurowich, P. M., 'The continuation of war by other means: Party and politics, 1855-1865', *Historical Journal*, Vol. 27, No. 3, 1984

Hart, J., 'Nineteenth century social reform: A Tory interpretation of history', *Past and Present*, No. 31, 1965

Harrison, B., 'Philanthropy and the Victorians', *Victorian Studies*, No. 9, 1965

Joyce, P. J., 'Factory politics in Lancashire in later nineteenth century', *Historical Journal*, Vol. 18, Issue 3, 1975

———— 'In search of the proletarians', *Times Literary Supplement*, 11 May, 1984

Kemnitz, T. M. and Jacques, F., 'J. R. Stephens and the Chartist Movement', *International Review of Social History*, Vol. 19, Part 2, 1974

Kemp, B., 'The General Election of 1851', *History*, Vol. 37, Issue 130, June, 1952

Kirk, N., 'Patrick Joyce: Work, Society and Politics', *Society for the Study of Labour History Bulletin*, No. 42, 1981

———— 'Challenge, crisis and renewal? Themes in the labour history of Britain, 1960-2010', *Labour History Review*, Vol. 75, No. 2, Summer 2010

Midwinter, E., 'Central and local government in mid-nineteenth century Lancashire', *Northern History*, Vol. 3, 1968

Mitchell, A., 'The Association Movement of 1792-3', *Historical Journal*, Vol. 4, Issue 1, 1961

Moore, D. C., 'Concession or cure: The sociological premises of the First Reform Act', *Historical Journal*, Vol. 9, Issue 1, 1966

_____ 'The other face of Reform', *Victorian Studies*, September, 1961

NAVICKAS, K., 'What happened to class? New histories of labour and collective action in Britain', *Social History*, Vol. 36, No. 2, May, 2011

O'GORMAN, F., 'Party politics in the early nineteenth century', *English Historical Review*, January, 1987

_____ 'Electoral deference in 'unreformed' England, 1760-1832', *Journal of Modern History*, No. 56, September 1984

_____ 'The Unreformed Electorate of Hanoverian England: The Mid-Eighteenth Century to the Reform Act of 1832', *Social History*, Vol. 11, No. 1, January 1986

_____ 'Party Politics in the Early Nineteenth Century', *English Historical Review*, Vol. 102, 1987

_____ 'The Electorate before and after 1832', *Parliamentary History*, Vol. 12, Issue 2, 1993

O'NEILL, M. AND MARTIN, G., 'A backbencher on parliamentary reform, 1831-1832', *Historical Journal*, Vol. 23, No. 3, 1980

PHILLIPS, J. A. AND WETHERELL, C., 'The Great Reform Act of 1832 and the Rise of Partisanship', *Journal of Modern History*, Vol. 63, No. 4, December 1991

_____ 'The Great Reform Act of 1832 and the Political Modernisation of England', *American Historical Review*, Vol. 100, No. 2, April 1995

ROBERTS, D., 'Tory paternalism and social reform in early Victorian England', *American Historical Review*, Vol. 63, No. 2, 1958

ROSE, M. E., 'The Anti-Poor Law Movement in the North of England', *Northern History*, 1966

ROTHBLATT, S., 'Some recent writings on British political history, 1832-1914', *Journal of Modern History*, Vol. 55, No. 3, 1983

ROWE, D. J., 'The London Working Mens Association and the 'People's Charter'', *Past and Present*, No. 36, 1970

SACK, J. J., 'The memory of Burke and the memory of Pitt: English Conservatism confronts its past, 1806-1929', *Historical Journal*, Vol. 30, No. 3, 1987

SALMON, P., 'Electoral Reform at Work: Local Politics and National Politics, 1832-1841', *Royal Historical Society Studies in History*, New Series, London, 2002

SANDERSON, M., 'Education and the factory in industrial Lancashire', *Economic History Review*, Second Series, No. 20, 1967

_____ 'Social change and elementary education in industrial Lancashire, 1780-1840', *Northern History*, No. 3, 1968

SCHWEIZER, K. W., 'Newspapers, Politics and Public Opinion in the Later Hanoverian Era', *Parliamentary History*, Vol. 25, Part 1, 2006

SEED, J., 'Unitarianism, political economy and the antinomies of Liberal culture in Manchester, 1830-1850', *Social History*, Vol. 7, No. 1, 1982

SOFFER, R. N., 'Attitudes and allegiances in the unskilled north, 1830-1850', *International Review of Social History*, Vol. 10, No. 3, 1965

STIGANT, P., 'Wesleyan Methodism and working class radicalism in the north, 1792-1821', *Northern History*, Vol. 6, 1971

STORCH, R. D., 'The plague of blue locusts: Police reform and popular resistence in northern England, 1840-1847', *International Review of Social History*, Vol. 20, No. 1, 1975

SYKES, R., 'Some aspect of working class consciousness in Oldham', *Historical Journal*, Vol. 1, No. 23, 1980

_____ 'Physical force Chartism: The cotton districts and the Chartist crisis of 1839', *International Review of Social History*, Vol. 30, No. 2, 1985

THOMAS, J. A., 'The system of registration and the development of party organization, 1832-1870', *History*, Vol. 35, Issue 3, 1950

THOMPSON, E. P., 'Time, work discipline and industrial capitalism', *Past and Present*, No. 38, 1967

_____ 'The moral economy of the English crowd in the eighteenth century', *Past and Present*, No. 50, 1970

_____ 'Eighteenth century society: class struggle without class?', *Social History*, Vol. 3, No. 2, 1978

THOMPSON, F. M. L., 'Social control in Victorian Britain', *Economic History Review*, Vol. 34, 1981

VINCENT, A., 'British Conservatism and the problem of ideology', *Political Studies*, Vol. 42, Issue 2, 1994

WARD, J. T., 'The factory reform movement in Lancashire, 1830-1855', *Lancashire and Cheshire Antiquarian*

Society, 1965-1966

3) BOOKS

ANDERSON, M., *Family Structure in Nineteenth Century Lancashire*, (London, 1971)

ARMSTRONG, W. A., *Stability and Change in an English County Town: A Study of York*, (London, 1974)

ASPINALL, A., (ed.), *Three Early Nineteenth Century Diaries*, (London, 1952)

_____ *Politics and the Press, 1780-1850*, (London, 1949)

BAGEHOT, W., *Essays on Parliamentary Reform*, (London, 1883)

BEATTIE, A., *English Party Politics: 1660-1906*, (London, 1970)

BELCHEM, J., *'Orator' Hunt: Henry Hunt and English Working Class Radicalism*, (Oxford, 1985)

_____ *Popular Radicalism in Nineteenth-Century Britain*, (London, 1995)

BELCHEM, J. AND KIRK, N., *Languages of Labour*, (London, 1997)

BIERNACKI, R., *The Fabrication of Labor: Germany and Britain, 1640-1914*, (California, 1995)

BOHSTEDT, J., *Riots and Community Politics in England and Wales, 1790-1810*, (Harvard, 1983)

_____ *The Politics of Provision: Food Riots, Moral Economy, and Market Transition in England 1550–1850*, (Farnham, 2010)

BOYSON, R., *The Ashworth Cotton Enterprise*, (Oxford, 1970)

BRIGGS, A., (ed.), *Chartist Studies*, (London, 1977 edition)

BROCK M., *The Great Reform Act*, (London, 1973)

BUTLER, J. R. M., *The Passing of the Great Reform Bill*, (London, 1914)

CANNADINE, D., *Class in Britain*, (London, 1998 edition)

CANNON, J., *Parliamentary Reform, 1640-1832*, (Cambridge, 1973)

CHADWICK, E., (WATSON, R., ed.), *Poor Law Reform and Public Health*, (London, 1969)

CHASE, M., *Chartism: A New History*, (Manchester, 2007)

CLARK, J. C. D., *Revolution and Rebellion*, (Cambridge, 1986)

COLE, G. D. H. AND FILSON, A.W., (eds.), *British Working Class Select Documents, 1798-1875*, (London, 1950)

COX, G. W., *The Efficient Secret: The Cabinet and the Development of Political Parties in Victorian England*, (Cambridge, 1987)

DAUNTON, M. J., *Progress and Poverty, an Economic and Social History of Britain, 1700-1850*, (Oxford, 1995)

_____ *House and Home in the Victorian City*, (London, 1984)

DINWIDDY, J. R., *From Luddism to the First Reform Bill: Reform in England, 1810-1832*, (Oxford, 1986)

DONAJGRODSKI, A. P., *Social Control in Nineteenth Century Britain*, (London, 1977)

DOZIER, R. R., *For King, Constitution and Country*, (Kentucky, 1987)

DRIVER, C. H., *Tory Radical: The Life of Richard Oastler*, (Oxford, 1946)

DUTTON, H. L. AND KING, J. E., *Ten Per-Cent and No Surrender: The Preston Strike of 1853-1854*, (Cambridge, 1971)

EDSALL, N. C., *The Anti-Poor Law Movement*, (Manchester, 1971)

EPSTEIN, J. AND THOMPSON, D., (eds.), *The Chartist Experience*, (London, 1982)

FARNIE, D. A., *The English Cotton Industry and the World Market*, (Oxford, 1969)

FOSTER, J., *Class Struggle and the Industrial Revolution*, (London, 1974)

FRASER, D., *Urban Politics in Victorian England*, (Leicester, 1976)

_____ *Power and Authority in the Victorian City*, (Oxford, 1979)

GARNETT, R. G., *Co-operation and the Owenite Socialist Communities in Britain, 1825-1845*, (Manchester, 1972)

GARRARD, J. A., *Leadership and Power in Victorian English Towns, 1830-1880*, (Manchester, 1983)

GASH, N., *Politics in the Age of Peel*, (London, 1953)

_____ *Mr Secretary Peel*, (London, 1961)

_____ *Reaction and Reconstruction in English Politics, 1832-1852*, (Oxford, 1965)

_____ *Sir Robert Peel*, (London, 1972)

_____ *Aristocracy and the People*, (London, 1979)

Glen, R. *Urban Workers and the Industrial Revolution*, (London. 1983)

GOURVISH, T. R., AND O'DAY, A., *Later Victorian Britain, 1867-1900*, (London, 1988)

GREGO, J. A., *History of Parliamentary Elections and Electioneering*, (London, 1892)

GUNN, S., *Public Culture of the Victorian Middle Class: Ritual and Authority in the English Industrial City, 1840-1914*, (Manchester, 2000)

HALL, R. G., *Voices of the People: Democracy and Chartist Political Identity, 1830-1870*, (Monmouth, 2007)

HARRISON, B. F., *Drink and the Victorians*, (London, 1972)

HARRISON, J. F. C. AND THOMPSON, D., *Bibliography of the Chartist Movement*, (Brighton, 1978)

HARRISON, R., *Before the Socialists: Studies in Labour and Politics*, (London, 1965)

HEWITT, M., *The Emergence of Stability in the Industrial City: Manchester, 1832-1867*, (London, 1996)

HOLLIS, P., (ed.), *Pressure from Without in Early Victorian England*, (London, 1974)

HOPWOOD, E. A., *History of the Lancashire Cotton Industry and the Amalgamated Weavers Association*, (Manchester, 1969)

HOVELL, M., *The Chartist Movement*, (Manchester, 1970 edition)

HOWE, A., *The Cotton Masters, 1830-1860*, (Oxford, 1984)

HUDSON, P., (ed.), *Regions and Industries: A Perspective on the Industrial Revolution in Britain*, (Cambridge, 1989)

JENKINS, M., *The General Strike of 1842*, (London, 1980)

JONES, D., *Chartism and the Chartists*, (London, 1975)

JOYCE, P. J., *Work, Society and Politics*, (Brighton, 1980)

_____ *The Rule of Freedom: Liberalism and the Modern City*, (London, 2003)

_____ *The Oxford Reader on Class*, (Oxford, 1995)

_____ *Democratic Subjects: The Self and the Social in 19th Century England*, (Cambridge, 1994)

_____ *Visions of the People: Industrial England and the Question of Class*, (Cambridge, 1991)

KIRK, N., *The Growth of Working Class Reformism in Mid-Victorian England*, (Beckenham, 1985)

_____ *Change, Continuity and Class: Labour in British Society, 1850-1920*, (Manchester, 1998)

_____ *The Conservative Mind*, (London, 1954)

KRAMINK, I., *The Rage of Edmund Burke: A Portrait of an Ambivalent Conservative*, (New York, 1977)

HILL, R. L., *Toryism and the People*, (London, 1929)

LUBENOW, W. C., *The Politics of Government Growth*, (Newton Abbot, 1971)

LUKACS, G., *History and Class Consciousness*, (London, 1977 edition)

McPHILLIPS, K., *Oldham: The Formative Years*, (Oldham, 1997 edition)

MACDOWELL, R. L., *British Conservatism, 1932-1914*, (London, 1949)

MACKENZIE, R. AND SILVER, A., *Angels in Marble*, (London, 1968)

MANDLER, P., *Aristocratic Government in the Age of Reform: Whigs and Liberals, 1830-1852*, (Oxford, 1990)

MARTIN, D. AND RUBINSTEIN, D., (eds.), *Ideology and the Labour Movement*, (New Jersey, 1979)

MIDWINTER, E. C., *Social Administration in Lancashire*, (Manchester, 1969)

MILLER, G. C., *Bygone Blackburn*, (Blackburn, 1950)

_____ *Blackburn: Evolution of a Cotton Town*, (Blackburn, 1951)

MOORE, D. C., *The Politics of Deference*, (Brighton, 1976)

MORRIS, R. J., *Class Consciousness and the Industrial Revolution*, (London, 1979)

MUMBY, L. M., *The Luddites*, (Edgeware, 1971)

NAVICKAS, K., *Loyalism and Radicalism in Lancashire, 1798-1815*, (Oxford, 2009)

NEAL, F., *Sectarian Violence: The Liverpool Experience, 1819-1914*, (Manchester, 1988)

NEALE, R. S., *Class and Ideology in the Nineteenth Century*, (London, 1972)

_____ *Class in English History*, (Oxford, 1981)

_____ *History and Class*, (London, 1983)

NEWBOLD, I., *Whiggery and Reform, 1830-1841: The Politics of Government*, (Stanford, 1990)

NEWBY, H., *The Deferential Worker*, (London, 1977)

NORDLINGER, E. A., *Working Class Tories*, (London, 1968)

NORMAN, E. R., *Anti-Catholicism in Victorian England*, (London, 1968)

NOWLAN, K. B., *The Politics of Repeal*, (London, 1965)

NOSSITER, T. J., *Influence, Opinion and Political Idioms in Reformed England*, (Brighton, 1975)

NEUMAN, S., *Modern Political Parties*, (Chicago, 1960)

O'GORMAN, F., *Edmund Burke: His Political Philosophy*, (London, 1973)

_____ *The Emergence of the British Two Party System*, (London, 1982)

_____ *The Long Eighteenth Century: British Political and Social History, 1688-1832*, (London, 1997)

O'SULLIVAN, N., *Conservatism*, (London, 1976)

PERKIN, H., *The Origins of Modern English Society, 1780-1880*, (London, 1978 edition)

PHILLIPS, J. A., *Electoral Behaviour in Unreformed England: Plummers, Splitters, and Straights*, (Princeton, 1982)

_____ *The Great Reform Bill in the Boroughs: English Electoral Behaviour, 1818-1841*, (Oxford, 1992)

PICKERING, P., *Chartism and the Chartists in Manchester and Salford*, (London, 1995)

RANDALL, A., *Before the Luddites*, (Cambridge, 1991)

_____ *Riotous Assemblies: Popular Protest in Hanoverian England*, (Oxford, 2006)

REDFORD, A., *Labour Migration in England*, (Manchester, 1976 edition)

ROBERTS, D., *Paternalism in Early Victorian England*, (London, 1979)

ROGERS, N., *Crowds, Culture and Politics in Georgian Britain*, (Oxford, 1998)

ROSE, M. E., *The Relief of Poverty, 1834-1914*, (London, 1972)

ROSENBLATT, F. F., *The Chartist Movement in its Social and Economic Aspects*, (New York, 1967)

ROTHSTEIN, T., *From Chartism to Labourism*, (London, 1983 edition)

ROYLE, E., *Victorian Infidels*, (Manchester, 1974)

_____ *Radical Politics, 1790-1900*, (London, 1979 edition)

_____ *Chartism*, (London, 1981)

RUDÉ, G., *The Crowd in History, 1730-1848*, (New York, 1964)

SCHMIECHEN, J. A., *Sweated Industry and Sweated Labour*, (London, 1981)

SMELSER, N. J., *Social Change and the Industrial Revolution*, (London, 1959)

SMITH, E. A., *Reform or Revolution? A Diary of Reform in England, 1830-32*, (Stroud, 1992)

SMITH, O., *The Politics of Language, 1791-1819*, (Oxford, 1984),

STEDMAN-JONES, G., *Languages of Class*, (Cambridge, 1983)

STEINBERG, M. W., *Fighting Words: Working Class Formation, Collective Action and Discourse in Early Nineteenth-Century England,* (Ithaca, 1999)

STEWART, R., *The Foundation of the Conservative Party*, (London, 1978)

_____ *The Politics of Protection*, (London, 1974)

THOMIS, M. I., *The Luddites*, (London, 1970)

THOMPSON, D., *The Early Chartists*, (London, 1971)

THOMPSON, E. P., *The Making of the English Working Class*, (London, 1978 edition)

_____ *Customs in Common*, (London, 1991)

TIMMINS, G., *Made in Lancashire: A History of Regional Industrialisation*, (Manchester, 1998)

TURNER, M., *Reform and Respectability: The Making of a Middle Class Liberalism in early nineteenth-century Manchester*, (Manchester, 1995)

WALMSLEY, R., *Peterloo: The Case Re-opened*, (Manchester, 1966)

WARD, J. T., *The Factory Movement*, (London, 1962)

_____ (ed.), *Popular Movements*, (London, 1970)

_____ *Chartism*, (London, 1973)

WARD, J. T. AND HAMISH-FRASER, W., *Workers and Employers*, (London, 1980)

WEST, J., *The History of the Chartism Movement*, (London, 1920)

WIGLEY, J., *The Rise and Fall of the Victorian Sunday*, (Manchester, 1980)

VERNON, J., *Politics and the People: A Study in English Political Culture, 1815-1867*, (Cambridge, 1993)

Index

Preston Conservative Registration
 Committee, 163
Preston Constitutional Reform
 Association, 163
Preston Guardian, 149
Preston Pilot, 81, 94, 156, 157, 159, 163,
 165, 167, 169
Preston Radical Association, 155, 164,
 216
Primitive Methodists, 56, 151, 219
primitive socialists, 124
primogeniture, 67
Prince Regent, 27, 53
printers, 49
Proclamation of the General Convention,
 85
progressive Liberals, 35, 72, 106, 123,
 125, 127, 135, 160, 169, 187, 207, 208
property qualification, 63, 105, 137, 153,
 154, 193, 196
protectionism, 26, 27, 29, 30
Protestant Association, 91, 218
Protestant Church, 30
Protestantism, 30, 91, 103, 106, 162, 167,
 170, 180, 192, 208, 218
Public Ledger and Guardian, 73, 75

Quakers, 89, 151
Queen Ann, 21

Radical Toryism, 66, 165, 176, 186, 187,
 195, 201, 210
radicalism, 2, 3, 9, 32, 33, 38, 57, 82-4,
 94, 101, 105, 107, 112, 155-7, 160,
 164, 170, 183, 187, 191, 192, 200, 205-
 8, 210, 216, 217, 219
radicals, 62, 100, 111, 119, 127, 136, 156,
 157, 195, 196, 199, 201, 217
Rand, John, 126
Rawlinson, Robert, 144
Rawtenstall, 173
Red Publican, The, 56
Redesdale, Lord, 78
Reeves Societies, 25, 208
Reeves, John, 86
reform crisis, 11, 15, 54, 56, 62, 80, 119,
 121, 130, 138, 155, 177, 193, 201, 206,
 218, 220
Reid, A. J., 16
Reid, Alastair, 209
Reid, Sir John, 76
religious toleration, 9, 22, 150
republicanism, 32, 61, 85, 89
Revolution Settlement of 1688, 21, 22, 23,
 70, 71
revolutionary consciousness, 60
revolutionary underground, 39
Ricardo, David, 124

Richardson, John, 144
riots, 57, 69, 191
 Anatomy Act riots, 197
 Bolton, 191
 Bristol, 65, 194
 Chadderton, 173
 Church and King riots, 25
 Derby, 65
 food riots, 38
 East Anglia, 34
 Little Bolton, 198
 Manchester, 48
 Nottingham, 65
 Preston, 161, 168
 Plug Strikes, 1842, 187
 Priestley riots, 25
 Spa Fields, 34, 54
 Swing riots, 84
Ripon, Lord, 78
Roberts, W. P., 187
Robinson, Dixon, 27, 35, 179, 194
Roby, John, 93
Rochdale, 48, 74, 90, 93, 96, 97, 100, 104,
 108, 112, 113, 118, 188, 189, 198, 211,
 219, 220
Rockingham, 22, 24
romantic atavism, 37, 93
 romantic Conservatism, 88
 romantic Toryism, 89, 119
Rome, 21, 29, 81
Romilly, Sir Samuel, 33, 35
Rosslyn, Lord, 78
Rothwell, Charles, 195, 196, 198, 199
Royal Proclamation, 32, 63, 84, 194, 207
Royds, C., 97
Russell, Lord, 63, 70, 157, 197
Russell Rads, 157

Sacred Month, 1839, 108, 112, 164, 187,
 197, 198, 199
Sadler, Michael, 121
Sadler, Richard, 124, 159, 176
Salford, 45, 47, 90, 96, 107-9, 111, 118,
 147-8, 171, 180, 188, 198, 200, 201,
 210, 211, 220, 222
Salisbury, Lord, 28
Salisbury, Marquis of, 92
Sandon, Lord, 76
Saunders, Joseph, 102
Saxton, J. T., 55
Schneider, H. W., 214
Scot and Lot, 67, 102, 111, 129, 146
Scotland, 96
Secret Service, 80
Seddon, John, 45
Segar, Robert, 152-3, 157
'September Massacres' in Paris, 85

Seven Years War, 21
Sharp, Edward, 145
Sheffield, 20, 91, 107
shoemakers, 59, 133, 175
shopocracy, 63
Short Time Movement, 66
Sick and Burial Clubs, 108, 109, 181, 209
Sick and Burial Fund, 187
Sidmouth, Lord, 27, 31, 53
Silvester, Colonel, 48
Simpson, William, 106
Singleton, John, 45
Six Points, 112, 122, 124
Skelmersdale, Lord, 92, 162
Skelton, Joseph, 191
Slave Trade, 10
Smith, Adam, 35, 114, 124
 Wealth of Nations, 114
Smith, George, 154
Smith, John, 145
Smith, William, 121, 181
social control, 48, 59, 60, 147, 178, 206
social deference, 60, 113, 126, 218
Socialism, 2, 42, 192
Somerset, 57, 173
Somerset, Lord Granville, 75, 76, 79, 83,
 90
South Lancashire Association Conference,
 107
Sowler, Robert Scarr, 79, 180
Spence, Thomas, 61
Spencer, K. M., 147
Spencer, Lawrence, 168
spinners, 37, 49, 59, 123, 148, 149, 151,
 156, 159, 160, 163, 169, 172, 175, 185,
 187, 190-6, 199, 217
Spitalfields Weavers, 50
Standard, 177, 184
Stanley, Lord, 30, 81, 93, 94
Starkie, Richard, 192
State Opening of Parliament, 1795, 32
Staten, 195
Stedman Jones, Gareth, 41-3, 125
 Languages of Class, 41, 42
Steinberg, Marc, 45
Stephens, Joseph Raynor, 121, 123, 124,
 126, 134, 176, 182, 196, 209, 210, 219
Stewart, Patrick, 136
Stockport, 45, 48, 52, 56, 90, 96, 97, 108,
 121, 173, 181, 211, 219, 220
Stokes, Donald, 104
Stormont, Viscount, 78
Stowell, Hugh, 220, 222
Strathfieldsaye, 65, 76
Strickland, Sir George, 166
strike, 48, 95, 134, 149, 164, 169, 185,
 191, 198, 216, 217

Also available from
Breviary Stuff Publications

Ralph Anstis, Warren James and the Dean Forest Riots, *The Disturbances of 1831*
£14.00 • 242pp *paperback* • 191x235mm • ISBN 978-0-9564827-7-8

The full story of the riots in the Forest of Dean in 1831, and how they were suppressed, is told here for the first time. Dominating the story is the enigmatic character of Warren James, the self-educated free miner who led the foresters in their attempt to stave off their increasing poverty and unemployment, and to protect their traditional way life from the threats of advancing industrial change.

John E. Archer, 'By a Flash and a Scare', *Arson, Animal Maiming, and Poaching in East Anglia 1815-1870*
£12.00 • 208pp *paperback* • 191x235mm • ISBN 978-0-9564827-1-6

'By a Flash and a Scare' illuminates the darker side of rural life in the nineteenth century. Flashpoints such as the Swing riots, Tolpuddle, and the New Poor Law riots have long attracted the attention of historians, but here John E. Archer focuses on the persistent war waged in the countryside during the 1800s, analysing the prevailing climate of unrest, discontent, and desperation.

John Belchem, 'Orator' Hunt, *Henry Hunt and English Working Class Radicalism*
£14.00 • *paperback* • 191x235mm • ISBN 978-0-9564827-8-5

In the early 19th century, Henry Hunt became one of the most stirring orators of English Radicalism. His speech following the "Peterloo" massacre cost him three years in prison and gave him a reputation for inciting the rabble to violence. This book considers his place in the radical movement.

Bob Bushaway, By Rite, *Custom, Ceremony and Community in England 1700-1880*
£14.00 • 206pp *paperback* • 191x235mm • ISBN 978-0-9564827-6-1

Bringing together a wealth of research, this book explores the view that rural folk practices were a mechanism of social cohesion, and social disruption. Through them the interdependence of the rural working-class and the gentry was affirmed, and infringements of the rights of the poor resisted, sometimes aggressively.

Malcolm Chase, The People's Farm, *English Radical Agrarianism 1775-1840*
£12.00 • 212pp *paperback* • 152x229mm • ISBN 978-0-9564827-5-4

This book traces the development of agrarian ideas from the 1770s through to Chartism, and seeks to explain why, in an era of industrialization and urban growth, land remained one of the major issues in popular politics. Malcolm Chase considers the relationship between 'land consciousness' and early socialism; attempts to create alternative communities; and contemporary perceptions of nature and the environment. *The People's Farm* also provides the most extensive study to date of Thomas Spence, and his followers the Spenceans.

Malcolm Chase, Early Trade Unionism, *Fraternity, Skill and the Politics of Labour*
paperback • 191x235mm • ISBN 978-0-9570005-1-3

Once the heartland of British labour history, trade unionism has been marginalised in much recent scholarship. In a critical survey from the earliest times to the nineteenth century, this book argues for its reinstatement. Trade unionism is shown to be both intrinsically important and to provide a window onto the broader historical landscape; the evolution of trade union principles and practices is traced from the seventeenth century to mid-Victorian times.

Barry Reay, The Last Rising of the Agricultural Labourers, *Rural Life and Protest in Nineteenth-Century England*
£12.00 • 192pp *paperback* • 191x235mm • ISBN 978-0-9564827-2-3

The Hernhill Rising of 1838 was the last battle fought on English soil, the last revolt against the New Poor Law, and England's last millenarian rising. The bloody 'Battle of Bosenden Wood', fought in a corner of rural Kent, was the culmination of a revolt led by the self-styled 'Sir William Courtenay'. It was also, despite the greater fame of the 1830 Swing Riots, the last rising of the agricultural labourers.

Buchanan Sharp, In Contempt of All Authority, *Rural Artisans and Riot in the West of England, 1586-1660*
£12.00 • 204pp *paperback* • 191x235mm • ISBN 978-0-9564827-0-9

Two of the most common types of popular disorders in late Tudor and early Stuart England were the food riots and the anti-enclosure riots in royal forests. Of particular interest are the forest riots known collectively as the Western Rising of 1626-1632, and the lesser known disorders in the Western forests which took place during the English Civil War. The central aims of this volume are to establish the social status of the people who engaged in those riots and to determine the social and economic conditions which produced the disorders.

Roger Wells, Insurrection, *The British Experience 1795-1803*
£17.50 • 364pp *paperback* • 191x235mm • ISBN 978-0-9564827-3-0

On the 16 November 1802 a posse of Bow Street Runners raided the Oakley Arms, a working class pub in Lambeth, on the orders of the Home Office. Over thirty men were arrested, among them, and the only one of any social rank, Colonel Edward Marcus Despard. Despard and twelve of his associates were subsequently tried for high treason before a Special Commission, and Despard and six others were executed on 21 February 1803. It was alleged that they had planned to kill the King, seize London and overturn the government and constitution.

Roger Wells, Wretched Faces, *Famine in Wartime England 1793-1801*
£18.00 • 412pp *paperback* • 191x235mm • ISBN 978-0-9564827-4-7

"The history of riots reaches its full maturity when riots break out of monographic case studies to be incorporated into full histories. Roger Wells includes riot as one dimension of his rich attempt to comprehend the whole range of responses of British society to the famines of 1794-96 and 1799-1801. These famines *dramatically revealed the fragile equilibrium underpinning national subsistence*, and its propensity to collapse. Wells explains how and why the archaic structure of state and society in Britain did just manage not to collapse."

Lightning Source UK Ltd.
Milton Keynes UK
UKOW05f2220120716

278229UK00017B/409/P